THE WORLD ECONOMY

THE WORLD ECONOMY

GLOBAL TRADE POLICY 2010

Edited by
David Greenaway

A John Wiley & Sons, Ltd., Publication

This edition first published 2011
Originally published as Volume 33, Issue 11 of *The World Economy*
Chapters © 2011 The Authors
Editorial organization © 2011 Blackwell Publishing Ltd

Blackwell Publishing was acquired by John Wiley & Sons in February 2007.
Blackwell's publishing program has been merged with Wiley's global Scientific,
Technical, and Medical business to form Wiley-Blackwell.

Registered Office
John Wiley & Sons Ltd, The Atrium, Southern Gate, Chichester, West Sussex, PO19
8SQ, United Kingdom

Editorial Offices
350 Main Street, Malden, MA 02148-5020, USA
9600 Garsington Road, Oxford, OX4 2DQ, UK
The Atrium, Southern Gate, Chichester, West Sussex, PO19 8SQ, UK

For details of our global editorial offices, for customer services, and for information
about how to apply for permission to reuse the copyright material in this book please
see our website at www.wiley.com/wiley-blackwell.

The right of David Greenaway to be identified as the author of the editorial material in
this work has been asserted in accordance with the Copyright, Designs and Patents Act
1988.

Wiley also publishes its books in a variety of electronic formats. Some content that
appears in print may not be available in electronic books.

Designations used by companies to distinguish their products are often claimed as
trademarks. All brand names and product names used in this book are trade names,
service marks, trademarks or registered trademarks of their respective owners. The
publisher is not associated with any product or vendor mentioned in this book. This
publication is designed to provide accurate and authoritative information in regard to
the subject matter covered. It is sold on the understanding that the publisher is not
engaged in rendering professional services. If professional advice or other expert
assistance is required, the services of a competent professional should be sought.

Library of Congress Cataloging-in-Publication data is available for this book.

9781444339062 (paperback)

A catalogue record for this book is available from the British Library.

This book is published in the following electronic formats: ePDFs (9781444343960);
Wiley Online Library (9781444343991); ePub (9781444343977); Kindle
(9781444343984)

Set in 11/13 pt Times by Toppan Best-set Premedia Limited
Printed and bound in Malaysia by Vivar Printing Sdn Bhd

01   2011

Contents

CONTENTS

REGIONAL TRADING AGREEMENTS

Foreword

Every year *The World Economy* publishes a Special Issue on developments in global trade policy. It has done so for almost two decades. In terms of coverage there are several elements that repeat each year, most notably the features on WTO Trade Policy Reviews which have been published over the previous year. Other components are driven by topical issues and specially commissioned mini-symposia. It is an issue which receives a lot of attention, so much so that it is subsequently published as a stand-alone book.

Global Trade Policy 2011 includes three new appraisals of WTO Trade Policy Reviews: for Turkey, China and the Dominican Republic. There is also a comprehensive survey of the links between trade policy and economic growth. Either side of that survey are two mini-symposia. The first focuses on WTO / GATT issues, including the stalled Doha Round and modelling the extensive margin of trade; the subject of the second is regional trading arrangements and some of their side effects.

This collection makes for a broadly based *Global Trade Policy 2011* and I am grateful both to the authors of the contributions and to Wiley-Blackwell for their expeditious processing of the manuscript.

David Greenaway
University of Nottingham

Contributors

David Blandford	Penn State University
Antoine Bouët	IFPRI, Washington DC
Gabriel Felbermayr	University of Hohenheim
Caroline Freund	World Bank, Washington DC
Ivar Gaasland	IREBA, Bergen
Roberto Garcia	Norwegian University of Life Sciences
Patrick Georges	University of Ottawa
Henrik Horn	RIIE, Stockholm
Wilhelm Kohler	Tubingen University
David Laborde	IFPRI, Washington DC
Changyuan Luo	Fudan University
Petros C. Mavroidis	University of Neuchates
Amelia U. Santos-Paulino	WIDER, Helsinki
André Sapir	Universite Libre de Bruxeller
Tarlock Singh	Griffith University Brisbane
Sübidey Togan	Bilkent University, Ankara
Erling Vårdal	University of Bergen
Jun Zhang	Fudan University

1

Turkey: Trade Policy Review, 2007

Sübidey Togan

1. INTRODUCTION

THE *Trade Policy Review: Turkey 2007*, the fourth of its kind, provides a comprehensive survey of trade policy developments and practices in Turkey. The review brings together a considerable amount of information on trade and tariff structures, exports, sector and trade-related policies in Turkey. This chapter examines the status of Turkey's trade policy regime following the approach of the *Trade Policy Review: Turkey 2007*. As highlighted in the chapter Turkey is pursuing a strategy of trade liberalisation through negotiations at the multilateral, regional and bilateral levels. As of 2009 tariffs in Turkey are a non-issue in the non-agricultural sector, but technical barriers to trade are still a major problem that hinders the attainment of free trade in industrial goods.

The chapter is structured as follows. The next section of the chapter describes the main developments in Turkey's trade regime and the third section considers the Turkish trade performance. Section 4 examines the trade policy under the headings of measures affecting imports, exports and foreign direct investment. The fifth section discusses technical barriers to trade, and the sixth and final section offers conclusions.

2. MAIN DEVELOPMENTS

After pursuing inward-oriented development strategies for 50 years Turkey switched over to outward-oriented policies in 1980. The policy of further opening up the economy was pursued with the aim of integrating into the world economy through membership in the World Trade Organization (WTO) and close association with the European Union (EU).

The World Economy: Global Trade Policy 2010, First Edition. Edited by David Greenaway.
© 2011 Blackwell Publishing Ltd. Published 2011 by Blackwell Publishing Ltd.

Turkey, which became an original Member of the WTO on 26 March 1995, accords at least Most Favoured Nation (MFN) treatment to almost all WTO Members. Turkey is not a signatory to any of the plurilateral agreements that resulted from the Uruguay Round but is an observer in the Committees on Government Procurement and Trade in Civil Aircraft, and party to the Information Technology Agreement. Turkey attaches great importance to the Doha Development Agenda (DDA). Its main interests in the DDA are attaining a fair, competitive and predictable trading environment where trade-distorting support measures are eliminated. For Turkey, agriculture is the key issue of the DDA, and Turkey attaches utmost importance to non-agricultural market access negotiations and trade facilitation.

Turkey's application for association with the European Economic Community was made in 1959. The application ultimately resulted in the signing of the Association Agreement in 1963. The Additional Protocol to the Ankara Agreement was signed in 1970, and became effective in 1973. The basic aim of the Additional Protocol is the establishment of a customs union. In 1995 it was agreed at the Association Council meeting under Decision No. 1/95 (CUD) that Turkey would create a customs union with the EU starting on 1 January, 1996. According to CUD all industrial goods, except products of the European Coal and Steel Community (ECSC), that comply with the European Community (EC) norms could circulate freely between Turkey and the EU as of 1 January 1996. For ECSC products, Turkey signed a free trade agreement (FTA) with the EU in July 1996, and, as a result, ECSC products have received duty-free treatment between the parties since 1999. The CUD does cover processed agricultural products, but not the agricultural commodities and services.

In 1999 the Helsinki European Council recognised Turkey as a candidate for EU membership on equal footing with other potential candidates. In December 2002 the Copenhagen European Council decided that 'the EU would open negotiations with Turkey "without delay" if the European Council in December 2004, on the basis of a report and a recommendation from the Commission, decides that Turkey fulfils the Copenhagen political criteria'. The EU leaders agreed on 16 December 2004 to start accession negotiations with Turkey from 3 October 2005. Right after the official launching of the EU accession negotiations the screening process started which lasted until October 2006. Thereafter the Commission prepared the screening reports for each of the 35 policy chapters. The first chapter to be negotiated, Chapter 25 on 'Science and Research', was opened and provisionally closed on 12 June 2006. In November 2006, the EU expressed concern over restrictions to the free movement of goods, including restrictions on means of transport to which Turkey had committed by signing the Additional Protocol to the Ankara Agreement. With no solution found, the European Council decided on 14–15 December 2006 to suspend negotiations on eight chapters relevant to Turkey's restrictions with regard to the Republic of

Cyprus.[1] It was also decided that no chapter would be provisionally closed until Turkey fulfils its commitments under the additional protocol to the EU–Turkey Association Agreement. However, this did not mean that the process of negotiations was blocked. As of January 2007, the negotiations were back on track on the chapters that were not suspended.[2]

The CUD required Turkey to implement the EC's Common Customs Tariffs on imports of industrial goods from third countries as of 1 January 1996, to adopt by 2001 all of the preferential trade agreements the EU has concluded over time, and to implement on the commercial policy side measures similar to those of the European Community's commercial policy. As a result Turkey signed FTAs with the European Free Trade Association countries, Israel, Macedonia, Croatia, Bosnia-Herzegovina, Palestinian Authority, Tunisia, Morocco, Syria, Egypt, Albania and Georgia. Under these agreements, bilateral trade was to be liberalised on industrial goods at the end of a transition period, and mutual concessions were granted on selected agricultural and processed agricultural goods.[3] As part of the CUD, Turkey has based its Generalised System of Preferences (GSP) on the EC's. Under Turkey's GSP regime, preferences are granted to selected nonagricultural goods, including raw materials and semi-finished goods. On the commercial policy side Turkey has adopted EC competition law, established the Competition Board, adopted the EC rules on protection of intellectual and industrial property rights, and established the Patent Office.

In addition to its trade relations with the EC, Turkey also participates in the Economic Cooperation Organisation (ECO), the Black Sea Economic Cooperation (BSEC), and in the Euro-Mediterranean Partnership, a political, economic and social programme aimed at creating an area of shared prosperity, including a Euro-Mediterranean Free Trade Area by 2010.[4]

---

[1] The eight chapters are: Chapter 1 on free movement of goods, Chapter 3 on the right of establishment and freedom to provide services; Chapter 9 on financial services; Chapter 11 on agriculture and rural development; Chapter 13 on fisheries; Chapter 14 on transport policy; Chapter 29 on customs unions; and Chapter 30 on external relations.

[2] Chapter 20 on 'Enterprise and Industrial Policy' was opened for negotiation at the end of March 2007, and two more negotiation chapters were opened thereafter, namely Chapter 18 on 'Statistics' and Chapter 32 on 'Financial Control' at the end of March 2007. At the end of December 2007 Chapter 21 on 'Trans-European Networks' and Chapter 28 on 'Health and Consumer Protection', and during June 2008 Chapter 6 on 'Company Law' and Chapter 7 on 'Intellectual Property' were opened. Lately, with the opening of Chapter 4 on 'Free Movement of Capital' and Chapter 10 on 'Information Society and Media' the number of policy chapters opened has increased to 10.

[3] Negotiations are in progress with the Faroe Islands, Gulf Cooperation Council, Jordan, Lebanon and Montenegro, while exploratory talks have been held with Chile, Mexico, the Southern African Customs Union and Ukraine.

[4] The ECO is an inter-governmental regional organisation established in 1985 by Iran, Pakistan and Turkey for the purpose of sustainable socio-economic development of member states. In 1992, the Organisation was expanded to include Afghanistan, Azerbaijan, Kazakhstan, the Kyrgyz Republic, Tajikistan, Turkmenistan and Uzbekistan. On 17 July 2003 the ECO Trade Agreement (ECOTA) was signed between Afghanistan, Iran, Pakistan, Tajikistan and Turkey. The Agreement foresees the

3. TRADE PERFORMANCE AND INVESTMENT

Until the early 1980s Turkey was a fairly closed economy. At that time – as part of more wide-ranging economic reforms – the trade policy of protection and import substitution was replaced by a much more open trade regime. As a result, exports and imports increased considerably over time. While Turkey's merchandise exports (imports) amounted to US$2.9 (7.9) billion in 1980, they increased to US$131.97 (201.96) billion in 2008. On the other hand, exports (imports) of goods and services increased during the same period from US$3.4 (7.8) billion in 1980 to US$187.2 (227.7) billion in 2008. This amounts to an average annual rate of growth of merchandise exports (imports) of 14.6 (12.3) per cent, and of exports (imports) of goods and services of 15.4 (12.8) per cent, respectively. As a per cent of GDP merchandise, exports (imports) increased from 4.5 (12.1) per cent in 1980 to 16.6 (25.4) per cent in 2008, and exports (imports) of goods and services from 5.2 (11.9) per cent in 1980 to 23.6 (28.7) per cent in 2008. These are remarkable increases by any standards achieved within the context of a liberal trade regime.

Kaminski and Ng (2007) note that countries take advantage of opportunities offered by global markets successfully as long as three conditions are satisfied: macroeconomic stability, contestable and competitive domestic markets that are open to external competition, and well-functioning backbone services. Although Turkey historically failed on the macroeconomic test, the condition seems to be satisfied after the stabilisation measures taken during and after 2001. On the other hand, the liberalisation measures taken during the 1980s, CUD and the EU accession process have contributed immensely to the emergence of contestable domestic markets and to improved efficiency in service sectors.

Table 1 shows that in 2008 exports to the EU15 formed 48.4 per cent of total exports. The table further reveals that the three export commodities with the highest shares in total exports were 'automotive products' with a share of 13.4 per cent, 'iron and steel' with a share of 12.6 per cent, and 'clothing' with a share of 10.2 per cent. The three export commodities with the highest shares in exports to the EU were 'automotive products' with a share of 20.8 per cent, 'clothing' with a share of 17.1 per cent, and 'other semi-manufactures' with a share of 7.9 per cent. During the period 1995–2008 total exports grew at an annual rate of 13.9

---

reduction of tariffs to a maximum of 15 per cent within a maximum period of eight years. ECOTA has binding provisions on state monopolies, state aid, protection of intellectual property rights, dumping and anti-dumping measures. On the other hand, the BSEC aims to improve and diversify economic and trade relations among its 11 members. The member countries are Albania, Armenia, Azerbaijan, Bulgaria, Georgia, Greece, Moldavia, Romania, the Russian Federation, Turkey and Ukraine. The BSEC Declaration was signed on 25 June 1992, and on 7 February 1997 a declaration of intent for the establishment of a BSEC free trade area was adopted. Recently, BSEC launched projects to eliminate non-tariff barriers on regional trade and to harmonise trade documents in the region.

TABLE 1
Exports from Turkey

SITC	Commodity	Total Exports, 2008 (US$ million)	Percentage Distribution, Total Exports	Annual Growth Rate of Exports, 1995–2008 (%)	Exports to the EU 2008 (US$ million)	Percentage Distribution, Exports to EU	Share of Exports to EU of Sectoral Exports	Annual Growth Rate, Exports to Eu 1995–2008 (%)
	Agricultural products							
0+1+4+22	Food	10,694	8.02	6.33	4,238	6.57	39.63	6.84
2–22–27–28	Agricultural raw materials	768	0.58	6.31	332	0.52	43.28	4.88
	Mining products							
27+28	Ores and other minerals	2,463	1.85	13.28	838	1.30	34.02	10.75
3	Fuels	7,531	5.65	21.21	2,073	3.21	27.52	9.36
68	Non-ferrous metals	2,094	1.57	15.31	1,169	1.81	55.83	17.66
	Manufactures							
67	Iron and steel	16,844	12.63	15.84	3,550	5.50	21.08	18.98
	Chemicals							
51	Organic chemicals	462	0.35	8.15	287	0.44	62.17	9.41
57+58	Plastics	2,365	1.77	19.67	876	1.36	37.06	20.42
52	Inorganic chemicals	673	0.50	4.32	256	0.40	38.08	2.20
54	Pharmaceuticals	470	0.35	13.98	193	0.30	41.04	16.88
53+55+56+59	Other chemicals	2,152	1.61	12.15	540	0.84	25.08	20.52
6–65–67–68	Other semi-manufactures	12,254	9.19	16.78	5,090	7.89	41.54	16.27
	Machinery and transport equipment							
71–713	Power-generating machinery	2,369	1.78	20.92	1,494	2.32	63.04	17.13

(Continued)

TABLE 1 (Continued)

SITC	Commodity	Total Exports, 2008 (US$ million)	Percentage Distribution, Total Exports	Annual Growth Rate of Exports, 1995–2008 (%)	Exports to the EU 2008 (US$ million)	Percentage Distribution, Exports to EU	Share of Exports to EU of Sectoral Exports	Annual Growth Rate, Exports to Eu 1995–2008 (%)
72+73+74	Other non-electrical machinery	6,097	4.57	20.57	2,451	3.80	40.20	20.27
75+76+776	Office machines and tel. equipment	2,433	1.82	19.13	2,081	3.23	85.53	20.84
77–776–7783	Electrical machinery and apparatus	7,062	5.30	17.71	3,520	5.46	49.85	17.82
78–785–786 +7132+7783	Automotive products	17,845	13.38	27.61	13,415	20.79	75.17	32.83
79+785+786+7131 +7133+7138+7139	Other transport equipment	4,674	3.51	21.44	3,036	4.70	64.94	20.28
65	Textiles	9,403	7.05	10.22	4,795	7.43	50.99	10.04
84	Clothing	13,595	10.20	7.22	11,027	17.09	81.11	9.23
8–84–86–891	Other consumer goods	6,896	5.17	17.83	2,970	4.60	43.08	20.31
9+891	Other products	4,208	3.16	41.93	291	0.45	6.91	29.43
Total		133,352	100.00	13.87	64,520	100.00	48.38	14.74

Note:
SITC = Standard International Trade Classification.
Source: Own calculations based on data provided by the State Institute of Statistics.

per cent. The export commodities with the highest annual growth rates were 'other products' with a growth rate of 41.9 per cent, 'automotive products' with a growth rate of 27.6 per cent, and 'other transport equipment' with a growth rate of 21.4 per cent. Similarly the export commodities to the EU with the highest growth rates were 'automotive products' with a growth rate of 32.8 per cent, 'other products' with a growth rate of 29.4 per cent, and 'office machines and equipment' with a growth rate of 20.8 per cent. Finally, we note that the share of the EU in total sectoral exports has been highest in the cases of 'office machines and telecommunications equipment' with a share of 85.5 per cent, 'clothing' with a share of 81.1 per cent, and 'automotive products' with a share of 75.2 per cent. Among the sectors considered the share of the EU in total sectoral exports has been the lowest in the cases of 'other products', 'iron and steel' and 'other chemicals'.

Table 2 shows that imports from the EU15 formed 37.2 per cent of total imports. The table further reveals that the three import commodities with the highest shares in total imports were 'fuels' with a share of 23.8 per cent, 'automotive products' with a share of 7.5 per cent, and 'iron and steel' with a share of 7.4 per cent. The three import commodities with the highest shares in imports from the EU were 'automotive products' with a share of 15.7 per cent, 'other non-electrical machinery' with a share of 12.7 per cent, and 'other semi-manufactures' with a share of 7.0 per cent. During the period 1995–2008 total imports grew at an annual rate of 12.4 per cent. The imported commodities with the highest annual growth rates were 'other products' with a growth rate of 36.2 per cent, 'clothing' with a growth rate of 22.9 per cent, and 'non-ferrous metals' with a growth rate of 17.5 per cent. Similarly the imported commodities from the EU with the highest growth rates were 'fuels' with a growth rate of 18.9 per cent, 'pharmaceuticals' with a growth rate of 17.4 per cent, and 'automotive products' with a growth rate of 15.7 per cent. Finally, we note that the share of the EU in total sectoral imports has been highest in the cases of 'automotive products' with a share of 77.8 per cent, 'pharmaceuticals' with a share of 68.6 per cent, and 'other non-electrical machinery' with a share of 64.5 per cent. Among the sectors considered, the share of the EU in total sectoral imports has been the lowest in the cases of 'other products', 'fuels' and 'clothing'.

Turning to consideration of foreign direct investment (FDI) flows we note that Turkey until recently was not successful in attracting FDI inflows. Annual FDI inflows amounted to only US$791 million during 1990–2000. The country's failure to attract large foreign investment inflows was mainly due to economic and political uncertainties surrounding the country in the 1990s and early 2000s, and the unfavourable investment climate in particular to foreign investors. With the introduction of the 2001 programme of economic stabilisation, implementation of its privatisation programme, the EU's 2004 decision to begin membership negotiations with Turkey, and liberalisation measures introduced during the last seven years, FDI inflows have increased considerably. They reached US$20.2 billion in 2006, US$22.1 billion in 2007 and US$18.2 billion in 2008.

TABLE 2
Imports from Turkey

SITC	Commodity	Total Imports, 2008 (US$ million)	Percentage Distribution, Total Imports	Annual Growth Rate of Imports, 1995–2008 (%)	Imports from EU, 2008 (US$ million)	Percentage Distribution, Imports from EU	Share of Imports from EU of Sectoral Imports	Annual Growth Rate, Imports from EU, 1995–2008 (%)
	Agricultural products							
0+1+4+22	Food	8,502	4.20	6.69	1,887	2.51	22.20	6.76
2-22-27-28	Agricultural raw materials	4,535	2.24	7.09	1,418	1.88	31.26	6.83
	Mining products							
27+28	Ores and other minerals	10,345	5.11	15.57	3,965	5.27	38.33	12.30
3	Fuels	48,207	23.81	12.97	3,531	4.69	7.32	18.94
68	Non-ferrous metals	6,382	3.15	17.50	1,452	1.93	22.76	13.11
	Manufactures							
67	Iron and steel	15,031	7.42	15.61	5,070	6.74	33.73	12.83
	Chemicals							
51	Organic chemicals	4,169	2.06	9.21	2,026	2.69	48.60	8.65
57+58	Plastics	8,486	4.19	15.63	4,749	6.31	55.97	13.15
52	Inorganic chemicals	1,667	0.82	8.67	537	0.71	32.22	6.28
54	Pharmaceuticals	4,738	2.34	16.51	3,250	4.32	68.59	17.36
53+55+56+59	Other chemicals	6,481	3.20	10.04	3,884	5.16	59.93	9.67

SITC								
6−65−67−68	Other semi-manufactures	9,071	4.48	11.74	5,267	7.00	58.06	10.90
	Machinery and transport equipment							
71−713	Power-generating machinery	2,991	1.48	10.59	1,740	2.31	58.19	11.51
72+73+74	Other non-electrical machinery	14,767	7.29	9.16	9,524	12.66	64.49	8.80
75+76+776	Office machines and tel. equipment	8,079	3.99	11.62	2,535	3.37	31.38	4.76
77−776−7783	Electrical machinery and apparatus	6,869	3.39	13.67	3,562	4.73	51.86	10.07
78−785−786 +7132+7783	Automotive products	15,155	7.49	15.47	11,794	15.67	77.82	15.72
79+785+786+7131 +7133+7138+7139	Other transport equipment	4,327	2.14	5.10	2,478	3.29	57.26	9.47
65	Textiles	5,797	2.86	9.64	1,713	2.28	29.55	7.00
84	Clothing	2,216	1.09	22.89	465	0.62	20.97	13.04
8−84−86−891	Other consumer goods	8,961	4.43	12.41	4,133	5.49	46.12	10.20
9+891	*Other products*	5,685	2.81	36.16	269	0.36	4.74	15.44
	Total	202,461	100.00	12.42	75,249	100.00	37.17	11.19

Note:

SITC = Standard International Trade Classification.

Source: Own calculations based on data provided by the State Institute of Statistics.

TABLE 3
Sectoral Distribution of Foreign Direct Investment Inflows (US$ million)

Sectors	2004	2005	2006	2007	2008
Agriculture, hunting and forestry	4	5	5	5	26
Fishing	2	2	1	3	19
Mining and quarrying	73	40	122	336	173
Manufacturing	190	785	1,866	4,210	3,828
Manufacture of food products and beverages	78	68	608	766	1,279
Manufacture of textiles	9	180	26	232	190
Manufacture of chemicals and chemical products	38	174	601	1,109	202
Manufacture of machinery and equipment	6	13	54	48	223
Manufacture of electrical optical equipment	2	13	53	117	243
Manufacture of motor vehicles, trailers and semi-trailers	27	106	63	70	67
Other manufacturing	30	231	461	1,868	1,624
Electricity, gas and water supply	66	4	112	567	1,053
Construction	3	80	222	285	720
Wholesale and retail trade	72	68	1,166	169	2,073
Hotels and restaurants	1	42	23	33	27
Transport, storage and communications	639	3,285	6,696	1,116	169
Financial services	69	4,018	6,957	11,662	5,925
Real estate, renting and business activities	3	29	99	560	673
Health and social services	35	74	265	177	150
Other community, social and personal service activities	33	103	105	13	59
Total	1,190	8,535	17,639	19,136	14,895

Source: Undersecretariat of the Treasury.

Table 3, showing the sectoral distribution of FDI inflows into Turkey over the period 2004–08, reveals that during the last five years the sectors attracting the highest amount of FDI have been services and manufacturing. While the average share of services in total FDI inflows over the period 2006–08 amounted to 79.2 per cent, the average share of manufacturing in total FDI inflow over the same period was 19.4 per cent. In services the 'financial services' and 'transport, storage and communications' received the highest amount of investment with 59.7 and 17.3 per cent, respectively. In manufacturing the highest amount of investment was received by 'manufacture of food products and beverages' and 'manufacture of chemicals and chemical products' with 28.1 and 21.3 per cent, respectively. On the other hand, Table 4, showing the FDI inflows by country of origin over the period 2004–08, reveals that the EU has been the largest investor in Turkey. While the share of the EU in total FDI inflows over the period 2006–08 amounted to 74.6 per cent, the share of the US was 10.9 per cent and the share of Gulf countries

TABLE 4
Foreign Direct Investment Inflows by Country of Origin (US$ million)

	2004	2005	2006	2007	2008
EU countries	1,027	5,006	14,489	12,600	11,281
Germany	73	391	357	954	1,217
France	34	2,107	439	368	685
Netherlands	568	383	5,069	5,443	1,738
United Kingdom	126	166	628	702	2,294
Italy	14	692	189	74	222
Other EU countries	212	1,267	7,807	5,059	5,125
Other European countries	6	1,646	85	373	291
African countries	–	3	21	5	82
USA	36	88	848	4,212	863
Canada	61	26	121	11	24
Americas	–	8	33	494	60
Asia	60	1,756	1,927	1,405	2,292
Near and Middle Eastern countries	54	1,678	1,910	608	2,132
Gulf countries	43	1,675	1,783	311	1,911
Other Near and Middle Eastern countries	11	2	3	196	96
Other Asian countries	6	78	17	797	160
Other countries	–	2	115	36	2
Total	1,190	8,535	17,639	19,136	14,895

Source: Undersecretariat of the Treasury.

8.2 per cent. In the EU the largest investors have been those from the Netherlands with a share of 31.2 per cent in total FDI inflows from the EU over the period 2006–08, and United Kingdom with a share of 10.1 per cent.

Finally, we note that Turkey's annual FDI outflows amounted to US$0.92 billion in 2006, US$2.11 billion in 2007 and US$2.59 billion in 2008, averaging US$1.87 billion over the period 2006–08.

4. TRADE POLICY

Over the last 13 years Turkey has been quite successful in amending its domestic legislation to reflect both its EU and WTO commitments.

a. Measures Affecting Imports

Goods imported into Turkey are subject to various charges: customs taxes and levies (customs tariffs, and the mass housing fund levy); and internal taxes (excise duties, i.e. special consumption tax, value-added tax (VAT), and stamp duty). As of 2009 Turkey's tariff comprises 16,800 lines at the Harmonised Commodity Description and Coding System (HS) 12-digit level.

As a result of the Uruguay Round, 46.3 per cent of tariff lines in Turkey are now bound (all tariff lines for agricultural products and some 36 per cent of the lines for non-agricultural products). Final bindings range from zero to 225 per cent on agricultural products, and from zero to 102 per cent on non-agricultural goods. The simple average bound tariff rate amounts to 33.9 per cent.

In Turkey there are two other sets of tariff rates besides the bound tariff rates. These are the applied tariff rates and the statutory tariff rates. Law No. 474 on Customs Tariff Schedule has set the so-called statutory tariff rates. The law enables the government to increase the applied MFN tariff rates for a given year when they are deemed not high enough to provide 'adequate' protection to domestic industries. Under the law, the government can replace applied MFN tariff rates by 150 per cent of the corresponding rates of the statutory tariff with a view to ensuring higher protection to local industries. In the case of products subject to tariff bindings, when the new rate is higher than the corresponding bound tariff rate, then the latter applies. But in cases where the tariff rate is specified as 'exempt', the equivalent applied tariff rate is zero per cent and the government cannot increase the applied tariff rate above zero per cent. Hence, the 'exempt' status in the tariff schedule provides added protection to Turkey's trade liberalisation commitments.

The applied tariff schedule in Turkey is rather complex.[5] It consists of a large number of lists specifying the tariff lines classified at the HS 12-digit level, for different country groups and countries. List I displays customs duties applied to imports of agricultural products, excluding fish and fishery products. List II shows customs duties to be applied to imports of industrial products and products covered by the ECSC. List III lays down customs duties applied to imports of processed agricultural products, and List IV the customs duties applied to imports of fish and fishery products. List V displays reduced customs duties applied to imports of certain products used as raw materials in the fertiliser, chemical, plastics, textile and electrical machinery industries. Finally, List VI lists the commodities that could be imported by the civil air transportation sector with zero tariff rates. The six lists are accompanied by six annexes. Annexes 1 and 2 show the specific tariff rates applied to imports of processed agricultural products distinguished by the content of milk fat and cornstarch/glucose. While Annex 3 lists the three groups of countries benefiting from the GSP regime, Annexes 4 and 5 list the sensitive and non-sensitive sectors benefiting again from the GSP regime.

Turkey's tariff comprises *ad valorem* and non-*ad valorem* rates consisting of specific, mixed, compound and formula duties. Most of the tariffs are *ad valorem*. Specific taxes (Mass Housing Fund levy) are applied on the imports of certain fish and fishery products specified in List IV as well as on the imports of certain prod-

---

[5] I would like to thank Şinasi Demirbaş and Taşkın Barış Ergün of the Undersecretariat of Foreign Trade for explaining certain aspects of this complex tariff schedule.

ucts in List II. On the other hand, the mixed, compound and formula duties apply
on processed agricultural commodities specified in List III. In List III the duties
range between 0 and 368.25 euro/100 kg depending on the content of milk fat and
cornstarch/glucose.[6] Finally, we note that products listed in List V are in general
more specific than those listed in List II. For products listed in both List V and
List II we take the minimum of the two tariff rates.

For the calculation of nominal protection rates we introduce the following nota-
tion. Let t_c^i denote the rate of *ad valorem* customs duty on commodity i; M_i c.i.f.
value of the import of commodity i measured in Turkish lira; m_i quantity of the
import of commodity i measured in units the Mass Housing Fund levy is reported;
$FUND_1^i$ the euro-denominated Mass Housing Fund levy on commodity i; $FUND_2^i$
ad valorem Mass Housing Fund tax rate on commodity i; and E exchange rate
(Turkish lira per euro).[7] The base of the customs duty on commodity i is the c.i.f.
value of the import of commodity i. Therefore, this duty is calculated as $t_c^i M_i$. The
Mass Housing Fund levy is usually specific. For these specific tariff rates the *ad
valorem* equivalents of these rates need to be calculated. Given the foreign price
of the commodity, $P_j^{Euro} = M_j/m_j E$, the Turkish lira equivalent of the euro-
denominated levy is calculated from the relation $FUND_1^i m_i E = (M_i(FUND_1^i/p_i^{Euro}))$
. Hence, the *ad valorem* equivalent is given by $(FUND_1^i/p_i^{Euro})$. On the other hand,
when the Mass Housing Fund tax is specified in *ad valorem* terms the equivalent
tariff revenue is given by $FUND_2^i M_i$. The sum total of all the above taxes and
surcharges is then denoted by $t_i = (t_c^i + (FUND_1^i/p_i^{Euro}) + FUND_2^i)$.

On imported commodities Turkey imposes value-added tax (VAT) as well as
special consumption tax (SCT). The base of SCT is the value of imported commodities inclusive of import taxes and surcharges, i.e. $(1 + t_i)M_i$. On the other
hand, the base of VAT is the value of imported commodities inclusive of import
taxes, surcharges and the SCT. Letting vat_i be the value-added tax rate on commodity i, sct_i the special consumption tax rate on commodity i, the special consumption tax rate on imported commodity i is calculated as

$$SCT_i = sct_i(1 + t_c^i + (FUND_1^i/p_i^{Euro}) + FUND_2^i).$$

Similarly, the VAT rate on imported commodity i is determined as

$$VAT_i = vat_i[(1 + t_c^i + (FUND_1^i/p_i^{Euro}) + FUND_2^i) + SCT_i].$$

[6] Here it should be emphasised that in line with the CUD, processed agricultural products imported
into Turkey from the EU are subject to customs duties comprising an industrial and agricultural
component. While all industrial components enjoy duty-free treatment, few agricultural components
are subject to preferential treatment. MFN customs duties still apply to most agricultural components, where these components are calculated by multiplying the quantity of primary agricultural
product used in processing, according to an agreed set of ratios, by the specific rate charge.
[7] Note that the Mass Housing Fund levy is denominated in euros.

Noting that domestically-produced commodities are subject to VAT and SCT at the rates vat_i and sct_i, respectively, the nominal protection rate (NPR) on imported commodity i (NPR_i), measuring the protection provided to commodity i relative to domestic production of commodity i, equals

$$NPR_i = t_i + SCT_i + VAT_i - vat_i(1 + sct_i) - sct_i.$$

When we consider the average protection rate in a particular sector j with k commodities in the sector the simple average protection rate is calculated as $\sum_{i=1}^{k} NPR_i^j / k$, where NPR_i^j denotes the average protection rate on commodity i of sector j.

It was stated above that Annexes 1 and 2 of the tariff schedule show among others the specific tariff rates applied to imports of processed agricultural products distinguished by the content of milk fat and cornstarch/glucose, and that the specific tariff rate for a specific 12-digit HS commodity indicated as T1 and T2 in List III may vary between 0 and 368.25 euro/100 kg depending on the content of milk fat and cornstarch/glucose. Thus, one cannot obtain the *ad valorem* equivalent of the specific tariff rate for those 12-digit HS commodities unless one has information on the milk fat and cornstarch/glucose contents of those commodities imported. To obtain the *ad valorem* equivalent of the specific tariff rates for each 12-digit HS commodity in List III, for which the specific tariffs are stated as T1 and T2, we first determine the total Housing Fund taxes collected on each 12-digit HS commodity under consideration by country groups (EU + EFTA, and other countries). Next we divide the Housing Fund tax collected on each 12-digit HS commodity under consideration by country groups by the value of import of the corresponding 12-digit HS commodity again by country group, and obtain the *ad valorem* tariff equivalent for each 12-digit HS commodity in List III, for which the specific tariffs are stated as T1 and T2.[8]

Table 5 shows the NPRs prevailing in 2009, where all non-*ad valorem* tariffs have been converted to *ad valorem* equivalents and incorporated into NPRs. In the table, average tariffs for two groups, of countries are listed. These are the EU, and countries for which the MFN tariffs apply. In the table the average NPRs are shown for 19 aggregated HS commodity groups such as 'chemical products', 'textile and textile articles' and 'transport equipment'. The table reveals that in trade with the EU, the overall simple average NPR is 9.12 per cent and the overall simple average MFN protection rate is 13.86 per cent.

In trade with the EU, 17 out of the total of 19 sectors have zero NPRs. The highest protection rates apply in the cases of 'agricultural commodities', and

---

[8] I am grateful to Rasim Kutlu of the Undersecretariat for Customs for providing the essential data required for the estimation of the *ad valorem* equivalent tariff rates for commodities for which the specific tariffs are stated as T1 and T2 in List III.

TABLE 5
Nominal Protection Rates, 2009 (per cent)

HS Code	Commodity Description	Number of Tariff Lines	Applied Mean Tariffs (Simple) EU	Range Tariff EU	Standard Deviation EU	Mean MFN Tariffs (Simple) Others	Range Tariff Non-EU	Standard Deviation Non-EU	Imports 2008 (US$ million)
01–24	Agricultural Products	2,931	52.22	0–243	54.54	56.50	0–243	55.08	8,758.8
25–27	Mineral Products	414	0.00	0–0	0.00	1.26	0–14.8	2.02	49,555.2
28–38	Chemical Products	3,072	0.08	0–18.4	1.10	5.41	0–40.8	3.23	17,384.7
39–40	Plastics and Rubber	543	0.00	0–0	0.00	4.54	0–7.0	2.88	11,604.7
41–43	Leather and Travel Goods	218	0.00	0–0	0.00	3.46	0–10.6	2.92	1,158.0
44–46	Wood Products	320	0.00	0–0	0.00	2.23	0–11.8	2.91	1,178.5
47–49	Cellulose Products, Paper and Paper Products	446	0.00	0–0	0.00	0.00	0–0	0.00	3,246.6
50–63	Textile and Textile Articles	2,341	0.00	0–0	0.00	8.93	0–14.2	3.98	9,630.0
64–67	Footwear and Miscellaneous Manufactures	156	0.00	0–0	0.00	8.03	0–18.4	5.69	769.2
68–70	Articles of Stone, Ceramics, Glass and Glass Products	437	0.00	0–0	0.00	4.36	0–15.6	3.39	1,403.1
71	Precious and Semi-precious Articles	104	0.00	0–0	0.00	1.20	0–4.7	1.91	5,653.8
72–83	Base Metals and Articles of Base Metal	1,915	0.00	0–0	0.00	5.36	0–27.6	6.41	33,417.3
84	Non-electric Machinery	1,479	0.00	0–0	0.00	1.95	0–10.5	1.69	22,515.4
85	Electric Machinery	977	0.00	0–0	0.00	3.30	0–19.8	3.82	13,868.0
86–89	Transport Equipment	466	0.00	0–0	0.00	6.36	0–38.2	6.56	15,593.2
90–92	Precision	591	0.00	0–0	0.00	2.55	0–11.8	2.25	3,711.9
93	Arms and Ammunitions	33	0.00	0–0	0.00	2.85	0–4.5	1.39	60.2
94–96	Miscellaneous Manufactured Articles	343	0.00	0–0	0.00	3.05	0–9.1	1.90	1,900.1
97	Art and Antiques	14	0.00	0–0	0.00	0.00	0–0	0.00	414.2
	Total	16,800	9.12	0–243	30.20	13.86	0–243	30.50	201,822.9

Source: Author's own calculations.

'chemical products'. In those cases the NPRs are 52.22 per cent and 0.08 per cent, respectively. On the other hand, in the case of trade with countries for which the MFN tariffs apply, the NPR on 'agricultural products' is 56.5 per cent, 'textiles and textile articles' 8.93 per cent, and 'footwear and miscellaneous manufactures' 8.03 per cent. The figures show that in Turkey the agricultural sector is heavily protected.

Table 6 shows the NPRs for the agricultural commodities in more detail. The table reveals that in trade with the EU the simple average NPR is 50.7 per cent and in trade with countries for which MFN tariffs apply, 54.85 per cent. In the case of trade with the EU the highest average protection rates apply in the cases of 'meat and edible offal', 'milk and dairy products; eggs; honey' and 'products made from meat, fish and crustacea'. In those cases the NPRs are 147.65 per cent, 104.01 per cent and on 102.63 per cent, respectively. On the other hand, in the case of trade with countries for which the MFN tariffs apply the highest average NPRs are imposed on 'meat and edible offal', 'products made from meat, fish and crustacea', and 'milk and dairy products; eggs; honey'. These protection rates are not much different from the protection rates that apply on imports from the EU.

Comparison of the protection rates reported in Tables 5 and 6 with those given in the *Trade Policy Review: Turkey 2007* reveals that Turkey's protection rates are higher than those reported in World Trade Organization (2008) for some of the commodity groups. Although the figures in World Trade Organization (2008) refer to the year 2007 and our data to the year 2009, the difference in the result is due mainly to the way the protection rates in the two studies have been estimated. It is interesting to note that while the overall MFN simple average tariff rate in World Trade Organization (2008) is 11.6 per cent, it is 13.86 per cent in our case. Furthermore, when the WTO definition of agricultural products is used, the overall MFN simple average protection rate in agriculture is calculated as 47.6 per cent in World Trade Organization (2008), whereas it is 54.85 per cent in our case.[9] Divergence of the NPRs calculated through the two different studies is more pronounced in sectors where the tariff rates inclusive of all other taxes and surcharges, value-added tax rates and special consumption tax rates are relatively high, as in the cases of 'vehicles other than railway or tramway rolling stock, and parts and accessories thereof' (HS 87).

In Turkey, import prohibitions apply to 10 broad product categories such as narcotics, arms and ammunitions, and ozone-depleting substances for reasons such as environment, public security, health and public morals. Regarding licensing,

---

[9] WTO definition of agriculture: HS Chapters 01–24 less fish and fishery products (HS 0301–0307, 0509, 051191, 1504, 1603–1605 and 230120) plus some selected products (HS 290543, 290544, 290545, 3301, 3501–3505, 380910, 382311–382319, 382360, 382370, 382460, 4101–4103, 4301, 5001–5003, 5101–5103, 5201–5203, 5301 and 5302). But in our calculations we use the following definition of agriculture: HS Chapters 01–24, 4101–4103, 5101–5103 and 5201–5203.

TABLE 6
Protection in Agriculture, 2009

HS Code	Description	Number of Tariff Lines	Applied Mean Tariffs (Simple) EU	Range Tariff EU	Standard Deviation EU	Mean MFN Tariffs (Simple) Others	Range Tariff Non-EU	Standard Deviation Non-EU	2008 Imports (US$ million)
I. Live animals and animal products									
1	Live animals	83	44.84	0–136.4	51.40	44.84	0–136.4	51.40	41.45
2	Meat and edible offal	235	147.65	25.3–243	80.66	147.72	25.3–243	80.57	0.91
3	Fish and sea products	336	36.88	0–64.9	14.52	47.05	0–76.7	17.99	119.77
4	Milk and dairy products; eggs; honey	209	104.01	0–183.6	65.05	105.93	0–183.6	63.33	126.94
5	Other animal products	38	1.92	0–23.6	5.75	2.08	0–23.6	5.78	28.54
II. Vegetable products									
6	Plants and floriculture products	52	20.05	2.6–55.2	22.96	20.64	4.2–55.2	22.52	57.75
7	Vegetable, plants, roots and tubers	166	20.74	0–50	10.33	20.80	0–50	10.23	400.25
8	Edible fruits; citrus fruits	148	42.08	15.6–147.3	22.98	42.08	15.6–147.3	22.98	318.63
9	Coffee, tea, spices	57	40.93	0–156.6	35.72	41.20	0–156.6	35.51	72.74
10	Cereals	65	58.05	0–140.4	48.81	58.09	0–140.4	48.77	2,137.32
11	Products of the milling industry	102	42.18	4.3–82.8	15.39	42.46	4.3–82.8	15.14	25.19
12	Oilseeds, various seeds/fruits; industrial plants	125	19.01	0–41.3	11.63	19.94	0–41.3	11.63	1,465.17
13	Vegetable lacquers, resins, balsams	35	2.70	0–23.6	7.62	4.97	0–29.5	9.96	25.68
14	Vegetable plaiting materials	21	0.00	0–0	0.00	0.00	0–0	0.00	4.92
III. Animal or vegetable oils and fats									
15	Animal or vegetable oils and fats	198	25.43	0–59	19.55	26.13	0–59	18.90	1,657.56

(*Continued*)

TABLE 6 (Continued)

HS Code	Description	Number of Tariff Lines	Applied Mean Tariffs (Simple) EU	Range Tariff EU	Standard Deviation EU	Mean MFN Tariffs (Simple) Others	Range Tariff Non-EU	Standard Deviation Non-EU	2008 Imports (US$ million)
IV. Foodstuffs, beverages, tobacco									
16	Products made from meat, fish, crustacea	134	102.63	43.2–131.2	34.14	109.12	58.3–131.2	26.90	2.47
17	Sugar and sweets	64	73.07	0–145.8	69.21	78.28	0–145.8	64.93	86.84
18	Cocoa and cocoa products	29	8.58	0–28.1	7.61	10.53	0–32.1	6.32	284.17
19	Cereal products, wheat flour, pastries	88	6.20	0–40.0	9.19	16.24	4.1–68.2	12.65	151.28
20	Foods made of vegetable, fruits and other plants	371	58.60	0–146.8	19.31	59.16	0–146.8	17.95	87.64
21	Various foods	63	5.88	0–63.2	15.98	14.77	0–63.18	15.73	387.18
22	Alcoholic and non-alcoholic beverages	201	46.41	0–96.2	45.51	66.05	0–134.6	62.82	111.79
23	Residues of food industry; fodders	83	9.44	0–15.9	5.02	10.17	0–15.9	4.86	772.97
24	Processed tobacco and substitutes	28	12.64	0–29.5	14.87	61.51	18.6–139.6	48.04	391.69
V. Hides, wool and cotton									
4101–4103	Hides and skin	31	0.00	0–0	0.00	0.00	0–0	0.00	235.46
5101–5103	Wool and animal hair	44	0.00	0–0	0.00	0.00	0–0	0.00	46.67
5201–5203	Cotton	13	0.00	0–0	0.00	0.00	0–0	0.00	1,005.81
Total		3,019	50.70	0–243	54.46	54.85	0–243	55.10	10,046.78

Source: Author's own calculations.

we note that import licences are required for several categories of products, including some motor vehicles, transmission apparatus, chemicals, fertilisers, endangered species of wild fauna and flora, solvent and petroleum products, and certain sugar substitutes. Importers of these items must obtain permission from the relevant authorities. In addition, the importation of pharmaceuticals, drugs, some medical products, cosmetics, detergents, foodstuffs and packaging materials, fishery products, and agricultural, animal and veterinary products are subject to health and sanitary controls. Imports of agricultural products and foodstuffs require a 'control certificate' issued by the Ministry of Agriculture and Rural Affairs (MARA); and imports of pharmaceutical products, drugs, certain consumable medical products, cosmetics and detergents require a control certificate issued by the Ministry of Health.[10] Finally, we note that measuring and weighing instruments to be released for free circulation in Turkey are subject to control by the Directorate General of Measures and Standards of the Ministry of Industry and Trade; materials comprising cinematographic and musical works are inspected and examined by the Directorate of Copyright and Cinema with the aim of combating piracy. On the other hand, tariff preferences on agricultural products, granted under Turkey's trade agreements, are generally subject to quotas. Tariff quotas are applied on imports of various agricultural and processed agricultural products from the EU, Israel, Macedonia, Croatia, Bosnia-Herzegovina, Morocco, Syria, Tunisia, Egypt and Albania. In addition, Turkey is applying import quotas on certain textile and clothing products as a requirement for harmonising its import policy with that of the EC. Licensing is used again whenever quotas are imposed.

Regarding contingent protectionism we note that as of the end of 2008, Turkey had 107 anti-dumping duties in force. Most of the anti-dumping duties were imposed on imports from China (42 duties), Indonesia (10 duties), Chinese Taipei (9 duties), Thailand (8 duties) and India (7 duties), and measures have affected mostly textiles and clothing. The majority are specific duties, and some *ad valorem* duties as high as 100 per cent. Turkey is an important user of anti-dumping measures. As of 31 December 2008 it had 32 anti-dumping investigations in progress, and most of these investigations concerned imports from China. On the other hand, Turkey did not make extensive use of countervailing measures and safeguard actions. It has reported only one countervailing measure against imports from India, and it has not taken any safeguard actions under GATT Article XIX.

---

[10] Since 1996 MARA has not issued 'control certificates' for imports from countries considered to be risks for diseases. The decision was made on sanitary grounds, and was based on the World Organisation for Animal Health risk classification for live animals (dairy and beef cattle, sheep, goats and poultry) and meat (beef, sheep, goats and poultry).

b. Measures Affecting Exports

In Turkey the exportation of certain commodities is subject to registration, and the exportation of some other commodities is prohibited because of environmental, health or religious reasons. All other commodities can be exported freely. Exporters are required to register with the Exporters Union and their local chamber of commerce. According to the regulations of the export regime, export prohibitions have been imposed on 'antiques and archaeological works', 'Indian hemp', 'tobacco seedlings and tobacco plants', 'Angora goats', 'game and wild animals', 'walnut, mulberry, cherry, pear, plum, badger, ash, elm, and lime in logs, in timber, in plank and in sketch', 'natural flower bulbs', 'wood and wood charcoal', 'plants of olive, fig, hazelnut, pistachio, and grapevine', 'sahlep', 'liquidamber orientalis', 'pterocarya carpinifolia', and 'dates "Phoenix the ophrasti crenter"'. On the other hand, an export licence is required for 26 categories of products. Exporters of these items must obtain permission from the relevant authorities. The 26 categories include (as of 2009) commodity groups such as 'military weapons and ammunition', 'opium and poppy seeds', 'addictive and psychotropic substances', 'seeds', 'feeds covered by Feed Law', 'pharmaceuticals for veterinary purposes', 'technology and equipment used for nuclear purposes', 'goods covered by Missile Technology Controlling Regime' and 'sugar'. Finally, we note that Turkey applies export taxes at the rate of US$0.04 per kg on shelled hazelnuts, US$0.08 per kg on unshelled hazelnuts, and US$0.5 per kg on raw skins (HS 41.01, 41.02 and 41.03, excluding processed raw skins).

Regarding export incentives we note that as a result of the customs union between the EU and Turkey, as well as Turkey's commitments vis-à-vis the WTO, Turkey has progressively revamped the incentives provided to exporters. Currently, export subsidies are provided through the following programmes: 'cash subsidies', 'Investment Encouragement Program', 'Inward-Processing' scheme, state aid programmes under Ministerial Council Resolution on 'State Aids Related to Exports of 1994', 'export credit scheme of the Turk Eximbank' and 'free zones'.

Cash subsidies are extended to a number of agricultural products and processed agricultural goods including cut flowers, frozen vegetables, frozen fruit and olive oil. Table 7 shows the subsidies extended to these commodities. From the table it follows that subsidies are quite substantial for various commodities, but that the applied subsidy rates cannot exceed specified maximum rates. These rates are set between 5 and 20 per cent of the value of exports, and between 14 and 100 per cent of the quantities exported.

Duty concessions are granted under the 'Investment Encouragement Program' (IEP) which merged the previous 'General Investment Encouragement Program' and the 'Aids Granted to Small and Medium Enterprises' (SMEs) Investments'. The purpose of IEP is to encourage and orient investments, in order to reduce regional imbalances within the country, and to create new employment opportuni-

TABLE 7
Cash Export Subsidies

HS	Commodity	Cash Subsidies	Share of Exported Quantity Eligible for the Subsidy	Maximum Subsidy Rate
0207	Meat and edible offal of poultry (excluding 02071391, 02071399, 02071491, 02072691, 02072699, 020734, 02073591, 02072791, 02072799, 02073599, 02073681, 02073685, 02073689)	$186/tonne	14%	20%
040700	Eggs	$15/1,000 units	78%	10%
040900	Honey	$65/ton	32%	10%
060311, 12, 13, 14, 19	Fresh cut flowers and flower buds of a kind suitable for bouquets	$205/tonne	37%	10%
0710	Vegetables (uncooked or cooked by steaming or boiling in water) (excluding 071010)	$79/tonne	27%	12%
0712	Dried vegetables, whole, cut, sliced, broken or in powder	$370/tonne	20%	10%
080810	Apples	$50/ton	March–May 2009	15%
0811	Fruits and nuts, uncooked or cooked by steaming or boiling	$78/tonne	41%	8%
1509	Olive oil (including 15162091 0014 and 15162090 8011)	$180/tonne	100%	5%
16010099, 160231, 160232	Sausages made of poultry	$250/tonne	40%	10%
1604	Prepared or preserved fish	$200/tonne	100%	5%
1806	Chocolate and other food preparations containing cocoa	$119/tonne	48%	6%
1902	Pasta	$66/tonne	32%	10%
190531, 32	Sweet biscuits; waffles (including 19059045, 1905906000, 1905906014)	$119/tonne	18%	8%
2001, 2002, 2003 2004, 2005, 2006 2008	Vegetables, fruits, nuts and other edible parts of plants, tomatoes prepared or preserved, mushrooms, truffles, other vegetables prepared or preserved. Fruits, nuts, and other edible parts of plants (frozen) (excluding 200811, 20081911, 200819130011, 200819190014, 200819190039, 200819190049, 20081991, 200819930011, 200819950014, 200819950039, 200819950049, 20081999)	$75/tonne	51%	15%
2007	Jams, fruit jellies, marmalades, fruit or net purée (excluding 20079920, 20079970018)	$63/tonne	35%	5%
2009	Fruit juices	$150/tonne	15%	12%

Source: www.igeme.gov.tr.

ties, while using technologies with greater value-added. To qualify for the IEP, potential investors must apply for an investment encouragement certificate to be issued by the Undersecretariat of the Treasury. In principle, all investment projects are eligible. If granted a certificate, the project can benefit from incentives which cover (i) exemption from customs duties and fund levies on imported machinery and equipment that are part of the investment project and appear on the machinery and equipment list approved by the Undersecretariat of Treasury; (ii) VAT exemption for imported and locally purchased machinery and equipment; (iii) 'interest support', by certain percentage points of the interest rate, on credits obtained on commercial terms by investors to finance their investment projects; and (iv) electricity cost support for tourism investments and establishments. Furthermore, foreign exchange earning activities are exempt from stamp duties and related charges. SME investments can also benefit from the encouragement measures offered under the IEP.

In addition to the IEP scheme, the Inward-Processing (IP) scheme also benefits exporters. Goods imported under the IP scheme are intended for re-export from the customs territory of Turkey in the form of 'compensating products'.[11] The system works through suspension of duties and VAT until the exportation of the products, or reimbursement based on a drawback method. The suspension system is used whenever there is a 'substantiated' intention to re-export the goods in the form of compensating products. Under the drawback system, used mainly for inward processing, repayment of the import duty and VAT can be reclaimed when the compensating products are exported.

Under Ministerial Council Resolution on 'State Aids Related to Exports of 1994', Turkey provides nine different state aid programmes, carried out by various public bodies/institutions and organisations. The programmes are 'state aid for organising domestic fairs with international participation', 'state aid for environmental protection activities', 'state aid for research and development projects', 'state aid for encouraging employment in sectoral foreign trade companies', 'state aid for participation in international fairs and exhibitions', 'state aid for operating stores abroad', 'state aid for promoting Turkish trade marks and improving the image of Turkish goods', 'state aid for market research projects' and 'state aid for vocational training'.[12]

---

[11] Compensating products are all goods obtained from processing operations.

[12] 'State aid for organising domestic fairs with international participation' provides up to 50 per cent of promotional activities not exceeding US$25,000; 50 per cent of transportation expenses of representatives of foreign companies not exceeding US$15,000; and 50 per cent of expenses regarding activities during the fair not exceeding US$5,000. 'State aid for environmental protection activities' covers up to 50 per cent of the relevant certification expenses. 'State aid for research and development projects' provides 50 per cent and up to a maximum of 60 per cent grant for R&D activities for three years. In addition, capital support is provided in the form of support for two years up to US$1 million, and a soft loan up to US$100,000 for one year to be paid back in US$ with interest.

Preferential export credits are extended by the Export Credit Bank of Turkey (Turk Eximbank), which operates a large number of export credit, guarantee and insurance schemes. Short-term financial assistance through Turk Eximbank is made available to exporters at the pre-shipment and post-shipment stages with a term up to 360 days for credits in Turkish lira and 540 days for credits in foreign currency. Credits are allocated through the Turkish commercial banks or directly by the Turk Eximbank. Turk Eximbank's medium- and long-term financial support programmes have been developed mainly for the export of capital goods and turnkey investment projects to be undertaken by Turkish and Turkey-based contractors. The majority of these programmes involve extending financing facilities to buyers outside of Turkey for the purchase of Turkish goods and/or services. For many medium- and long-term operations, a sovereign guarantee in favour of Turk Eximbank has been a prerequisite for extension of the facility. Moreover, export receivables are discounted in order to promote sales on deferred payment conditions and to increase export trade volumes. The Turk Eximbank also offers Turkish exporters, investors and overseas contractors a variety of insurance policies against commercial and political risks. Commercial risk-based losses are indemnified by Turk Eximbank from its own resources, while political risks are, in principle, backed by the government. Since 2000, short-term political risks have also been ceded to the reinsurance panel within certain country limits.

Since the passage of the law on free zones in 1985, 20 zones have been established in Turkey. The zones are open to a wide range of activities. Offshore banking, insurance business and customs brokers are not allowed, but all industrial, other commercial and service operations deemed appropriate by the Supreme Planning Board may be conducted. There is no limitation on foreign capital participation in investment within the free zones, and 100 per cent repatriation of

---

'State aid for encouraging employment in sectoral foreign trade companies' provides 75 per cent of the pre-tax salary for one manager and two staff with professional experience, for one year. 'State aid for participation in international fairs and exhibitions' includes, in the case of national participation, 50 per cent of participation fees not exceeding US$10,000–15,000; and 50–75 per cent of the rental cost of empty stands not exceeding US$10,000–15,000. In addition, 75 per cent of promotional expenses will be covered not exceeding US$80,000–120,000. 'State aid for operating stores abroad' covers 50–60 per cent of the advertisement, rent, office inventory and decoration expenditures of companies operating a store abroad depending on the type of firm involved. In those cases promotional expenses up to certain limits will also be covered by the aid programme. 'State aid for promoting Turkish trade marks and improving the image of Turkish goods' provides 50 per cent of consultancy fees, rental fees, advertisement, certification expenses and fees for the registration of trade marks. The upper limit of support depends on the type of organisation involved. 'State aid for market research projects' provides support for buying market research projects, reports and statistics; financial assistance for companies participating in trade missions abroad, and for becoming members of e-trade websites in order to market their products abroad. The amount of support provided depends on the type of activity. Finally, 'state aid for vocational training' covers support for improving quality, productivity, management techniques, design, international marketing and foreign trade operations. The support amount to 90 per cent of training costs for programmes up to six months, 75 per cent of consultancy services costs up to one year, and one-year tuition costs of selected designers.

capital is allowed without prior permission, tax, duty or fee. In addition, financial incentives are available to free zone companies, and these include exemption from payment of customs duties and fees, and value-added taxes; no restrictions on profit transfer and for foreign exchange transactions. Under Law No. 5084 of 2004 on the 'Encouragement of Investments and Employment' only free zone users that operate under a production licence are exempted from the income or corporate taxes until the end of the taxation period of the year in which Turkey becomes a full member of the EC.[13] For other free zone users that obtained an operating licence before February 2004, the income or corporate tax exemption will apply for the validity period of the operating licence, and income tax on wages will not be paid until 2009. On the other hand, free zone users that had obtained an operating licence other than for production after February 2004, do not enjoy income or corporate tax exemption. In contrast to most other free zones, sales to the Turkish domestic market are allowed. But goods and revenues transported from the zones into Turkey are subject to all relevant import regulations.

c. Foreign Direct Investment Framework

Until very recently annual FDI inflows into Turkey amounted to less than $1 billion. The result was mainly due to economic and political uncertainties surrounding the country and the enormous institutional, legal and judicial obstacles faced by foreign investors. Furthermore, the inadequate functioning of regulatory bodies that foresaw competition in service and infrastructure industries such as telecommunications, energy and finance made entry and exit into these markets extremely difficult.[14] The situation improved considerably with the introduction of the 2001 programme of economic stabilisation, implementation of its privatisation programme, the EU's 2004 decision to begin membership negotiations with Turkey, and liberalisation measures introduced over recent years.

The Decree on Improving the Investment Environment in Turkey was enacted at the end of 2001 as a part of the national strategy to increase domestic and foreign investments by improving the business environment, increasing the overall level of income and productivity, and raising the level of competitiveness. The Decree also established the Coordination Council for the Improvement of the Investment Environment and technical subcommittees to identify and remove the remaining regulatory and administrative barriers to private investment. Since then, the authorities have implemented several legislative measures to further improve the business and investment climate, including the adoption of the Foreign Direct

---

[13] Under the prevailing regulations for operations and practices in the zones the validity period of an operating licence is a maximum of 10 years for tenant users, and 20 years for users who wish to build their own offices in the zone; if the operating licence is for production, the terms are 15 and 30 years for tenant users and investors, respectively.

[14] See Izmen and Yılmaz (2009).

Investment Law No. 4875 in 2003, and the establishment of the Turkish Investment Support and Promotion Agency in June 2006.[15]

The aim of the 2003 Foreign Direct Investment Law is to: (i) encourage FDIs in the country; (ii) protect foreign investors' rights; (iii) bring investors and investments in line with international standards; (iv) establish a notification-based rather than approval-based system for FDIs; and (v) increase the volume of FDI through established policies. The law provides a definition of foreign investors and foreign direct investments, and explains the important principles of FDIs, such as freedom to invest, national treatment, expropriation and nationalisation, transfers, access to real estate, dispute settlement, valuation of non-cash capital, employment of expatriates, and liaison offices. The new law has removed the screening and pre-approval procedures for FDI projects, re-designed the company registration process on an equal footing for domestic and foreign firms, facilitated the hiring of foreign employees, included FDI firms in the definition of 'domestic tenderer' in public procurement, and authorised foreign persons and companies to acquire real estate in Turkey. All companies established under the rules of the Turkish Commercial Code are regarded as Turkish companies. Therefore, equal treatment is applicable to all such companies, both in rights and responsibilities as stated in the Constitution and other laws. According to the law a company can be 100 per cent foreign owned in almost all sectors of the economy. However, a number of sectors are still subject to FDI restrictions. Establishments in broadcasting, aviation, maritime transportation, port services, fishing, accounting, auditing and bookkeeping services, financial sector, petroleum, mining, electricity, education and private employment offices require special permission, according to appropriate laws. Finally, regarding acquisition of land we note that until 2003, foreigners were not allowed to acquire property in Turkey. With the new FDI Act foreigners can acquire land in accordance with the mutuality principle. But, acquisition of land of between 2.5 and 30 hectares is subject to permission from the Council of Ministers.[16]

The Investment Promotion and Support Agency provides information to interested investors, as well as incentives such as the provision and development of investment sites for specific investment projects. The agency aims to function in the future as a one-stop shop where all bureaucratic procedures can be handled within a very short period of time. Finally, note that Turkey has been a member of the International Centre for Settlement of Investment Disputes and the Multilateral Investment Guarantee Agency since 1987. Furthermore, since 1991 Turkey has been a member of the Convention on the Recognition and Enforcement of Foreign Arbitral Awards, and of the European Convention on International

---

[15] See World Trade Organization (2008).

[16] As a result US$2.9 billion on average annually have been invested in real estate during the period 2006–08.

Commercial Arbitration. In addition, Turkey has developed since 1962 an impressive network of bilateral agreements with 80 countries, the main purpose of which has been to promote investment flows between parties, ensure a more stable investment environment, provide economic and legal assurance to foreign investors, and to establish a favourable environment for economic cooperation. Turkey has also signed double taxation prevention treaties with 68 countries, which enables tax paid in one of two countries to be offset against tax payable in the other, thus preventing double taxation, and Social Security Agreements with 22 countries, which make it easier for expatriates to move between countries.

Although the investment climate in Turkey has improved considerably over the last seven years, the change is still not reflected in the various international competitiveness studies such as the IMD (International Institute for Management Development) *World Competitiveness Report*. While Turkey was ranked as the 48th country in the IMD *World Competitiveness Report* for 2001, it was ranked again as the 48th country in 2007 and 2008, and it is lagging far behind many of its competitors: the Czech Republic ranks 28th, the Slovak Republic 30th, Spain 33rd, Portugal 37th, Hungary 38th, Greece 42nd and Poland 44th. This poor record is also confirmed by the Doing Business Survey of the World Bank which ranks Turkey as the 57th country among 178 countries. On the other hand, according to a 2006 study conducted by the OECD's overall FDI regulatory restrictiveness index, Turkey's most restrictive sectors are air and maritime transport, followed by electricity, and its most liberal sectors are in manufacturing, together with some service sub-sectors, such as telecommunications, insurance services and certain business services.[17]

As emphasised above, FDI inflows into Turkey during the last five years have increased considerably. They reached US$20.2 billion in 2006, US$22.1 billion in 2007 and US$18.2 billion in 2008. But an important shortcoming of these inflows has been its composition. Almost all of the FDI inflows over the last four years have been composed of mergers and acquisitions, and directed towards service sectors and real estate. From a longer-term growth perspective Turkey needs to attract greenfield investments.[18] In order for Turkey to participate in international producers' networks the current investment environment should further be improved by the implementation of long-delayed judicial and legal reforms.

5. TECHNICAL BARRIERS TO TRADE

The above considerations reveal that Turkish protection rates are very low except for agricultural commodities. Hence, one could state that tariffs for Turkey

---

[17] See OECD (2006).
[18] See Izmen and Yılmaz (2009).

are largely a non-issue in the non-agricultural sector. Currently there is free movement of industrial products between the EU and Turkey – with the exception of contingent protectionism measures and technical legislation. Regarding contingent protectionism we note that both the EU and Turkey have been active users of contingent protection measures, but more so the EU. The formation of the customs union has not provided protection from EC anti-dumping, and the EU has continued to protect its sensitive sectors through contingent protection measures. But the development of free trade between the EU and Turkey has been hindered mainly because of non-elimination of technical barriers to trade (TBT). Although 13 years have passed since the formation of the EU–Turkey customs union, TBTs between Turkey and the EU could still not be eliminated, although considerable effort has been made by Turkey.[19]

Different approaches are available for countries to raise standards and to address TBTs. Countries can unilaterally upgrade standards by adopting international standards. But some of the returns to adopting the international standards – in terms of greater market access – only materialise if the country's trading partners also accept products produced to that standard in the country under consideration. A second approach requires cooperation between a specified number of countries to upgrade standards by agreeing that products satisfying particular standards will be accepted in each other's markets. Turkey has adopted the second approach for elimination of TBTs when it formed the customs union with the EU in 1995. This section, discussing the policies pursued by Turkey towards the elimination of TBTs, consists of three sub-sections. While the first sub-section is on standards, conformity assessment and trade in general terms, the second sub-section discusses the EU approach to elimination of TBTs and the third sub-section the Turkish approach to elimination of TBTs.

a. Standards, Conformity Assessment and Trade

Product standards, technical regulations and conformity assessment systems are essential ingredients of functioning modern economies. While a 'standard' is defined as a set of characteristics or quantities that describes features of a product, process, service or material, 'technical regulation' is a mandatory requirement imposed by public authorities. Technical regulations and standards, despite many similarities, have different impacts. If a product does not fulfil the requirements of a technical regulation, it will not be allowed to be put on sale. In the case of standards, non-complying products will be allowed on the market but, then, the volume of sales may be affected if consumers prefer products that meet the standards. While the distinction between product standards and technical regulations is

---

[19] This section draws heavily on the joint work with Saadettin Doğan. I am grateful to Frederic Misrahi for his detailed and constructive comments on an earlier draft of the chapter.

useful for policy purposes, in the following we use the term 'standards' to refer to both mandatory requirements and voluntary specifications. Finally, 'conformity assessment' is the comprehensive term for measures taken by manufacturers, their customers, regulatory authorities and independent third parties to assess conformity to standards.

Product and process standards serve the functions of fostering commercial communication, diffusing technology, raising productive efficiency, enhancing market competition, ensuring physical and functional compatibility, and enhancing public welfare.[20] Standards reduce the transaction costs for buyer and seller by conveying information regarding the inherent characteristics and quality of products. They facilitate market transactions. Under standardisation, products become closer substitutes, increasing the elasticity of substitution in demand between versions of similar products. As a result, standards enhance competition by allowing products that conform to a given standard to compete directly with each other. Moreover, standardisation in manufacturing enables efficiency-increasing measures such as repetitive production, reduced inventories and flexibility in substituting components on the assembly line, bringing about significant economies of scale. The economies of scale, in turn, benefit the producer through cost reductions, which can then be passed on to the consumer as lower prices. In addition, compatibility standards are important in industries that are organised into networks, such as telecommunications. The more widespread a given network standard becomes, the greater the incentive becomes for additional users to adopt that standard. Moreover, standards diffuse technical information embodied in products and processes, when a technological advance by a designer, researcher or developer at one firm is incorporated into a standard used by others. Thereby, standards help to raise productivity and industrial competitiveness. They also contribute to the provision of public goods. While emission standards can contribute to cleaner air, health standards can raise the average heath status in the economy. Since a standard can be used any number of times without depleting its utility, it is also a public good, raising questions about the provision of standards by the private sector only.

Standards are developed in three main ways. First, a standard may arise from a formal coordinated process, in which key participants in a market, such as producers, designers, consumers, corporate and government purchasing officials, and regulatory authorities seek consensus on the best technical specifications to meet customer, industry and public needs. The resulting standards are then published for voluntary use throughout industry. Second, a standard may arise from uncoordinated processes in the competitive marketplace. When a particular set of products or process specifications gains market share, such that it acquires influence, the set of specifications is considered a *de facto* standard. Third, a standard

---

[20] See National Academy of Sciences (1995), Stephenson (1997) and Maskus and Wilson (2001).

may be set by the government for which compliance is required, either by regulation or in order to sell products or services to government agencies. In this context, a procurement standard may specify requirements that must be met by suppliers to the government, and a regulatory standard may set safety, environmental or related criteria.

Conformity assessment enhances the value of standards by increasing the confidence of buyers, users and regulators that products actually conform to claimed standards. Over time, the definition of conformity assessment has gained different meanings, as developments occurred in conformity assessment procedures. Currently, it requires the close interrelation between 'parties assessing conformity to standards', accreditation, calibration and metrology.

Testing is the determination of the characteristics of a product, process or service, according to certain procedures, methodologies or requirements; the aim of testing may be to check whether a product fulfils specifications such as safety requirements or characteristics relevant for commerce and trade. The extent of the controls that a product must undergo varies according to the risk attached to the use of the product. Requirements may range from a declaration by the manufacturer stating that certain standards have been applied to extensive testing and certification. In a large number of cases, tests are carried out by the manufacturer, based on internal testing and quality assurance mechanisms. In such cases, the purchaser takes the manufacturer's word that the product conforms. However, in more risky situations, the manufacturer's declaration of conformity may not be sufficient. The use of independent laboratories may be required by the customer as a condition of sale or mandated by a regulatory agency. Alternatively, through testing and other means, the purchaser may insist on formal verification by an unbiased third party that a product conforms to specific standards. In this case, certification is the procedure by which a third party gives written assurance that a product, process or service conforms to specified requirements. In sectors with high demands for safety and reliability, certifiers may require a relatively intensive certification process involving multiple tests, one or more factor inspections, and testing large numbers of product samples.

Conformity assessment systems consist not only of testers and of certifiers evaluating products, processes and services, but they also incorporate accreditation and recognition. While accreditation refers to the procedure by which an authoritative body gives formal recognition that a body responsible for conformity assessment is competent to carry out specific tasks, recognition is the evaluation of the competence of the accreditors. Many large manufacturers require their suppliers' testing laboratories to be accredited as a condition for accepting suppliers' products. As emphasised by the National Academy of Sciences (1995), accreditation of a laboratory's or certifier's competence in a particular field typically involves a review of technical procedures, staff qualifications, product sample handling, test equipment calibration and maintenance, quality control, independence, and financial stability. To maintain accredited status, periodic reassessment, with follow-up testing and site visits, may also be required.

One of the most significant factors in any conformity assessment system is the reliability of measurements. This reliability can only be achieved by calibrating the measuring devices. Almost all countries have national metrology centres, the main objectives of which are to build and maintain national standards for all measurements carried out within the country and to calibrate the measurement standards and devices of lower-level laboratories. National centres with accredited laboratories form the national measurement system and coordinate their activities. Thus, metrology delivers the basis for the comparability of test results, e.g. by defining the units of measurement and by providing traceability and associated certainty of the measurement results. In many countries, a National Metrology Institute exists, which maintains primary standards of measurement used to provide traceability to customers' instruments through calibration.[21]

The benefits of standards and conformity assessment systems apply also across borders. However, standards and conformity assessment systems can also impose additional costs to exporters and act as barriers to trade. TBTs are said to exist as long as countries impose different product standards as conditions for the entry, sale and use of commodities; as long as the different countries have different legal regulations on health, safety and environmental protection; and as long as different parties have dissimilar procedures for testing and certification to ensure conformity to existing regulations or standards.[22]

Stephenson (1997) points out that many disputes over technical barriers arise from mandatory government requirements for standards, due to differing national interpretations of the reasonableness of the regulations in question, such as the scientific interpretation of tolerable health and safety risks for consumers of various products. Non-tariff barriers also arise through increased product costs created by the often redundant testing and certification for different national markets; increased transportation costs, if the product is deemed not to comply with the importer's regulatory requirements; and time and administrative delays caused by costly and lengthy inspection visits by the importing country's authorities.

Technical barriers have two aspects: (i) the content of the norms (regulations and standards); and (ii) the testing procedures needed to demonstrate that a product complies with a norm. The TBTs thus come in two basic forms, content-of-norm TBTs and testing TBTs. In either case, the costs of the product design adaptations, the reorganisation of production systems, and the multiple testing and certification needed by exporters can be high. These costs are, on the one hand, up-front and one-time and, on the other, ongoing. While the up-front costs are associated with

---

[21] See Howarth and Redgrave (2003).
[22] See Sykes (1995) on technical barriers to trade.

learning about the regulations and bringing the product into conformity with the regulations, the ongoing costs are related to periodic testing. TBTs are said to distort trade when they raise the costs of foreign firms relative to those of domestic firms. As emphasised by Baldwin (2001), liberalisation requires closing the gap between the costs of the foreign and domestic firms. The two main dimensions to such a step are liberalisation of the content of norms and liberalisation of conformity assessment. Liberalisation of the content of norms involves making product norms more cosmopolitan and, thus, narrowing the cost advantage of domestic firms. Liberalisation of conformity assessment involves lowering the excess costs that foreign firms face in demonstrating the compliance of their goods to accepted norms.

b. The EU Approach to Elimination of Technical Barriers to Trade

The European Commission (1998) divides traded products into regulated and non-regulated commodities. Regulated products are those whose commercialisation is governed by the regulations of Member States, and non-regulated products are those for which no regulations have an impact on commercialisation. Regulated products are further divided into commodities under the harmonised sphere and under the non-harmonised sphere. Products under the harmonised sphere are covered by European rules for the harmonisation of regulations and mandatory specifications, and commodities under the non-harmonised sphere are governed by national rules.[23]

(i) Mutual recognition principle

Mutual recognition refers to the principles enshrined in the Treaty of Rome, interpreted by the European Court of Justice, as set out in the 1979 Cassis de Dijon judgment. In this ruling, the court stated that Germany could prohibit imports of a French beverage (Cassis de Dijon) only if it could invoke mandatory requirements such as public health, protection of the environment, and fairness of commercial transactions. In other words, the court introduced a broad definition of Article 28 (ex 30) of the Treaty of Rome, which prohibits quantitative restrictions on imports between Member States and 'all measures having equivalent results'. Because of this ruling, the European Commission stated that a product lawfully produced and marketed in one Member State should be admitted to other Member States for sale, except in cases of mandatory requirements. Thus, the basic EU approach under the mutual recognition principle (MRP), considered as the first line

---

[23] The general principle of the free movement of goods implies that products must be traded freely from one part of the EU to another. This principle is enshrined in the EC Treaty, in particular Articles 28 to 30, 95(4) to 95(9), 296 to 298, as interpreted in the case law of the European Court of Justice as well as in Commission Directive 70/50/EEC and interpretative communications.

of defence against technical barriers in the regulated non-harmonised sphere, has been to promote the idea that products manufactured and tested in accordance with a partner country's regulations could offer levels of protection equivalent to those provided by corresponding domestic rules and procedures. Mutual recognition, in other words, reflects the existence of *ex ante* trust between the trading partners.

The Directive 98/34/EC, covering all industrial and agricultural commodities which fall outside the 'harmonised' area, aims to eliminate or reduce the barriers to the free movement of goods which can arise from the adoption of different national technical regulations, by encouraging transparency of national initiatives vis-à-vis the European Commission, European standardisation bodies and other Member States. According to the Directive, Member States are obliged to notify to the Commission, in draft, proposed technical regulations and to observe a three-month standstill period before the regulation is made or brought into force.[24] The Commission circulates the notified drafts to all Member States. In order to allow the Commission and other Member States to react, the Member States must refrain from adopting any draft technical regulations for three months from the date of receipt by the Commission. The standstill period is extended to four months for drafts in the form of a voluntary agreement and for six months for all others where the Commission delivers a detailed opinion indicating that the draft may impede the free movement of goods. This notification procedure is to provide an opportunity for the Commission and other Member States to comment if they consider that the proposed regulation has the potential to create a technical barrier to trade.

According to the European Commission (2007) national technical rules adopted by various Member States lead to substantial obstacles to the free movement of goods within the EU, resulting in extra administrative controls and tests, and the system of market surveillance needed considerable improvement, as there was no consistency of approach. As a result, the European Parliament and the Council adopted the Resolution (EC) No. 764/2008, which defines the rights and obligations of national authorities and enterprises wishing to sell in a Member State products lawfully marketed in another Member State, when the competent authorities intend to take restrictive measures about the product in accordance with national technical rules. The Regulation concentrates on the burden of proof by setting out the procedural requirements for denying mutual recognition.

---

[24] Technical regulations refer to 'technical specification', a specification contained in a document which lays down the characteristics required of a product such as levels of quality, performance, safety or dimensions, including the requirements applicable to the product as regards the name under which the product is sold, terminology, symbols, testing and test methods, packaging, marking or labelling and conformity assessment procedures. The term 'technical specification' also covers production methods and processes. Other requirements include a requirement, other than a technical specification, imposed on a product for the purpose of protecting, in particular, consumers or the environment, and which affects its life cycle after it has been placed on the market, such as conditions of use, recycling, reuse or disposal, where such conditions can significantly influence the composition or nature of the product or its marketing.

(ii) Harmonisation of national regulations and standards

EU legislation on harmonising technical specifications has followed two distinct approaches: the old approach and the new approach.

The old approach was based on the idea that the EU would become a unified economic area functioning like a single national economy. It dealt with the content-of-standards issue via negotiated harmonisation. The regulations were implemented by the directives of the European Council, and the designated bodies in EU nations performed the conformity assessments. Technical regulations were harmonised using the old approach for foodstuffs, motor vehicles, chemicals, pharmaceuticals, cosmetics, textiles, footwear labelling, crystal glass, legal metrology and pre-packaging. Under this approach, separate directives for different products detailed EU specifications that applied to the related products and their testing requirements. Under the old approach, European standards institutions such as CEN (Comité Européen de Normalisation), CENELEC (Comité Européen de Normalisation Electrotechnique) and ETSI (European Telecommunications Standards Institute) were not mandated to draw up supplementary technical specifications.[25] The old approach involved extensive product-by-product or even component-by-component legislation, and was carried out by detailed directives. Achieving this type of harmonisation was slow, as emphasised by the World Bank (2005), for two reasons. First, the process of harmonisation became highly technical, with attention given to very detailed product categories. Consultations were often drawn out. Second, the adoption of directives required unanimity in the Council, which meant that they were slow to be adopted.[26] Over time, the need was recognised by economic units to reduce the intervention of the public

---

[25] CEN (European Committee for Standardisation), based in Brussels, has a membership consisting of the national standards-writing organisations of European countries and the members of the EU and EFTA. CEN develops voluntary European standards in all product sectors excluding electrical standards covered by CENELEC. The sectors are air and space, information and communications technologies, chemistry, materials, construction, measurement, consumer products, mechanical engineering, energy and utilities, nanotechnology, environment, security and defence, food, services, health and safety, transport and packaging, healthcare, heating, cooling and ventilation. These standards are also national standards in each of its member countries. With funding from the European Commission, CEN also writes standards to meet the 'essential requirements' for product safety mandated in EU product directives. *CENELEC* (European Committee for Electrotechnical Standardisation), based in Brussels, has European national electrotechnical committees as members. CENELEC develops European standards for electrotechnology. CENELEC also develops standards that meet EU product directives, with funding from the European Commission. On the other hand, ETSI produces globally applicable standards for Information & Communications Technologies including fixed, mobile, radio, broadcast, internet and several other areas. Currently, ETSI is recognised as an official European Standards Organisation by the European Commission, enabling valuable access to European markets.

[26] With the entry into force of the 1985 Single European Act, a qualified majority voting system was adopted in the decision-making process for internal market-related legislation. As a result when new old-approach directives or Acts revising existing old-approach directives are adopted, qualified

authorities prior to a product being placed on the market and to change the decision-making procedure to allow for the adoption of harmonisation directives by a qualified majority. Therefore, the 'new approach' was adopted, and it applied to products with 'similar characteristics' that were subject to a widespread divergence of technical regulations in EU countries.

Under the new approach, only 'essential requirements' are indicated. This approach gives manufacturers greater freedom on how they satisfy those requirements by dispensing with the 'old' type of exhaustively detailed directives. Directives under the new approach provide for more flexibility, by using the support of the established standardisation bodies – CEN, CENELEC, ETSI and the national standard bodies. This standardisation work is easier to update and involves greater participation from industry.

Under the new approach, the European Council issues a directive that outlines 'essential requirements'. So far, 26 directives have been adopted based on this approach, and 21 of these directives require the affixing of the CE (Conformité Européene) marking, explained in more detail below. This new approach to product legislation covers the areas of non-automatic weighing instruments and measuring instruments, low voltage equipment, electromagnetic compatibility, toys, machinery, lifts, noise emissions by outdoors equipment, emissions of pollutants from non-road mobile machinery engines, personal protective equipment, equipment and protective systems intended for use in explosive atmospheres, medical devices, gas appliances, pressure vessels, cableway installations, construction products, recreational craft, eco-design requirements for energy-using products, and radio and telecommunications terminal equipment. Once a new approach directive has been issued, Member States must make their national laws and regulations conform to it. The European Commission is empowered to determine whether the national measures are equivalent to the 'essential requirements'. The Council refers the task of formulating detailed standards that meet the essential requirements to CEN, CENELEC and the ETSI.

(iii) Conformity assessment

To ensure that products meet the requirements laid down in the new approach directives, special conformity assessment procedures have been established. They describe the controls to which products must be subjected before they are considered compatible with the essential requirements and thus placed on the internal market. The extent of the controls a product must undergo varies, according to the risk attached to the use of the product. Requirements may range from a declaration

---

majority voting is used. Furthermore, the decision-making procedure for internal market-related legislation currently is typically co-decision between the European Parliament and the Council of Ministers.

by the manufacturer stating that certain standards have been applied, to extensive testing and certification by third parties, called notified bodies in the EU.[27]

In 1993, Council Decision 93/465/EEC was adopted in connection with the new approach directives. It provides an overview of all conformity assessment procedures available under the directives, divided up into modules and grouped by category of risk. By standardising the conformity assessment procedures the Decision ensures coherence and transparency in the application of the directives. It divides conformity assessment into eight different modules, which cover the design and production phases. The modules specify how conformity assessment procedures used in new approach directives are organised. In setting the range of possible choices open to the manufacturer, the directives (i) take into consideration, in particular, such issues as the appropriateness of the modules to the type of products, the nature of the risks involved, the economic infrastructures of the given sector, the types and importance of production, etc., and (ii) attempt to leave as wide a choice to the manufacturer as is consistent with ensuring compliance with the requirements. The specifications of the eight modules are as follows:

Under Module A on 'internal control of production' covering internal design and production control, the manufacturer prepares technical documentation and declares conformity with the directive.[28] The module does not require the intervention by a notified body. Under Module B on 'EC type-examination' covering the design phase, the manufacturer prepares technical documentation and the notified body ascertains conformity. The module is followed by one of the Modules C, D, E and F providing for the assessment in the production phase.

- Module C on 'conformity to type' provides for conformity with the type as described in the EC type-examination certificate issued according to Module B. The module does not require the intervention of a notified body.[29]
- Module D on 'production quality assurance' derives from the quality assurance standard EN ISO 9002, with the intervention of a notified body responsible for approving and controlling the quality system for production, final product inspection and testing set up by the manufacturer.
- Module E on 'product quality assurance' derives from quality assurance standard EN ISO 9003, with the intervention of a notified body responsible for approving and controlling the quality system for final product inspection and testing set up by the manufacturer.

---

[27] Notified bodies are explained in more detail in the following.

[28] Technical documentation and the EC declaration of conformity are explained in more detail in the following.

[29] Type examination is the comparison of the design specification of a product against the requirements of a standard specification, informed by physical examination of a sample and the performance of tests as may be necessary according to the particular standard.

- Under Module F on 'product verification' a notified body controls conformity to the type as described in the EC type-examination certificate issued according to Module B, and issues a certificate of conformity.

Module G on 'unit verification' covers the design and production phases. Each individual product is examined by a notified body, which issues a certificate of conformity. Finally, Module H on 'full quality assurance' covers the design and production phases. It derives from quality assurance standard EN ISO 9001, with the intervention of a notified body responsible for approving and controlling the quality system for design, manufacture, final product inspection and testing set up by the manufacturer.

The new approach directives oblige the manufacturer to draw up a technical file (technical documentation), which provides information on the design and manufacturing phases of the product. The contents of the technical documentation are laid down with the requirements of the directive to be assessed.[30] The details included in the documentation depend on the nature of the product and on what is considered as necessary, from the technical point of view, for demonstrating the conformity of the product to the essential requirements of the relevant directive. The manufacturer must also draw up an EC declaration of conformity as part of the conformity assessment procedure provided for in the new approach directives. The EC declaration of conformity should contain all relevant information to identify the directives according to which it is issued, as well as the manufacturer, the notified body if applicable, the product, and where appropriate a reference to harmonised standards or other normative documents.[31] The technical file and the

---

[30] The following might be required to be included in technical documentation: (i) a general description of the product; (ii) overall drawing of a product, design and manufacture drawings and diagrams of components, sub-assemblies, control circuits, etc., together with descriptions and explanations needed to understand those drawings and diagrams; (iii) risk analysis and a description of methods adopted to eliminate hazards presented by the product; (iv) the essential requirements of the applicable directives; (v) a list of the standards used, in full or in part, and a description of the solutions employed to meet the essential requirements of applicable directives; (vi) other technical specifications, which were used; (vii) results of design calculations and of checks carried out, etc.; (viii) test reports and/or certificates, which may be available, either by the manufacturer or a third party (depending on the requirements of the directives); and (ix) a copy of the instructions (for use, for maintenance, other instructions).

[31] As a minimum the following information should be provided by the EC declaration of conformity: (i) the name and address of the manufacturer; (ii) the identification of the product (name, type or model number, and any relevant supplementary information, such as lot, batch or serial number, sources and numbers of items); (iii) all relevant provisions complied with; (iv) the referenced standards or other normative documents (such as national technical standards and specifications) in a precise, complete and clearly defined way; (v) all supplementary information that may be required (for example, grade, category), if applicable; (vi) the date of issue of the declaration; (vii) signature and title or an equivalent marking of authorised person; and (viii) the statement that the declaration is issued under the sole responsibility of the manufacturer and, if applicable, the authorised representative.

EC declaration of conformity must be kept for at least 10 years from the last date of manufacture of the product, unless the directive expressly provides for any other duration, and this is the responsibility of the manufacturer.

For products regulated by the new approach directives, the mandatory CE marking confirms conformity with the essential requirements of the directives and is required for a product to be placed on the internal market. The CE marking indicates not only that the product has been manufactured in conformity with the requirements of the directive, but also that the manufacturer has followed all the prescribed procedures for conformity assessment. It ensures free access to the entire EU.

The above considerations reveal that conformity assessment varies in levels of difficulty and complexity, depending on the level of risk associated with the product. For example, Module A permits the manufacturer to assume total responsibility for conformity assessment. If the product is manufactured to harmonised standards, and if the risk is not unusually high, the manufacturer may rely on internal manufacturing checks. The manufacturer compiles the technical file, issues a declaration of conformity to the appropriate directives, and, if appropriate, standards, applies the CE marking, and places the product on the market. On the other hand, as the risk of injury associated with a product increases, the level of complexity of the conformity assessment process and the associated cost increases with it. Certain high-risk products may not be self-certified, but must be subjected to an EC type-examination. This examination involves the inspection of a representative example by a notified body.[32]

Notified bodies are independent testing houses, laboratories or product certifiers authorised by the EU Member States to perform the conformity assessment tasks specified in directives. A notified body is designated by a Member State and must have the necessary qualifications to meet the testing and/or certification requirements set forth in a directive. A notified body not only needs to be technically competent and capable of carrying out the specified conformity assessment procedures, but it must also demonstrate independence, impartiality and integrity. Accreditation, according to the EN ISO 45000 series of standards, is a support to the technical part of notification and, although it is not a requirement, it remains an important and privileged instrument for evaluating the competence, impartiality and integrity of the bodies to be notified.

In order to build and maintain confidence between the Member States concerning the assessment of notified bodies, it is essential to apply the same assessment criteria. It is also important that the bodies performing the assessment of notified

---

[32] Delaney and van de Zande (2000) note that modules for active implantable medical devices could call for a type-examination of the product, plus a production quality assurance system that conforms to the ISO 9002 (EN 29002) standard. Another choice for a medical device manufacturer would be a complete quality assurance programme that would conform to ISO 9001 (or EN 29001). In those cases where the risk is high, the modules will call for the involvement of the notified body.

bodies have the capability to do so and can demonstrate an equivalent competence and operate according to the same criteria, and that such requirements are laid down in EN ISO 45003 and EN ISO 45010. The European Commission (1997) emphasises that accreditation systems at a national level should be set up under the aegis of the public authorities. It maintains that accreditation systems must be commercially independent and that accreditation services be offered in a competent, transparent, neutral, independent and nondiscriminatory manner. Furthermore, the national accreditation bodies should become members of a European organisation covering all countries of the EU and EFTA, to ensure proper coordination as well as the development of appropriate mutual recognition mechanisms. Such an organisation was formed in 2000 as the European Co-operation for Accreditation (EA), which resulted from the merger of the European Accreditation of Certification (EAC) and the European Co-operation for Accreditation of Laboratories (EAL).

Finally, note that conformity assessment procedures differ for classical approach and new approach directives. The above text describes the procedures for new approach directives. The general procedures, however, also apply to a large extent for bodies working with conformity assessments under old approach directives. There are, however, some differences. Since the old approach directives contain specified technical requirements, 'product standards' as defined formally above are used to a very limited extent. Conformity assessment bodies that deal with new approach directives officially are named 'Notified Bodies', while bodies working with old approach directives officially are named 'Technical Services'. The new approach directives are based on essentially private pre-market certification. However, notified bodies may also be public. Thus, in the new approach pre-market certification is competitive as opposed to exclusively public authority-based certification in the old approach.

(iv) Market surveillance

The final stage of implementation of the new approach system consists of market surveillance procedures that develop a common approach to enforcement. The main objective of market surveillance is to place only safe products on the market. Market surveillance consists of the control that the relevant authorities in the Member States are required to carry out to ensure that the criteria for CE marking have been satisfied – after the products have been placed on the market.

For areas under the new approach directives, the system in use is in-market control. Under this system, the responsibility for placing a product on the market is left to the producer, as long as the product is certified to satisfy the minimum requirements set under the directives. Market surveillance is the responsibility of public authorities. As emphasised by the European Commission (2000), each Member State can decide upon the market surveillance infrastructure. There is no limitation on the allocation of responsibilities between authorities on a functional or geographical basis, as long as surveillance is efficient and covers the whole territory. Market surveillance authorities must perform their operations in an impartial and non-discriminatory way. They must have the power, competence and resources to visit commercial, industrial and storage facilities regularly; to visit regularly, if appropriate, workplaces and other premises where products are put into service to organise random checks and spot checks; to take samples of products and subject them to examination and testing; and to require all necessary information. Thus, market surveillance is carried out in the form of random inspections to ensure that the technical documentation, as required by the directive, is available, but it may also include examination of the documentation or the product itself. The control is intended to prevent misuse of the CE marking, to protect consumers and to secure a level playing field for producers. New approach directives provide for two different tools that enable surveillance authorities to receive information on the product: the EC declaration of conformity and the technical documentation. These must be made available by the manufacturer, the authorised representative established within the community, or under certain circumstances by the importer or person responsible for placing the product on the market. Monitoring of products placed on the market may be divided between several authorities at the national level, for example, functionally or geographically. Where the same products are subject to control by more than one authority, coordination between services within a Member State is necessary.

The coordination task between different market surveillance bodies in a Member State can be accomplished by a market surveillance authority. Regarding personnel resources, this authority needs to have, or have access to, a sufficient number of suitably qualified and experienced staff, with the necessary professional integrity. The testing facilities should comply with the relevant criteria of the EN ISO 45001 standard. The authority should be independent and carry out its operations in an impartial and non-discriminatory way.[33] For market surveillance to be efficient, resources should be concentrated where risks are likely to be higher or non-compliance more frequent, or where a particular interest can be identified.

Through the market surveillance system described above, measures are taken in the EU to ensure that products meet the requirements of the applicable directives, that action is taken to bring non-compliant products into compliance, and that sanctions are applied when necessary. Member States are free to choose the type of sanction to use. The only requirement is that the penalties be effective, proportionate and dissuasive. But the above text describes the surveillance procedures for the new approach directives. For other commodities surveillance could be discussed in terms of the general safety directive (2001/95/EC), rapid exchange

---

[33] See European Commission (2000).

of information (RAPEX), and the principle of product liability as developed by Directive 85/374/EEC.

The General Product Safety Directive 2001/95/EC is aimed at ensuring that consumer products placed on the market are safe. The Directive obliges the Member States to take the measures necessary to enforce the safety requirements for which it provides and to notify any such measures taken. To that effect, the Directive sets up a system for rapid exchange of information (RAPEX) concerning products posing a serious risk to consumers.[34] The General Product Safety Directive also imposes obligations on producers and distributors. Producers and distributors are to inform the national authorities if they know or ought to know, on the basis of information in their possession and as professionals, that a product they have placed on the market is dangerous. On the other hand, Directive 85/374/EEC establishes the principle of objective liability or liability without fault of the producer in cases of damage caused by a defective product. According to the Directive, people injured by defective products may have the right to sue for damages, the injured person can take action against producers as well as importers, and liability applies to all goods used at a place of work and food.

(v) Epilogue

According to the European Commission (2007) almost all the promises on the internal market for goods that were made in the 1985 White Paper on the completion of the Internal Market were kept. Almost all technical barriers to intra-EU trade in goods were eliminated through the application of Articles 28 to 30 EC Treaty and through secondary EC legislation. After determining that the Internal Market for goods was still not complete as of 2007, a new legislative framework was adopted in 2008. The new package of measures has the objective of removing the remaining obstacles to free circulation of products. The legal texts include

---

[34] RAPEX is the EU rapid alert system for dangerous consumer products with the exception of food, pharmaceutical and medical devices, which are covered by other mechanisms. It facilitates the rapid exchange of information between Member States and the Commission on measures taken to prevent or restrict the marketing or use of products posing a serious risk to the health and safety of consumers. RAPEX works as follows. When a product is found to be dangerous, the competent national authority takes appropriate action to eliminate the risk. It can withdraw the product from the market, recall it from consumers or issue warnings. The National Contact Point then informs the European Commission about the product, the risks it poses to consumers and the measures taken by the authority to prevent risks and accidents. The European Commission disseminates the information that it receives to the National Contact Points of all other EU countries. It publishes weekly overviews of dangerous products and the measures taken to eliminate the risks on the internet. The National Contact Points in each EU country ensure that the authorities responsible check whether the newly notified dangerous product is present on the market. If so, the authorities take measures to eliminate the risk, either by requiring that the product be withdrawn from the market, by recalling it from consumers or by issuing warnings.

Regulation (EC) No. 765/2008 setting out the requirements for accreditation and market surveillance relating to the marketing of products, and Regulation (EC) No. 768/2008 on a common framework for the marketing of products. The objective of the package is to facilitate the functioning of the internal market for goods and to strengthen and modernise the conditions for placing a wide range of industrial products on the EU market. The package builds upon existing systems to introduce clear Community policies which will strengthen the application and enforcement of internal market legislation.

c. Turkish Approach to Elimination of Technical Barriers to Trade

According to Decision 1/95 of the EC–Turkey Association Council of 1995 establishing the Customs Union, Turkey must harmonise its technical legislation with that of the EU.[35] Decision 2/97 of the Association Council of 1997 listed the areas in which Turkey must align its legislation. This work should have been finalised before the end of 2000, but, unfortunately, due to the lack of suitable legal infrastructure, it was not completed during the specified period. According to Annex II of Decision 2/97, Turkey was supposed to incorporate into its internal legal order 300 instruments that correspond to various EEC or EC regulations and directives. Currently, Turkey has incorporated into its legal order only 236 of these instruments.

Turkey has adopted all 21 new approach directives that require affixing the CE conformity marking, and 20 of the directives have entered into force up to the present time. They cover commodities and product groups such as low-voltage equipment, toys, simple pressure vessels, electromagnetic compatibility, gas appliances, personal protective equipment, machinery, medical devices, non-automatic weighing instruments, telecommunications terminal equipment, hot-water boilers, civil explosives, lifts and recreational crafts.

To align with the *acquis*, Law 4703 on the 'Preparation and Implementation of Technical Legislation on Products', published in 2001, entered into force in January 2002, and it has been supplemented by secondary legislation. This greatly enhanced harmonisation works, as it provides the legal basis for harmonisation with the EC legislation. It defines the principles for product safety and for implementation of the old and new approach directives, including the conditions for

---

[35] Within the framework of Articles 5–7 of the Association Council Decision (ACD) No. 1/95, the signatories shall eliminate not only classical trade-restricting measures such as tariffs and quotas, but also the barriers to trade arising from different regulatory practices on goods in both Turkey and the EU. On the other hand, within the framework of Articles 8–11 of the ACD No. 1/95, Turkey shall progressively adopt the relevant *acquis communautaire* on the removal of TBTs and all other related technical regulations.

placing products on the market; the obligations of the producers and distributors, conformity assessment bodies, and notified bodies; market surveillance and inspection; withdrawal of products from the market; and notification procedures.[36] The legislation on market surveillance, the use and affixing of the CE conformity mark, working principles and procedures for the conformity assessment bodies and notified bodies and notification procedures between Turkey and the EU for technical regulations and standards, which apply to the non-harmonised regulated area, entered into force during 2002.[37]

(i) Quality infrastructure

In the EU, national quality infrastructures are critical to the free circulation of goods in the Single Market. Turkey, as a member of a customs union with the EU and as a candidate country, must align its national quality infrastructure with the European one. It has to complete the establishment of the so-called quality infrastructure, a generic term encompassing the operators and operation of standardisation, testing, certification, inspection, accreditation and metrology. Products manufactured in Turkey must satisfy the same requirements prevailing in the EU, and conformity to these requirements must be demonstrated in the same way and according to same the principles. Furthermore, it is important to create confidence on an international level in the testing, inspection and certification bodies in Turkey and to create reliability in the tests they perform and in the certificates they issue.

After the formation of the customs union in 1995, private conformity assessment bodies started to invest in Turkey in order to provide international certificates and markings such as the ISO 9000 series and CE marking for Turkish producers. The Turkish Accreditation Body (TURKAK), founded in 1999, started accepting

---

[36] Law 4703 is based on Council Directive 92/59/EEC on general product safety, Council Regulation 85/C136/01 on the new approach to technical harmonisation and standards and the Council resolution of December 1989 on the global approach to conformity assessment.

[37] The legislation on market surveillance was prepared using Council Directive 92/59/EEC on general products safety, the Council resolution of December 1989 on the global approach to conformity assessment, Council Directive 88/378/EEC on the approximation of the laws of the Member States on the safety of toys and the European Commission (2000). The legislation on working principles and procedures for the conformity assessment bodies and notified bodies was prepared using the material in Chapter 6 of the European Commission (2000). The legislation on the use and affixing of the CE conformity mark is based on Council Decision 93/465/EEC on the modules for the various phases of the conformity assessment procedures and the rules for the affixing and use of the CE conformity marking. Finally, the legislation on notification procedures between Turkey and the EU for technical legislation and standards is based on Council Directive 98/34/EC, which outlines a procedure for the provision of information in the field of technical standards and regulations, and the relevant section of Decision 2/97 of the EC–Turkey Association Council.

accreditation applications for conformity assessment bodies in 2001.[38,39,40] The relevant ministries are responsible for appointing notified bodies in their field of competence. These authorities work in cooperation with TURKAK to assess the capacity of the notified bodies, or accept those that are to be notified to the European Commission. In particular, the Ministry of Industry and Trade, the Ministry of Labour and Social Security, the Ministry of Health, the Ministry of Public Works and Settlements, the Undersecretariat for Maritime Affairs and the Telecommunication Authority have established cooperation protocols with TURKAK in this context. In 2002, TURKAK became a full member of the European Co-operation for Accreditation (EA). However, becoming a member of an international organisation is not sufficient to achieve international recognition of accreditation certificates, as an accreditation body must also be a signatory to specific multilateral agreements (MLAs) with other accreditation bodies.

In the past, the relatively large Turkish firms wishing to obtain CE marking for products exported to the EU market contacted the local subsidiaries of the European notified bodies that used their European laboratories for testing. However, for other Turkish companies, this process was expensive and slow. The small and medium-size enterprises (SMEs) that export products to the EU found it particularly difficult to pay the high costs.[41] In Turkey, marking and certification parallel to the EU system were implemented only in the automotive sector, which is subject to the old approach directives.[42] In addition, Turkey has long suffered from a lack

---

[38] The legal framework for accreditation consists of Law 4457 on the establishment and tasks of the Turkish accrediting agency of 1999.

[39] Note that with the increase in the number of conformity assessment bodies, two associations were established: Turkish Calibration and Experiment Laboratories Association (TUKLAB) and Association for Conformity Assessment (UDDer). While TUKLAB aims to improve the coordination and cooperation between Turkish laboratories and provide support for its members in accreditation and certification processes, UDDer aims to serve as a platform in which the above-mentioned stakeholders can effectively cooperate in tackling problems related to the conformity assessment sector.

[40] The legal framework for conformity assessment in Turkey consists of general provisions covered by Articles 7, 8 and 9 of Framework Law 4703 relating to the preparation and implementation of technical regulation on products, published in 2001. Detailed principles can be found in the implementing Regulation on Conformity Assessment Bodies and Notified Bodies.

[41] According to the World Bank (2005), the certification of organic nut production in Moldova exported to Germany must be renewed every six months, and each visit from an international certifying company costs US$5,000 plus US$2,000 per production test – once before processing and once after processing. This can amount to $18,000 per year, which is a heavy burden for firms in an economy such as Moldova, a small economy trying to compete in international markets.

[42] Istanbul Technical University does automotive testing under the authorisation of the Ministry of Industry and Trade, and it performs acoustic, emissions and other tests. The Turkish Standards Institute, Tofaş-Fiat and Ford-Otosan also have engine and emissions test facilities; Seger has an audible warning devices laboratory; Tam-Test is implementing testing and certification in the case of agricultural tractors; Fren Teknik has test facilities for brakes; and Brisa has a pneumatic tyres laboratory. Turkey is implementing all relevant automotive EC directives via these facilities. We

of certification bodies.[43] Although Turkey opened up the certification, testing and calibration market to other actors, Turkish firms were reluctant to enter the market for conformity assessment bodies as long as uncertainties prevailed regarding the acceptance of notified bodies by the European Commission.

In April 2006, TURKAK signed four out of seven multilateral agreements (MLAs) with EA members. These four MLAs cover the areas of test laboratories, calibration laboratories, quality systems management certification bodies and inspection bodies. Hence, certificates issued by all test, calibration, quality systems management and inspection bodies accredited by TURKAK have been recognised within the EU since April 2006. With the signing of the remaining three MLAs in 2008 TURKAK's full international recognition has been completed. These three MLAs are those for product certification, personnel certification and environmental management systems certification. Finally, we note that the right of Turkey to assign Notified Bodies was officially recognised by the EU by virtue of the Association Council Decision No. 1/2006.[44] Thereafter Turkish authorities have assigned a number of Turkish Notified Bodies for several New Approach Directives.[45]

Over time, competition among potential Turkish notified bodies will ensure lower costs for conformity assessment. The expense, time and unpredictability incurred in obtaining approvals will then be reduced by having products evaluated in Turkey. These savings can be particularly important when rejection of products in the EU can create delays and necessitate additional shipping or other costs. In addition, the SMEs can benefit from procedures in which all testing and certification steps are carried out locally at lower costs. Turkish firms, and in particular the SMEs, can then be expected to increase their competitiveness in the EU market, and more and more Turkish firms can be expected to participate in the free circulation of goods between Turkey and the EU.

Finally, note that the Turkish National Metrology Institute (UME) was founded in 1992, as part of the Scientific and Technological Research Council of Turkey (TUBITAK). The objectives of the UME are to: (i) establish and maintain national measurement standards in accordance with the International System of Units; (ii) ensure the traceability of national measurement standards to international standards; (iii) establish a national measurement system and provide services to the

---

note that for automotive products, the 'e' sign verifies conformity. Crash tests, electromagnetic compatibility (EMC) and other tests on complete cars are largely conducted abroad. The National Metrology Institute was able to run the EMC tests on vehicles. It has calibration laboratories in mechanics, physics, electricity, ionising radiation and chemicals. The laboratories under construction include EMC, acoustics and liquid flow.

[43] See European Committee for Standardisation (2003).

[44] The Association Council Decision (ACD) No. 1/2006 has been put into force on 15 May 2006 on the implementation of Article 9 of the 1/95 ACD. It regulates the rules and procedures on the allocation of identification numbers to the Turkish notified bodies.

[45] The six Turkish Notified Bodies recognised by the EU are

laboratories within this system in terms of calibration, training, consultancy and other mechanisms; (iv) ensure the suitability of the laboratories that apply to join the Turkish Calibration Service and organise their accreditation; (v) contribute to research and development in the areas of measurement techniques, calibration and basic metrology at the international level; (vi) develop high-technology products and disseminate them via its developed infrastructure; (vii) increase the quality of products produced in Turkey by providing the measurement infrastructure through the national measurement system; and (viii) represent Turkey at an international level in the field of metrology.

The above considerations reveal that, as of 2008, there is a relatively well-functioning quality certification system in place in Turkey, comprising the accreditation agency TURKAK, the National Metrology Institute UME, and the Turkish Standards Institute TSE, which is explained in more detail in the following. Because the transposition of harmonised European legislation into Turkish national legislation is nearing completion, what is needed as a last step is the establishment of a soundly functioning market surveillance system with improved administrative and technical infrastructure.

(ii) Market surveillance

The legal basis for market surveillance activities consists of Law 4703 on the 'Preparation and Implementation of Technical Legislation on Products' of 2001, the 'Regulation on Market Surveillance of Products' of 2002 and specific product legislation and administrative legislation by public authorities, in the form of circulars or communiqués. The Framework Law obliges producers to put on the market only safe products, and authorises public authorities to devise and implement product-specific legislation. Even if this legislation lacks in providing for complete safety, the related authority is still bound to monitor for complete product safety with respect to its legally-established competency area. The law leaves detailed procedures and principles of market surveillance to the Regulation on Market Surveillance. In addition, each competent authority may lay down detailed procedures for its market surveillance activities in a specific legislation, defining the duties and responsibilities of the inspectors and the procedures and principles

---

(i) Turkish Standards Institute (Lifts (95/16/EC), Construction Products (89/106/EEC), Appliances burning gaseous fuels (90/396/EEC), and Pressure equipment (97/23/EC)),
(ii) Turkish Cement Manufacturers Association (Construction Products (89/106/EEC)),
(iii) Turkish Lloyd Foundation (Appliances burning gaseous fuels (90/396/EEC), Pressure equipment (97/23/EC), and Recreational craft (94/25/EC)),
(iv) MEYER (Appliances burning gaseous fuels (90/396/EEC), and Pressure equipment (97/23/EC)),
(v) Chamber of Mechanical Engineers (Lifts (95/16/EC)), and
(vi) Turkish Ready Mixed Concrete Association (Construction Products (89/106/EEC)).

for market surveillance. In 2004, a communiqué was published in order to provide for a standard form to be used by all market surveillance authorities in registering the data collected during market surveillance.

There are 10 public authorities responsible for market surveillance and one coordinating body, which is the Undersecretariat for Foreign Trade. The public authorities are the Ministry of Industry and Trade, the Ministry of Health, the Ministry of Public Works and Settlement, the Ministry of Labour and Social Security, the Telecommunications Authority, the Ministry of Environment and Forestry, the Ministry of Agriculture and Rural Affairs, the Undersecretariat of Maritime Affairs, the 'Tobacco, Tobacco Products and Alcoholic Beverages Market Regulatory Authority' and the 'Energy Market Regulatory Authority'. An important role in the execution of market surveillance is played by the regional and provincial offices of most of the public authorities distributed all over Turkey. The provincial offices have different executive tasks, such as inspection and sampling of products and reporting of results, dealing with consumer complaints and advising the public and businesses.

For the coordination of market surveillance activities of the different public authorities, the Coordination Board on Market Surveillance was established in 2002 and is composed of members of the market surveillance authorities plus two members from the Ministry of Culture and Tourism and the Ministry of Transportation. The Board, which has no executive power, is chaired by the Undersecretariat for Foreign Trade.

As emphasised in a report prepared for the Undersecretariat for Foreign Trade (2008a), market surveillance in Turkey faces serious problems. It is emphasised that for a large percentage of consumer products, there is no market surveillance at all; the system is fragmented and in fact invisible; there is a substantial risk of conflict of interests; the activities are mainly focused on administrative issues, not on the safety of products, and have low priority as well; in most inspections the compliance with the General Product Safety Directive of the EU is absent and the enforcement by inspectors is hampered by logistic problems, lack of power and lack of experience. Thus, the report notes that the present system of market surveillance in Turkey is incomplete, ineffective and inefficient.[46]

---

[46] The report notes that in Turkey for a great part of product groups, there is hardly any sampling and analysis and that a large number of consumer products are not monitored at all. There is limited laboratory capacity, and this capacity is used only partially. Warnings and fines are seldom imposed, and withdrawals and recalls occur even less often. The market surveillance system is fragmented, both on a national level and even within authorities, and it is too complicated. Each authority has its own inspection body or even several bodies per type of product, and there are no obvious transverse links between the different inspection bodies. Policy at each authority is top-down, so that management and execution are determined centrally, with weak influence from the regions. As a result, the overall coordination between the market surveillance activities is fragile. Furthermore,

Recently, a new draft law has been prepared for market surveillance. It will take into account the latest version of the general product safety directive (2001/95/ EC). This draft law, called the 'Product Safety Law', will cover provisions related to mutual recognition, unregulated areas and the areas included in Law 4703, such as new and classical approaches, notified bodies and market surveillance in some detail.

(iii) Standardisation

The Turkish foreign trade regime concerning technical regulations and stand-ardisation was originally published in 1995 by the Undersecretariat for Foreign Trade as the 'Ministerial Decree on the Regime Regarding Technical Regulations and Standardisation for Foreign Trade' and supplementary legislation. This regime has been amended by Ministerial Decree No. 2005/9454 for Technical Regulations and Standardisation for Foreign Trade, a Regulation and related Communiqués. The Decree covers the technical regulations, standards, conformity assessment and inspections to which import and export products are subject, the obligations of the importers and exporters, the powers and the obligations of the customs authorities and related authorities, the sanctions to apply and the notifications related to these issues. The decree also defines the administration competent for issuing technical requirements for imports. Therefore, by force of this Decree and its implementing provisions, certain mandatory standards are still in place. On the other hand, the Regulation and the Communiqués are amended every year, except for the Communiqué on the Imports of CE Marked Products.[47] Furthermore, the Regulation is related to the controls of the agricultural products to be exported within the scope of the standards mandated in exports, and it determines the framework of the import controls, which are regulated by communiqués in more detail.[48]

---

market surveillance is usually based on conformity and consists of checks of CE marks and docu-ments. There are not checks on safety, and pro-active risk assessment is generally lacking. Although effective market surveillance requires powerful inspectors, who are authorised to make quick deci-sions at the place of inspection according to the risk occurred, inspectors are not in a position to fulfil these requirements. They are reluctant to make decisions, as the legal status of the inspectors is not sufficiently regulated. In addition, there is no implementing authority for the non-harmonised consumer products, and market surveillance activities in the case of these products are not carried out at all. Finally, the report stresses that there are no binding or result-oriented agreements on activities such as the number of inspections to be carried out, and there is no separate budget for samples or for lab analysis.

[47] The Communiqué on the Imports of CE Marked Products was published in the Turkish *Official Gazette* on 14 February 2004, No. 25373. The Regulation and the Communiqués for 2008 were promulgated in the Turkish *Official Gazette* on 31 December 2007, No. 26743.

[48] For more information on legislative alignment, see the website of the Undersecretariat for Foreign Trade: www.dtm.gov.tr.

Although, in principle, standards are voluntary in Turkey, in the absence of a proper market surveillance system, the technical ministries and the Undersecretariat of Foreign Trade have turned the process of standardisation and licensing before production into a mandatory regime for both domestic and imported products, in order to protect the market and the consumers. This pre-market control system gave the Turkish Standards Institute (TSE) a great deal of power.[49] According to the European Committee for Standardisation (2003), the TSE has misused its power in several cases of imports and has created TBTs. The TSE asked for the technical files of the imported products when they entered the Turkish market, and the processing of the files usually took a long time. There were also cases in which products bearing the CE marking were asked to be further inspected.

Since 2004, products covered by directives on toy safety, medical devices, active implantable medical devices, low-voltage electrical equipment, electromagnetic compatibility, machinery and construction products have not been subject to mandatory controls when imported and used in the internal market. With the Communiqué on Standardisation for Foreign Trade No. 2008/1, 190 commodities classified in the 12-digit harmonised system of tariff classification (HS) are, as of 2008, subject to inspection by the TSE.[50] All of these commodities refer to those in the unregulated area. The inspections are carried out in respect of minimum standards of health, safety and protection of the environment, providing adequate information to consumers.

Because of recent developments in the harmonisation works, the number of standards that are mandatory for the domestic market as well as for imports has substantially decreased, and it seems that the TSE's monopoly as an active player of the mandatory standards controls is ending. Thus, Turkey has replaced all national standards with EU and international standards and significantly reduced the number of mandatory standards applied to imports; this reduction brings Turkey close to having an EU-compatible control mechanism on imports from third countries. However, as of 2008, a remarkable difference exists between the intensity of controls over imported products and domestic products in Turkey. Since import control focuses on the surveillance of goods to be imported from third countries, and local products are expected to meet the same requirements as imported ones, the same directives could apply, in principle, for the surveillance of all products, whether imported or domestically produced. An obvious advantage of combining import control with the surveillance of the domestic market is that

---

[49] The Turkish Standards Institute (TSE) was established in 1954 to draft standards for all kinds of products and services. The TSE is responsible for issuing and implementing technical standards. So far, it has transposed close to 90 per cent of the CEN and CENELEC standards. The TSE is a member of the ISO and IEC as well as an affiliate member of CEN and CENELEC.

[50] See the *Official Gazette* of 31 December 2007 and No. 26743.

the available personnel capacity can be employed on a broader scale, and cooperation with customs can be smooth and uniform.

6. CONCLUSION

The *Trade Policy Review: Turkey 2007* is a comprehensive review of trade-related policies in Turkey. It has provided a wealth of information about the economic developments in Turkey in general, and the Turkish trade policies in particular. The well-developed format of *Trade Policy Reviews* (TPRs) successfully discerns what has been improved and what sort of issues remain.

As emphasised in WTO (2008), Turkey is pursuing a strategy of trade liberalisation through negotiations at the multilateral, regional and bilateral levels. It is actively participating in the Doha Development Agenda. Nonetheless, Turkey's membership in several arrangements makes its trade regime complex and seemingly difficult to manage. It is stressed that further multilateral trade liberalisation could reduce the need for preferential trade arrangements.

As of 2009 Turkey has a very liberal trade regime for industrial goods. Although tariffs for Turkey are largely a non-issue in the non-agricultural sector, free trade in industrial goods between Turkey and the EU could still not be established mainly because of NTBs and, in particular, because of the various problems faced in the elimination of TBTs.[51] The establishment of the quality infrastructure turned out to be a lengthy and complex process, as, until the formation of the customs union with the EU, Turkey had no such infrastructure nor did it have the required technical knowledge. Establishing public awareness of the problem, acquiring the necessary knowledge and establishing the infrastructure took some time. The development of market surveillance structure as in the EU turned out to be even more challenging than establishing the quality infrastructure. The reasons are again various. A successful consumer product safety-related market surveillance system requires independence, visibility, uniform surveillance policy, uniform enforcement policy, integration of market surveillance and import controls,

---

[51] The reasons for the non-elimination of TBTs between Turkey and the EU are various. Firstly, the task itself is a very challenging one. Secondly, the framework law and the associated legislation, which is the basis for the work of harmonisation of the EU's technical regulations, was put into effect only in January 2002, seven years after the formation of the customs union. Thereafter the adaptation process for both the new and classical approach regulations has accelerated and a large number of related regulations were adopted by Turkey. This time, however, Turkey faced another difficulty. There was not a mechanism between Turkey and the EU similar to the one provided by the 'EFTA Surveillance Body', which evaluates the regulations prepared by the EFTA countries and ascertains the acceptability of these regulations by the EU. Fourthly, the number of personnel in the responsible ministries and governmental bodies who were fluent in English and trained in matters related to TBTs was insufficient. Finally, financial resources provided for harmonisation of technical legislation were limited.

stronger regions, more acting power for inspectors, and sufficient technical infra-structure.[52] Unfortunately, the Turkish system does not meet these conditions. The continuation of these problems has adversely affected the elimination of TBTs in trade with the EU.

The costs of adjustment related with the elimination of TBTs in trade with the EU has been substantial for the Turkish public sector. These costs involve the costs associated with the adoption of technical legislation equivalent to that of the EU; the establishment of institutions required for efficient functioning of quality infra-structure as in the EU such as TURKAK, the National Metrology Institute, and market surveillance authorities; the training and employment of sufficient numbers of suitably qualified and experienced staff with the necessary professional integrity to be employed in those institutions; and the acquisition of the technical infra-structure (laboratories, cars, fuel) required for efficient functioning of the system. However, the task is not complete. Additional adjustment costs have to be incurred by the public sector. Turkey has incurred these costs with the hope of becoming a full member of the EU, and the associated costs were considered as the unavoid-able costs of the EU accession. But as the chances of EU membership have decreased over time, doubts have arisen in Turkey over whether the strategy adopted by the country for the elimination of TBTs has in fact been the right strategy.

REFERENCES

Baldwin, R. E. (2001), 'Regulatory Protectionism, Developing Nations and a Two-tier World Trade System', *Brookings Trade Forum*, **3**, 237–80.
Delaney, H. and R. van de Zande (2000), 'A Guide to EU Standards and Conformity Assessment', National Institute of Standards and Technology Special Publication 951 (Gaithersburg: NIST).
European Commission (1997), 'Accreditation and the Community's Policy in the Field of Conformity Assessment', CERTIF 97/4 – EN Rev. 2 (Brussels: European Commission).
European Commission (1998), *Dismantling of Barriers: Technical Barriers to Trade*, The Single Market Review, Subseries III: Volume I (Luxembourg: Office for Official Publications of the European Communities (OOPEC)).
European Commission (2000), *Guide to the Implementation of Directives based on the New Approach and the Global Approach* (Brussels: European Commission).
European Commission (2007), 'The Internal Market for Goods: A Cornerstone of Europe's Competitiveness', Communication from the Commission to the European Parliament, the Council and the European Economic and Social Committee, COM(2007)35 final (Brussels: European Commission).
European Committee for Standardization (2003), *Support to the Quality Infrastructure in Turkey: Country Report 2003* (Brussels: CEN).
Howarth, P. and F. Redgrave (2003), Metrology – In Short, document prepared for the European Commission.

---

[52] See Undersecretariat for Foreign Trade (2008b).

Izmen, Ü. and K. Yılmaz (2009), 'Turkey's Recent Trade and Foreign Direct Investment Performance', Economic Research Forum Working Paper 0902 (Istanbul: TÜSIAD-KOÇ University).

Kaminski, B. and F. Ng (2007), 'Turkey's Evolving Trade Integration into Pan-European Markets', *Journal of International Trade and Diplomacy*, **1**, 35–103.

Maskus, K. E. and J. S. Wilson (2001), 'A Review of Past Attempts and the New Policy Context', in *Quantifying the Impact of Technical Barriers to Trade: Can it be Done?* Keith E. Maskus and John S. Wilson (eds.), (Ann Arbor: University of Michigan Press).

National Academy of Sciences (1995), *Standards, Conformity Assessment, and Trade: Into the 21st Century* (Washington, DC: National Academy Press).

Organisation for Economic Co-operation and Development (2006), 'OECD's FDI Regulatory Restrictiveness Index: Revision and Extension to More Economies', Working Paper on International Investment No. 2006/4 (Paris: OECD).

Stephenson, S. M. (1997), 'Standards and Conformity Assessment as Non-tariff Barriers to Trade', Policy Research Working Paper 1826 (Washington, DC: World Bank).

Sykes, A. O. (1995), *Product Standards for Internationally Integrated Goods Markets* (Washington, DC: Brookings Institution).

Undersecretariat for Foreign Trade (2008a), 'Analysis Report on Market Surveillance System in Turkey with an Emphasis on Consumer Products "Report of the Present Situation"', report prepared within the context of the Twinning Project funded by the European Commission on 'Reinforcement of Institutional Capacity for Establishing a Product Safety System in Turkey', Ankara.

Undersecretariat for Foreign Trade (2008b), 'The Way Ahead', report prepared within the context of the Twinning Project funded by the European Commission on 'Reinforcement of Institutional Capacity for Establishing a Product Safety System in Turkey', Ankara.

World Bank (2005), *Global Economic Prospects 2005* (Washington, DC: World Bank).

World Trade Organization (2008), *Trade Policy Review: Turkey 2007*, WTO (Geneva: WTO Publications).

2

China Trade Policy Review:
A Political Economy Approach

Changyuan Luo and Jun Zhang

1. INTRODUCTION

ON 11 December 2001, China formally joined the World Trade Organization (WTO). According to the WTO Trade Policy Review Mechanism, China's trade policy will be reviewed biennially. The work is carried out by the Trade Policy Review Body on the basis of the self-presentation of the target country together with the report of the Trade Policy Review Division. The first two reviews of China's trade policy had already been completed by May 2006 and May 2008. Focusing largely on the second review, this chapter will comment on the trade policy of China in the last three years.

In 2008, China was the second largest exporter and third largest importer in the world. In terms of trade volume, it ranked third in the world, after the USA and Germany (Table 1). Within half a century, China's share of world imports and exports had risen from less than 1 per cent to 7 per cent and 9 per cent respectively (Figure 1); since its accession to the WTO, China's dependence on foreign trade had increased from less than 40 per cent to almost 70 per cent (Figure 2). As a developing country, China has made substantial economic progress in the past 30 years under an export-oriented growth strategy. Therefore, the review of its trade policy has provided not only a good opportunity for China itself to evaluate its own policy practice, but also a reference for other developing countries for policymaking. Different from Western democratic nations, China is politically centralised (Blanchard and Shleifer, 2001) so that internal competition of the system

The authors thank Ms. Cen Jiang for her excellent research assistance. Remaining errors are obviously ours.

The World Economy: Global Trade Policy 2010, First Edition. Edited by David Greenaway.

TABLE 1
Rank of Countries in Merchandise Trade 2008

Country	Exports			Country	Imports		
	Rank	Value (billion USD)	Share in the World (%)		Rank	Value (billion USD)	Share in the World (%)
Germany	1	1,462	9.1	USA	1	2,170	13.2
China	2	1,428	8.9	Germany	2	1,204	7.3
USA	3	1,287	8.0	China	3	1,133	6.9
Japan	4	782	4.9	Japan	4	763	4.6
Holland	5	633	3.9	France	5	706	4.3
France	6	605	3.8	UK	6	632	3.8
Italy	7	538	3.3	Holland	7	573	3.5
Belgium	8	476	3.0	Italy	8	555	3.4
Russia	9	472	2.9	Belgium	9	470	2.9
UK	10	459	2.9	Korea	10	435	2.7

Source: WTO.

FIGURE 1
China's Share of Exports and Imports in the World

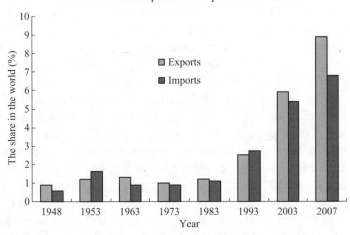

Source: WTO.

is insufficient and the internally motivated perfection of the system is slow.[1] In this case, the trade policy review has provided new impetus for improvement. Within the current political structure, the Chinese government has won political legitimacy through continuous economic development (Pei, 2009), which has, to

---

[1] Institutional experiment in the designated areas and copying to other places after achieving success is regarded as an important factor of China's rapid economic growth (Rodrik, 2006). However, the scope of such experiments is limited, instead of comprehensive and systematic.

FIGURE 2
Trade Dependency Ratio in China

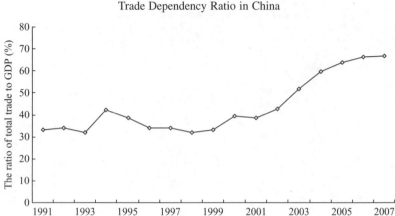

Source: *China Statistical Yearbook 2008.*

some extent, eliminated potential threats from the inside; while through improvement of the system by bringing it in line with the international practice, the acknowledgement of the international community has been gained and, also, potential threats from the outside weakened.

Since the first trade policy review, China's macroeconomic situation has undergone dramatic changes, the turning point of which is the global financial tsunami triggered by the 'subprime mortgage crisis'. The adjustment of trade policy, as one of the economic policies, is closely related to the macroeconomic climate, which in fact serves as the fundamental motivator for the change of China's foreign-related economic policy in the past three years. This chapter will adopt a political economy approach to comment on trade policies in this period. Since Grossman and Helpman (1994) proposed the model, the so-called 'Protection for Sale' (PFS model), understanding trade policies from the perspective of interaction between interest groups and the government has become the mainstream of research in this field. According to this model, empirical studies on trade policies of the USA, Canada, Australia, Mexico and Turkey, etc., were carried out such as Goldberg and Maggi (1999), Gawande and Bandyopadhyay (2000), Grether et al. (2001), Mitra et al. (2002), McCalman (2004) and Lopez and Matschke (2006). Likewise, Branstetter and Feenstra (2002) applied this PFS model to China's foreign trade and investment policies during 1984–95 as an empirical study.

In our opinion, to discuss China's trade policy over the past three years, adjustments must be made to the political economy approach. First of all, China's political reality must be taken into consideration. In democratic countries, trade policy is usually a result of the interaction between interest groups and government. In China, however, interest groups as well as their activities are informal and indirect.

Then how is a trade policy formed?[2] Moreover, pressure from trade partners should be considered. In the literature, external pressure does not play a significant role in trade policy. Nevertheless, trade between China and its main partners is seriously imbalanced, which has naturally resulted in pressure from the latter on China's trade policy. Last but not least, the changes in the international economic climate should be squarely faced. The above literature does not regard the external environment as an influential factor in making trade policy. Nonetheless, the world economy has undergone dramatic ups and downs in the last three years. So how will the responsibility of China, the engine for the world economy, affect its trade policy?

The remainder of the study is as follows: in Section 2, we discuss China's basic macroeconomic situation since the first trade policy review; in Section 3, we go over the changes of China's foreign trade and trade policy, and supplement what has not been either touched upon or fully discussed in the second trade policy review; in Section 4, we will follow a political economy approach to comment on trade policy from a global perspective; Section 5 concludes.

2. CHINA'S MACROECONOMY SINCE 2007

After joining the WTO, China has been on its third fast track of economic growth since reform and opening up (the first two emerged respectively in the mid-1980s and the pre-mid-1990s). China's economic growth had maintained straight double-digit growth in the five years since 2003, but fell to 9.0 per cent in 2008 (Figure 3) due to deterioration of the global economy. Another important macroeconomic variable is inflation. From the middle of 2007, this has upset China's economic model of 'low inflation, high growth' which lasted for 10 years. In February 2007, the consumer price index (CPI) was only 102.7, but a year after, it had already reached 108.7. In accordance with the Central Economic Work Conference at the end of 2007, the main task of the government was 'to prevent the fast-growing economy from overheating' and 'prevent the price from structural rise to remarkable inflation' with an emphasis on a 'prudent fiscal policy' and a 'tight monetary policy' should be implemented, and the goal of the economic development was modified from 'sound and fast' to 'giving priority to quality'. Against this background, the keynote of 2008 was set as 'to prevent an overheated economy, to prevent inflation, to attach importance to people's livelihood'. After that, a series of tight macroeconomic policies were gradually issued, and from the middle of 2008 the inflation rate began to decline month by month (Figure 4).

---

[2] He and Yao (2009) argue that the existence of a 'neutral government' that is not captured by interest groups is an important contributor to the success of the Chinese economy.

FIGURE 3
Growth Rate of Gross Domestic Product (GDP) in China

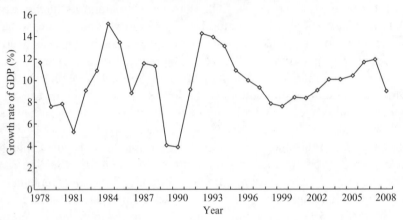

Sources: *China Statistical Yearbook 2008, Statistical Communiqué of the PRC 2008.*

FIGURE 4
Inflation Rate in China

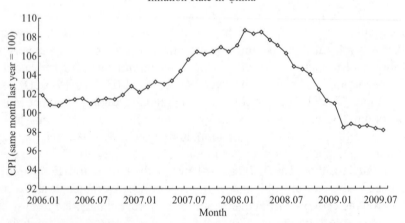

Source: Monthly data of the National Bureau of Statistics.

From 2003 to 2007, registered urban unemployment dropped from 4.3 per cent to 4.0 per cent. By the end of 2008, however, this had rebounded by 0.2 per cent. The macroeconomic variable associated with foreign-related economy is the change of foreign exchange reserves (Figure 5). Since implementation of a managed floating exchange rate in 1994, continuous growth of China's foreign exchange reserves has experienced three stages. In 1996, it broke 100 billion USD; 10 years later, it exceeded one trillion USD. Foreign exchange reserves then broke two trillion USD in less than three years. Rapid growth of foreign exchange

FIGURE 5
Foreign Exchange Reserves in China

Sources: *China Statistical Yearbook 2007, China Statistical Yearbook 2008, Statistical Communiqué of the PRC on 2008*, quarterly data of the National Bureau of Statistics.

reserves had something to do with the trade balance, and massive inflow of capital. However, the liquidity resulted from the continuous accumulation of foreign exchange reserves added more difficulty to China's macro control.

With the spread of the global financial crisis, China's macroeconomic situation deteriorated. According to the Central Economic Work Conference 2008, 'to ensure growth and promote development' became the new theme and 'prudent fiscal policy and tight monetary policy' were replaced by 'positive fiscal policy' and 'moderately easy monetary policy'. Within a year, macroeconomic goals and policy had changed significantly. According to information issued by the National Bureau of Statistics in July 2009, the overall macroeconomic situation is still harsh. In the first half of the year, gross domestic product saw growth of only 7.1 per cent; CPI saw a decline of 1.1 per cent; exports declined by 21.8 per cent and imports dropped by 25.4 per cent and the trade surplus saw a decline of 2.1 billion USD. The employment situation was also grave.

3. FOREIGN TRADE AND POLICIES SINCE 2007

a. Changes on China's Foreign Trade and Investment since 2007

In comparison with 2006, the trade volume of China in 2007 increased by 23.5 per cent, reaching a total of 2,173.8 billion USD (Table 2). Exports were 1,218 billion USD, an increase of 25.7 per cent; imports 955.8 billion USD, an increase of 20.8 per cent. The trade surplus was 262.2 billion USD, an increase of 84.7

TABLE 2
China's Exports and Imports, 2007–08

Item	2007		2008	
	Value (100 million USD)	Increase over 2006 (%)	Value (100 million USD)	Increase over 2007 (%)
Total imports and exports	21,738	23.5	25,616	17.8
Exports	12,180	25.7	14,285	17.2
of which: General trade	5,386	29.4	6,626	22.9
Processing trade	6,177	21.0	6,752	9.3
of which: Mechanical and electronic products	7,012	27.6	8,229	17.3
High- and new-tech products	3,478	23.6	4,156	13.1
of which: State-owned	2,248	17.5	2,572	14.4
Foreign-funded	6,955	23.4	7,906	13.6
Others	2,977	39.2	3,807	27.9
Imports	9,558	20.8	11,331	18.5
of which: General trade	4,286	28.7	5,727	33.6
Processing trade	3,684	14.6	3,784	2.7
of which: Mechanical and electronic products	4,990	16.7	5,387	7.9
High- and new-tech products	2,870	16.0	3,419	4.3
of which: State-owned	2,697	19.8	3,538	31.1
Foreign-funded	5,594	18.4	6,200	10.8
Others	1,267	35.1	1,593	25.7
Trade surplus	2,622	47.7	2,955	–
of which: General trade	1,099	32.2	–	–
Processing trade	2,493	32.0	–	–
Other trade	–970	2.6	–	–

Sources: *Statistical Communiqué of the PRC on 2007, Statistical Communiqué of the PRC on 2008.*

billion USD. As compared to 2007, trade value increased by 17.8 per cent in 2008, reaching a total of 2,561.6 billion USD. Export was 1,428.5 billion USD, an increase of 17.2 per cent; import was 1,133.1 billion USD, an increase of 18.5 per cent. Export surpassed import by 295.5 billion USD, an increase of 32.8 billion USD from the last year.

Processing trade increased at a slightly slower rate t, but still amounted to 51 per cent of the total volume in 2007. Electronic goods constituted 58 per cent of exports, whereas high-tech goods accounted for nearly 30 per cent. Regarding the ownership of enterprises involved in exporting, state-owned, foreign-invested and private enterprises took a share of 18 per cent, 57 per cent and 24 per cent, respectively. As for imports, processing trade accounted for 39 per cent. Electronic goods stood at 52 per cent, whereas high-technology goods had a share of 30 per cent. Imports of state-owned, foreign-invested and private firms shared 28 per cent, 59 per cent and 13 per cent, respectively. Processing trade was the largest contributor to the total trade surplus, amounting to 95 per cent of the latter.

The year 2008 saw a similar situation. Processing trade constituted 47 per cent of total exports, although its growth was still slower than that of general trade. Electronic goods accounted for 58 per cent of exports, whereas high-tech goods constituted only 29 per cent. With respect to the ownership of exporting enterprises, state-owned, foreign-invested and private firms stood at 18 per cent, 55 per cent and 23 per cent, respectively. As for imports, processing trade took a share of 33 per cent. The import of electronic goods and high-tech products were 48 per cent and 30 per cent, respectively. As regards the ownership, state-owned, foreign-invested and private firms obtained a share of 31 per cent, 55 per cent and 16 per cent, respectively.

With respect to volume, automatic data processing machines and components, clothes and clothing accessories, textile yarns and textile articles and rolled steel ranked ahead in the exports (Table 3). As for the growth rate, coal, rolled steel, motor vehicles, furniture, footwear and textile yarns and textile articles were highest. Crude oil, iron ore, plastics in primary forms, refined petroleum products, rolled steel and soybean were listed as the most important import products. In growth rates, soybean ranked first, followed by refined petroleum products, iron ore, crude oil and edible vegetable oil. From Table 3, we also see: first, automatic data processing machines and components replaced textile yarns and textile articles to be the top export product. This suggests that China's comparative advantage has shifted towards more capital-intensive and technology-intensive products, in line with findings in Rodrik (2006) and Schott (2006); second, primary products as the main import, to a certain extent reflects China's role as 'the factory of the world' (Fallow, 2007); third, coal and rolled steel ranked as the first two seats for their growth rate in export, whereas soybeans, refined petroleum products took the first two seats for their growth rate in imports. This shows the impact on import and export of terms-of-trade change triggered by the price surge of primary goods. The evidence is that the values of these products went up, yet quantity went down. Export quantity for coal and rolled steel declined by 14.6 per cent and 5.5 per cent, respectively, in 2007, while the quantity of seven out of 13 top import products reduced.

According to the trade volume, China's top five trade partners were the EU, USA, Japan, ASEAN and South Korea (Table 4). Due to its uniqueness as a re-export centre, Hong Kong will not be discussed here.[3] The EU, USA, Japan and ASEAN were the top four markets for China's exports, whereas Japan, the EU, ASEAN and South Korea were the leading four sources of China's imports. China's trade surplus mainly came from the USA and EU, whereas Taiwan, South Korea, Japan and ASEAN were the main sources of trade deficit. As a 'factory of

---

[3] Ferrantino and Wang (2008) recently discussed the discrepancies between America and China when each came up with its own statistics on USA–Sino bilateral trade. The intermediary role that Hong Kong had played in transit trade was also discussed.

TABLE 3
Main Export and Import Commodities, 2008

Exports				Imports		
Item	Value (100 million USD)	Increase over 2007 (%)		Item	Value (100 million USD)	Increase over 2007 (%)
Automatic data processing machines and components	1,350	9.1		Crude oil	1,293	62.0
Clothes and clothing accessories	1,198	4.1		Iron ore	605	79.1
Textile yarns and textile articles	654	16.6		Plastics in primary forms	341	5.3
Rolled steel	634	43.8		Petroleum products refined	300	82.7
Handheld mobiles and car telephones	385	8.2		Rolled steel	234	14.0
Footwear	297	17.2		Soybean	218	90.1
Furniture	269	21.5		Copper and copper alloys	192	−2.3
Integrated circuit	243	3.3		Edible vegetable oil	90	44.0
Liquid crystal display panels	224	13.9		Paper pulp	67	20.9
Containers	91	3.6		Natural rubber (including latex)	43	32.0
Motor vehicles (including a complete set of spare sets)	89	32.5		Synthetic rubber (including latex)	33	17.5
Coal	52	58.9		Aluminium oxide	18	−9.7
				Cereals and cereal flour	7	37.0

Source: *Statistical Communiqué of the PRC on 2008.*

TABLE 4
China's Merchandise Trade with Major Partners (100 million USD)

Country or Region	2007			2008		
	Export Value	Import Value	Trade Surplus	Export Value	Import Value	Trade Surplus
EU	2,452	1,110	1,342	2,929	1,327	1,602
USA	2,327	694	1,633	2,523	814	1,709
HK	1,844	128	1,716	1,907	129	1,778
Japan	1,021	1,340	−319	1,161	1,507	−346
ASEAN	942	1,084	−142	1,141	1,170	−29
South Korea	561	1,038	−477	740	1,122	−382
Russia	285	197	88	330	238	92
India	240	146	94	315	203	112
Taiwan	235	1,010	−775	259	1,033	−774

Sources: *Statistical Communiqué of the PRC on 2007, Statistical Communiqué of the PRC on 2008.*

the world', China has bound the world's economy together: it imports raw materials and intermediate goods from its neighbours in Asia, transporting assembled products to the EU and the USA. As a result, China has trade deficits with its partners in Asia. On the other hand, it has a trade surplus with the EU and the USA (Lum and Nanto, 2007).[4] Frequent trade disputes between China and the USA, EU and India undoubtedly relate to imbalanced trade. As the second largest trade partner of the EU, China has been the largest export country to the EU since 2003. It has also been the fourth import country from the EU since 2005. In 2007, the EU's trade deficit with China reached 250 billion USD, 86 per cent of its total trade deficit. In 2008, China was the biggest exporter to the USA and third largest importer of the USA. The USA's trade deficit amounted to 882.1 billion USD in this year, while its deficit with China alone amounted to one-third of this figure.[5] China continued its trade surplus with the EU and the USA while maintaining a trade deficit with neighbouring partners. This results from China's position in the international division of labour, and is also consistent with its diplomatic strategy of 'fostering an amicable, peaceful and prosperous neighbourhood'.

In 2007, foreign direct investment (FDI) inflow amounted to 74.77 billion USD, an increase of 13.6 per cent from the previous year (Table 5). More than half of

---

[4] From 1995 to 2008, China underwent 677 cases of anti-dumping investigation, a far cry from what Korea suffered. Korea incurred 252 cases and has been ranked second after China. In 2008, China suffered from 73 cases of anti-dumping investigation, of which 6, 5 and 15 came respectively from the EU, USA and India.
[5] The data here regarding the EU/USA trade balance with China are from the WTO, not China's statistics (Table 4). These two data sources have big differences, a controversial issue often confronted but beyond the scope of our chapter.

TABLE 5

The Sectoral Distribution of Foreign Direct Investment in China, 2007–08

Sector	2007		2008	
	Actually Utilised Value (100 million USD)	Increase over 2006 (%)	Actually Utilised Value (100 million USD)	Increase over 2006 (%)
Total	747.7	13.6	924.0	23.6
Farming, Forestry, Animal Husbandry and Fishery	9.2	54.2	11.9	28.9
Mining and Quarrying	4.9	5.4	5.7	17.0
Manufacturing	408.6	-4.6	498.9	22.1
Production and Supply of Electricity, Gas and Water	10.7	-16.6	17.0	58.1
Construction	4.3	-36.9	10.9	151.6
Transport, Storage, Post and Telecommunication	20.1	1.1	28.5	42.1
Information Transmission, Computer Services and Software	14.9	38.7	27.7	86.8
Wholesale and Retail Trade	26.8	49.6	44.3	65.6
Lodging and Catering Services	10.4	25.8	9.4	-9.9
Banking	2.6	-12.4	5.7	122.5
Real Estate	170.9	107.3	185.9	8.8
Leasing and Business Services	40.2	-5.2	50.6	25.9
Scientific Research, Technical Services and Geological Prospecting	9.2	81.8	15.1	64.2
Water Conservancy, Environment Protection and Public Facilities Management	2.7	39.8	3.4	24.7
Services to Households and Other Services	7.2	43.0	5.7	-21.1
Education	0.3	10.4	0.4	12.2
Health, Social Security and Social Welfare	0.1	-23.7	0.2	63.1
Culture, Sports and Entertainment	4.5	86.9	2.6	-42.8
Public Management and Social Organisation	0.0	–	0.0	–
International Organisation	–	–	6.0	–

Sources: *Statistical Communiqué of the PRC on 2007, Statistical Communiqué of the PRC on 2008.*

this was concentrated in manufacturing, followed by real estate with around 23 per cent. Although manufacturing topped the list, its growth rate fell by 4.6 per cent compared to 2006. On the other hand, FDI in real estate experienced a 107.3 per cent growth. In 2008, China's FDI continued to boom, reaching 92.4 billion USD, an increase of 23.6 per cent from 2007. Manufacturing accounted for 54 per cent, a growth of 22.1 per cent. Real estate accounted for 20 per cent but its growth rate fell to 8.8 per cent. Apparently, the measures taken in controlling investment in real estate during that period exerted a negative impact. In 2009, adverse effects of the global financial tsunami affected China. During the first five months, 7,890 newly approved foreign-funded enterprises were established, a fall of 33.78 per cent. Actual FDI stood at 34.048 billion USD, a fall of 20.41 per cent. With regard to China's overseas investment, non-financial outward investment amounted to 18.7 billion USD in 2007, a growth of 6.2 per cent compared to 2006. In 2008 this rose to 40.7 billion USD, an increase of 63.6 per cent from 2007. China remains an important host for foreign investment, while it has at the same time become an important source for capital outflow.

b. Changes in Foreign Trade Policies since 2007

With the macroeconomy heating up, China began to take tightening measures in 2007. The Ministry of Finance (MOF) and State Administration of Taxation (SAT) adjusted export duty rebates of 2,831 products on 1 July. They accounted for 37 per cent of the commodities covered by the custom tariff. Export duty rebate rates of 2,268 products easily provoking trade disputes were lowered, while rebates for 553 types of 'high energy-consuming products, high pollution products and resource products' were removed. The Ministry of Commerce (MOFCOM) and the General Administration of Customs (GAS) twice changed the catalogue of prohibited commodities in processing trade in 2007. The 2007 Catalogue was released on 5 April with a list of 1,140 items, among which 184 items were newly added. The 2007 Second Batch of Prohibited Commodities Catalogue was released on 21 December, with a list of 589 items. On 23 July 2007, The 2007 Catalogue of Restricted Commodities in Processing Trade was released with a list of 2,247 commodities, among which 1,853 items were newly included. The 2008 Catalogue of Prohibited Commodities in Processing Trade was released and enforced on 5 April 2008, including 1,816 items, while 39 items were newly added. It is obvious that from mid-2007 to mid-2008, the government strove to control the production and export of low-value-added products (Table 6).

The global financial crisis greatly impacted the USA and EU. As a result, China's exports met with unprecedented pressure. China is a country with a trade dependency ratio of 70 per cent, which suggests that export decline will definitely lead to recession. The government did not take any action until it realised the destructive power of the crisis in the second half of 2008. On 1 August 2008, the

TABLE 6
Foreign Trade Policy Change, 2007–09

Year	Date of Enforcement	Content
Export duty rebates		
2009	1 June	To uplift the export duty rebate rate of competitive products, labour-intensive products, high-tech products and deeply processed products
	1 April	To raise the export tax rebate rates of calcium hypochlorite, sanitary ceramics, methanol, leather products, textiles and clothes and CRT colour TV
	1 February	To raise the export duty rebate rates for textile and clothing
	1 January	To increase the export tax rebate rates for 553 types of mechanical and electrical products with high technical content and added value
2008	1 December	To further raise the export tax rebate rates for some labour-intensive, mechanical and electrical products
	1 November	To raise the tax rebate rate for 3,486 items from labour-intensive industries such as textile, garment, toy, high-tech and high added value sectors like anti-AIDS drugs and tempered glass
	1 August	To raise tax rebates for certain textiles and garments, including silk, wool yarn, chemical fibre and cotton products
2007	1 July	To eliminate the export tax rebates for 553 'highly energy-consuming and resource-intensive' products, such as cement, fertiliser and non-ferrous metals. To slash the rebates for another 2,268 products, which are 'easy to trigger trade frictions' and include garments, toys, steel products and motorcycles
The catalogue of commodities for processing trade		
2009	3 June	The 2009 Catalogue of Prohibited Commodities in Processing Trade included 1,759 items
	1 February	The Catalogue of Prohibited Commodities in Processing Trade included 1,789 items. A total of 27 items were taken away from the previous catalogue
	1 February	The Catalogue of Restricted Commodities in Processing Trade included 500 items. A total of 1,747 items were taken away from the previous catalogue
2008	5 April	The 2008 Catalogue of Prohibited Commodities in Processing Trade included 1,816 items. A total of 39 new items were newly included
	21 January	The 2007 Second Batch of Prohibited Commodities Catalogue (prohibited exports) included 589 items
2007	23 August	The 2007 Catalogue of Restricted Commodities in Processing Trade included 2,247 items, an increase of 1,853 items from the previous catalogue
	27 April	The 2007 Catalogue of Prohibited Commodities in Processing Trade included 1,140 items, an increase of 184 items from the previous catalogue

Source: MOFCOM.

MOF and SAT began to raise export duty rebate rates on textiles, apparels and other products. Since then, they have raised it on 1 November 2008, 1 December 2008, 1 January 2009, 1 February 2009, 1 April 2009 and 1 June 2009. Take the adjustment on 1 November 2008 as an example. Export duty rebate rates for 3,486 items were increased. The commodities involved accounted for 25.8 per cent of the commodities the custom tariff covered. An official from the MOF even pointed out that 'the adjustment on export duty rebates this time is the largest, most intensive one since 2004' (source: *China Times*, 1 November 2008). The MOFCOM and the GAS announced in 31 December 2008 that in the catalogue of restricted commodities for processing trade, only 500 items were kept. On 3 June 2009, *The 2009 Catalogue of Prohibited Commodities in Processing Trade* was announced with the number of items reducing to 1,759, far less than that included in *The 2008 Catalogue*.

Since China adopted reform and opening up, attracting foreign investment has always been the priority. Nevertheless, with economic development going on, the negative side of China's foreign investment policy has been revealed. The 'FDI race' between local governments leaves foreign investors as 'the big winner' of China's growth. But the costs are exclusively shouldered by Chinese people. To prevent the macroeconomy from overheating, China also introduced a series of laws, regulations and documentations related to foreign investment (Table 7).

The Standing Committee of the National People's Congress (SCNPC) passed three laws in 2007, all of which went into effect a year later. *The Enterprise Income Tax Law* was passed on 16 March 2007. The key point is to unify tax rates at 25 per cent to eliminate the discriminating tax treatment to domestic and foreign enterprises. Adapting this to all kinds of firms is a general rule practised worldwide. It is also helpful in improving the quality of China's FDI inflow in the long run. Especially, those FDI seeking tax incentives will be discouraged. On 29 June 2007, the *Labour Contract Law* was passed, which brings new costs to firms such as lay-off pay, on-leave pay, etc. Nevertheless, building a sound legal system including *Labour Contract Law* will reduce the uncertainties for business-making, which is in favour of FDI for long-time horizons. On 30 August 2007, the Anti-monopoly Law was passed, which further regulates the behaviour of foreign investors. Specifically, foreign enterprises involved in merge and acquisition are required to pass the review of the concentration of business operators. If needed, they also should pass the national security review. In comparison with the USA and other countries, China's legal framework is still in the primary stages. This law will, however, allow the behaviour of foreign investors to be reviewed formally, preventing cases like 'Carlyle Group LP's Unsuccessful Acquisition of Xuzhou Construction Machinery Group' from recurring. NDRC and MOFCOM released the *Catalogue for the Guidance of Foreign Investment Industries* (amended in 2007) on 31 October 2007, which has direct influence on the sectoral distribution of FDI. Especially, it encouraged FDI to enter the advanced manufacturing

TABLE 7
Documents Related to Foreign Direct Investment (FDI), 2007–09

Year	Department (Date of Enforcement)	Documents	Key Point
2009	MOFCOM (22 January)	Reply of the General Office of the State Council to Issues concerning Facilitation of Service Outsourcing Industry	To develop service outsourcing
	NDRC, MOFCOM (1 January)	Catalogue of Priority Industries for Foreign Investment in Central and Western Regions (amended in 2008)	To promote utilising FDI in mid-west China
2008	MOFCOM (22 December)	Guidance on the Establishment of a Comprehensive Evaluation System for Attracting Foreign Investment	To move from 'attracting FDI' to 'selecting FDI'
	MOFCOM (1 July)	Circular on Better Implementation of the Filing of Foreign Investment in Real Estate Sector	To strengthen the supervision of foreign investment in real estate
	SCNPC (1 August)	Anti-monopoly Law	Review of concentration of business operators, national security review
	SCNPC (1 January)	Labour Contract Law	Open-ended employment contract
	SCNPC (1 January)	Enterprise Income Tax Law	To unify the tax rates
2007	NDRC, MOFCOM (1 December)	Catalogue for the Guidance of foreign Investment Industries (amended in 2007)	The sectoral distribution of foreign capital

Source: The websites of related departments.

sector and outsourcing service sector, but restricted FDI in rare and non-renewable natural resource areas. On the other hand, the *Circular on Better Implementation of the Filing of Foreign Investment in Real Estate Sector* was released by MOFCOM on 18 June 2008, which was expected to raise the regulatory efficiency in foreign capital in the real estate sector.

Shortly after these documents were issued, the negative impact of the global financial crisis on China's FDI inflow began to surface. Consequently, related ministries and departments started to make adjustments on policies again. MOFCOM released a *Guidance on the Establishment of a Comprehensive Evaluation System for Attracting Foreign Investment* on 22 December 2008, which stressed that China should move from 'attracting FDI' towards 'selecting FDI'.

To promote FDI in central and western China, the NDRC and MOFCOM released the *Catalogue of Priority Industries for Foreign Investment in Central & Western Regions* (amended in 2008) on 23 December 2008. It emphasised that FDI should be compatible with the resource endowment and industrial structure in these areas. In addition, MOFCOM forwarded the *Reply of the General Office of the State Council to Issues concerning Facilitation of Service Outsourcing Industry* on 22 January 2009. It pointed out that, to utilise FDI in the service sector, China should become an important centre for international service outsourcing.

c. China's Bilateral Trade Agreements with Other Countries and Regions

China is an important country in promoting global free trade. In addition to participating in multilateral trade negotiations, China has committed itself to bilateral free trade with other partners. So far, China has signed free trade agreements (FTAs) with New Zealand as well as eight other trade partners; it is carrying out FTA negotiations with Australia as well as another five partners; the FTA with South Korea and India are at the stage of a feasibility study (Table 8).

A Closer Economic Partnership Arrangement (CEPA) with Hong Kong/Macao is the first fully implemented free trade agreement. It sheds new light for Hong Kong/Macao on their dealing with structural challenges and facilitates these two special administrative regions in their integration with the Mainland (especially with Pan-Pearl River Delta Regions). The China–ASEAN Free Trade Area is the first of its kind, which China negotiated with foreign countries; it is also the first FTA, which ASEAN as a whole negotiated. With the CAFTA Investment Agreement signed on 15 August 2009, the goal of building up a free trade area in the year 2010 is now on the horizon. If China's FTAs with its Asian neighbours are to some extent mixed with political considerations, its FTAs with Chile and Peru are mainly signed for the security of energy and resources. As the CCFTA between China and Chile was brought into effect in October 2006, China has become the largest importer of Chilean copper. By the first half of 2009, China has already replaced the USA as Chile's biggest trade partner. Peru also ranks high for its abundant mineral reserves. China has become its second biggest trade partner and importer. In the year 2004, China entered into negotiations with GCC. The latter has abundant reserves of petroleum, whose proven oil reserves account for about 45 per cent of the total world reserves. China's free trade talks with developed countries are closely related to its endeavour to promote the acceptance of the so-called 'market economy status'. The agreement signed with New Zealand on 7 April 2008 was the first between China and a developed country, and New Zealand was the very first country to acknowledge China's market economy status. China's free trade agreement negotiations with countries such as Australia, Iceland and Norway are now well under way, and Switzerland has decided to start its negotiation in the second half of 2009. These four developed countries have all

TABLE 8

Free Trade Agreements (FTAs) between China and Its Partners

Start-up Time	Partners	Implementation
The free trade areas that have already signed the free trade agreement		
2002	ASEAN	The first FTA, for which China has negotiated with foreign countries; it is also the first FTA, for which ASEAN as a whole has negotiated with foreign countries. The FTA negotiation was started in 2002; the FTA will be set up as scheduled by 2010
2003	Hong Kong, Macau	CEPA is a free trade agreement between Hong Kong, Macao and the Mainland which is the first fully implemented free trade agreement in the Mainland. The FTA negotiation was started in 2003. By 2009, six supplemental agreements have been signed
2004	Chile	China–Chile Free Trade Agreement was signed in 2005; China–Chile FTA on Trade in Services Agreement was signed in 2008
2005	Pakistan	China–Pakistan Free Trade Agreement and China–Pakistan FTA Trade in Services Agreement have already been signed
2005	Laos et al.	Asia–Pacific Free Trade Agreement was signed by China, Bangladesh, India, Laos, South Korea and Sri Lanka in 2005
2007	Peru	China–Peru Free Trade Agreement was signed in 2009
2008	New Zealand	China–New Zealand Free Trade Agreement was signed in 2008, which was the first free trade agreement with a developed country
2008	Singapore	China–Singapore Free Trade Agreement was signed in 2008
The free trade areas that are under negotiation		
2004	GCC	Consensus has already been reached in most fields of trade in goods negotiation; and trade in services negotiation has been launched
2004	SACU	Up to now, it has not entered the substantial stage
2005	Australia	By the end of 2008, 13 rounds of FTA negotiation had been completed
2007	Iceland	By 2008, the fourth round of negotiation had been completed
2008	Norway	Up to now, the fourth round of negotiation has been completed
2008	Costa Rica	Till now, the third round of negotiation has been completed
The free trade areas that are under consideration		
2004	Korea	FTA feasibility study is being jointly carried out by government departments, enterprises and academic institutions. The fifth round had been completed by 2008
2005	India	The report of joint study had been completed by 2007
2009	Switzerland	FTA negotiation will be launched in the second half of 2009

Note:
The Start-up Time refers to the beginning of the FTA negotiation; as for South Korea and India, the Start-up Time indicates the beginning of the feasibility study.
Source: MOFCOM.

recognised China's market economy status. On 23 March 2009, Uruguay also announced its acknowledgement of China's full market economy status. Up to now, there have been 79 countries which have accepted China's full market economy status. It is a pity that China's main trade partners such as the USA, the EU, Japan and India are still absent from the list.

4. FACTS REVISITED AND POLITICAL ECONOMY

a. Facts on Foreign Trade and Investment

In 2007 and 2008, China continued its strong growth in foreign trade and investment. During these years, total trade volume ranked third in the world. Its import value ranked second in the world. Its export value was less than only the USA and Germany. At the same time, FDI experienced growth of 13.6 per cent and 23.6 per cent in 2007 and 2008, respectively. However, in 2006, FDI had a 4.1 per cent drop. Since 2009, foreign trade and FDI have declined dramatically. From January to June 2009, the total value of trade dropped by 23.5 per cent; 10,419 newly approved foreign-funded enterprises were established, a drop of 28.36 per cent; and the FDI was 43 billion USD, a drop of 17.9 per cent (source: MOFCOM).

Processing trade accounted for 50 per cent of exports and 35 per cent of imports, 60 per cent by foreign-funded enterprises. Electronic products were the main commodities, amounting to 50–60 per cent. High-tech products accounted for around 30 per cent. Most of the trade surplus came from processing trade. Private enterprises were the largest source of trade surplus, accounting for around 70 per cent. State-owned enterprises were the only type of enterprises that incurred trade deficit. China's main trade partners were the EU, USA, Japan and ASEAN. Trade surplus came mainly from the EU and the USA, while Korea, Japan and ASEAN were the main sources of trade deficit. More than half of FDI inflow was concentrated in manufacturing, while real estate took a second place. The real estate sector, however, underwent greater fluctuations. Besides 'tax heavens', the major sources for China's FDI inflow were Singapore, Japan, Korea and the USA. More than half of China's outflow was concentrated in leasing and business services as well as wholesale and retail trade. Latin America surpassed Asia to become the top destination for China's overseas investment.

b. Foreign Trade and Investment Policies

To deal with the overheated economy, 'tightening' trade policies were introduced from mid-2007 to mid-2008. Measures included reducing the scope and rates of export duty rebates, increasing prohibited and restricted commodities as well as imposing temporary export tariffs. New laws were deemed unfavourable to FDI inflow, especially for those aiming at preferential policies. Adjustment on the industrial catalogue for foreign investment further pointed out the areas in which FDI was encouraged, limited or prohibited. Regulations related to foreign investment in real estate were issued to prevent speculation. However, with the global financial crisis, China's economy was hit hard. Since the second half of 2008, the government started to readjust its foreign trade policies, especially broadening the scope of export duty rebates, raising export duty rebates, reducing

prohibited and restricted commodities for processing trade, removing the temporary export tariffs, etc. To attract FDI, the government issued guidance for investors to Central and Western China.

c. Bilateral Trade Agreements

China established 14 Free Trade Zones with 31 partners. Seven FTAs are
already in effect. Besides Hong Kong and Macau, other partners include ASEAN,
Chile, Pakistan, New Zealand and Singapore. China is also pushing talks with the
Gulf Cooperation Council, Australia, Iceland, Norway and the Southern African
Customs Union. China and India have already completed the feasibility research
on free trade arrangements. In addition, China has been conducting similar research
with South Korea. In the second half of 2009, free trade talks with Switzerland
will be initiated. China and ASEAN signed a bilateral investment agreement on
15 August 2009. This signified that they had completed major talks on FTA, setting
an example in the fight against the reemergence of global trade protectionism.

d. Top Down versus Bottom Up

Trade policies in developed countries are 'bottom up', which means that interest
groups are the main forces pushing change. Policy formed in this way is strong
and cannot be changed in a short period. In contrast, the formal and open activity
of interest groups is 'absent' in China. As a result, there is a 'top-down' feature
in Chinese trade policy. This approach mainly reflects the preference of the leadership in economic development. The CCP has published 'Resolution on Major
Issues Regarding Building of Harmonious Socialist Society' on 11 October 2006,
which gives prominence to 'scientific development' and actually paves the road
for the following policy (including trade policy) adjustment.

Because the information policymakers are able to acquire about the market is
limited, policies in favour of the 'top-down' approach cannot produce the desired
effects. Guangdong is a good case in this regard. Its export-oriented economy is
the earliest to have been developed and the most successful. It is also one of the
provinces which are quickly under pressure from structural transition. In December
2006, Wang Yang, the former top leader of Chongqing City, has been nominated
as Party chief of Guangdong Province. His position as a member of the Political
Bureau ensures that reform at the local level is consistent with the top leaders (Bai
et al., 2008). He called for elimination of so-called 'obsolete production capacity'
as soon as he took office. With the global economy in recession, the Pearl River
Delta heavily relying on processing trade is severely affected. The predicament in
this region shocked top officials. Since the second half of 2008, Premier Wen
Jiabao has visited Guangdong three times. Big changes in policies have followed.
From this case, we infer that, in view of the fact that industrial groups understand

the market better than government, had they been given the opportunities to participate in policy design, the measures would not have had to undergo 'drastic changes' within such a short period.

e. Inside Out versus Outside In

Trade policies in developed countries are also 'inside out'. As old members of the WTO, they do not have to face international pressures of new members like China. In these countries, pressure for policy change mainly comes from interest groups within countries. We call this the 'inside-out' trade policy. By contrast, China's trade policy is obviously 'outside in'. This refers to the situation where, when domestic interest groups are absent, the pressure from outside plays a critical role. China's fast growth in exports is seen as a major source of global imbalance. Under such circumstances, pressure from the international community must be considered when adjustments are made to trade policies.[6] In addition, China has vast trade surpluses with the EU and USA. Due to their significant influence over the global trade system, pressure from both has also to be taken into account. In other words, trade policy changes between mid-2007 and mid-2008 have something to do with these external pressures.

Nevertheless, the 'tightening' policy on processing trade affects the supply of China's exports only, which cannot basically improve global disequilibrium. Even if China could reduce exports to the USA, the 'appetite' of Americans still could be satisfied by other developing countries. More ironically, an 'outside-in' trade policy has actually not anticipated the effects of the change in foreign demand imposed on China. The real estate bubble burst, reducing households' wealth in developed countries. Undoubtedly, this will have negative spillover effects on China's exports. The worsening of the external environment weakens China's ability to embark on structural reform. As a result, 'reversing' the policies is the only way out. Domestic interest groups are closer to the market, having newer and more information about supply and demand in global and domestic markets. Had their needs been respected, the cycle of 'adoption and abandonment' in trade policy would not have been necessary.

f. Pro-market versus Pro-government

In recent years, export tax rebates have become an important macroeconomic tool (Xiong, 2009). Although adjustments made can stimulate or control exports in the short run, efficiency usually gets worse. Since 2006, government has adjusted export tax rebates 15 times. Therefore, it is inevitable that the costs both

---

[6] Foreign-funded firms play important roles in China's economy, enjoying a higher 'bargaining power'. They have a great impact on trade polices as well (Kennedy, 2005, 2006).

for tax collectors and taxpayers have risen. Till now, the rates of export tax rebates have seven levels, while there were only three levels when tax reform was initiated in 1994. Too many rates provide incentives for rent-seeking. Adjustments on the commodity catalogue for processing trade also have similar problems. Adjustment at least once every year not only increases uncertainty, but also renders economic policies out of control by laws.

Although these 'pro-governmental' policies raise government's flexibility in decision-making, they fail to make any breakthrough in structural reforms. To transform its development model successfully, China should make improvements in the following respects. First, it should take steps for further privatisation. In China, this has already gone a long way in the last 30 years. Nevertheless, the worrying cases of 'further nationalisation and lesser privatisation' have resurfaced during the financial crisis.[7] It is necessary to enlarge the scope for private capital in natural resources, advanced manufacturing and modern service industries, preventing them from being locked in processing trade and competition. Second, the financial sector should be reformed. Delayed financial reform will result in an unacceptable structure, with the financial sector dominated by state-owned firms, yet the real sector controlled by private firms. Being risk averse, banks still give most of their loans to public firms. This has led to serious over-capacity in state-owned enterprises. The overproduction in the steel industry monopolised by public firms is an example. Because private enterprises do not have enough financial support, they have to accumulate capital with 'assembling fees' via export. This is one reason why they are the largest contributor to China's trade surplus. Finally, high-quality human resources are also necessary for structural reform. Employment training is especially important for the reallocation of resources in the process of transition. Due to positive externalities, enterprises sometimes lack incentives to train their workforce. There is thus a need for the government to be much more involved in this.

g. Long Run versus Short Run

In the long run, the efforts made by each country to carry out structural reforms are necessary for global equilibrium. Nevertheless, without the government's helping hand, structural adjustment regulated by market forces will possibly exacerbate the sluggishness of the economy. Although structural reform can be accomplished when the market reaches a new equilibrium, it will take a rather long time. Therefore, there is a trade-off between long-term restructuring and short-term economic growth. Trade policy changes since 2007 reflect the government's

---

[7] Li (2009) has revealed in detail in an essay for *China Business News* (4 August) that state-owned enterprise Shandong Iron and Steel will take over the privately-owned Rizhao Iron and Steel, although the former is losing money.

dilemma. The final choice depends on the wisdom of policymakers and the public and is contingent on other factors as well. At present, the Chinese government puts 'people's livelihood' on the top of the agenda, requiring that more employment opportunities should be created. In addition, 2008 was very special. It was the Olympics year and also the 30th anniversary of China's reform and opening. The year 2009 was also special. It was the 60th anniversary of the founding of new China. Taking these factors into account, the government has to avoid social unrest instigated by climbing unemployment. According to Okun's law, economic growth is a necessary condition for increased employment. During the economic downturn, that means expansionary policies have to be timely. Since the second half of 2008, loosening export tax rebates and processing trade is the example of these kinds of policies in the foreign trade area.

That structural reform yields to economic growth is a 'second-best' option when the outside environment gets worse. Nevertheless, China's recovery in growth is no doubt good news for a blighted global economy. As the world's largest developing country and largest economy of the 'Golden BRICs', China's economic growth not only creates profit opportunities for international capital, but also provides markets for developing countries to expand their exports. As an important destination for FDI, the investment opportunities found in China will reduce uncertainty faced by international capital and is also helpful in bringing financial resources back into the real economy. As a large importer of natural resources, parts and intermediate goods, China's recovery will have positive spillovers to other countries, especially developing countries. For China, the best reward is a free trade environment that the international community should maintain. Trade will bring about growth opportunities for each country and render structural reform easier.

5. CONCLUSION

From mid-2007 to mid-2008, the most important task for China was the fight against inflation. As a result, tightening of export duty rebates, shrinkage of the catalogue for processing trade and other trade polices were introduced. In the past few years, the so-called 'harmonious society' has become China's new guiding ideology in economic development. Making changes to the outward-oriented development model is the priority of the government. Nevertheless, the global financial tsunami triggered by the 'subprime crisis' quickly took its toll on China. The constraining trade policies and the downturn in the international market have given processing trade a 'double blow' in terms of supply and demand. Coastal provinces heavily reliant on international markets found themselves in a tight corner. The favourable surroundings available for China to carry out structural reform ceased to exist. Under these conditions, some policies adopted earlier have been called off in the second half of 2008 and many old measures, discarded previously, have been picked up again. When the economy has integrated with the global market, China is caught in a dilemma: in order for healthy and continuous economic development, structural reform remains the top priority; but without desirable external surroundings (international and domestic), structural reform cannot take a further step. The global financial crisis at the moment is just a 'natural experiment' for China, which proves that structural reform is highly sensitive to the outside climate. This outcome is not surprising, but still worrying.

Within the past three years, trade policy in China has experienced an 'adoption and abandonment' cycle. This situation is closely related to its political structure and external circumstances. First, leaders' will decides where trade policy should go. Without pressure from the bottom, the forces pushing trade policy come from the top and the international community. This means domestic interest groups do not play major roles in policy design. Compared with these groups, policymakers have less information regarding supply and demand in domestic and international markets. Hence, policies introduced often do not achieve desired results. Second, the discretionary power in using trade policy strengthens the government's role in the economy. However, this does not help in making breakthroughs in structural reforms. Adjusting export duty rebates and catalogues for processing trade frequently does increase the government's flexibility in policymaking and also leads to inefficiency and even induces rent-seeking activities. From our viewpoint, the more essential tasks for structural reform are further privatisation, faster financial reconstruction and more effective human resource development. Finally, unexpected shocks both inside and outside force China to return to its short-term goal in trade policy design. Structural reform is unavoidable for long-run economic equilibrium. However, it cannot be finished overnight. Due to political constraints, the government cannot but place importance on economic growth.

Economic policies, including trade policies, are loosened up again. The quick recovery of China's economy has positive externalities. If the international community can cooperate to protect free trade, that will be the best reward for China's contribution in driving the global economy out of recession. Free trade brings about growth opportunities for every country, and growth will create conditions for successful structural reform.

REFERENCES

Bai, C.-E., Z. Tao and Y. S. Tong (2008), 'Bureaucratic Integration and Regional Specialization in China', *China Economic Review*, **19**, 308–19.
Blanchard, O. and A. Shleifer (2001), 'Federalism with and without Political Centralization: China versus Russia', NBER Working Paper 7616 (Cambridge, MA: NBER).
Branstetter, L. G. and R. C. Feenstra (2002), 'Trade and Foreign Direct Investment in China: A Political Economy Approach', *Journal of International Economics*, **58**, 335–58.

Fallow, J. (2007), 'China Makes, the World Takes', *Atlantic Monthly*, **300**, 48–72.

Ferrantino, M. J. and Z. Wang (2008), 'Accounting for the Discrepancies in Bilateral Trade: The Case of China, Hongkong and the United States', *China Economic Review*, **19**, 502–20.

Gawande, K. and U. Bandyopadhyay (2000), 'Is Protection for Sale? A Test of the Grossman–Helpman Theory of Endogenous Protection', *Review of Economics and Statistics*, **82**, 139–52.

Goldberg, P. K. and G. Maggi (1999), 'Protection for Sale: An Empirical Investigation', *American Economic Review*, **89**, 1135–55.

Grether, J.-M., J. de Melo and M. Olarreaga (2001), 'Who Determines Mexican Trade Policy?' *Journal of Development Economics*, **64**, 343–70.

Grossman, G. and E. Helpman (1994), 'Protection for Sale', *American Economic Review*, **84**, 833–50.

He, D. and Y. Yao (2009), 'Equality and Neutral Government: An Interpretation on China's Economic Growth during the Past 30 Years', *World Economic Papers*, **1**, 103–20 (in Chinese).

Kennedy, S. (2005), 'China's Porous Protectionism: The Changing Political Economy of Trade Policy', *Political Science Quarterly*, **120**, 407–32.

Kennedy, S. (2006), 'The Political Economy of Standards Coalitions: Explaining China's Involvement in High-tech Standards Wars', *Asia Policy*, **2**, 41–62.

Li, G. (2009), 'Loss-making Shandong Steel Group to Take Over Profit-making Rizhao Steel Group', China Business Review, 4 August (in Chinese).

Lopez, R. and X. Matschke (2006), 'Food Protection for Sale', *Review of International Economics*, **14**, 380–91.

Lum, T. and D. K. Nanto (2007), 'China's Trade with the United States and the World', *CRS Report for Congress RL31403* (Washington, DC: Congressional Research Service).

McCalman, P. (2004), 'Protection for Sale and Trade Liberalization: An Empirical Investigation', *Review of International Economics*, **12**, 81–94.

Mitra, D., D. D. Thomakos and M. A. Ulubasoglu (2002), ' "Protection for Sale" in a Developing Country: Democracy vs. Dictatorship', *Review of Economics and Statistics*, **84**, 497–508.

Pei, M. (2009), 'Will the Chinese Communist Party Survive the Crisis?' www.foreignaffairs.com, 12 March.

Rodrik, D. (2006), 'What's so Special about China's Exports?' NBER Working Paper 11947 (Cambridge, MA: NBER).

Schott, P. K. (2006), 'The Relative Sophistication of Chinese Exports', NBER Working Paper 12173 (Cambridge, MA: NBER).

Xiong, L. (2009), 'Structural Tax Deduction and its Consequence', *China Finance*, **14**, 36–8 (in Chinese).

3

The Dominican Republic Trade Policy Review 2008

Amelia U. Santos-Paulino

1. INTRODUCTION

THE Dominican Republic (DR) is regarded as a successful liberaliser. The most recent *Trade Policy Review* conducted in 2008 clearly states the country's commitment to continuous trade liberalisation. However, the potential benefits from a more open trade regime recognised in the trade and development literature depend on minimum economic and institutional conditions for liberalisation to be successful in enhancing economic performance and welfare (e.g. Greenaway, 1993; Santos-Paulino and Thirlwall, 2004). As Winters (2004) argues, trade liberalisation by itself is unlikely to boost economic growth, unless openness reduces corruption, institutional constraints and is accompanied by improved macroeconomic policymaking.[1]

This chapter assesses the DR's 2008 *Trade Policy Review* conducted by the Review Body of the World Trade Organization (WTO). It summarises and discusses the *Trade Policy Review* (2008), and evaluates the development challenges faced by the country in view of continuous liberalisation and economic integration processes. The rest of the chapter proceeds as follows. Section 2 sets the stage by overviewing the trade liberalisation efforts and previous trade policy reviews. Section 3 reviews the 2008 *Trade Policy Review*. Section 4 discusses some future challenges for trade policy in the DR and provides concluding remarks.

---

[1] For reviews of the evidence on trade liberalisation and economic performance, see Greenaway et al. (1998) and Santos-Paulino (2005).

The World Economy: Global Trade Policy 2010, First Edition. Edited by David Greenaway.
© 2011 Blackwell Publishing Ltd. Published 2011 by Blackwell Publishing Ltd.

2. STRUCTURAL REFORMS AND TRADE LIBERALISATION

The WTO completed its first *Trade Policy Review* of the Dominican Republic in 1996, just midway through vital economic reforms and trade policy adjustments that started in the early 1990s. Following the 'lost decade', an extensive programme of macroeconomic reforms was launched in 1990 aimed at improving national policies and hence the country's economic performance.

The programme focused mostly on fiscal and trade policy reforms, and the main targets were increasing the efficiency of the existing tariff and tax structure and eliminating price distortions, reducing asymmetries in the incentives provided to specific industries and sectors (particularly that between the industrial and agricultural sectors competing with imports), and at the same time maintain a fiscal equilibrium. Crucially, the existing anti-export bias needed attention, to increase exports' competitiveness, as well as to achieve a better allocation of resources and a higher participation of the private sector in productive activities.

At the onset of structural reforms, the trade regime featured a complex structure and difficult administration, as well as by the discretionary nature of its application. Specifically, trade policy was typified by the use of import substitution strategy based on a dense tariff code, additional duties applied to specific products, contingents, licences, prohibitions, exemptions and concessions to specific industries, and a multiple exchange rate system with various rates applied to different transactions (see Santos-Paulino, 2006). Before the reform, imports were ruled by over 27 laws, and 140 taxes and duties, and were subject to three different types of exchange rates.[2]

The 1990 tariff reform simplified the tariff structure and reduced tariff dispersion, therefore lowering the effective rate of protection. Also, a new tariff code based on the 'Harmonised System of Goods Codification' was introduced.[3] Tariff exemptions granted to specific sectors under special agreements with the government were eliminated. Import prohibitions were also removed, with the exception of several products competing with domestic production, whereby these commodities represented around 40 per cent of agricultural output and 12 per cent of manufacturing production. Domestic taxes applied to imports were also reformed, particularly the value-added tax.

Importantly, the exchange rate for different imports was unified, and the system of custom administration was improved reducing inefficiencies and corruption. In

---

[2] Import prohibitions included textiles, food and electronic products, shoes, cars and luxury items. These prohibitions were justified on the grounds of encouraging national production, and to enable the country to balance its trade account.

[3] Although tariff rates were significantly reduced, the government implemented temporary tariff surcharges to counteract the impact of liberalisation on the protective structure of 'sensitive' sectors, and at the same time to allow them to adapt gradually to foreign competition. The additional tariffs were eliminated by 1995.

1995 Congress approved a new foreign direct investment (FDI) law, which eliminated restrictions on foreign companies investing in certain economic sectors, and allowed the repatriation of profits and the channelling of long-term loans. This signified determinant of future FDI inflows. Following the restoration of macroeconomic stability in 1991, the DR entered a new period of remarkable economic growth.

Following several years of confrontation, in December 2000 the Congress approved a programme of trade and tax policy reforms, which intertwined the different existing proposals, under a *Tariff Reform and Fiscal Compensation Programme*. The application of the programme started in January 2001. The new programme further reduced tariffs and trade duties, the value-added tax and the tax on selective consumption. The further liberalisation effort was the highlight of the second *Trade Policy Review* in 2002.

Reforms also eliminated most non-tariff barriers and converted them into explicit taxes, such as import prohibitions, quotas, licences and exemptions, to comply with the WTO agreements; consequently, the import tax base was extended. However, tariff contingents for some agricultural products (beans, corn, chicken, milk, rice, sugar and garlic) regarded as sensitive for Dominican producers continued to be applied. The protection schedule for these products was bound at the time of the country's accession to the WTO.[4]

Table 1 reports the evolution of the tariff schedules as a result of the trade liberalisation programmes. The reduction in tariff rates and in their dispersion is evident, but the government yet uses tariffs and temporary excises as a means of protection for some industries/sectors, mainly agricultural products and raw materials that compete with imports.[5] This reduction in trade barriers has stimulated a higher growth of exports and imports, but the net trade balance has deteriorated progressively (see Figure 1).

3. THE 2008 *TRADE POLICY REVIEW*

Since the *Trade Policy Reviews* preceding 2008's, the DR has continued liberalising its trade policy regime. Important measures include streamlining customs

---

[4] During the Uruguay Round of multilateral trade negotiations (1986–94), a tariff of 40 per cent was consolidated for these agricultural products. In 1998, the government established the quotas (approved by the WTO in February 1999), and the tariffs on imports in excess of the quotas. The government also stated the schedule under which these contingent tariffs will be reduced to between 40 and 99 per cent by 2005.

[5] During this period, the selective consumption tax for vehicles and alcoholic beverages was also increased, with marginal rates between 10 and 95 per cent. This increased the operative costs of sectors such as tourism, affecting the sector's comparative advantages, and consequently the demand for that service.

TABLE 1
Tariff Schedule Before and After 2001 Trade Reform

Type of Imports	Tariff (%)	
	Before	After
Final consumption	20–35	20
Agricultural goods (final consumption or agro industrial)	30–35	20
Inputs (which are not produced in the country)	5	3
Inputs (which are produced in the country)	10–20	8
Capital goods	10–20	8
Inputs for construction (luxurious)	15–25	20
Inputs for construction (not luxurious)	15–25	14
Pharmaceutical products and inputs required for their fabrication	3–5	3
Vehicles for transport	30	20
Other vehicles for commercial use	10–15	8
Memorandum		
Average tariff rate (simple)[a]		18.6

Note:
[a] Includes the selective tax on consumption applied to imports.

Source: Santos-Paulino (2006).

FIGURE 1
Exports, Imports and Trade Balance (1990–2007)

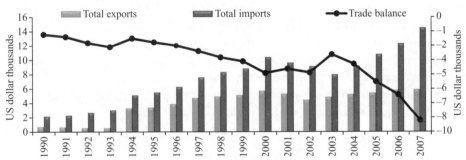

Source: IMF–DOT (2009).

procedures, further reducing tariffs, eliminating import surcharges and export taxes, and notable improvements in the legal framework by adopting a new legislation on government procurement, and new laws on competition policy and intellectual property rights. The improvement in the legislation signifies a major step to establishing a comprehensive system and the public sector transparency. Traditionally, government procurement in the DR has been conducted without reference to any uniform set of regulations, and has mainly been done by unrestricted administrative purchasing. The problems with this system are obvious. That is, wasteful use of fiscal funds, no uniform procurement proceedings or efficient supervisory procedures, and lack of transparency have been a source of corruption in the past.

This has resulted from sovereign efforts, as well as by binding commitments from the economic integration agenda, as will become clear later in the chapter.

The DR's involvement in the global economy has remained strong, as shown by the evolution of trade in goods and services, investment flows and family remittances, which have a significant share in the economy.

Notwithstanding ongoing trade liberalisation, the incentive framework continues to be characterised by significant bias in favour of selective productive sectors. In this regard, the WTO and government reports (WTO, 1996, 2002, 2008) recognise that most exporters of goods are exempt from the general trade and fiscal schemes in an attempt to counteract the anti-export bias of these regimes. This has also been noted in previous trade policy reviews, conveying that this restricted strategy, alongside persistent market inefficiencies mostly in infrastructure – notably in electricity supply – are significant obstacles for sustained improvements in living standards, and hence development.

In the manufacturing sector some firms supply the domestic market, while the favoured part of the sector consist of firms producing under the free trade zones (FTZ) regime, and this is apparent in Figure 2. FTZ production account for most of the DR's merchandise exports but its main industry, textiles and clothing, has been recently affected by the pressures of a more competitive global environment (see also Figure 3). In contrast to manufacturing, agriculture continues to be supported through measures like higher-than-average applied tariffs, direct payments, quotas, and marketing and price control programmes.

The assistance granted to certain agricultural activities merit revision, to facilitate its transparency and minimise its impact on consumers and taxpayers. A more optimal strategy could be to enhance competition in the domestic market and rationalising the fiscal incentive programmes to discourage agency problems and improve economic efficiency. Despite this incentive bias, manufactures represent

FIGURE 2
Dominican Republic's National and Free Trade Zone Exports

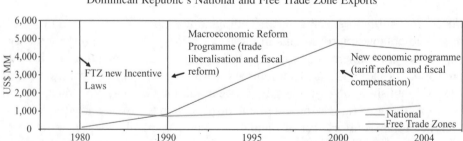

Source: Santos-Paulino (2006).

FIGURE 3

Free Trade Zone Manufactures Exports by Economic Activity

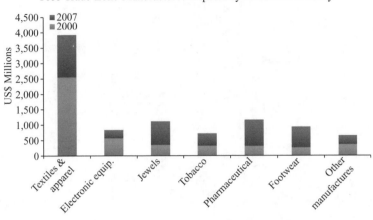

Source: Central Bank of the Dominican Republic, Statistical Reports (various issues).

above 30 per cent of gross domestic product (GDP), and over 50 per cent of total national exports, compared to the lower value added in agriculture (Tables 2 and 3). But it is the services industry that dominates the Dominican economy, mainly via tourism-related activities.

Recently, in addition to export promotion programmes, the DR has introduced new fiscal incentive schemes to promote the competitiveness of its domestic industry and to reduce the gap with the incentives given under the export promotion regimes. Other programmes have been also fostered to aid small and medium-sized enterprises, technological innovation and regional development, mainly consisting of tax incentives, financing on preferential terms, technical assistance and support for research and development. But the concerns about distortions and allocation of resources remain.

As noted, overall, trade liberalisation has resulted in the reduction of the average applied most-favoured-nation (MFN) tariff rates, as seen in Figures 4 and 5. Although the share of duty-free tariff lines decreased manifestly, tariffs' dispersion has increased implying that certain products could be benefiting from higher effective protection. The DR has bound its entire tariff schedule, mostly at 40 per cent; and the WTO Secretariat Report (1996, 2002, 2008) suggests that reducing the average gap of around 28 percentage points between bound and applied rates would further enhance the predictability of the DR's trade regime.

Trade policy measures continue to be used as short-term instruments for counteracting macroeconomic crises and business cycle fluctuations, and this affects the reliability of the regime. That was the case as the Dominican economy's 1990s boom ended abruptly, due to a major banking crisis in 2003 costing over 20 per

TABLE 2
Selected Macroeconomic Indicators (1990–2007, averages)

Indicators	Dominican Republic				Latin America and Caribbean			
	1990–99 Average	1990–99 Std. Dev.	2000–07 Average	2000–07 Std. Dev.	1990–99 Average	1990–99 Std. Dev.	2000–07 Average	2000–07 Std. Dev.
GDP per capita (2000 US$)	3,809	460.1	5,363	501.12	7,540	359.2	8,459	531.9
GDP growth (annual %)	4.6	4.1	5.5	4.3	3.0	2.1	3.6	2.6
Agriculture, value added (% of GDP)	12.8	0.9	11.6	0.5	7.7	1.1	6.4	0.5
Industry, value added (% of GDP)	32.5	1.1	29.9	3.3	31.7	2.8	32.0	2.1
Services, etc., value added (% of GDP)	54.9	0.3	58.5	2.7	60.7	3.8	61.8	2.3
Foreign direct investment, net inflows (% of GDP)	2.9	2.0	4.7	0.5	2.2	1.4	3.0	0.8
Gross fixed capital formation (% of GDP)	22.1	2.4	22.1	1.5	18.8	0.8	18.5	1.2
External debt stocks (% of GNI)	43.6	14.2	33.0	8.8	37.8	3.3	35.8	8.6
Total debt service (% of GNI)	3.4	0.8	4.5	1.0	5.3	1.7	7.3	1.6

Source: World Bank–WDI (2009).

TABLE 3
Domestic Trade Structure (By sectors)

Description	2002		2006	
	Exports	Imports	Exports	Imports
Total (US$ million)	971	6,001	1,982	9,401
		(% of total)		
Total primary products	56.0	37.9	47.3	44.2
Agriculture	43.9	15.3	27.3	13.1
Food	42.5	13.3	26.7	11.6
Agricultural raw materials	1.5	2.0	0.7	1.4
Mining	12.0	22.6	19.9	31.1
Ores and other minerals	0.9	0.3	1.6	0.3
Non-ferrous metals	0.5	0.6	0.3	0.8
Fuels	10.6	21.6	18.0	30.0
Manufactures	35.0	61.9	50.4	55.6
Iron and steel	18.6	2.6	40.3	3.9
Chemicals	5.3	9.7	3.3	9.6
Other semi-manufactures	2.7	10.0	3.0	8.7
Machinery and transport equipment	1.3	32.1	0.6	24.5
Textiles	0.1	1.2	0.1	1.0
Articles of apparel and clothing accessories	1.3	1.3	0.3	1.9
Other consumer goods	5.6	5.0	2.9	6.0
Other	8.8	0.1	2.2	0.2
Gold	0.1	0.0	0.0	0.0

Source: WTO Secretariat (1996, 2002, 2008) estimates based on data provided by the Government of the Dominican Republic.

FIGURE 4
Distributions of Average Applied Most-favoured-nation (MFN) Tariffs by
Main Trading Partner (2006)

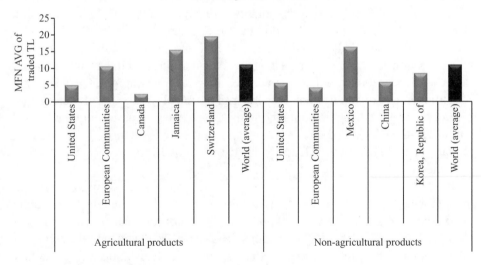

Source: WTO World Tariff Profiles (2008).

FIGURE 5

Tariff Lines and Duty Ranges for Agricultural and Non-agricultural Imports (2006)

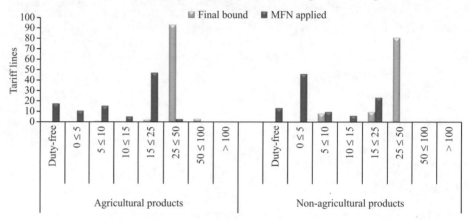

Source: Based on Figure 4.

cent of GDP along with adverse international conditions such as the slowdown in tourism after the 11 September attacks on the USA, the reduced growth rate of the US economy, and higher petroleum import prices. The latter, exacerbated by the considerable degree of informal dollarisation of the Dominican economy, generated exchange rate instability, high inflation, and weakened the effectiveness of macroeconomic (stabilisation) policies during 2003. Critically, as a result of the economic crisis the DR signed a standby agreement with the International Monetary Fund (IMF). It also introduced temporary trade protective measures – which were eliminated afterwards, notably surcharges on import duties of 10 and 13 per cent, and a transitional import tax rate of 2 per cent.

Importantly, the DR has modernised its legal and institutional framework for the elaboration and application of technical regulations, similar to international standards. Since 2002, the DR has adopted new laws to improve the protection and enforcement of intellectual property rights, mostly reflecting the entry into force of the free trade agreement among the DR, Central America and the United States (DR–CAFTA). And, in some cases, the domestic regulations go beyond the standards established by the Trade Related Intellectual Property Rights (TRIPS) Agreement.

The DR does not subscribe to the WTO's Agreement on Government Procurement. But in 2006 new legislation was adopted to regulate most public procurement of goods, services, works and State concessions (in line with the DR–CAFTA requirements). But revisions need to be completed, and the country's capacity should be strengthened, in areas such as the legislation ruling sanitary and phytosanitary measures, as well as other technical barriers to trade. This would benefit producers and consumers. New legislations have also been approved in the areas of air and maritime transports, which further enhance the country's ability to internationally trade goods and services.

At the national level, following over a decade of debate in Congress, a General Law on Competition was adopted in 2007 and it is expected to enter into force in 2009. This represents an important development in promoting the efficiency of the Dominican economy.[6] Finally, lack of basic infrastructure and the provision of key services remain a critical issue affecting the DR. The telecommunications sector is one of the most dynamic in the Dominican economy and receives large flows of foreign investment. But the electricity sector is still in a profound crisis, and this lingers as one of the country's main economic challenges.[7]

The financial sector has recovered from the 2003–04 crisis, and prudential indicators have improved markedly, largely because of measures to strengthen the supervisory framework. However, according to financial market indicators, the sector suffers from high operation costs and limited competition – and it is expected that this would be improved under DR–CAFTA.

The contribution of tourism to the Dominican economy is crucial, and the sector has recovered from its depression in the early 2000s. There are no restrictions to foreign investment in this sector, and investors in certain tourism projects are granted incentives, including import and income tax exemptions; such incentives are conditioned on employing Dominican professionals.

a. International Trade and Economic Integration

Over and above trade openness, mostly through tariff and tax reductions and eliminations of quantitative barriers, one of the most noticeable features of the DR's trade policy in recent years has been its embracing of international trade relationships, both bilaterally and multilaterally. Until recently, Dominican exports benefited from an extensive preferential access to US market under the Generalised System of Preferences, which encompassed 26 different schemes under which developed countries granted market access to developing countries; and the Multi-Fibre Agreements, both dating back to 1974. It has also been a beneficiary of the Caribbean Basin Initiative since 1983, providing preferential access to the USA. The DR was also a signatory of the 'Lomé Convention' between the European

---

[6] For instance, the DR applies price controls on electricity and certain agricultural products; the price of hydrocarbons is set on the basis of a formula and varies according to fluctuations on the international market.

[7] The consumption of selected types of energy is highly subsidised, undermining public finances and rational energy use. Some incentives granted under a 2007 law aimed at increasing domestic energy production from alternative sources are contingent on the use of domestic inputs. The law also prohibits biofuel imports when domestic production meets demand.

Union, and the African, Caribbean and Pacific countries (ACP), and later the Cotonou agreement.

These preferential agreements have faced out and evolved into free trade and economic integration treaties. But most of the market access facilities under the preferential trade schemes have been extended, to minimise the transaction costs of the elimination of such preferences. The rights of preferential access to developed markets – notably the USA – have been a key factor in attracting foreign investment, particularly in the export processing zones, which benefit from a competitive package of fiscal incentives, and access to industrial space and infrastructure, as discussed earlier.

Treaties pursued by the DR proliferate from bilateral to regional schemes, and from partial to full trade and economic integration (see Table 4), and the country has further liberalised its trade regime selectively through preferential agreements. In addition to agreements in force, the DR completed negotiations on the Partial Scope Agreement with Panama, the DR–CAFTA and the Economic Partnership Agreement (EPA) between the European Union and Caribbean States Forum (CARIFORUM).[8] The DR grants at least MFN treatment to all its trading allies, compliant with the WTO rules.

The DR also participates in the Doha Development Round negotiations, where it has submitted numerous proposals, either individually or in conjunction with other Members, particularly in Agriculture and Services (tourism, financial services and basic telecommunications) and on export subsidies. Conscious of its innate vulnerabilities, the country also subscribes to the issue of 'small economies' and supports a variety of proposals on the definition and measures that could be taken to implement special and differential treatment for those economies in the various negotiating areas of the Doha Development Round. The DR has made specific commitments to the General Agreement on Trade in Services (GATS), i.e. a fraction of the sectors covered by the GATS Agreement, and signed the GATS Agreement, Protocols on financial services and telecommunications.[9]

b. Free Trade and Economic Integration Arrangements

As already noted, the DR participates in various bilateral and regional trade agreements as part of its international integration strategy. The free trade agreements establish cross-border free trade for most products, but excluding those in

---

[8] The DR bas embarked upon negotiations to establish free trade agreements with Canada (2007) and with Chinese Taipei (2006); and is exploring the possibility of negotiating preferential agreements with Mexico, Mercosur and Cuba.

[9] Despite the significant modernisation of the regulatory framework, there is a sizeable difference between the DR's multilateral commitments and its applied regime. And it is expected that the country would continue enhancing its service regime by expanding its multilateral obligations. This would also be affected by the commitments bound under the DR–CAFTA.

TABLE 4
Trade Agreements Subscribed by the Dominican Republic (DR)

Agreements	Countries	Date of Signature	Entry into Force
Free Trade Agreements and Economic Integration Agreement			
CARICOM–DR		22 August 1998	
Central America Common Market	Costa Rica, El Salvador, Guatemala, Honduras, Nicaragua, Dominican Republic	16 April 1998	01 March 2001 (05 February 2002 for the DR)
DR–Central America– United States Free Trade Agreement (CAFTA–DR)[a]	Costa Rica, Dominican Republic, El Salvador, Guatemala, Honduras, Nicaragua and the United States	05 August 2004	01 March 2006 (1 March 2007 for the DR)
European Community CARIFORUM States EPA[a]	Antigua and Barbuda, Austria, Belgium, Bulgaria, Cyprus, Czech Republic, Denmark, Estonia, Finland, France, Germany, Greece, Hungary, Ireland, Italy, Latvia, Lithuania, Luxembourg, Malta, Netherlands, Poland, Portugal, Romania, Slovak Republic, Slovenia, Spain, Sweden, United Kingdom, Bahamas, Barbados, Belize, Dominica, Dominican Republic, Grenada, Guyana, Jamaica, Saint Kitts and Nevis, Saint Lucia, Saint Vincent and the Grenadines, Suriname, Trinidad and Tobago	15 October 2008	01 November 2008
Partial Preferential Agreements			
Panama		17 July 1985	July 1985
Bilateral Investment Agreements			
Argentina		16 March 2001	
Chile		28 November 2000	
China (Taiwan)		05 November 1998	27 November 2001
Ecuador		26 June 1998	
France		14 January 1999	30 October 2002
Panama		06 February 2003	November 2003
Spain		16 March 1995	07 October 1996

Notes:
[a] Agreement has been notified to the WTO.
CARICOM, Carribbean Community.

Source: Author's elaboration.

the sensitive list agreed with the WTO. Despite the variety of agreements, the DR–CAFTA and the EPA with the European Community and the CARIFORUM states are the most relevant, representing significant challenges to the country's economic structure and trading patterns. What follows overviews each of these agreements' key features.

c. DR–CAFTA

The DR–CAFTA is particularly important inasmuch as the majority of the DR's overall trade in goods is carried out with the parties to this agreement, mostly the USA.[10] The DR–CAFTA, which has been notified to the WTO, created an FTZ by eliminating most tariffs and other trade barriers in the margin between the United States (the DR's main trade partner) and Central America. This agreement has driven the DR's trade policy strategies since the negotiation started.[11]

The treaty contains 22 chapters and their respective annexes. These chapters itemise the elements of the agreement: that is, national treatment and market access for goods (with special provisions on agricultural products, textiles and clothing);[12] rules of origin and related procedures; customs administration; sanitary and phyosanitary measures; technical barriers to trade; trade protection; government procurement; investment; cross-border trade in services; financial services; telecommunications; electronic commerce; intellectual property; transparency; labour and environmental issues; and other administration and final provisions issues.

The DR–CAFTA is applicable multilaterally, which implies that most of the mutual obligations are identical for all parties. There are certain obligations, however, such as tariff quotas, which are applied bilaterally between the United States and each of the partner countries (World Bank, 2005). The most significant component of the agreement is tariff elimination and the perpetuation of preferences under the US–Caribbean Basin Trade Partnership. The agreement would also immediately remove tariffs from 80 per cent of US consumer and industrial goods and more than half of US agricultural products exported to the FTA countries. Sensitive products – mostly agricultural – that are protected by subsidies and

---

[10] The DR–CAFTA entered into force for the United States and El Salvador on 1 March 2006, for Honduras and Nicaragua on 1 April 2006, for Guatemala on 1 July 2006 and for the DR on 1 March 2007. The agreement had not entered into force in Costa Rica.

[11] However, the impacts on welfare (i.e. poverty, employment, productivity, etc.) are still to be assessed. But is evident that certain groups might require assistance to adapt to the more competitive environment.

[12] The market access conditions established in the agreement between the DR and Central America were incorporated as a special regime in an annex to the DR–CAFTA. Furthermore, importers can choose between two preferential regimes granted by the USA, provided that the corresponding rule of origin is fulfilled, either the multilateral tariff reduction programme, or the programme contained in the FTA between the DR and Central America. Also, certain provisions on financial services and government procurement apply only between the DR and its Central American counterparts.

import quotas – tariffs would be phased out over a 15- to 20-year implementation period.

The DR–CAFTA also entails the removal of barriers to investments, including on several sectors governed by Central American countries and the DR, notably energy, transport and telecommunications. The agreement also guarantees the protection of patents, trademarks and other forms of intellectual property. Importantly, the enforcement of labour regulation in the developing country parties of the agreement is *a tour de force*, particularly in industries directly linked to FDI-related activities. But, the conditionalities, mostly not related to trade, were attached to the agreement to facilitate its approval by the US Congress. Labour and environmental standards are the most notorious examples.

The agreement has served as a discipline device and has determined significant reforms of the DR's legal and institutional systems. It has also contributed to solidifying ongoing economic reforms and prompting further reform efforts. Therefore, it is expected that investors should respond positively to the modernisation of key regulations in such areas as trade in services, government procurement and intellectual property rights – mostly provisions for greater transparency in government regulations.

Preliminary studies suggest that the gains from trade, as has been found with other free trade agreements, will depend on the ability of the Central American economies to adjust successfully to the changes that the agreement will bring (including changes in relative prices) and to manage effectively the ensuing restructuring of the economy (e.g. World Bank, 2005). The welfare gains might be further conditioned by losses in sensitive sectors such as agriculture and other commodities and goods highly protected by the largest trading partner.

d. Economic Partnership Agreement with the EU and Caribbean and ACP Countries

As a member of the CARIFORUM, the DR is part of the EPA between the European Union and the group of ACP. The EPA replaces the former Cotonou Agreement between these parties. The agreement evolves from non-reciprocal relationships, reflecting WTO rules regarding tariff exemptions and preferences granted under the previous regime, which expired in December 2007. This is the most significant challenge for the developing partners, particularly the least developed ones.

That is, the EPA will progressively establish an FTZ based on reciprocity among the members. In addition to eliminating cross-border tariffs, the agreement introduces disciplines in several areas, including safeguards and trade disputes; technical barriers to trade; services; investment; intellectual property; government procurement; and stipulations on technical and financial assistance.

The EPA raise challenges to ACP countries. These mostly relate to the potential competition resulting from the preferential access to EU products under reciprocal terms, which would affect developing countries' producers in numerous sectors. The second challenge is the ensuing loss of tariff revenues due to the reduction of tariffs for EU products. And, the scope and time of liberalisation has, and how intra-integration will be linked to ACP–EU liberalisation.

However, reciprocity is not the only objective of the EU–ACP EPA, and the parties have been vigilant in securing other elements, including support for 'deep integration', which entails establishing or expanding the institutional environment in order to facilitate trade and location of production regardless of national borders. Development assistance is also a key element, therefore, encompassing development objectives in the agreement. Overall, it is expected that EPA will have very different outcomes, depending on countries and their specific initial conditions, economic structures and regional context.

4. POLICY CHALLENGES AND CONCLUDING REMARKS

Globalisation has brought about benefits for the Dominican economy, but these benefits entail unavoidable challenges. The DR has made significant progress towards a more open trade regime, particularly through the elimination of non-tariff barriers, by simplifying its tariff structure and by reducing the rates of duties. The DR's membership in the WTO has been influential over trade reforms. In this sense, the structure of the trade policy required important unilateral adjustments in response to the multilateral agenda, particularly with reference to the instruments that affect the productive sectors and the export strategies of the country. The 2008 *Trade Policy Review* clearly pictures that trade and payments liberalisation has been a continuous process, but economic efficiency ought to be improved.

The subscription to a variety of free trade and EPA has driven the DR's recent trade policy efforts. For instance, the DR–CAFTA contributed to furthering necessary institutional reforms, complementing the enforcement of multilateral rules. The improvements in the legal frameworks are important for institutional capabilities and the country's competitiveness. However, the integration strategy has been very much focused on perpetuating the preceding preferential regimes and market access schemes, leaving too little to nurturing the country's comparative advantages, and / or promoting trade diversification.

This is particularly relevant to reduce the country's exposure and vulnerability to a limited number of income sources. This affects not only the DR, but also other middle-income countries, which need to diversify their productive and trade structures, and evolve from labour intensive–low skill production (e.g. the FTZ model) to higher value added, and more skill–technology-intensive activities.

Eliminating the sources of distortions created by incentives to specific industries is a major challenge for the DR. It is well known that Agriculture is supported by measures like higher-than-average applied tariffs, direct payments, and marketing and price control programmes, creating distortions that impact mostly the consumers. The duality in the manufacturing sector merits also revision. But what is more critical is overcoming basic infrastructural constraints, such as high cost and poor quality of energy supply and some services, which affect the producers' cost structures and detriment the country's comparative advantages.

REFERENCES

Greenaway, D. (1993), 'Liberalising Foreign Trade through Rose-tinted Glasses', *Economic Journal*, **103**, 208–22.
Greenaway, D., C. W. Morgan and P. Wright (1998), 'Trade Liberalisation Adjustment and Growth: What Does the Evidence Tell Us?', *Economic Journal*, **108**, 1547–61.
International Monetary Fund (2009), *Direction of Trade Statistics* (Washington, DC: IMF).
Santos-Paulino, A. U. (2005), 'Trade Liberalisation and Economic Performance: Theory and Evidence', *The World Economy*, **28**, 783–821.
Santos-Paulino, A. U. (2006), 'Trade Liberalisation and Trade Performance in the Dominican Republic', *Journal of International Development*, **18**, 925–44.
Santos-Paulino, A. U. and A. P. Thirlwall (2004), 'Trade Liberalisation and Economic Performance in Developing Countries – Introduction', *Economic Journal*, **114**, F1–3.
Winters, L. A. (2004), 'Trade Liberalisation and Economic Performance: An Overview', *Economic Journal*, **114**, F4–21.
World Bank (2005), *DR–CAFTA: Challenges and Opportunities for Central America* (Washington, DC: World Bank).
World Bank (2009), *World Development Indicators* (Washington, DC: World Bank).
World Trade Organization (1996, 2002, 2008), *Dominican Republic Trade Policy Review*, Secretariat Reports (Geneva: World Trade Organization).
World Trade Organization (1996, 2002, 2008), *Dominican Republic Trade Policy Reviews*, Government Reports (Geneva: World Trade Organization).
World Trade Organization (2008), *World Tariff Profiles*. Available at www.wto.org (Geneva: World Trade Organization).

4

Modelling the Extensive Margin of World Trade: New Evidence on GATT and WTO Membership

Gabriel Felbermayr and Wilhelm Kohler

1. INTRODUCTION

THE World Trade Organization (WTO) is commonly regarded as epitomising a transparent and predictable world trading environment that features open markets. Although its practical importance is sometimes questioned, most people would agree that, overall, it plays an important role for securing gains from trade liberalisation and avoiding harmful protection.[1] The cornerstones of this environment are: (i) most-favoured nation treatment, (ii) national treatment of foreign goods, services and intellectual property rights, (iii) multilateral negotiations on reciprocal reductions of trade barriers, (iv) fair competition rules related to dumping and subsidies, including a mechanism of dispute settlement and (v) preferential treatment of developing countries.[2] Formal WTO membership implies that countries adhere to these principles, which is also seen as a key vehicle to enhance the growth and development perspectives of less developed countries.

Established in 1994 and put into effect in 1995, the WTO grew out of the General Agreement on Tariffs and Trade (GATT), which had served as an institutional

---

The authors gratefully acknowledge comments and helpful criticism from anonymous referees. They thank Davide Sala and Philipp Schröder for discussion and constructive suggestions, as well as Inga Heiland for very able research assistance.

[1] See Bagwell and Staiger (2003) for an in-depth analysis of the efficiency-enhancing potential of a WTO-like world trading system.

[2] See the WTO's self-characterisation on http://www.wto.org/, as well as Chapter 3 in Bagwell and Staiger (2003).

backbone of multilateral trade liberalisation ever since the end of the Second World War. In 1947, there were 23 founding signatories of the GATT. Presently, as many as 153 countries are members of the WTO. The GATT/WTO was remarkably successful in reducing the level of trade barriers through eight successive rounds of multilateral negotiations. On average, the import tariffs applied by GATT/WTO members have fallen to levels that are a mere quarter of what they were after the Second World War.[3] Thus, there has been a widening, as well as deepening, of trade liberalisation throughout the six decades that the GATT/WTO has been in existence. This was paralleled by a remarkable increase in world trade, relative to world production. Between 1950 and 2005, the average annual growth rate of the volume of world exports was 6.2 per cent (7.5 per cent for manufactures), compared with a real gross domestic product (GDP) growth of 3.8 per cent.[4] The GATT and the WTO almost routinely receives credit as a *causal* factor for this.

Somewhat surprisingly, however, when Rose (2004a) set out to quantify the trade-enhancing role of WTO membership in an econometric study of world trade based on the gravity equation, he ended up concluding that 'we currently do not have strong empirical evidence that the GATT/WTO has systematically played a strong role in encouraging trade'. In a companion paper, Rose (2004b) has studied the trade policies pursued, concluding that WTO member countries also do not follow more liberal trade policies than non-members. These papers have drawn a lot of attention, questioning the conventional view of the GATT/WTO as an important trade-promoting institution.

However, subsequent literature has readdressed the issue, adding pieces of revisionist evidence more in line with received wisdom. Thus, Subramanian and Wei (2007) have shown that WTO membership appears to be a more effective vehicle of trade creation for industrial countries than for developing countries. Tomz et al. (2007) have argued that WTO membership does come out as a strong

---

[3] The negotiations are about tariff *ceilings* (or *bindings*). *Applied* tariffs are typically below the ceilings. The WTO estimates that prior to the first round of negotiations (Geneva 1947), the average applied tariff rate across all member countries was between 20 and 30 per cent. The Geneva Round has brought a weighted US tariff reduction by 26 per cent, with a cumulative further cut by 15 per cent through the next four rounds of negotiation (Annecy 1949, Torquay 1951, Geneva 1956, Dillon 1962). Next came three more ambitious rounds of negotiations (Kennedy 1967, Tokyo 1979 and Uruguay 1994), each with average applied tariff cuts by well above 30 per cent for industrial countries, affecting an ever larger amount of world trade. Thus, for the US, Canada and the major European countries, the *import-weighted average applied tariff rate* came down from 15 per cent in 1952 to 4.1 per cent in 2005. For the entire world, the World Bank estimates a reduction of the *unweighted average of import tariffs* tariff from 26.3 per cent in 1986 to 8.8 in 2007; see the Data and Research Website of the World Bank. More recent negotiations have also included reductions in quantitative restrictions and other non-tariff barriers, as well as export subsidies. Arguably, the most important step came with the Uruguay Round, which has added two new agreements: the General Agreement on Trade in Services (GATS) and the agreement on Trade-Related Intellectual Property Rights (TRIPs). Perhaps most importantly, it has led to the establishment of the WTO. For more details, see the *WTO World Trade Report 2007*.
[4] See again the *WTO World Trade Report 2007*.

driving force of trade, if defined to include non-formal (or *de facto*) compliance with GATT/WTO rules, in addition to formal membership status. However, doubts remain. Rose (2007) points out certain puzzles that cast doubt on the trade-promoting role of non-formal membership. Eicher and Henn (2008) question the findings of Subramanian and Wei (2007) on the grounds of a more comprehensive treatment of preferential trade agreements alongside WTO membership, as well as on econometric grounds.[5]

By restricting his sample to country pairs where trade is strictly positive, Rose (2004a) has ignored the possibility that WTO membership may be important for whether or not two countries trade with each other at all. This is the so-called *extensive* margin of world trade, as opposed to the *intensive* margin relating to how existing trading relationships evolve through larger or smaller quantities traded. Felbermayr and Kohler (2006) present detailed evidence on the relative importance of these two margins, concluding that the post-war increase of world trade took place through both, larger quantities traded (the intensive margin) and an increase in the number of country pairs that engage in trade (extensive margin). The question then is whether WTO membership comes out as a stronger trade-promoting force, if movements at the extensive margin of trade are adequately taken into account. Evidence pointing in this direction is presented in Felbermayr and Kohler (2006), Helpman et al. (2008) and in Liu (2009).

This chapter contributes to the literature in several ways. First, we review open theoretical and methodological issues related to the gravity model, which researchers have invariably used to explore the trade-promoting power of WTO membership. Second, we present a new strategy for estimating the gravity model that is fully grounded in theory and accounts for the extensive margin of trade, yet is intuitive and easy to implement. We identify WTO membership effects on both the intensive and extensive margins of trade. We show that such effects arise in a direct way, but also indirectly through the so-called multilateral trade resistance terms of the gravity equation.

Based on our 'corner-solutions' version of the gravity model, we then reexamine the empirical evidence on WTO membership and trade, with special attention to disentangling the extensive and intensive margins, respectively, of world trade. We estimate our model using a Poisson approach, to deal with the inherent non-linearity of any gravity model of bilateral trade that involves zero trade relationships, as with the extensive margin of trade. Our empirical strategy duly addresses the concerns raised in Subramanian and Wei (2007) about appropriate country pooling, as well as the issue of informal participation in the GATT/WTO raised by Tomz et al. (2007). However, our dataset includes more recent observations up to 2008, and we slice our sample in line with the formative subperiods of GATT history, covering successive rounds of trade liberalisation.

---

[5] See also Rose (2010) for a comprehensive reply to the literature subsequent to Rose (2004a).

We find that GATT membership was successful on the extensive margin of world trade but not on the intensive margin. For the recent WTO episode (1995–2008), we find consistent and robust evidence for a substantial tradecreating role of membership. This is an important result which is new to the literature. It strongly suggests that forming the WTO, with the new agreements on services and intellectual property rights added to the GATT, and with a more effective dispute settlement mechanism, has ushered in a new era, where being a formal member of the multilateral trading system is a more powerful driving force of trade than in earlier episodes of the GATT. Interestingly, and in stark contrast to Subramanian and Wei (2007), this holds true also, indeed more strongly, for developing countries than for industrial countries. Moreover, it holds for formal membership and does not rely on informal compliance, as suggested in Tomz et al. (2007). Also, it is driven primarily by the intensive margin, and not the extensive margin. On average, WTO membership results in higher bilateral trade of about 40 per cent.

The structure of the chapter is as follows. In Section 2, we discuss the present state of the literature, focusing on open methodological questions. In Section 3, we develop our 'corner-solutions' version of the gravity model that highlights zero bilateral trade between certain country pairs as an equilibrium outcome, determined among other things by GATT/WTO membership. In Section 4, we discuss our database for econometric estimation, including some preliminary descriptive exploration that guides our estimation strategy. Section 5 takes a Probit look at the extensive margin of trade, whereas Section 6 presents results from a comprehensive estimation of the non-linear gravity model. Section 7 will summarise and draw conclusions from our findings.

2. STATE OF THE LITERATURE: OPEN ISSUES

Given the aforementioned consensus view of the GATT/WTO, it is not surprising that Rose's (2004a) finding has caught a great deal of attention. It seems to cast doubt on the GATT/WTO as a 'success story' that exemplifies the virtues of multilateral trade liberalisation. But perhaps one should not be too surprised. It is well known that the GATT/WTO was only partly successful in delivering trade policies towards freer trade. There were sectoral exemptions, most notably in agriculture and textiles, and there were country exemptions as well. For instance, up until 1995 developing countries were facing little demand for liberalisation when they became members. Moreover, member countries have partly undone negotiated tariff cuts by introducing non-tariff barriers. They have also made extensive use – sometimes abusively – of antidumping and safeguard provisions, as well as the WTO's dispute settlement mechanism, with disruptive effects on trade.

In a companion paper, Rose (2004b) has substantiated this concern by examining whether GATT/WTO member countries have systematically followed more liberal trade policies than non-members. His conclusion is that 'there is little evidence that membership in the GATT/WTO has actually liberalised trade policy'. Hence, the lack of a significant and robust *trade effect* demonstrated by Rose (2004a) may simply reflect the lack of a liberalising *trade policy effect* of the WTO. But this explanation is not entirely convincing, as it is obvious from the previous characterisation that WTO membership involves more than what is observable in terms of its members' trade policies. At any rate, such an explanation would still leave us with a troubling verdict on the GATT/WTO, whose primary mandate is to foster more liberal trade policies.

Several contributions have questioned that such a verdict is justified. Subramanian and Wei (2007) argue that there is a systematic pattern of asymmetry in this nexus of WTO membership and trade policies. They conduct a Rose-type empirical analysis, but allow for WTO membership to play a different role for developing and industrial countries. They find a strong positive trade volume effect for the latter, 175 per cent in their preferred specification, but not for the former. This reflects a policy asymmetry in that developing countries did not utilise their WTO membership towards trade liberalisation, whereas developed countries typically did. Indeed, this type of asymmetry has for a long time been enshrined in the GATT itself, through the so-called special and differential treatment (SDT). Thus, Subramanian and Wei (2007) find larger membership effects also for developing countries subsequent to 1995 when the SDT was reduced. They also disaggregate along sectoral lines, to find positive membership effects for trade in liberalised manufacturing (for all countries) and for trade in non-liberalised manufacturing (for developed countries). Unsurprisingly, no positive effect was found for textiles, footwear and food. What are we to conclude from this exercise of disaggregation? Although the results are certainly revealing, in our view they can hardly be interpreted as unequivocal support of a trade-increasing effect of WTO membership. Rather, they provide a gravity-based documentation of the partial failure/success of the GATT/WTO. Allowing *all* data to speak up in a unified way, Rose's (2004a) finding that there is no robust positive WTO membership effect on trade remains upheld, even after Subramanian and Wei (2007); see also Rose (2010).[6]

But a negative verdict on the GATT/WTO is still unjustified according to a further criticism raised by Tomz et al. (2007). Rose's results might partly be due to the fact that WTO-type most favoured nation (MFN) treatment was sometimes also granted to non-members. In a similar vein, the attempt to secure WTO acces-

---

[6] Some studies have taken the concern about excessive country pooling to the extreme by looking at individual countries. Thus, Lissovolik and Lissovolik (2006) have found Russian trade with WTO members to be less than that would be expected given its 'gravity position'. The explanation offered by the authors can be interpreted as evidence in the spirit of Subramanian and Wei (2007). Evenett and Gage (2005) have found mixed effects for WTO accession of Angola, Bulgaria, Ecuador and Jordan.

sion might have triggered more liberal trade policies ahead of formal membership. In Rose's empirical strategy, either of these two cases militates against a significant trade effect of WTO membership, provided that MFN treatment and pre-accession liberalisation did in fact lead to more trade. Tomz et al. (2007) therefore suggest to look at *de facto* participation, in addition to *formal* membership. They point out that the WTO explicitly provides for such participation by member countries' colonies, as well through provisional membership status during a country's accession negotiation. Redoing Rose's analysis with extended WTO coding of the data (including non-membership participation), they find positive trade effects that are significant, both statistically and economically. For instance, the difference between bilateral trade volumes of non-member participants of the WTO and non-participants is 140 per cent. These 'revisionist' results make the GATT/WTO appear in a more favourable light than was the case in Rose (2004a), as well as Subramanian and Wei (2007). However, Rose (2007) points out that closer inspection reveals certain puzzles that continue to cast doubt on a trade-promoting effect of WTO membership. For instance, it seems difficult to imagine why non-membership participation in the WTO should have a larger effect than membership. Moreover, the bilateral trade effects found by Tomz et al. (2007) do not appear to show up in aggregate trade.

From a methodological perspective, the point raised by Tomz et al. (2007) is that Rose's (2004a) analysis involves a measurement error in WTO membership, leading to a downward bias in coefficient estimates, whereas Subramanian and Wei (2007) point to country heterogeneity among WTO members, measuring heterogeneity through the state of development. But there is additional *unobserved* country heterogeneity, also among non-members, which may give rise to biased coefficient estimates. Baier and Bergstrand (2007) have thoroughly addressed this issue with respect to preferential trading agreements (PTAs). In the present context, their argument is that there may be *unobserved* country characteristics that influence trade, and which are at the same time systematically correlated with WTO membership. Conventional estimation of the WTO membership effect would then suffer from an omitted variables bias. Baier and Bergstrand (2007) suggest using dyadic fixed effects in a panel dataset to avoid a bias from such endogeneity. In addition to controlling for endogeneity, this would also control for the time-invariant component of unobserved multilateral trade resistance.[7] Their empirical study demonstrates that in much of the earlier literature endogeneity has indeed caused a downward bias in the estimated coefficients for the trade effects of PTAs. In principle, the same could hold true also for the estimated WTO membership

---

[7] The notion of multilateral trade resistance was introduced into the gravity approach by Anderson and van Wincoop (2003). Their estimation involves non-linear constraints. Importer and exporter country fixed effects are an easier way to control for multilateral resistance. Subramanian and Wei (2007) do this as well.

effects, although they do not address this in their paper. It is interesting to note that Rose (2004a) did run estimations with country fixed effects, which have consistently generated larger membership effects than those without. However, he still regards these coefficients as small, relative to other effects; see Rose (2010).[8]

Generally, however, true *endogeneity* seems a less severe problem with WTO membership as such than with PTAs. An upward bias would arise, for instance, if there is some unobserved dyad-specific variable which is positively correlated with both WTO membership and bilateral trade. Baier and Bergstrand (2007) list several examples in this vein for PTAs. Basically, the endogeneity concern arises if certain country pairs are more natural trading partners than others, and are therefore more likely to reach a regional trading arrangement (in addition to trading more), for reasons other than those observed 'on the right-hand side'. But this type of concern seems far less convincing for the WTO which is a multilateral, not a regional, trading arrangement. The reason is that jointly entering a *multilateral* agreement like the GATT/WTO is a very unlikely response to being natural *bilateral* trading partners. In a similar vein, the notion that certain countries are more natural trading partners than others for the 'whole world' (instead of bilaterally) seems far-fetched. However, even if endogeneity of WTO membership is absent, heterogeneity along the lines of 'natural trading partners' or PTAs might still involve *de facto* correlations, such that ignoring PTAs as an explanatory variable for bilateral trade will lead to an omitted variables bias. *A priori*, an upward bias seems more likely than a downward bias. The initial studies by Rose (2004a, 2005) did include PTA regressors, but still failed to deliver a robust WTO membership effect on trade.

From a broader perspective, the WTO status is but one element of the trading arrangement that governs bilateral trade. Adding PTAs and the generalised system of preferences (GSP), one obtains a rich pattern of possible arrangements. Some authors have argued in favour of a *mutually exclusive* coding of trading arrangements. This means classifying trading arrangements in such a way that any country pair belongs to one and only one arrangement. Bilateral trading arrangements relying only on GATT/WTO membership would then be identified in isolation, and the corresponding coefficient could be interpreted as a 'pure' WTO effect. Alternatively, PTA and WTO membership could be coded *independently*, as in the original studies by Rose (2004a, 2005). If cumulative arrangement effects (e.g. from WTO membership plus PTAs) are *additive*, then independent and mutually exclusive coding should deliver the same effects. However, additivity might be questioned. For instance, one may argue that membership effects are *hierarchical*.

---

[8] Rose (2010) also emphasises the difference in interpretation between fixed effects (within) estimation of WTO coefficients and estimates that also use cross-section evidence. 'Within' estimation asks whether accession increases trade for a given country pair, whereas cross-section estimation compares across different country pairs.

Thus, Subramanian and Wei (2007) argue that a PTA dominates all WTO effects, meaning that WTO membership does not further increase bilateral trade if two countries already belong to a PTA. Identification of the true WTO effect then requires hierarchical coding, whereby WTO membership is coded only for country pairs that do not also belong to the same PTA (and similarly for importer GSP status). If the trading arrangements in fact work in a hierarchic manner, then independent coding would lead to an underestimation of the pure WTO effect. A truly general estimation of arrangement effects requires mutually exclusive coding. Having estimates based on such data at hand, one can then use an additivity (or some other) assumption to calculate composite effects.

Eicher and Henn (2008) do this for the hierarchy assumption employed by Subramanian and Wei (2007), similarly distinguishing between industrial and developing country PTA effects. They corroborate the finding that the WTO works for industrial countries, but not for developing countries. Their composition exercise adds a further insight. Industrial countries find almost no additional PTA effect, whereas developing countries see an average PTA effect equal to 214 per cent, which is even more than the WTO effect for developing countries. Eicher and Henn (2008) also distinguish between different types of PTAs, and they add bilateral fixed effects. This gives full control over all unobserved country pair heterogeneity, in addition to controlling for the time-invariant component of multilateral resistance. Estimation of WTO and PTA effects is then based entirely on within variation (time dimension). Their main message is that almost all significant WTO affects found by Subramanian and Wei (2007) and Tomz et al. (2007) vanish, once other trading arrangements are controlled for. This is a severe blow to the 'revisionist' conclusions suggested by recent literature. Importantly for our purpose, however, Eicher and Henn (2008) restrict their data to positive trade pairs. The extensive margin of trade thus remains unexplored in their analysis.[9]

This leads us to what thus seems to be the ultimate line of defence for the WTO; that is, the extensive country margin of world trade. Rose (2004a) and most of the subsequent literature estimate the gravity equation on data that exclude country pairs where bilateral trade is zero. Intuitively, however, WTO membership may play a role, not only for how much two countries trade with each other, but also for whether they trade with each other at all. Technically speaking, estimating a gravity equation on non-zero observations alone suffers from an omitted variables bias, as pointed out in Felbermayr and Kohler (2006). Unfortunately, the standard theoretical underpinning of the gravity equation used in this type of literature does not allow for zero trade. Felbermayr and Kohler (2006) suggest an *ad hoc*

---

[9] It is worth pointing out here that 'revisionist' conclusions have also been drawn based on nonparametric methods. Thus, Chang and Lee (2007) use non-parametric matching techniques to check for a trade effect of 'WTO treatment', coming up with large positive effects of WTO membership on trade. Ambiguity still seems to prevail.

modification of the gravity model where zero trade emerges as a 'corner-solution' in the sense of Wooldridge (2002). Estimating this model using Tobit techniques they have generally found the omitted variables bias to be empirically important.[10] They also find that including the extensive margin does make a difference for the estimated trade effect of WTO membership, generating more evidence for a positive trade effect from membership. Helpman et al. (2008) use a framework with heterogeneous firms which also involves an extensive country margin of trade, and they run a Heckmantype procedure for empirical estimation. Although they look at the WTO issue only in a peripheral way, they do find a significant effect of joint WTO membership in their Heckman selection equation. According to their estimate, the likelihood of positive trade increases by 15 percentage points if two countries belong to the WTO. Liu (2009) runs panel regressions, also including zero trade country pairs in his sample when looking at WTO membership effects. He finds strong WTO effects at the extensive margin of world trade.

This chapter is thus not the first to explore WTO membership effects at the extensive margin of world trade. However, discussing the research that has followed his seminal contribution, Rose (2010, p. 212) concludes: 'I'm now persuaded that membership in the GATT/WTO encourages the creation of trading links where none might otherwise exist. How important this is to world trade and welfare is currently unclear to me; I look forward to more work in the area'.

3. A SIMPLE MODEL OF THE EXTENSIVE MARGIN

Empirical analysis of WTO membership requires a theoretical model that allows us to control for all other determinants of trade. The literature almost invariably uses the gravity model. The problem is that in its usual formulation this model cannot explain zero trade between any pair of countries. Put bluntly, the model simply does not have an extensive country margin of trade. In this section, we reformulate the gravity model, so that such a margin arises, which in turn allows us to identify extensive margin trade effects of WTO membership.

A gravity equation for bilateral trade arises if demand satisfies the Inada conditions and if the equilibrium is such that any one good is produced in only one country. In a world of comparative advantage, this condition is met if the equilibrium happens to involve complete specialisation, as noted by Deardorff (1998). However, researchers mostly rely on a theoretical underpinning with monopolistic competition, enriched by features of geography, where complete specialisation is

---

[10] The empirical implementation of this approach in Felbermayr and Kohler (2006) has revealed that the increasing force of distance as a trade barrier, transpiring from recent gravity estimates of the distance coefficient (distance puzzle), can partly be explained as reflecting an omitted variables bias from ignoring the extensive margin.

a necessary outcome because of product differentiation. The most complete derivation of the gravity equation along these lines is found in Anderson and van Wincoop (2003). Importantly, this derivation features trade barriers only of the iceberg cost type, whence all goods are sold everywhere, albeit for different c.i.f. prices. It also features Dixit–Stiglitz preferences which satisfy the Inada conditions, hence there is positive trade between any pair of countries.

Empirically, however, there are many country pairs where bilateral trade is zero.[11] Acknowledging the lack of an extensive margin in the underlying theory, existing literature mostly estimates the gravity equation on data that are restricted to country pairs with positive trade. This risks misspecification of the regression and ignores potentially important information. Exploiting this information requires a model allowing for zero trade. Felbermayr and Kohler (2006) suggest a simple *ad hoc* modification of the gravity approach where zero trade cases arise as 'corner-solutions', and which may be estimated using Tobit techniques. The modification rests on a threshold level of bilateral trade that needs to be surpassed for governments' willingness to incur the investment cost for *public* infrastructure required to support trade. If trade falls short of this threshold level, it will fall all the way down to zero, for lack of necessary infrastructure.

Helpman et al. (2008) develop a model of monopolistic competition with *private* fixed cost of serving foreign markets. Their model combines such cost with firm heterogeneity along the lines of Melitz (2003), to generate two extensive margins of trade. There is an extensive *country* margin separating zero trade country pairs from trading pairs.[12] In addition, for each country pair the model also generates an extensive *firm* margin that separates firms exporting to the partner country from those who do not. There is multiple selection of *existing* firms into potential export markets. The model is geared towards estimation of a generalised gravity approach, including the two extensive margins. Helpman et al. (2008) follow a two-step estimation procedure à *la* Heckman (1979).

For the purpose of this chapter and for many other applications, a much simpler model without firm heterogeneity suffices to motivate the empirical strategy. On the demand side, we assume Dixit–Stiglitz-type preferences, identical for all countries, with a constant elasticity of substitution $\sigma > 1$ between different varieties of goods. Preferences are fully symmetric across all potential varieties,

---

[11] As indicated before, Felbermayr and Kohler (2006) present a decomposition of the post-war evolution of world trade into the extensive and intensive margins.

[12] An extensive country margin of world trade also arises in Eaton and Kortum (2002) who employ a stochastic representation of the pattern of (Ricardian) comparative advantage among many countries with perfect competition. Adding geography in the form of trading cost, they arrive at a gravity-type equation for bilateral trade. The key difference to the standard gravity model is that for any good all countries are perfect substitutes as sources of supply. In their model, two countries end up with zero bilateral trade, if for the entire range of goods each of them finds cheaper supply from third countries, because of their idiosyncratic technology and geography.

independent on the country of origin. Throughout this section, we use i to indicate an exporting country, and j to indicate an importing country. Denoting the c.i.f. price for a variety originating in country i and arriving in country j, demand for this variety may be written as: $D^{ji} = A^j (p^{ij})^{-\sigma}$, where $A^j := Y^j (P^j)^{\sigma-1}$. In this expression, Y^j is equal to country j's GDP, and P^j is the exact price index (unit expenditure function), depending on prices of all varieties shipped to market j.[13]

We assume that there are $C + 1$ countries. Each firm produces its own variety, using a well-defined bundle of inputs, with an associated minimum unit cost c^i, which is specific to the country where a firm is located, and determined from factor market clearing; see below. We use a to denote the constant marginal input requirement of this bundle, identical for all firms worldwide. Analogously, f denotes a fixed input requirement.

Serving a foreign market entails two types of costs. One is variable trade costs, assumed to be of the iceberg type and captured by a parameter $\tau^{ij} > 1$, where i and j indicate the sending and receiving countries, respectively. In addition, there is a fixed cost f^{ij} that each firm located in country i has to bear when entering an export market j.[14] Fixed costs are in terms of the input bundle with minimum unit cost c^i. Domestic sales do not require any of these costs, whence $\tau^{ii} = 1$ and $f^{ii} = 0$. Variable and fixed *trade costs* are defined to include both natural as well as policy-induced factors of trade resistance.

Profit maximisation by a representative firm located in country i, assuming that the price index P^j for export market j is unaffected by its own pricing, implies a mark-up price equal to:

$$p^{ij} = \tau^{ij} c^i a / \rho, \tag{1}$$

where $\rho := (\sigma - 1)/\sigma$ from the Dixit–Stiglitz preferences. The price for domestic sales is equal to $p^{ii} = c^i/\rho$.[15] A firm located in country i perceives maximum profits to be earned on exports to country j equal to

$$\pi^{ij} = (1-\rho)\rho^{\sigma-1} A^j \left(c^i a \tau^{ij}\right)^{1-\sigma} - c^i f^{ij}. \tag{2}$$

Obviously, the firm will choose to export to country j only if $\pi^{ij} \geq 0$. This condition may be rewritten as:

$$(1-\rho)\rho^{\sigma-1}\left(c^i a\right)^{1-\sigma} \geq f^{ij}\left(\tau^{ij}\right)^{\sigma-1} A^j. \tag{3}$$

We can now envisage all potential trading partners of country i as being ranked, such that $f^{ij}(\tau^{ij})^{\sigma-1}/A^j$ falls monotonically, as $j \neq i$ increases from 1 up to C. Note

---

[13] GDP replaces the level of expenditure, assuming balanced trade.

[14] The model bears some resemblance to Schmitt and Yu (2001) who introduce firm heterogeneity in fixed costs of exporting into a single export market.

[15] Remember that we have scaled units such that $a = 1$.

that this ranking is specific to the exporting country i. Then, there is a marginal country j^i, such that for all countries $j \leq j^i$ condition (3) is satisfied, whereas for all countries $j > j^i$ it is violated. This is the *extensive country margin* for exports of country i. We introduce an integer-valued function

$$j^i = j^i\left(c^i, \boldsymbol{\tau}^i, \mathbf{f}^i\right) \tag{4}$$

to indicate that country i's extensive margin of trading partners j^i depends on its entire pattern of iceberg and fixed trade resistance, appearing in vector form through $\boldsymbol{\tau}^i$ and $\mathbf{f}^i$ in equation (4). We use J^i to denote the index set of all $j \leq j^i$. Thus, country i will have positive exports only to countries $j \in J^i$. Notice that even if trade costs are symmetric in both directions, trade flows may be unidirectional, as c^i is country-specific, and the trade resistance terms need not be symmetric in terms of direction. The key 'relative price' determining profitability of bilateral exports is $(c^i \tau^{ij} a)/P^j$, in addition to the size of the market relative to fixed cost, A^j/f^{ij}.

We now introduce a latent variable $\rho^{\sigma-1} A^j (c^i \tau^{ij})^{1-\sigma}$, which is the *potential* value of exports shipped by a representative country i firm to consumers of country j. The *actual* value of exports by this firm then is:

$$p^{ij} x^{ij} = \begin{cases} \rho^{\sigma-1}\left(c^i a \tau^{ij}\right)^{1-\sigma} A^j & \text{if } i \in J^i, \\ 0 & \text{otherwise.} \end{cases} \tag{5}$$

This is the *corner-solutions* formulation of bilateral exports, whereby $c^i f^{ij}/(1-\rho)$ is a threshold value for the *latent* variable $\rho^{\sigma-1}(c^i a \tau^{ij})^{1-\sigma} A^j$ that determines zero 'corner-solutions' of bilateral exports to all countries $j > j^i$ (or, equivalently, $j \notin J^i$). Aggregate bilateral exports are $X^{ij} = N^i p^{ij} x^{ij}$, evaluated at c.i.f. prices in country i.[16]

We now introduce two aggregate measures of the export markets served by a country i firm:

$$\Theta^i := \frac{1}{A^i} \sum_{j \in J^i} A^j \left(\tau^{ij}\right)^{1-\sigma} \quad \text{and} \quad F^i := \sum_{j \in J^i} f^{ij}. \tag{6}$$

The variable Θ^i measures the 'aggregate size' of foreign markets reached by a representative firm of country i, relative to country i's domestic market. Thus, A^j, scaled down by the iceberg trade cost term $(\tau^{ij})^{1-\sigma}$, is used to measure the size of market j, viewed from country i's perspective. It is closely related to what is

---

[16] In this chapter, the term 'corner-solutions' is used to designate any model explaining zero trade as an equilibrium outcome of the same mechanisms that also determine the volume of trade. Any such model involves a non-linear relationship between trade (allowing for zeros) and the covariates. Wooldridge (2002) uses the term 'corner-solutions' to describe Tobit estimation techniques to incorporate the non-linearity. In our empirical analysis, we rely on a Poisson pseudo-maximum likelihood (PPML) estimator; see next section.

sometimes called the nominal export market potential of country i. In what follows, domestic sales are indicated by $p^{i0}x^{i0}$. The variable F^i is a simple measure of the entire fixed cost of exporting incurred by each firm in country i, again measured in units of the input bundle with a per unit cost c^i. For given trade costs, both Θ^i and F^i are increasing in $j^i(\tau^i, f^i)$.

It is important to make a distinction between the impact of infra-marginal trade liberalisation which operates through τ^{ij} and f^{ij} for $j \in J^i$, and the impact of trade liberalisation at the margin, which increases j^i through either a reduction in τ^{ij} or f^{ij} for some $j > j^i$. However, we first continue describing the equilibrium for a given j^i.

Profits on actual exports from i to $j \leq j^i$ are equal to $[(c^i\tau^{ij}/\rho) - c^ia\tau^{ij}]x^{ij} - c^if^{ij}$. Moreover, denoting domestic sales by a representative country i firm by x^{i0}, market clearing, $D^{ji} = x^{ij}$, requires $x^{ij} = (A^j/A^i)(\tau^{ij})^{-\sigma}x^{i0}$ and $p^{ij}x^{ij} = (A^j/A^i)(\tau^{ij})^{1-\sigma}p^{i0}x^{i0}$, since $p^{ij} = \tau^{ij}p^{i0}$. The following zero profit condition describes a free entry equilibrium

$$x^{i0}\frac{1-\rho}{\rho}(1+\Theta^i)-(F^i+f)=0. \tag{7}$$

This determines the level of firm-level domestic sales in a familiar way, except for the appearance of the aggregate market potential and fixed cost of exports, Θ^i and F^i: $x^{i0} = (\sigma - 1)(F^i + f)/[1 + \Theta^i]$.[17] From the GNP identity $Y^i \equiv N^ix^{i0}c^i(1 + \Theta)/\rho$, we have

$$p^{i0}x^{i0} = \frac{Y^i}{N^i(1+\Theta^i)}. \tag{8}$$

We now close the model by introducing endowments and factor market clearing. Using the scalar V^i to denote country i's endowment with the input bundle, the equilibrium number of firms emerges from the full employment condition which is written as: $N^i[X^{i0}(1 + \Theta^i) + f + F^i] = V^i$. In view of equation (6), this simplifies to:

$$N^i = \frac{V^i}{(F^i+f)\sigma}. \tag{9}$$

Thus, the equilibrium number of firms is unaffected by Θ^i, but it falls with an increase in $F^i + f$, relative to the resource base V^i. On the other hand, the equilibrium volume of domestic sales per firm is independent on the resource base V^i.

Finally, factor prices are determined such that the cost-minimising input levels per unit of the input bundle add up to the country's endowment for each of the factors present. We use $c(w)$ to denote the dual characterisation of technology, common to all countries; that is, the unit-cost function for the input bundle behind

---

[17] It may seem strange that this condition does not include variable cost, but remember that we have scaled units such that $a = 1$.

the variable and fixed costs of production and trade, whereby w indicates a vector of K primary input prices.[18] Using a subscript to denote a partial derivative, $c_k(w)$ gives the cost-minimising quantity of factor k to generate a unit of the input bundle. Factor market equilibrium in country i then requires

$$c_k(w) = V_k^i/V^i, \quad k = 1, \ldots, K \tag{10}$$

for all $k = 1, \ldots, K$, where V_k^i denotes the endowment of country i with factor k. The factor cost advantage of country i introduced above then emerges as $c^i = c(w^i)$, where w^i is the factor price vector satisfying the aforementioned factor market equilibrium condition.

We are now ready to derive a gravity equation for bilateral trade. Aggregate bilateral exports X^{ij} from i to j are given by $N^i p^{ij} x^{ij} = N^i (A^j/A^i)(\tau^{ij})^{1-\sigma} p^{i0} x^{i0}$. Replacing for $p^{i0} x^{i0}$ from equation (8), we have

$$X^{ij} = \begin{cases} Y^i Y^j \dfrac{(\tau^{ij})^{1-\sigma}}{\Pi^i Q^j} & \text{if } j \in J^i, \\ 0 & \text{otherwise,} \end{cases} \tag{11}$$

whereby

$$\Pi^i := A^i(1+\Theta^i) = A^i + \sum_{j \in J^i} A^j (\tau^{ij})^{1-\sigma}, \tag{12}$$

$$Q^j := (P^j)^{1-\sigma} = N^j (p^{j0})^{1-\sigma} + \sum_{i \in I^j} N^i (p^{i0} \tau^{ij})^{1-\sigma}. \tag{13}$$

Π^i is what Anderson and van Wincoop (2003) call the exporting country i's *multilateral trade resistance term*. Notice that in this model multilateral trade resistance depends on bilateral trade costs of the exporter country i vis-à-vis all countries belonging to the set J^i. Thus, it depends on the extensive country margin of i's exports determined before; see equation (4). In turn, P^j is the importing country j's exact price index, whereby we have replaced $p^{ij} = p^{i0} \tau^{ij}$ and taken into account that the price index includes prices and trade costs only from countries whose firms decide to serve country j. I^j denotes the index set for all such countries i who find country j to be within their extensive country margin of exports. Obviously, $i \in I^j$ iff $j \in J^i$. By complete analogy to Π^i, Q^j measures multilateral trade resistance for the importer country j.

Remember that $A^j := Y^j (P^j)^{\sigma-1}$. Hence, Π^i also depends on all importer country price indices P^j for $j \in J^i$. We may now use the demand function and condition

---

[18] Nothing of what we do here depends on the assumption of a uniform technology. We could allow for country-specific minimum cost functions $c^i(w)$. But this would only make for more cumbersome presentation, without adding any insight.

(7) to write $p^{i0}x^{i0} = A^i(p^{i0})^{1-\sigma}$, which allows us to replace $(p^{i0})^{1-\sigma} = Y^i[A^iN^i(1 + \Theta^i)]$ (and analogously for $(p^{j0})^{1-\sigma}$) appearing in equation (13), hence we may write

$$\left(P^j\right)^{1-\sigma} = \sum_{i \in I^j} \frac{Y^i}{A_i\left(1 + \Theta^i\right)}\left(\tau^{ij}\right)^{1-\sigma}. \tag{14}$$

From the definition of Q^j in equation (13), we now have $\Pi^i = Y^iQ^i + \sum_{j \in J^i}Y^j\left(\tau^{ij}\right)^{1-\sigma}Q^j$ and $Q^j = Y^j\Pi^j + \sum_{i \in I^j}Y^i\left(\tau^{ij}\right)^{1-\sigma}\Pi^i$. This is a system of $2 \times (1 + C)$ equations that determines an equal number of multilateral trade resistance terms Π^i and Q^j as non-linear functions of all bilateral trade costs. Our model with an endogenous country margin of each country's exports thus leads to a solution of the gravity model which is perfectly analogous to Anderson and van Wincoop (2003).[19] The solution involves an 'importer-view' of the extensive margin with the index set I^j. But this is just a different angle on the same margin, not an independent choice of source countries by importing countries.

Turning to WTO membership, we now realise that there is a *direct* tradepromoting effect of membership at the intensive margin through a lower τ^{ij}, if countries i and $j \in J^i$ are *both* members of the WTO. According to equation (11), these countries should have more bilateral trade than country pairs that are otherwise similar, but where both are outside the WTO or only one is a member. Importantly, there is a perfectly analogous effect at the extensive margin, making positive trade for member country pairs a more likely event than for a non-member pair. In terms of our model, lower τ^{ij} and/or lower f^{ij} may move country j into the set J^i. Notice that f^{ij} plays no role for the intensive margin effects of WTO membership, but may be important for extensive margin effects.

In addition, there are *indirect* ('third-country') effects that operate through the multilateral trade resistance channel. Suppose, for instance, that two countries i and $j \in J^i$ are *both* members of the WTO, and there is a third country $k \notin J^i$ with no exports from i to k. Now suppose that k joins the WTO and, through lower τ^{ik} and or lower f^{ik}, it jumps the extensive export margin of country i. This means that k moves into J^i in equation (11). Other things equal, this obviously raises Π^i and thus reduces X^{ij}. Intuitively, this may be interpreted as a *trade diversion effect* that comes about through the resource constraint of the exporting country. Newly established trade between i and k draws away resources from exports to existing trading partners. Obviously, there is a similar effect also for the importing country. No such trade diversion will occur, if i and j are a non-member country pair. However, exporter trade diversion or importer trade diversion does occur, respectively, if the exporter or importer country alone is a member of the WTO.

---

[19] A straightforward manipulation, dividing and multiplying equation (11) by world GDP, leads to a formulation with income shares instead of national GDPs appearing in Π^i and Q^j, as in Anderson and van Wincoop (2003).

4. AN EMPIRICAL MODEL

Our goal is to empirically quantify the effect of WTO membership. Our emphasis lies on an appropriate treatment of the extensive country margin of trade, based on the gravity model developed before. A key feature of the 'corner-solutions' gravity equation (11) is that it is *non-linear*. A possible estimation approach to such an equation is to rely on Tobit techniques, as in Felbermayr and Kohler (2006). This chapter uses a different approach, recently suggested by Santos Silva and Tenreyro (2006), that has a number of advantages over the Tobit estimation.

According to this approach, the empirical model based on equation (11) is as follows. Recognising that X^{ij} can be zero, we write equation (11) as an exponential model:

$$X^{ij} = \exp\left[(1-\sigma)\ln \tau^{ij} + K^i + K^j\right], \tag{15}$$

where $K^i := \ln Y^i - \ln \Pi^i$ and $K^j := \ln[Y^j/Q^j]$. Note again that i and j denote the exporter and importer countries, respectively. The estimation strategy proposed by Anderson and van Wincoop (2003) and Feenstra (2004) amounts to using an array of exporter- and importer-specific dummy variables to control for K^i and K^j. This approach perfectly controls for the multilateral trade resistance terms, which cannot be directly measured in the data and would otherwise have to be simulated. Failing to control for the multilateral resistance term is likely to cause severely biased estimates, as Anderson and van Wincoop (2003) have shown. The use of dummy variables does away with the awkward question of proper discounting of trade and GDP values and allows inclusion of country pairs where GDP data is not available (or unreliable) for either the importer or the exporter. Importantly, the country dummies are perfect controls for country-specific policies that apply to all trading partners, regardless of WTO membership. Many non-tariff and technical barriers to trade have this characteristic.

Typically, researchers add a multiplicative error term ε^{ij} to equation (1), take logs and then substitute dummy variable vectors v^i and v^j for K^i and K^j, respectively. This yields the familiar log–log gravity equation $\ln X^{ij} = \alpha \ln \tau^{ij} + v^i + v^j + \ln \varepsilon^{ij}$, where $\alpha := 1 - \sigma$ is interpreted as the trade cost elasticity of bilateral exports. In a typical empirical gravity equation, real trade costs τ^{ij} are specified as some multiplicative function of policy-induced trade barriers and a host of geographic variables. We stipulate

$$\tau^{ij} = \left(1 + t^{ij}\right) \cdot \left(\text{DIST}^{ij}\right)^{\delta} \cdot \exp\left[(1 - \mathbf{CAT}^{ji})\gamma\right], \tag{16}$$

where $(1 - \text{CAT}^{ji})$ is a row vector of ones minus relevant categorical variables (with associated coefficients in γ) affecting real trade costs τ^{ij}, in addition to distance DIST^{ij} and *ad valorem* tariffs t^{ij}.

The problem with this procedure is that unless the *variance* of ε^{ij} is independent on the variables $Z^{ij} := \{\tau^{ij}, v^i, v^j\}$, the *expectation* of $\ln \varepsilon^{ij}$ will depend on these same regressors, leading to inconsistent ordinary least square (OLS) estimates. Moreover, taking logs generates 'missing values' if for some country pairs bilateral trade is zero, as in the 'corner-solutions' before. This, in turn, may bias estimates, as the data may no longer be viewed as randomly sampled.[20]

Santos Silva and Tenreyro (2006) suggest an approach that avoids these problems. Given that the log of a stochastic variable also depends on its variance, the estimation should be guided by the assumed relationship between $E[X^{ji}|Z^{ij}]$ and $V[X^{ji}|Z^{ij}]$, where Z^{ij} denotes the entire vector of explanatory variables. A reasonable hypothesis is that the conditional variance of X^{ji} is proportional to its conditional mean; that is, $E[X^{ji}|Z^{ij}] \propto V[X^{ji}|Z^{ij}]$. Santos Silva and Tenreyro (2006) show that equation (15) can then be estimated by solving the following set of first-order conditions:

$$\sum_{r=1}^{C(C-1)} \left[X^r - \exp\left(Z^r \hat{\beta}\right) \right] z_h^r = 0 \quad h = 1, \ldots, H, \tag{17}$$

where r indexes bilateral import relationships (ji). In this estimation criterion, Z^r denotes an $H \times 1$-dimensional vector of covariate observations (with elements z_h^r), and $\hat{\beta}$ denoting the corresponding vector of parameter estimates. This estimator is equivalent to the PPML estimator. It is consistent under the correct specification of the conditional mean. Importantly, the data need not themselves be Poisson,[21] and X^r need not be integer-valued. Our econometric strategy relies on this PPML estimator.

5. DATA AND ECONOMETRIC STRATEGY

a. Trade

Our trade data are from the September 2009 CD-ROM of the IMF's *Direction of Trade Statistics* (DoTS). Some of the literature (e.g. Rose, 2004a) estimates the gravity equation on gross trade (exports plus imports). In line with theory, our model has bilateral exports as the dependent variable. However, we estimate the gravity equation on bilateral import data, measured in c.i.f. terms, as this data is usually deemed of higher quality. In other words, we use observations on imports from country i recorded by country j to measure X^{ij}. With the number of countries

---

[20] Tobit- and Heckman-type procedures can deal with the 'corner-solutions' nature of equation (11); they are, however, not robust to misspecification of the error term.
[21] A maximum likelihood estimator is called a pseudo-maximum likelihood estimator, if it remains consistent even if the likelihood function is misspecified (Winkelmann, 2003).

FIGURE 1

The Relative Importance of the Extensive Margin of World Trade, 1948–2008

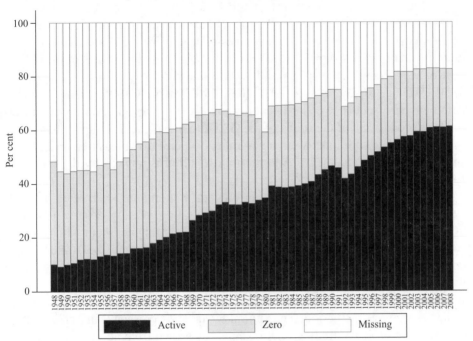

$C = 192$ for the year 2000, we thus have $C(C - 1) = 36,672$ bilateral trade relationships. Trade values are missing for 25.71 per cent of these country pairs.
Figure 1 provides an illustration of missing, zero and positive trading relationships
for the years 1948–2008. The data exhibit considerable discrete jumps in the share
of missing observations, owing to decolonialisation or owing to the break-up of
countries, such as the Soviet Union in the 1990s. However, as a general trend, the
share of active trading relationships has increased strongly over time, both measured in terms of total potential relationships and non-missing ones.[22]

One must be cautious in interpreting variations at the extensive margin of trade
across time. Many country pairs exhibit frequent switches between active
trade, zero trade and missing. For example, between 1948 and 2008 we observe
as many as 26 such switches for the Malta–Paraguay country pair; similarly for
Sri Lanka–Tunisia. For 5 per cent of all country pairs, switches occur more than
12 times. These frequent switchers are usually small, poor countries. Exploring

---

[22] The IMF provides historical data on a separate CD-ROM for the years 1948–80, and regular
updates for the subsequent period. Note the discontinuity between these two datasets around the
year of 1980 visible in Figure 1.

the likelihood of switches across time, we find that a Probit model explaining zero trade does equally well in predicting the occurrence of missing observations and zeros. Hence, it seems unwise to focus too much on time variance, at least in an analysis that explicitly focuses on the role of the extensive margin.[23] In our econometric analysis, we therefore take averages over longer time spans. Instead of an arbitrary slicing of our sample, we focus on the big formative stages of the GATT: pre-Kennedy Round (1948–67), pre-Tokyo Round (1968–79), pre-Uruguay Round (1980–94) and, finally, the (post-Uruguay) WTO period (1995–2004). The first period covers a sequence of tariff-cutting rounds. The second period is characterised by a broadening of the scope of the GATT to include anti-dumping measures. The third period additionally involves rules on non-tariff measures and the so-called framework agreements. And the fourth period is marked by the transition from the GATT to the WTO.[24]

Within these time intervals, missing bilateral imports are interpreted as zeros whenever we encounter at least one year with a non-missing observation. This procedure should reduce measurement error, as it straightens out idiosyncratic switches between zero, positive trade and missings although the strategy does reduce the amount of zero trade observations, relative to a year-by-year treatment of the data. Hence, a 'corner-solution' of zero trade is defined as a case where, subject to the previous treatment of missings, we observe zero trade for each year of the respective time period. The summary statistics presented in Table 1 show that the share of active trading relationships has grown from about 46 per cent in the pre-Kennedy period to 90 per cent in the post-Uruguay times.

b. GATT/WTO Membership

Tomz et al. (2007) emphasise the distinction between *formal* membership of the GATT or the WTO, and *informal* participation in the institution, for example, of colonies through their metropolitan colonisers, or through *de facto* compliance during negotiation ahead of formal membership. They find factual membership (i.e. compliance with GATT rules through either formal or informal participation) is significantly related to higher trade, whereas participation defined as formal membership does not. In this section, we focus on formal membership. In the Appendix, we contrast regression results based on formal and factual membership. Our results are robust with respect to extending the definition of membership to informal participation.

---

[23] Indeed, comparing the raw data from Comtrade with the DoTS reveals that the latter often has zeros and missing where the Comtrade has small values (e.g. $1,000,000). Our view on the information content of short-run extensive margin variation is also corroborated in Head et al. (2010).

[24] The Appendix reports results obtained from averaging across decades rather than across different stages of the world trading system.

TABLE 1
Summary Statistics

Variable	Pre-Kennedy		Kennedy–Tokyo		Tokyo–Uruguay		Post-Uruguay	
	(1948–67)		(1968–78)		(1979–94)		(1995–2008)	
	N = 15,377		N = 16,615		N = 24,431		N = 23,230	
	Mean	SD	Mean	SD	Mean	SD	Mean	SD
$I(M > 0)$ indicator variable	0.46	0.50	0.66	0.47	0.80	0.40	0.90	0.31
ln Imports	13.06	2.75	13.06	3.75	13.24	4.06	13.68	4.49
Imports (USD mn)	6.75	85.80	34.90	419.00	95.30	1,140.00	277.00	3,160.00
WTO (formal)	0.13	0.26	0.31	0.45	0.34	0.44	0.59	0.46
WTO (formal) × IND	0.04	0.16	0.10	0.29	0.08	0.27	0.11	0.31
WTO (formal) × DEV	0.08	0.22	0.21	0.40	0.26	0.40	0.47	0.47
Regional trade agreement (dummy)	0.00	0.04	0.01	0.10	0.02	0.13	0.08	0.22
Currency union (dummy)	0.05	0.21	0.02	0.13	0.01	0.09	0.01	0.10
ln Distance	8.74	0.77	8.73	0.78	8.68	0.81	8.69	0.80
Contiguity (dummy)	0.02	0.15	0.02	0.14	0.02	0.14	0.02	0.14
Common language (dummy)	0.20	0.40	0.20	0.40	0.16	0.37	0.15	0.36
Ever colony (dummy)	0.02	0.13	0.02	0.13	0.01	0.12	0.01	0.11
Common coloniser (dummy)	0.12	0.33	0.13	0.33	0.12	0.32	0.11	0.31
Currently colony (dummy)	0.00	0.03	0.00	0.03	0.00	0.02	0.00	0.02
Same country (colony)	0.01	0.10	0.01	0.11	0.01	0.10	0.01	0.10

c. Other Covariates

Our control variables are identical to those typically used in the literature. They include dummies for joint membership in a regional trade agreement and a strict currency union.[25] The information about WTO membership and regional trade agreements (RTAs) is taken from the WTO homepage.[26] These variables represent trade policy controls and may vary over time. The estimated equation also includes geographical or cultural variables, such as geographical distance, contiguity, the existence of a common language and a host of dummies reflecting the colonial relationship between an importer and the exporter. These data are from CEPII, Paris.

---

[25] In the working paper version, we have also included a dummy for whether the importer grants GSP status to the exporter. That variable is available only for the 1948–99 period and is therefore not present in our analysis. However, its inclusion does not make a noteworthy difference.
[26] We are grateful to Jose de Sousa for providing a STATA code for the computation of the RTA and the currency union dummies.

d. Econometric Strategy

Our strategy differs from existing literature in several respects. First, unlike Rose (2004a), Subramanian and Wei (2007), Tomz et al. (2007) and Eicher and Henn (2008), we place emphasis on the extensive margin of trade. In a recent paper that looks at the extensive margin, Liu (2009) employs a panel framework, controlling for time-invariant bilateral effects (e.g. unobserved bilateral components of trade policy). He thus draws exclusively on within-variance (switches from outsider into member status over time). We have argued before that a close inspection of the data leads us to question the reliability of time series variation at the extensive margin of trade. We therefore propose an econometric strategy that relies on cross-section variation rather than a panel framework. In that sense, our results are best viewed as complementary to Liu's. Our strategy has the further advantage that it allows us to trace the behaviour of the WTO effect over time. It also avoids having to deal with the fact that over time new countries have been created through decolonialisation and the break-up of the Soviet Union.[27]

We proceed in two steps. First, we look at the extensive margin in isolation, employing a cross-section Probit estimation framework for the aforementioned subperiods representing characteristic episodes in the history of the GATT/WTO. In doing so, we also investigate whether there are differences between developing and industrial countries. The second step then estimates the full 'corner-solutions' gravity model, relying on PPML procedure, to capture the non-linearity implied by 'corner-solutions'; see above. We avoid what Baldwin and Taglioni (2006) call the 'gold medal mistake' by consistently using country fixed effects to control for unobserved variables.[28] Moreover, our specification is theory-grounded in the sense that we use bilateral imports, rather than total trade (exports plus imports) as our dependent variable. This also increases the number of observations for each period; see Table 1 for details.[29]

6. ESTIMATION RESULTS

a. A Probit View on the Extensive Margin

In this section, we investigate WTO membership at the extensive margin of world trade by means of a Probit analysis of a cross-section in the aforementioned formative periods of GATT/WTO history. The dependent variable is an indicator variable I^{ij} that takes the value 1 if country i has strictly positive imports from country j, that is, if $X^{ij} > 0$, and the value of 0 otherwise. We present results from

---

[27] In Felbermayr and Kohler (2006), this is called the 'pseudo-extensive margin'.
[28] Liu (2009) tries to solve this problem by proxying unobserved variables.
[29] Rose (2004a) and Tomz et al. (2007) use total trade. Subramanian and Wei (2007) also use imports.

the Probit model, but the logistic and linear probability model gives comparable results. All our regressions include country effects, but these are not shown to save space. We decompose the effect of WTO membership according to whether the importer country is a developing or an industrial country. Using the country classification of Subramanian and Wei (2007), we define a dummy IND_i, such that $IND_i = 1$ if country i is industrialised and $IND_i = 0$ otherwise. We compute the interactions $WTO_{ij} \times IND_i$ and $WTO_{ij} \times (1 - IND_i)$ and jointly use them in our regressions, where $WTO_{ij} = 1$ indicates that countries i and j are both members of the WTO. For the sake of comparison, the variables included in the regression are the same as those by Subramanian and Wei (2007) and Tomz et al. (2007). Whenever a variable perfectly predicts an outcome, it is dropped. Moreover, observations are dropped also for countries which import from all other countries.

Table 2 reports the estimated marginal effects, with different time periods lined up as different columns. All coefficients come with the expected signs whenever they are statistically significant. Comparing across time periods, we note that distance becomes ever less important as a determinant of the extensive margin of world trade. This may reflect the fact that trading relationships are becoming more and more far-reaching geographically. This is an interesting result that has not been noted before. It contrasts with the 'distance-puzzle' found in intensive margin models surveyed in Disdier and Head (2008), meaning that gravity estimates reveal distance to play an ever-increasing role in restricting trade over the past decades.[30] In a similar vein, the trade-creating effect of colonial variables is weakening over time.

(i) Pooling all countries

We first treat all countries in a unified way. Odd-numbered columns report the marginal effect on bilateral trade of formal GATT/WTO membership. In the pre-Kennedy Round period, formal membership has had a fairly strong positive impact on the likelihood of an average importer having an active trade relationship with other WTO members. Membership raises those odds by about 18 percentage points. This is a large effect compared with other determinants of the probability of positive trade, such as the existence of a common language, which increases this likelihood by about 8 per cent. Colonial ties matter strongly. Having had a common coloniser in the past increases the odds of positive trade between any two countries by about 26 per cent. Over time, however, these effects all tend to wear out. WTO membership generally matters less in the Kennedy–Tokyo period and does not seem to play any role at all, at least not for the extensive margin of world trade, in the time period after Tokyo.[31]

---

[30] On the extensive margin, see Felbermayr and Kohler (2006).
[31] This is mainly because of the fact that the dependent variable exhibits decreasing variance over time.

TABLE 2

World Trade Organization (WTO) Membership and the Extensive Margin of Trade

	(1)	(2)	(3)	(4)	(5)	(6)	(7)	(8)
	Pre-Kennedy		Kennedy–Tokyo		Tokyo–Uruguay		Post-Uruguay	
WTO	0.184***		0.0841***		0.00853		−0.00400	
	(0.0344)		(0.0160)		(0.00681)		(0.00440)	
WTO × IND		0.225***		0.132***		0.0724***		0.0172*
		(0.0660)		(0.0240)		(0.0186)		(0.0104)
WTO × DEV		0.180***		0.0736***		0.00505		−0.00466
		(0.0353)		(0.0165)		(0.00666)		(0.00433)
Regional trade agreement			0.306***	0.302***	0.468**	0.451**	0.0246***	0.0244***
			(0.0832)	(0.0822)	(0.209)	(0.203)	(0.00713)	(0.00702)
Currency union	0.0689**	0.0695**	0.145***	0.147***	0.0186	0.0188	0.0131	0.0131
	(0.0328)	(0.0328)	(0.0390)	(0.0388)	(0.0218)	(0.0211)	(0.0102)	(0.0100)
ln Distance	−0.329***	−0.329***	−0.206***	−0.205***	−0.0838***	−0.0811***	−0.0319***	−0.0313***
	(0.0112)	(0.0112)	(0.00731)	(0.00729)	(0.00476)	(0.00472)	(0.00216)	(0.00213)
Contiguity	0.130**	0.130**	−0.0164	−0.0160	0.000838	0.000787	−0.0132	−0.0129
	(0.0508)	(0.0508)	(0.0463)	(0.0460)	(0.0174)	(0.0169)	(0.0133)	(0.0131)
Common language	0.0786***	0.0785***	0.0546***	0.0542***	0.0283***	0.0273***	0.0113***	0.0111***
	(0.0182)	(0.0182)	(0.0116)	(0.0115)	(0.00461)	(0.00447)	(0.00227)	(0.00223)

	(1)	(2)	(3)	(4)	(5)	(6)	(7)	(8)
Ever colony	0.336***	0.336***	0.108***	0.108***	0.00461	0.00455	-0.205*	-0.209*
	(0.0514)	(0.0513)	(0.0406)	(0.0403)	(0.0335)	(0.0325)	(0.121)	(0.119)
Common coloniser	0.262***	0.262***	0.136***	0.135***	0.0465***	0.0449***	0.00628**	0.00613**
	(0.0195)	(0.0195)	(0.0105)	(0.0104)	(0.00423)	(0.00411)	(0.00255)	(0.00251)
Same country	-0.0646	-0.0640	0.0554	0.0557	0.0432***	0.0416***	0.0118	0.0115
	(0.0722)	(0.0722)	(0.0506)	(0.0501)	(0.0138)	(0.0132)	(0.00891)	(0.00876)
N	14,547	14,547	16,615	16,615	24,431	24,431	23,230	23,230
Adjusted R^2	0.486	0.486	0.369	0.369	0.339	0.339	0.384	0.385
χ^2	4,146.3	4,141.7	4,302.9	4,303.6	4,879.8	4,814.4	3,648.8	3,631.4
χ^2 (IND = DEV)	0.50	0.50	6.89***	6.89***	13.14***	13.14***	4.96**	4.96**
Observed p	0.4593	0.4593	0.6587	0.6587	0.7961	0.7961	0.8961	0.8961
Predicted p	0.4867	0.4866	0.6611	0.6610	0.7908	0.7908	0.8704	0.8704

Notes:
All coefficients are to be read as marginal effects (evaluated at sample averages). Robust standard errors are in parentheses (corrected for clustering at country pair level); *** $p < 0.01$, ** $p < 0.05$ and * $p < 0.1$. All specifications include importer and exporter effects and a constant (not shown). Pre-Kennedy refers to averages for the period 1948–67; Kennedy–Tokyo to 1968–78; Tokyo–Uruguay to 1979–94; and post-Uruguay to 1995–2008. Number of observations reflects observations that are not perfectly predicted by covariates. Chi-squared ($IND = DEV$) tests equality of coefficients $WTO \times IND$ and $WTO \times DEV$.

(ii) Industrial versus developing importers

The even-numbered columns separate the total GATT/WTO effect according to the development status of countries. Across all time periods, GATT/WTO membership of industrialised importers was more effective in activating trade relationships with other GATT/WTO partners than if the importer was a developing country. However, the difference between industrialised and developing countries was not statistically significant in the pre-Kennedy period. Overall, Table 2 tells us that to some extent the conclusions drawn by Subramanian and Wei (2007) for the intensive margin carry over to the extensive margin. However, the effect weakens over time.

(iii) Robustness check – yearly effects

Figure 2 plots WTO coefficients obtained by running regressions of the type discussed in Table 2 as yearly cross-sections, rather than taking averages over the formative GATT periods. This substantially increases the number of zeros in

FIGURE 2

The Extensive Margin, Year-by-Year Estimates

(Dashed lines indicate confidence intervals for two standard deviations)

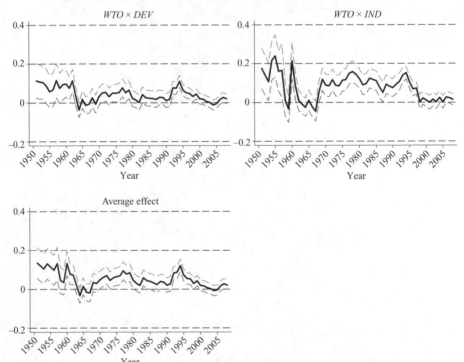

the data, but presumably comes at the cost of substantial measurement error.[32] The top row depicts the effects of formal membership, distinguishing between industrialised and developing countries, whereas the bottom row shows the pooled effect for all countries. The overall message from this analysis is that GATT/WTO membership did help activate trading relationships in the period 1970–2000, with the strongest effects in the period of decolonialisation and dissolution of the Soviet Union. However, the positive effect is mostly driven by industrialised countries. In the period 1970–98, their odds of positive trade flows rose by about 15 per cent as a result of GATT membership. Developing countries have benefited less.

We should bear in mind that the amount of trade creation at the extensive margin over the entire evolution of world trade after formation of the GATT has been relatively small; see Felbermayr and Kohler (2006) and Helpman et al. (2008). To eliminate the 'pseudo-extensive margin' owing to formation of new countries, Felbermayr and Kohler (2006) use a sample of countries that have been in existence ever since 1965. They find that 15 per cent of total world trade in 2004 is because of bilateral relationships that have not existed in 1965. Hence, although WTO membership does indeed increase the odds that two members engage in trade, the contribution of the extensive margin to total world trade growth cannot be very large. In the next section, we therefore study the intensive margin of world trade, but allowing for trade to be zero, as in the 'corner-solutions' version of the gravity model presented in Section 3 above. Using a PPML estimation approach allows us to see to what extent the extensive margin changes the total pro-trade effect of WTO membership.

(iv) Factual versus formal WTO membership

Table A1 follows Tomz et al. (2007) and defines WTO membership on factual rather than formal grounds. As the Tomz data are not available beyond the year 2004, and country coverage is somewhat lower than in our sample, the number of observations in the regressions is lower for each period. Odd-numbered columns refer to the Probit estimates. The results suggest that – compared with Table 2 – factual membership was not more likely to activate trade than formal membership. Also, across all periods, the effect is larger for industrialised countries than for developing ones. Hence, we do not find that broadening the definition of membership to factual (as opposed to formal) participation makes the advantage of being associated to the GATT/WTO any more visible in an econometric analysis of the extensive margin. This is an important piece of new information relative to Tomz et al. (2007) who find this type of effect at the intensive margin. Our results are

---

[32] Measurement problems appear larger before the year 1970. Therefore, it makes sense to focus on the post-1970 era, where idiosyncratic switches between zeros, positive trade values and missings are far less frequent than in the years before.

quite plausible. Why should a country bother about going beyond informal membership, if formal membership has a lower trade-promoting effect?[33]

(v) Robustness check – averages over 10-year windows

Finally, Table A2 presents results based on an alternative definition of time periods. Rather than following the intervals between important multilateral trade negotiations, the 1948–2008 period is split into six periods of equal lengths of 10 years. The upper panel in Table A2 looks at Probit estimates, reporting only the interesting coefficients. Row [A] reports a single coefficient obtained in one regression per time period; coefficients marked [B] are from a single regression for each time period. The results confirm the overall picture obtained in Table 2. There is evidence that GATT/WTO membership has activated trade relationships in early times, but the effect is watered down and finally vanishes over time. Moreover, industrialised countries tend to benefit more from membership than developing ones.

b. Estimating the Full Non-linear Model

We have argued in Section 4 that the potential of zero trade as an equilibrium outcome gives rise to a non-linear gravity model of bilateral trade. Following Santos Silva and Tenreyro (2006), we now proceed to estimating this model using a PPML procedure.

(i) Pooling all countries – OLS versus PPML

Table 3 sets estimates from the standard log–log OLS procedure against PPML estimates. Columns labelled (A) present conventional results where the dependent variable is the log of bilateral imports. Columns labelled (B) use PPML on the same sample as in (A), whereas columns labelled (C) extend the sample to zero trade observations which for obvious reasons drop out in the OLS approach. The OLS results look familiar. The elasticity of distance is fairly large and almost doubles in magnitude over time. Cultural proximity (colonial ties, common language) boosts trade considerably. Formal GATT/WTO membership increases bilateral trade in all time spans considered, except for the time between the Kennedy and the Tokyo Rounds of the GATT.

Running PPML on the same sample (i.e. excluding zero trade observations), the distance coefficient is much smaller, the dummy for colonial ties is less frequently significant, and the regional trade agreement dummy comes with comparable size. As to WTO/GATT membership, the results are generally somewhat bleaker than those from OLS estimation. PPML also generates stronger variation

---

[33] See also Rose's (2007) reply to Tomz et al. (2007).

TABLE 3

Trade Creation and the Extensive Margin: Ordinary Least Squares (OLS) versus Poisson Pseudo-maximum Likelihood (PPML)

Dependent Variable	Pre-Kennedy			Kennedy–Tokyo			Tokyo–Uruguay			Post-Uruguay		
	(A) $\ln M_{ij}$ OLS	(B) $M_{ij} > 0$ PPML	(C) M_{ij} PPML	(A) $\ln M_{ij}$ OLS	(B) $M_{ij} > 0$ PPML	(C) M_{ij} PPML	(A) $\ln M_{ij}$ OLS	(B) $M_{ij} > 0$ PPML	(C) M_{ij} PPML	(A) $\ln M_{ij}$ OLS	(B) $M_{ij} > 0$ PPML	(C) M_{ij} PPML
WTO	0.186* (0.0962)	−0.249 (0.217)	−0.467** (0.223)	−0.132 (0.0891)	−0.763*** (0.193)	−0.874*** (0.190)	0.629*** (0.0795)	−0.0870 (0.166)	−0.141 (0.166)	0.371*** (0.134)	0.362** (0.170)	0.340** (0.168)
Regional trade agreement	−0.469 (0.366)	0.517** (0.225)	0.467** (0.228)	−0.496*** (0.184)	0.521*** (0.116)	0.479*** (0.118)	−0.292** (0.124)	0.500*** (0.102)	0.491*** (0.103)	0.0861 (0.0809)	1.027*** (0.0885)	1.033*** (0.0882)
Currency union	0.549*** (0.114)	1.716*** (0.202)	1.768*** (0.202)	1.187*** (0.187)	0.522*** (0.186)	0.558*** (0.187)	0.725*** (0.189)	−0.713*** (0.213)	−0.704*** (0.214)	−0.0607 (0.158)	−0.318*** (0.105)	−0.319*** (0.105)
ln Distance	−0.942*** (0.0308)	−0.597*** (0.0544)	−0.614*** (0.0574)	−1.347*** (0.0314)	−0.661*** (0.0373)	−0.676*** (0.0383)	−1.513*** (0.0262)	−0.606*** (0.0330)	−0.607*** (0.0331)	−1.649*** (0.0285)	−0.489*** (0.0338)	−0.488*** (0.0337)
Contiguity	0.276** (0.122)	0.228** (0.115)	0.194* (0.118)	0.223 (0.143)	0.209** (0.0888)	0.187** (0.0897)	0.488*** (0.108)	0.394*** (0.0791)	0.391*** (0.0795)	0.482*** (0.119)	0.338*** (0.0671)	0.336*** (0.0671)
Common language	0.397*** (0.0613)	0.477*** (0.105)	0.506*** (0.108)	0.487*** (0.0636)	0.403*** (0.0820)	0.419*** (0.0830)	0.398*** (0.0544)	0.428*** (0.0765)	0.437*** (0.0766)	0.536*** (0.0535)	0.273*** (0.0690)	0.273*** (0.0689)
Ever colony	1.397*** (0.112)	0.741*** (0.151)	0.758*** (0.155)	1.580*** (0.111)	0.510*** (0.106)	0.523*** (0.109)	1.460*** (0.104)	0.246*** (0.0906)	0.244*** (0.0914)	1.122*** (0.106)	0.311*** (0.0893)	0.313*** (0.0895)
Common coloniser	0.792*** (0.0914)	−0.395 (0.243)	−0.452* (0.238)	0.654*** (0.0901)	−0.339** (0.150)	−0.354** (0.151)	0.910*** (0.0708)	0.0906 (0.125)	0.0773 (0.125)	0.897*** (0.0697)	0.304** (0.144)	0.305** (0.144)
Same country	0.897*** (0.184)	−0.563** (0.258)	−0.509* (0.265)	1.190*** (0.198)	0.515*** (0.167)	0.420** (0.211)	0.763*** (0.170)	0.993*** (0.206)	1.005*** (0.206)	0.657*** (0.174)	0.517*** (0.110)	0.519*** (0.110)
Observations	7,063	7,063	15,377	10,944	10,944	16,615	20,020	20,020	25,147	25,854	25,854	28,853
R^2	0.728			0.744			0.734			0.736		
F/χ^2		39,222.9	39,222.9	121.0	54,609.9	62,138.5	167.2	72,565.8	74,382.0	222.9	78,295.2	79,717.2

Notes:

Robust standard errors are in parentheses (corrected for clustering at country pair level); *** $p < 0.01$, ** $p < 0.05$ and * $p < 0.1$. All specifications include importer and exporter effects and a constant (not shown). Pre-Kennedy refers to averages for the period 1948–67; Kennedy–Tokyo to 1968–78; Tokyo–Uruguay to 1979–94; and post-Uruguay to 1995–2008. Number of observations reflects observations that are not perfectly predicted by covariates.

across GATT periods. Thus, in the Kennedy–Tokyo window, joint GATT member-ship even appears to *lower* bilateral trade. In the pre-Kennedy and the Tokyo–Uruguay windows, GATT membership simply does not seem to matter at all. It is only in post-Uruguay Round times that abiding by rules of the WTO appears to boost bilateral trade. The effect is statistically significant and economically important. On average, the volume of trade is about 36 per cent larger for WTO members than for outsiders.

(ii) The role of the extensive margin

Columns labelled (C) include zero trade observations, thus allowing for WTO membership to enhance trade also at the extensive country margin. Including zero trade country pairs more than doubles the number of observations in earlier years. In more recent periods with increased utilisation of potential trade relationships, the number of observations still increases by 15 per cent. The OLS results in columns (A) suffer from two problems. First, the log–log model yields consistent estimates only under very strong assumptions regarding the error term. And second, the results may be biased as the extensive margin is ignored. Columns (B) remedy the first problem and columns (C) help with both issues. With the exception of the GATT/WTO variable, columns (B) and (C) look fairly similar. It appears safe to conclude that the extensive margin *per se* does not play an impor-tant role in explaining the difference between OLS and PPML. In particular, for the post-Uruguay period the estimates are most plausible and very consistent across columns (A)–(C), indicating that WTO membership increases bilateral trade by about 40 per cent (i.e. $e^{0.340} - 1$), whether zeros are included or not. Note that this magnitude is smaller than the findings in Subramanian and Wei (2007), but it does make sense. As in their analysis, the comprehensive inclusion of country-specific fixed effects guarantees that multilateral trade resistance is duly taken into account; see Section 3 above. Given the fact that most countries today are WTO members, it is tempting to interpret our WTO coefficient as the cost of non-membership.

Our results are in contrast to the panel estimates reported by Liu (2009), which seem to suggest that including zeros increases the trade-creating potential of WTO membership by about 30 per cent. The difference is potentially due to three fea-tures of our approach. First, we include importer and exporter country fixed effects, to control for multilateral trade resistance as a determinant of bilateral trade. This turns out to be crucial for the results obtained. Second, for reasons outlined above we average the data over formative GATT periods, whereas Liu uses yearly observations. To see what this implies, Figure 3 reports results for the WTO coefficients in specifications (B) to (C) in Table 3, but from *yearly* regres-sions. It compares estimates on a sample restricted to non-zero trade with those from an unrestricted sample for the years 1948–2008, with 95 per cent confidence

FIGURE 3
Poisson Pseudo-maximum Likelihood Estimates of World Trade Organization Coefficient on
Non-zero Trade Observations (solid lines) and Including Zero Trade Observations (dashed lines),
with Confidence Intervals for Two Standard Deviations

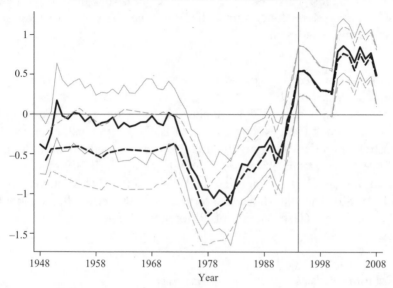

intervals. It turns out that averaging as such is not responsible for the weak WTO
effect at the extensive margin, at least not in cross-sections. This leaves Liu's
reliance on variance across time (within variance) in a panel estimation framework
as an explanatory factor for a seemingly robust positive role of WTO membership
at the extensive margin of trade. However, as pointed out above, a close inspection
of our data leads us to question the reliability of time-series evidence on the occurrence of zero trade.[34]

Figure 3 highlights a further striking result that appears to have gone almost
unnoticed in existing literature: the WTO makes a difference. In the GATT period
(1948–94), there is little evidence that the multilateral trading regime has increased
members' bilateral trade; quite the opposite seems to hold true. From 1995 onwards,
the picture is much brighter. The WTO has consistently increased its members'
trade by 35–50 per cent.

(iii) Industrial versus developing importers
Finally, Table 4 distinguishes between industrialised and developing WTO
members. The sign of our coefficient estimates is consistently negative for the first

---

[34] Liu's finding also does not square with the low quantitative importance of new trade relationships
in the 2004 total trade volume found by Felbermayr and Kohler (2006) and Helpman et al. (2008).

three time spans considered and turns positive only in the post-Uruguay Round era and, most strikingly, for developing countries. We find that developing importers' trade grows by almost 70 per cent ($e^{0.52} - 1$), whereas industrialised importers' trade barely changes. This finding is in stark contrast to Subramanian and Wei (2007) where the general conclusion is that WTO membership works less well for developing than for industrial countries.

(iv) Robustness check – yearly effects

Figure 4 provides a robustness check, depicting the WTO coefficients from yearly regressions, where WTO membership is defined on formal grounds. The lines depict coefficient estimates for GATT/WTO membership for developing and industrial countries, respectively, in a specification corresponding to column (C) in Table 4, again with 95 per cent confidence intervals. It turns out that the coefficients for developing countries tend to be somewhat higher in the early period (1948–80). The opposite is true for the 1980–90 period. In the more recent period, there is no clear pattern of differences between the two groups of countries.

(v) Robustness check – factual WTO membership

Table A1 reports Poisson estimates for factual rather than formal GATT/WTO membership. As explained above, the sample contains fewer countries and ends earlier. Hence, results are not fully comparable with those reported in Table 4. However, the analysis confirms two key findings. First, we find positive membership effects only for the WTO period. And second, developing countries have a higher coefficient in this period than industrialised countries. In contrast to Table 4, factual membership defined over the sample in question has larger effects than formal membership in the sample used for Table 4. Note, however, keeping the sample constant, factual and formal memberships have very similar effects.[35]

(vi) Robustness check – averages over 10-year windows

Finally, Table A2 slices the time period into arbitrary intervals of 10 years in length, rather than using periods between important GATT/WTO Rounds. The analysis confirms that we find consistently positive GATT/WTO effects only in more recent times. Interestingly, although in the 1988–97 period developing countries benefited more from membership than industrialised countries, this pattern reverses in the last decade (1998–2007). This is consistent with Figure 4. Moreover,

---

[35] See the working paper version of this chapter (Table A1 therein).

TABLE 4

Trade Creation and the Extensive Margin: Industrialised versus Developing Countries

Dependent Variable	Pre-Kennedy (A) ln Mij — OLS	Pre-Kennedy (B) Mij > 0 — PPML	Pre-Kennedy (C) Mij — PPML	Kennedy–Tokyo (A) ln Mij — OLS	Kennedy–Tokyo (B) Mij > 0 — PPML	Kennedy–Tokyo (C) Mij — PPML	Tokyo–Uruguay (A) ln Mij — OLS	Tokyo–Uruguay (B) Mij > 0 — PPML	Tokyo–Uruguay (C) Mij — PPML	Post-Uruguay (A) ln Mij — OLS	Post-Uruguay (B) Mij > 0 — PPML	Post-Uruguay (C) Mij — PPML
wto_ind	0.331***	−0.332	−0.574***	−0.163	−0.812***	0.944***	0.942***	−0.0784	−0.139	0.263*	0.319*	0.293
	(0.110)	(0.217)	(0.222)	(0.0993)	(0.194)	(0.191)	(0.0921)	(0.173)	(0.173)	(0.144)	(0.181)	(0.180)
wto_dev	0.0192	0.241	0.164	−0.108	−0.473**	−0.478**	0.470***	−0.133	−0.150	0.412***	0.533***	0.520***
	(0.130)	(0.269)	(0.275)	(0.105)	(0.239)	(0.239)	(0.0878)	(0.180)	(0.180)	(0.140)	(0.186)	(0.185)
Regional trade agreement	−0.537	0.510**	0.459**	−0.483***	0.535***	0.501***	−0.394***	0.495***	0.490***	0.0954	1.026***	1.032***
	(0.369)	(0.228)	(0.231)	(0.186)	(0.116)	(0.118)	(0.128)	(0.103)	(0.104)	(0.0811)	(0.0872)	(0.0868)
Currency union	0.563***	1.672***	1.706***	1.180***	0.504***	0.533***	0.773***	−0.702***	−0.702***	−0.0586	−0.310***	−0.311***
	(0.114)	(0.199)	(0.199)	(0.187)	(0.186)	(0.187)	(0.189)	(0.212)	(0.214)	(0.158)	(0.106)	(0.106)
ln Distance	−0.938***	−0.606***	−0.625***	−1.348***	−0.664***	−0.679***	−1.513***	−0.606***	−0.607***	−1.647***	−0.489***	−0.488***
	(0.0309)	(0.0547)	(0.0576)	(0.0314)	(0.0373)	(0.0383)	(0.0263)	(0.0330)	(0.0331)	(0.0286)	(0.0334)	(0.0333)
Contiguity	0.271**	0.246**	0.218*	0.223	0.216**	0.196**	0.487***	0.393***	0.390***	0.483***	0.343***	0.342***
	(0.122)	(0.115)	(0.117)	(0.143)	(0.0887)	(0.0896)	(0.108)	(0.0790)	(0.0795)	(0.119)	(0.0671)	(0.0670)
Common language	0.396***	0.466***	0.489***	0.487***	0.399***	0.414***	0.401***	0.428***	0.437***	0.536***	0.274***	0.274***
	(0.0613)	(0.105)	(0.108)	(0.0636)	(0.0820)	(0.0829)	(0.0543)	(0.0765)	(0.0766)	(0.0535)	(0.0683)	(0.0682)
Ever colony	1.397***	0.768***	0.793***	1.580***	0.516***	0.530***	1.457***	0.246***	0.244***	1.122***	0.310***	0.312***
	(0.113)	(0.148)	(0.151)	(0.111)	(0.105)	(0.107)	(0.105)	(0.0907)	(0.0914)	(0.106)	(0.0885)	(0.0886)
Common colonizer	0.785***	−0.334	−0.377	0.654***	−0.323**	−0.333**	0.908***	0.0889	0.0770	0.896***	0.281**	0.280**
	(0.0914)	(0.238)	(0.235)	(0.0901)	(0.150)	(0.152)	(0.0708)	(0.125)	(0.125)	(0.0697)	(0.143)	(0.143)
Same country	0.919***	−0.644**	−0.613**	1.186***	0.487***	0.386*	0.780***	0.988***	1.004***	0.650***	0.520***	0.523***
	(0.185)	(0.263)	(0.271)	(0.198)	(0.172)	(0.213)	(0.170)	(0.203)	(0.205)	(0.174)	(0.112)	(0.112)
Observations	7,063	7,063	15,377	10,944	10,944	16,615	20,020	20,020	25,147	25,854	25,854	28,853
R^2	0.728			0.744			0.734			0.736		
F/χ^2	120.8	38,786.4	38,786.4	120.8	53,781.5	60,590.8	165.8	72,907.9	74,908.8	223.2	78,791.8	80,165.2

Notes:

Robust standard errors are in parentheses (corrected for clustering at country pair level); *** $p < 0.01$, ** $p < 0.05$ and * $p < 0.1$. All specifications include importer and exporter effects and a constant (not shown). Pre-Kennedy refers to averages for the period 1948–67; Kennedy–Tokyo to 1968–78; Tokyo–Uruguay to 1979–94; and post-Uruguay to 1995–2008. Number of observations reflects observations that are not perfectly predicted by covariates.

FIGURE 4

Poisson Pseudo-maximum Likelihood Estimates of World Trade Organization Coefficients for Industrialised (solid lines) and Less Developed Countries (dashed lines), including Zero Trade Observations, with Confidence Intervals for Two Standard Deviations

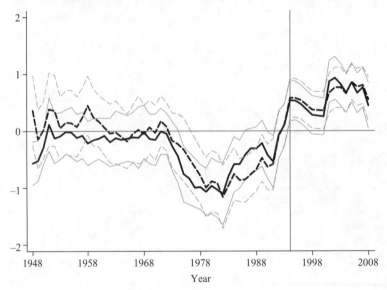

as in our earlier analyses, broadening the focus to include the extensive country margin of trade does not make a qualitative difference (compare the middle and lower panels in Table A2).

7. CONCLUSION

World trade has evolved over the past five decades at both the intensive and extensive margins. Most existing bilateral trading relationships have seen an increase in the amounts traded, and new trading relationships have been established over time. Existing studies exploring the role of GATT/WTO membership for trade have mostly focused on the intensive margin, thus ignoring the possibility that membership has promoted trade through the formation of trading relationships between countries who had not been trading with each other before. The results are mixed, but trade-promoting influence of GATT/WTO membership remains in doubt. However, consistent estimation of the trade-promoting influence of GATT/WTO membership requires an empirical framework that allows for variation at the extensive margin that separates positive from zero trade country pairs. In this chapter, we have developed what is probably the simplest possible gravity model that serves this purpose. We have estimated this model on a conventional dataset of bilateral trade and the usual gravity controls, including in particular a set of dummy variables for trading arrangements, such as WTO membership.

Our theoretical model clearly identifies extensive margin effects of WTO membership, including 'third-country' effects running through the multilateral trade resistance terms of the gravity equation. Our estimation strategy duly responds to the issues raised in recent literature. Thus, we account for multilateral trade resistance, and we differentiate between country groups (developing and industrial countries), as well as between formal membership as opposed to factual participation in the GATT/WTO. Moreover, responding to concerns about the reliability of trade data at the extensive margin, we abstain from panel estimation and rely on cross-sectional evidence instead, averaging our data for the important phases of GATT/WTO history. Recognising the non-linear nature of our 'corner-solutions' version of the gravity model, our estimation relies on the PPML estimator.

What, then, is the conclusion that we may draw from our empirical exercise? First, our Probit results do generate some evidence for WTO membership to raise the odds that countries trade with each other at all, but the effect is by no means robust across country groups and time. Nor does a broader definition of membership that includes *de facto* participation make much of a difference. The asymmetry, both across country groups and types of membership, changes erratically over subperiods considered. A significantly positive Probit coefficient estimate emerges in less than half the number of specifications considered. The positive findings of WTO membership reported in Subramanian and Wei (2007) and Tomz et al. (2007) for the intensive margin thus do not carry over in any robust way to our Probit view on the extensive margin of world trade.

Things do not improve in any reassuring way if we turn to the non-linear PPML estimation. Indeed, running PPML on the entire sample of countries gives rise to an even bleaker picture for formal WTO membership than do conventional OLS estimates relying on positive trade only. It is only for the aftermath of the Uruguay Round that we obtain a significantly positive effect for formal membership. Broadly speaking, the same result is obtained if we differentiate between types of membership and country groups.

The broad conclusion, then, is that the extensive margin does not prove a powerful line of defence for WTO membership as a trade-promoting force in a model which otherwise seems to work fine in terms of explanatory power, and in terms of the magnitude and significance of coefficient estimates. Moreover, our results strongly suggest that the transition from the GATT to the WTO has amounted to a qualitative change in the world trading system that makes membership in this system more profoundly trade promoting than was the case for earlier periods of GATT history.

APPENDIX

TABLE A1

Robustness Checks – Factual GATT/WTO Membership

Dependent Variable	(1)	(2)	(3)	(4)	(5)	(6)	(7)	(8)
	Pre-Kennedy		Kennedy–Tokyo		Tokyo–Uruguay		Post-Uruguay	
	Factual Probit	Factual PPML	Factual Probit	Factual PPML	Factual Probit	Factual PPML	Factual Probit	Factual PPML
Membership status								
WTO × IND	0.00356	−0.974***	0.0712***	−1.034***	0.0580**	0.275	0.0700	1.017***
	(0.0524)	(0.189)	(0.0254)	(0.193)	(0.0292)	(0.220)	(0.0438)	(0.340)
WTO × DEV	−0.0212	−0.0144	0.0177	−1.127***	0.0395***	−0.185	0.0199	1.285***
	(0.0350)	(0.212)	(0.0178)	(0.235)	(0.0122)	(0.242)	(0.0173)	(0.337)
Regional trade agreement		−0.0167	0.537*	0.249		0.135	0.478**	0.561***
		(0.358)	(0.318)	(0.161)		(0.122)	(0.213)	(0.159)
Generalised system of preferences	1.772	−8.576***	0.263***	0.442***	0.241***	0.334***	−0.0786	0.365***
	(1.239)	(2.649)	(0.0301)	(0.0775)	(0.0595)	(0.0575)	(0.0790)	(0.116)
Currency union	0.674***	1.976***	0.367***	0.892***	0.101	−0.380	0.496***	−1.907**
	(0.168)	(0.283)	(0.0845)	(0.198)	(0.0617)	(0.335)	(0.187)	(0.774)
ln Distance	−0.391***	−0.609***	−0.176***	−0.713***	−0.127***	−0.693***	−0.0760***	−0.681***
	(0.0146)	(0.0461)	(0.00714)	(0.0363)	(0.00604)	(0.0328)	(0.00402)	(0.0288)

	(1)	(2)	(3)	(4)	(5)	(6)	(7)	(8)
Contiguity	0.125*	0.313***	−0.0197	0.229**	−0.0196	0.400***	−0.0314	0.427***
	(0.0641)	(0.117)	(0.0475)	(0.100)	(0.0386)	(0.0841)	(0.0352)	(0.0834)
Common language	0.0586***	0.572***	0.0300***	0.424***	0.0450***	0.432***	0.0284***	0.292***
	(0.0221)	(0.0958)	(0.00952)	(0.0842)	(0.00683)	(0.0809)	(0.00475)	(0.0765)
Every colony	0.378***	0.843***	0.0812***	0.418***	0.0225	0.131	0.0225	0.0780
	(0.0479)	(0.139)	(0.0209)	(0.109)	(0.0671)	(0.0990)	(0.0671)	(0.102)
Common coloniser	0.318***	−0.195	0.0921***	−0.00900	0.0587***	0.263	0.0215***	−0.0471
	(0.0193)	(0.190)	(0.00706)	(0.148)	(0.00621)	(0.175)	(0.00502)	(0.198)
Same country	−0.0686	−0.455*	0.00853	0.434**	0.0788***	0.568**	0.0460***	0.443***
	(0.0939)	(0.259)	(0.0478)	(0.201)	(0.0164)	(0.248)	(0.0117)	(0.141)
N	12,147	13,155	14,131	14,364	16,453	20,388	15,212	22,516
Adjusted R^2	0.559		0.490		0.423		0.440	
χ^2	3,700	29,114	4,000	99,630	4,155	64,661	3,687	85,479

Notes:
Robust standard errors are in parentheses (corrected for clustering at country pair level); *** $p < 0.01$, ** $p < 0.05$ and * $p < 0.1$. All specifications include importer and exporter effects and a constant (not shown). Pre-Kennedy refers to averages for the period 1948–67; Kennedy–Tokyo to 1968–78; Tokyo–Uruguay to 1979–94; and post-Uruguay to 1995–2004. Number of observations reflects observations that are not perfectly predicted by covariates.

TABLE A2
Robustness Checks – Different Time Periods

	(1) 1948–57	(2) 1958–67	(3) 1968–77	(4) 1978–87	(5) 1988–97	(6) 1998–2007
Probit – dependent variable: $I(M > 0)$						
[A] WTO	0.155***	0.144***	0.0812***	0.0203*	0.0149**	0.000642
	(0.0449)	(0.0293)	(0.0161)	(0.0121)	(0.00663)	(0.00479)
[B] WTO × IND	0.218***	0.223***	0.129***	0.119***	−0.00148	0.0189*
	(0.0712)	(0.0446)	(0.0240)	(0.0227)	(0.0107)	(0.0103)
[B] WTO × DEV	0.129**	0.128***	0.0705***	0.00949	0.0170**	−0.0000521
	(0.0506)	(0.0301)	(0.0166)	(0.0121)	(0.00678)	(0.00473)
PPML – dependent variable: $M > 0$						
[A] WTO	−0.118	−0.380	−0.874***	−0.943***	0.341**	0.421**
	(0.261)	(0.248)	(0.218)	(0.236)	(0.164)	(0.206)
[B] WTO × IND	−0.195	−0.419*	−0.912***	−0.928***	0.303*	0.472**
	(0.260)	(0.249)	(0.220)	(0.237)	(0.167)	(0.206)
[B] WTO × DEV	0.253	−0.171	−0.706***	−1.023***	0.437**	0.297
	(0.301)	(0.266)	(0.227)	(0.241)	(0.170)	(0.222)
PPML – dependent variable: $M \geq 0$						
[A] WTO	−0.339	−0.582**	−0.946***	−0.903***	0.331**	0.382*
	(0.263)	(0.251)	(0.213)	(0.242)	(0.165)	(0.206)
[B] WTO × IND	−0.430	−0.632**	−0.992***	−0.891***	0.291*	0.433**
	(0.263)	(0.251)	(0.215)	(0.244)	(0.168)	(0.206)
[B] WTO × DEV	0.0840	−0.315	−0.751***	−0.956***	0.427**	0.261
	(0.302)	(0.268)	(0.222)	(0.248)	(0.172)	(0.221)

Note:
***: Significance at the 2 per cent level; **: Significance at the 5 per cent level; *: Significance at the 10 per cent level.

REFERENCES

Anderson, J. E. and E. van Wincoop (2003), 'Gravity with Gravitas: A Solution to the Border Puzzle', *American Economic Review*, **93**, 170–92.

Bagwell, K. and R. W. Staiger (2003), *The Economics of the World Trading System* (Cambridge, MA: MIT Press).

Baier, S. L. and J. H. Bergstrand (2007), 'Do Free Trade Agreements Actually Increase Members' International Trade?' *Journal of International Economics*, **71**, 72–95.

Baldwin, R. E. and D. Taglioni (2006), 'Gravity for Dummies and Dummies for Gravity Equations', NBER Working Paper No. 12516, Cambridge, MA.

Chang, P. and M. Lee (2007), 'The WTO Trade Effect', mimeo, Singapore Management University.

Deardorff, A. V. (1998), 'Determinants of Bilateral Trade: Does Gravity Work in a Neoclassical World?' in J. A. Frankel (ed.), *The Regionalization of the World Economy* (Chicago, IL: University of Chicago Press), 33–57.

Disdier, A. and K. Head (2008), 'The Puzzling Persistence of the Distance Effect on Bilateral Trade', *Review of Economics and Statistics*, **90**, 37–41.

Eaton, J. and S. Kortum (2002), 'Technology, Geography, and Trade', *Econometrica*, **70**, 1741–79.

Eicher, T. and C. Henn (2008), 'In Search of WTO Trade Effects: Preferential Trade Agreements Promote Trade Strongly, but Unevenly', mimeo, University of Washington.

Evenett, S. J. and J. Gage (2005), 'Evaluating WTO Accessions: The Effect of WTO Accession on National Trade Flows', Chapter II, in M. Kennett, S. J. Evenett and J. Gage (eds.), Evaluating WTO Accessions: Legal and Economic Perspectives, prepared for an IDRC-sponsored research project entitled, 'Evaluating and Preparing for WTO Accessions'. Available at http://www.evenett.com/research/workingpapers/evaluatingWTOaccessions.pdf (accessed 1 September 2010).

Feenstra, R. C. (2004), *Advanced International Trade: Theory and Evidence* (Princeton, NJ: Princeton University Press).

Felbermayr, G. J. and W. Kohler (2006), 'Exploring the Intensive and Extensive Margin of World Trade', *Review of World Economics*, **142**, 642–74.

Head, K., T. Mayer and J. Ries (2010), 'The Erosion of Colonial Trade Linkages after Independence', *Journal of International Economics*, **81**, 1–14.

Heckman, J. J. (1979), 'Sample Selection Bias as a Specification Error', *Econometrica*, **47**, 153–61.

Helpman, E., M. J. Melitz and Y. Rubinstein (2008), 'Estimating Trade Flows: Trading Partners and Trading Volumes', *Quarterly Journal of Economics*, **123**, 441–87.

Lissovolik, B. and Y. Lissovolik (2006), 'Russia and the WTO: The "Gravity" of Outsider-Status', *IMF Staff Papers*, **53**, 1–27.

Liu, X. (2009), 'GATT/WTO Promotes Trade Strongly: Sample Selection and Model Specification', *Review of International Economics*, **17**, 428–46.

Melitz, M. J. (2003), 'The Impact of Trade on Intraindustry Reallocation and Aggregate Industry Productivity', *Econometrica*, **71**, 1695–725.

Rose, A. K. (2004a), 'Do We Really Know that the WTO Increases Trade?' *American Economic Review*, **94**, 98–114.

Rose, A. K. (2004b), 'Do WTO Members Have More Liberal Trade Policy?' *Journal of International Economics*, **63**, 209–35.

Rose, A. K. (2005), 'Which International Institutions Promote International Trade?' *Review of International Economics*, **13**, 682–98.

Rose, A. K. (2007), 'Do We Really Know that the WTO Increases Trade? Reply', *American Economic Review*, **97**, 2019–25.

Rose, A. K. (2010), 'The Effect of Membership in the GATT/WTO on Trade: Where Do We Stand?' in Z. Drabek (ed.), *Is the World Trade Organisation Attractive Enough for Emerging Economies: Critical Essays on the Multilateral Trading System* (Basingstoke: Palgrave Macmillan), 195–216.

Santos Silva, M. C. J. and S. Tenreyro (2006), 'The Log of Gravity', *Review of Economics and Statistics*, **88**, 641–58.

Schmitt, N. and Z. Yu (2001), 'Economies of Scale and the Volume of Intra-industry Trade', *Economics Letters*, **74**, 127–32.

Subramanian, A. and S. Wei (2007), 'The WTO Promotes Trade, Strongly but Unevenly', *Journal of International Economics*, **72**, 151–75.

Tomz, M., J. L. Goldstein and D. Rivers (2007), 'Do We Really Know that the WTO Increases Trade? Comment', *American Economic Review*, **97**, 2005–18.

Winkelmann, R. (2003), *Econometric Analysis of Count Data* (Berlin: Springer-Verlag).

Wooldridge, J. M. (2002), *Econometric Analysis of Cross Section and Panel Data* (Cambridge, MA: MIT Press).

5

How Effective are WTO Disciplines on Domestic Support and Market Access for Agriculture?

David Blandford, Ivar Gaasland, Roberto Garcia and Erling Vårdal

1. INTRODUCTION

𝔄 NEW round of trade negotiations under the World Trade Organization (WTO) was launched in 2001. One of the major aims of the Doha Development Round is to reduce agricultural protection and impose greater discipline on domestic agricultural subsidies, particularly those that are most trade distorting. In this chapter, we examine whether the proposed WTO modalities for agriculture will actually achieve this aim in the case of Norway. Norwegian agriculture, which accounts for less than 1 per cent of GDP and 3 per cent of domestic employment, is among the most heavily protected in the world (NILF, 2007). The OECD's Producer Support Estimate for Norway was 62 per cent in 2008, the highest among the Organization's member countries (OECD, 2009). Norway has a complex system of farm subsidies involving deficiency payments, structural income support, acreage and headage payments, and a range of indirect supports. The system is buttressed by substantial import protection, which limits market access. Consequently, the extent to which Norway will have to change its agricultural

The authors are grateful to an anonymous referee for useful comments. In addition, we thank participants at the annual meeting of IATRC 2009, Scottsville, Arizona, for encouraging comments on an earlier version of this chapter. Financial support from the Research Council of Norway, through the programme Area and Nature-based Industrial Development, is gratefully acknowledged.

support policies in response to new WTO disciplines provides an important indicator of how successful these are likely to be.

2. CURRENT AND PROPOSED WTO RULES FOR AGRICULTURE

One of the major achievements of the Uruguay Round (UR) of negotiations (1986–94) was an agreement on agriculture. Since the signing of the General Agreement on Tariffs and Trade in 1947, agriculture had largely been left out of multilateral trade negotiations. There had been little reduction in the protection provided through tariff and non-tariff trade barriers and support through domestic subsidies (Normile and Simone, 2001).

The UR Agreement on Agriculture (AoA) made modest progress in this regard, resulting in the conversion of non-tariff barriers to bound tariffs with some modest reductions. The AoA introduced limitations on the value of export subsidies and the volume of subsidised exports, and a cap on the value of the most trade-distorting domestic subsidies, again with a modest reduction in that cap. There were also several other innovations, including: a construct called tariff-rate quotas (TRQs) intended to provide a minimal level of market access for imports that would otherwise face prohibitive tariffs; the Aggregate Measurement of Support (AMS) that defines how trade-distorting subsidies are to be measured and how the value of support is to be quantified; and the classification of two categories of subsidy (*blue box* and *green box*) that were to be monitored but not subject to reduction commitments. *Blue box* support includes potentially trade-distorting subsidies that are subject to constraints on production, whereas *green box* support is a category of payments viewed to be minimally distorting for production and trade. The quantification of the total AMS includes all relevant product-specific and non-product-specific support, except when this is below 5 per cent of the corresponding value of production, a threshold defined as *de minimis* support.

Agriculture has continued to occupy a central position in the Doha negotiations. These focus on the three pillars of the UR AoA: domestic support, market access (tariffs and TRQs) and export competition (export subsidies). The AoA is 28 pages long. The summary of the draft modalities prepared by the chair of the WTO agricultural negotiating committee in December 2008 is over four times as long (123 pages). Although commitments in individual country schedules would have to be included in considering the respective lengths of the two agreements, the substantial increase in length of the body of the draft Doha agreement is indicative of the complexity of the new modalities.

Table 1 summarises the main features of the Doha Round proposals. The proposed cuts in domestic support are substantial. The biggest users of domestic support (defined in terms of the value of the total bound AMS in US dollars) have the largest reduction commitment. Norway's total bound AMS is less than US$2

TABLE 1

Summary of Proposed Doha Agricultural Commitments for Developed Countries

1. *Domestic support*[a]
    A. Overall Trade-distorting Domestic Support (OTDS)[b] calculated on the basis of an average for
        1995–2000, to be reduced according to the following:
        80 per cent for base OTDS levels greater than US$60 billion
        70 per cent for base OTDS levels between US$10 and 60 billion
        55 per cent for base OTDS levels less than US$10 billion
    B. Total AMS commitment to be reduced according to the following:
        70 per cent for final bound UR AoA levels of greater than US$40 billion
        60 per cent for levels between US$15 and 40 billion
        45 per cent for levels less than US$15 billion
        Furthermore, developed country members with high relative levels of final bound total AMS (i.e. at
        least 40 per cent of the average total value of agricultural production during 1995–2000) that are in the
        bottom tier (i.e. less than US$15 billion), are required to make an additional reduction of one-half of
        the difference between the reduction rates specified for the two lowest tiers (i.e. 0.5(60 – 45) or 7.5 per
        cent)
    C. Product-specific AMS limits
        AMS support on a product-specific basis will have a base rate calculated as the average for
        1995–2000. In cases where a member introduced product-specific AMS exceeding the *de minimis*
        level, but where the country did not have product-specific AMS support during the base period, the
        limit may be the average value for the two years prior to the adoption of the modalities. In cases
        where product-specific support for each year during the base period was below the *de minimis*, the
        base is the *de minimis* level
    D. *De minimis*
        The *de minimis* levels, either 5 per cent of the total value of agricultural production for non-product-
        specific support or 5 per cent of the total value of production of a basic agricultural product in the
        case of product-specific support, are to be reduced by no less than 50 per cent
    E. Blue box
        The value is capped at 2.5 per cent of the average total value of agricultural production for
        1995–2000. Countries with blue box support exceeding 40 per cent of the OTDS have a reduction
        commitment equal to that for the AMS. Blue box support for individual products is limited to the
        average value during 1995–2000
2. *Market access*
    A. Cuts in UR final bound tariffs according to the following:
        50 per cent for lines with *ad valorem* equivalents greater than 0 and less than or equal to 20 per cent
        57 per cent for lines with *ad valorem* equivalents greater than 20 per cent and less than or equal to 50
        per cent
        64 per cent for lines with *ad valorem* equivalents greater than 50 per cent and less than or equal to 75
        per cent
        70 per cent for lines with *ad valorem* equivalents greater than 75 per cent
        There is also a requirement that the minimum average cut across all final bound tariffs is 54 per cent
        and a tariff ceiling of 100 per cent
    B. Sensitive products
        Of the 1,354 agricultural tariff lines, 4 per cent can be designated as sensitive. An additional 2 per cent
        can be designated sensitive by members that have more than 30 per cent of their tariff lines in the top
        band. There is a requirement for TRQ expansion for sensitive products, depending on the deviation
        from the applicable tiered reduction formula in the final bound tariff rates on products designated as
        sensitive. If tariffs on sensitive products exceed 100 per cent *ad valorem* after the reduction, a higher
        quota expansion of 0.5 per cent of domestic consumption is required on those lines
    C. Other issues: TRQs
        In-quota tariffs are to be reduced either by 50 per cent or to a threshold of 10 per cent, whichever is
        lower. In cases where the TRQ was administered by the MFN bound rate, the member can eliminate
        the tariff quota. There is to be stricter administration of TRQ fill rates. Members have the right to
        request that unused import licences be reallocated to potential users in cases where the quota is not
        filled
3. *Export subsidies are to be eliminated*

Notes:
[a] Special provisions apply to the calculation of product-specific blue box limits for the US and there are some
provisions for shifting product-specific support from the AMS to the blue box (see Blandford et al., 2008). These
are not included in the table.
[b] There is an additional reduction for developed countries with an OTDS exceeding 40 per cent of the value of
production.

Source: WTO (2008b); for domestic support, see also Orden (2008).

billion, placing it in the lowest tier of cuts in domestic support. However, the notified AMS as a share of the value of agricultural production amounted to roughly 58 per cent during 1995–2000, requiring a further cut of 7.5 per cent. A cap on blue box subsidies is also proposed. There is also a new support concept, the *overall trade-distorting support* (OTDS), defined as the total AMS plus 10 per cent of the average total value of agricultural production in the 1995–2000 base period, plus the higher of average blue box payments, or 5 per cent of the average total value of agricultural production, in the 1995–2000 base period. The OTDS is capped and has a reduction commitment. The OTDS is intended to act as a constraint on policymakers' overall ability to support agriculture.

The main principles for the market access proposals are also summarised in Table 1. Under the draft modalities, countries would be required to reduce their highest most-favoured nation (MFN)-bound tariffs (those exceeding 75 per cent *ad valorem*) by 70 per cent and reduce overall MFN rates by 54 per cent. However, under the conditions for designating sensitive products, Norway would have the right to declare 81 product lines as sensitive. These would be subject to smaller tariff reductions, but would require a corresponding increase in any associated market access quota under a TRQ. Finally, the Doha draft modalities call for the phased elimination of export subsidies.

On the surface, the proposed changes seem dramatic for Norway. As we shall demonstrate, both the actual AMS and blue box support are currently high. In addition, border protection is extremely high (WTO, 2001). The applied average tariff on all agricultural products under Chapter 2 of the Harmonized Commodity Description and Coding System of the tariff nomenclature (HS) was 38 per cent in 2004 (WTO, 2004). However, 44 per cent of the bound MFN tariffs are in the range of 100–400 per cent. In addition, Norway has the highest number of TRQs negotiated of any WTO member country, 232 of a WTO total of 1,425. In-quota tariff rates also generally exceed 100 per cent.

Norway has WTO commitments on export subsidies for a range of agricultural products, primarily under the meat and dairy product lines, with the most important being the commitment on cheese. This is because of the absolute volume of subsidised exports involved and the near 100 per cent fill rate for the allowable export quota during 1995–2004. In its most recent export subsidy notification to the WTO (2008a) covering 2005–07, Norway indicated that it continued to use more than 90 per cent of its volume commitment on subsidised cheese exports of 16,208 tons, and 80 per cent, on average, of the commitment on the maximum value of export subsidies of 246 million Norwegian krone (NOK).[1]

---

[1] Norway's notifications to the WTO are reported in NOK. For readers who are unfamiliar with the value of the Norwegian currency, the approximate exchange rate against the USD in February 2010 was 6.00. However, a more representative value of the USD in terms of NOK would be to take the average value over the last 25 years, which is approximately 7.50.

3. THE WTO MODALITIES AND DOMESTIC SUPPORT IN NORWAY

a. How Norway has Adapted to the Uruguay Round

(i) Aggregate measurement of support

As a result of the UR negotiations, Norway established a base (1986–88 average) for its total AMS of NOK 14.3 billion. This was reduced by 20 per cent to NOK 11.4 billion over the implementation period, 1995–2000.

Norway's AMS is composed primarily of market price support, which is measured as the difference between domestic administrative prices and a fixed reference price, multiplied by eligible production. A binding reduction in the AMS would therefore translate into a reduction in administrative prices or eligible production or both.

Figure 1(a) highlights the development in Norway's total AMS through 2004. The bound rate is the kinked line that declines from 1995 to 2000 with the annual reduction commitment under the UR and then levels off at the new ceiling after 2000. The annual AMS, represented by the lower line, is below the bound rate for the entire period but the gap has narrowed, particularly after 2000, suggesting that the bound rate has the potential to become binding. In panel (b), the composition of total support in terms of the various boxes is shown. Total support is the aggregate of the AMS, the blue box and the green box support. Only the AMS and blue box components would be subject to reduction commitments in a Doha Round agreement.

(ii) Blue box support

Schemes classified under the blue box fall under three types: (i) payments based on fixed area and yields; (ii) payments made on 85 per cent or less of the base

FIGURE 1

Domestic Agricultural Support in Norway, 1995–2004

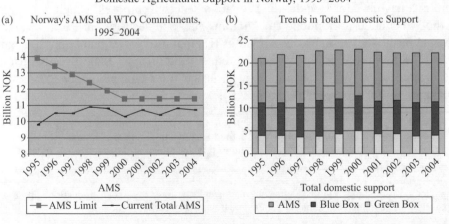

(a)   Norway's AMS and WTO Commitments, 1995–2004

(b)   Trends in Total Domestic Support

level of production; and (iii) livestock payments made on a fixed number of head. As with green box programmes, there was no WTO commitment on the total value of blue box support in the AoA.

From Figure 1(b), it may be seen that the share of blue box support in total Norwegian support is large, amounting to some 25 per cent. Together with the AMS, these two categories constitute roughly two-thirds of overall domestic support. Norway's most prominent blue box measure has been the 'acreage and cultural landscape scheme', a fixed area support payment. But 'headage support', a per unit livestock payment, is almost as high.[2]

(iii) Green box support

Support that has no or minimal production and trade-distorting effects can, according to Annex 2 of the AoA, be placed in the green box category. This type of support must be provided through a publicly funded government programme not involving transfers from consumers, and cannot have the effect of providing price support to producers (Blandford and Josling, 2007). There are no ceilings or reduction commitments on the value of support under the green box. The largest item notified by Norway under the category is the 'vacation and replacement scheme', which provides refunds for farm-related expenses when a farmer takes a vacation. This form of support is not explicitly mentioned in Annex 2. It is quite substantial, accounting for roughly one-third of Norway's green box total. Since, in reality, the scheme can have an effect equivalent to a farm labour subsidy it could be argued that it stimulates production. In addition, payments made under the scheme are based either on the number of animals or the acreage in production, which appears to be inconsistent with the production-neutral requirement of green box support. Member countries could challenge Norway's inclusion of this programme in the green box, requiring that it be notified under the AMS instead.

Another potentially controversial green box measure is the grain price support programme, which according to the government includes two items. The main item is a payment for stockholding for food security purposes, which is notified to the WTO under the 'public stockholding for food security purposes' heading. The payment is given to processing industries that use Norwegian grain. It is paid on a per kilogram basis, and, in effect, reduces the price to domestic grain users. According to the WTO, an important criterion for payments under the 'public stockholding for food security purposes' is:

Expenditures (or revenue foregone) in relation to the accumulation and holding of stocks of products which form an integral part of a food security programme identified in national legislation. This may include government aid to private storage of products as part of such a

---

[2] Smaller measures are 'regional deficiency payments' for milk and meat production. These are categorised as payments based on 85 per cent or less of base-level production.

programme. . . . Food purchases by the government shall be made at current market prices and sales from food security stocks shall be made at no less than the current domestic market price for the product and quality in question (GATT, 1994, p. 58).

The current Norwegian system does not satisfy this condition and its inclusion in the green box is also potentially subject to challenge.

b. The Doha Round Proposals for Domestic Support

Table 2 summarises the proposed commitments for the reduction in Norwegian domestic support, based on the most current draft report on modalities for agriculture prepared by the previous chair of the WTO agriculture committee, Crawford Falconer (WTO, 2008b), corresponding to the formula presented in Table 1. The OTDS value, NOK 21.1 billion, is the sum of the AMS ceiling, 10 per cent of the average value of agricultural production during 1995–2000 and the average blue box value during 1995–2000. Since Norway has a total AMS less than US$15 billion, its AMS reduction commitment is 45 per cent. However, countries such as Norway that have a high AMS as a share of total value of production face an additional 7.5 per cent reduction. This 52.5 per cent requirement means that Norway's total AMS binding has to be reduced from NOK 11.4 billion to NOK 5.4 billion. In addition, Norway currently has more than 40 per cent of its trade-distorting support under blue box measures, which requires the same reduction commitment as for the total AMS. This would reduce the maximum value of blue box support from NOK 7.5 billion to NOK 3.6 billion. Norway would be required to reduce its OTDS by 55 per cent, because the OTDS base is less than $US10 billion, resulting in a commitment of NOK 9.5 billion.[3]

TABLE 2
Current Base Rates of Support and Proposed Commitments (Billion NOK)

Domestic Support	Current Base Rate	Proposed Doha Commitment
AMS	11.4	5.4
Blue box	7.5	3.6
10 per cent of value of production	2.2	–
Overall trade-distorting support (OTDS)	21.1	9.5

Source: Own calculations based on current draft modalities, WTO (2008b) and MAF (2009, p. 9).

[3] It is likely that the NOK 9.5 billion in OTDS under the proposed Doha commitment would act as the binding constraint on domestic support. The sum of the new AMS and blue box ceilings would be NOK 9.0 billion, which is below the OTDS ceiling, and Norway could use the remaining NOK 0.5 billion as non-product-specific de minimis support. Norway began using around NOK 0.1 billion in de minimis support after 2002 (WTO, 2008c).

Norway's current total AMS is around NOK 10 billion. Blue box support has varied between NOK 7 and 8 billion through 2004, yielding an OTDS of roughly NOK 18 billion. Hence, if the proposed Doha Round commitments were to be agreed, the Norwegian agricultural sector would seem to face substantial change since the OTDS would be capped at NOK 9.5 billion. However, there are reasons to believe that the impact of the Doha Round commitments would not be so dramatic. These are discussed in the following sections.

c. Box Shifting

If a country is likely to have problems meeting WTO commitments on trade-distorting support, it may try to redefine its policy measures so that these can be notified as green box. Norway has undertaken considerable preparation to justify such box shifting. The 'acreage and cultural landscape scheme' is an example. This was the largest income-support payment listed under the blue box until 2005. It is supposed to even out differences in profitability among lines of production and farms of varying size. Together with part of the 'headage support', the programme was included in the National Environmental Programme in 2004 (MLSI, 2004, 2005; MAF, 2005, 2006), and re-classified as green box support from 2005 and onwards.[4] This resulted in a decrease in blue box support from an average of roughly NOK 7.5 billion per year during 1995–2004 to under NOK 4 billion from 2005.

d. Following the Japanese Example

In 1997, Japan reduced its notified total AMS substantially by changing its rice policy. Administered prices for rice were eliminated, although the government continued to acquire rice for food security stocks (Godo and Takahashi, 2008). There was little real change in the Japanese rice market since domestic producers were protected by prohibitive tariffs. Many other WTO countries have since lowered their AMS support by abolishing or re-defining the purpose of administered prices, thereby removing market price support from the AMS calculation (Orden, 2008).[5]

---

[4] For a farmer to be eligible for support an environmental plan must be followed and land must be managed in an environmentally friendly manner. The farmer receives a per hectare payment for compliance. There is additional support to help cover the cost of implementing certain types of production techniques, provided on an activity-specific basis. The national regulatory body, the Norwegian Agricultural Authority, has claimed that this support complies with green box criteria. This can be questioned because the green box compliance criteria state that payments can only compensate for additional costs or income foregone through complying with an environmental programme. The 'headage support' was re-classified even though the nature of the payment had not changed.

[5] According to Brink (2008), other countries, notably Australia, EU, Mexico, South Africa, Switzerland and the USA, have adopted this strategy.

When Norway notified its support for 2002–04, it changed the definition of some administered prices.[6] This re-definition had the effect of lowering the market price support component in the total AMS. Without this re-definition, it is likely that Norway would have exceeded its AMS ceiling (Mjørlund and Vårdal, 2008).

The Norwegian Ministry of Agriculture and Food has on several occasions announced that it will abolish certain domestic administered prices, as a means of reducing its AMS. From 1 January 2007, an equivalent reference price for poultry meat replaced the former administered price. In a proposition to the parliament (MAF, 2005), it was argued that this would remove market price support for poultry meat from the AMS calculation and reduce total AMS support by NOK 800 million. In May 2008, in negotiations between the farmers' unions and the Ministry of Agriculture and Food, it was agreed to increase prices on most agricultural products, an action that would likely have violated the AMS ceiling. The problem was solved by replacing administered prices by reference prices for sows, boars and mutton, thereby removing these products from the AMS support calculation. Since the market price support component of the total AMS was NOK 11.1 billion in 2007, Norway has plenty of space to pursue this strategy.

4. AN ASSESSMENT OF THE IMPLICATIONS OF THE DOHA MODALITIES FOR NORWAY

The reduction commitments under any of the three pillars in the Doha modalities could potentially affect Norwegian agricultural policies. For example, consider the effect of eliminating export subsidies for cheese. The inability to provide such subsidies would curtail cheese exports, which are a convenient avenue for removing surplus milk from the domestic market. Hence, the elimination of export subsidies seems to imply a cut in the price of milk to reduce production. This would reduce the market price support component in the AMS. Lower milk production could also reduce income support under the blue box.

Similarly, reductions in tariffs and increases in the market access quotas under TRQs across various product lines should lead to lower domestic prices through increased competition from imports. Therefore, increased market access should result in reductions in measured domestic support. A key issue is the extent to which the export competition and market access modalities would actually reduce

---

[6] In the 2002–04 domestic support notification (WTO, 2008c), the administered milk price was measured at the farm gate level, whereas in earlier notifications it was measured at the dairy-processing level. This accounts for one-third of the discrepancy between the old and new way of notifying. In addition, changes were made in the formulae used for calculating the value of compensation for concentrated feed. This accounts for a further one-third of the discrepancy.

measured support and, by extension, how much additional effort Norway might have to make to meet the Doha bindings summarised in Table 2.

a. The Model

To examine these issues, we use a price-endogenous model of Norwegian agriculture. The model includes the most important commodities produced by the Norwegian agricultural sector. For given input costs, demand functions and support systems, the model computes market-clearing prices and quantities. The model includes all major agricultural policies and generates estimates of production, use of inputs, domestic consumption and prices, imports and exports, measures of support, and economic surplus measured as the sum of producers' and consumers' surplus.[7]

The base year in the model is 2003. Since the structure and size of agricultural production, as well as agricultural support, has been relatively stable over the last decade, this can be viewed as a representative year. The notified AMS in 2003 amounted to 94 per cent of the ceiling set in the UR AoA.

b. Doha Assumptions and Implementation

The main features of the proposed modalities under the most recent draft agreement are summarised in Table 1. The relevant modalities and the assumptions used to determine the implications for Norway are given in Table 3. The final bound AMS as well as the average blue box support in the base period 1995–2000 has to be reduced by 52.5 per cent, whereas the maximum OTDS is to be reduced by 55 per cent. Compared with the levels in the base year, which differ from the base rates, AMS, blue box support and OTDS have to be reduced by 49.7, 52.1 and 47.9 per cent, respectively.

With respect to market access, MFN tariffs for products in the top tier that are not defined as sensitive are subject to a 70 per cent reduction, with a 100 per cent ceiling. For the principal Norwegian products, the 100 per cent ceiling will be binding. However, as pointed out below, since all principal Norwegian products could be defined as sensitive, the 100 per cent ceiling may not be relevant.

Products defined as sensitive are subject to lower tariff reductions, but at the expense of creating new market access opportunities through TRQs, which are additional to the existing TRQs under the UR agreement. We assume that Norway will choose to define 6 per cent of the total number of products listed under the HS at the six-digit level (HS-6) as sensitive. This means that all principal Norwegian products such as grain, meat and milk products are covered as sensitive products.

---

[7] More details and further references can be found in Brunstad et al. (2005). A technical description of the model is given in Brunstad et al. (1995).

TABLE 3
Main Assumptions in the Model

1. *Domestic support*
    A. OTDS: the base rate value of OTDS is reduced by 55 per cent
    B. AMS: the UR bound rate is reduced by 52.5 per cent (45 + 7.5 per cent)
    C. Product-specific AMS: the *de minimis* level based on the average value of production of the basic agricultural product
    D. *De minimis*: product-specific and non-product-specific *de minimis* are reduced by 50 per cent
    E. Blue box: reduced by 52.5 per cent from the 1995–2000 base

2. *Market access*
    A. MFN-bound tariff rates: 70 per cent reduction for the highest tariff lines and 100 per cent tariff ceiling for non-sensitive goods
    B. Sensitive products: the maximum number of tariff lines that qualify as sensitive products under agriculture is 6 per cent (4 plus an extra 2 per cent since Norway has more than 30 per cent of its tariff lines in the top tariff band) based on the total number of HS-6 tariffs lines under agriculture (WTO definition of agriculture)
    C. MFN tariffs for sensitive products: MFN-bound rates reduced by 23.33 per cent (a 2/3 deviation from the otherwise 70 per cent reduction)
    D. TRQ expansion: the market access quota is 6.5–7 per cent of domestic consumption (6 plus an extra 0.5 per cent because all sensitive products have tariff rates exceeding 100 per cent. For the additional 2 per cent of sensitive products from B, TRQs are expanded by an extra 0.5 per cent. This means that the TRQs are 6.5 per cent of domestic consumption for the first 4 per cent of the sensitive products and 7 per cent for the next 2 per cent)
    E. TRQ fill rate: a minimum fill rate of 65 per cent to avoid being challenged by other WTO members

3. *Export subsidies are eliminated*

Source: Gaasland et al. (2008) and WTO (2008b).

The ordinary tariffs for sensitive products are subject to a 23.33 per cent reduction in the MFN tariff rate (i.e. two-thirds deviation from the otherwise 70 per cent reduction), which yields tariffs that are still above 100 per cent. Concessions in the form of new TRQs amount to 6.5 per cent of domestic consumption, but with an additional 0.5 per cent for the additional 2 per cent of the product lines declared as sensitive products. We assume a quota fill rate of 65 per cent; if it were to fall below that level one could expect challenges to be made by other WTO members. Finally, export subsidies are abolished. More details with respect to the implementation of market access are given in Blandford et al. (2009, Appendix 4).

c. Results

The first column in Table 4 shows that domestic support in the base year 2003 was far above the new ceilings generated by the reduction commitments in

TABLE 4
Model Results of WTO Compliance with Proposed Doha Commitments

	Base Solution (1)	Box Shifting (2)	+ Export Subsidy Commitment (3)	+ Market Access Commitment (4)	+ Elimination of Administered Prices (Doha Solution) (5)
Commitment = 100					
AMS	199	199	191	162	56
Blue box	209	114	119	95	100
OTDS	192	157	155	129	69
Base solution = 100					
Production value	100	100	99	78	93
Economic welfare	100	100	105	132	113

Table 3. The total AMS exceeds the new ceilings by 99 per cent, blue support by 109 per cent and the OTDS by 92 per cent. The first strategy to minimise the impact on agricultural activity, which Norway already has followed, is to transfer subsidies from the blue to the green category. In 2005, two years after the base year of our analysis, roughly NOK 3.4 billion previously included in the 'acreage and cultural landscape' (NOK 3 billion) and 'headage support' (NOK 0.4 billion) schemes was shifted from the blue to the green box without any major change in how policy was implemented. The second column in Table 4 reflects this move. Although the value of production and economic welfare are unchanged, the amount of blue box support and the OTDS decrease substantially, with the former now only 14 per cent above the ceiling.

The next question is whether compliance with market access reduction commitments and the elimination of the export subsidy, as reported in Table 3, will be sufficient to bring support levels below the ceilings. The effect of eliminating export subsidies is shown in column (3) of Table 4. The present practice of subsidising exports of cheese by levies on domestic sales of fluid milk is assumed to be abolished. The implication is lower milk production which is accomplished by a cut in the farm gate price of milk. Since that price, interpreted as an administered price, enters into the market price support component of the total AMS, both the AMS and the OTDS are reduced (by 4 per cent and 1 per cent, respectively). Lower milk production and farm gate prices lead to a 1 per cent decline in the total value of agricultural production. However, the 5 per cent increase in economic welfare is indicative of the economic cost of the current policy regime.

If we now simulate the implementation of the market access commitments specified in Table 3, we generate the results in the fourth column of Table 4. Although blue box support is now below the ceiling, the AMS and the OTDS still exceed commitments by 62 per cent and 29 per cent, respectively. In other words, even if Norway complies with the market access and export subsidy commitments, the AMS and the OTDS values will violate their respective ceilings. Also, observe that the production value in agriculture would be 22 per cent below the present level, which suggests that further cuts in the total AMS and OTDS would have a major impact on Norwegian agriculture.

To minimise the effects on the sector, the obvious strategy would be to abolish the administered prices, which, as explained in Section *3d*, will remove market price support as defined by the UR AoA from the AMS calculation.[8] Since 98 per cent of Norway's total AMS is market price support, this provides substantial flexibility to compensate farmers through deficiency payments within the NOK 5.4 billion AMS ceiling specified in Table 2. The results in column (5) show that it is possible to maintain more than 90 per cent of the production value while meeting Doha commitments with safe margins. However, such a change in policy is costly since expensive Norwegian production substitutes for cheaper imports. This is reflected in the drop in the welfare index from 132 in scenario 4 to 113 in scenario 5.[9]

We can conclude that even though the proposed Doha commitments would allow Norway to maintain most of its current agricultural activity level, the framing of its agricultural policy would have to change. The present system of domestic market regulation will be put under pressure when administered prices and export subsidies are eliminated and import options increase. Furthermore, cuts in import tariffs and higher TRQs imply lower farm gate prices, and, consequently, lower market price support. It follows that relatively more of the support has to be provided by taxpayers. Table 5 shows that budgetary support increases, in

TABLE 5
Composition of Support (Billion NOK)

	Base Solution	*Doha Solution*
Budget support	11.3	13.7
Market price support (actual)	8.6	5.4
Total support	19.9	19.1

[8] The *de minimis* quantities in the OTDS would allow Norway a limited amount of additional flexibility if it were to adjust its support levels. For example, Norway could use non-product-specific support amounting to about NOK 1.1 billion providing that total trade-distorting support does not exceed the limit on the OTDS. However, given the amount by which the AMS exceeds its binding in column (4) of Table 4, the support provided under this category would have to be reduced substantially before this would become a viable option.

[9] We make the additional assumption in this scenario that Norway would choose to use its maximum allowable blue box support.

absolute terms, by NOK 2.4 billion, whereas market price support decreases by NOK 3.2 billion. As a result, total support is only NOK 0.8 billion below the base year level.

5. CONCLUSIONS

A major achievement of the UR was to include agriculture in the WTO system of multilateral trade rules. However, the agreement has had only a modest effect on Norway's agricultural production and trade. The agreed constraint on the AMS has not affected Norwegian agricultural programmes. Norway has, in fact, managed to expand agricultural output relative to the 1986–88 base period and the AMS and total support have remained stable during 1995–2004. The most that can be concluded is that there has been some reduction in the 'water' in the inflated binding on the total AMS.

The question raised in this chapter is whether a positive outcome in the ongoing Doha Round will require real policy change. At first sight, the Doha draft modalities appear to be a considerable advance on the weak disciplines in the UR AoA. Norway's total AMS, blue box and OTDS exceed the proposed Doha ceilings by 92–109 per cent, and either elimination of export subsidies or the required increase in market access are sufficient to bring support levels below their ceilings.

However, it is likely that Norway, like many other countries, will try to reduce the AMS and blue box support in ways that involve no major change in policy. First, Norway has already shifted roughly NOK 3.4 billion from the blue box to the green box with only modest changes in the requirements for receiving such support. Second, the market price component of the AMS is being reduced by abolishing administered prices for selected products while maintaining real market price support through market access restrictions. This provides substantial flexibility to compensate producers through deficiency payments within the AMS ceiling.

By using such approaches, our empirical analysis suggests that Norway will be able to maintain most of the current activity in agriculture. However, the framing of agricultural policy will have to change. The present system of domestic market regulation will be put under pressure when export subsidies are eliminated and market access improves. Most important, cuts in import tariffs and expanded TRQ volumes imply lower farm gate prices, and, consequently, lower market price support. Relatively more of the support will have to be provided by taxpayers, and to sustain current agricultural activity budgetary support will have to increase substantially compared with the current level. Such a shift in the use of policy instruments could be challenging for Norwegian policymakers since budgetary support is more transparent than market price support and hence exposed to public scrutiny. Norway's policies may also be more exposed internationally if WTO member countries begin to look more closely at Norwegian notifications and question whether its 'green box' programmes actually meet WTO rules.

In conclusion, on the basis of our analysis, it is difficult to envisage that any fundamental liberalisation of Norwegian agricultural policy will result from the implementation of the Doha Round modalities as currently drafted. Unless Norway decides to implement reform unilaterally, pressure for any real policy change through WTO disciplines will to have to wait for a future round of trade talks.

REFERENCES

Blandford, D. and T. Josling (2007), 'Should the Green Box be Modified?' IPC Discussion Paper, March 2007 (Washington, DC: International Food & Agricultural Trade Policy Council).

Blandford, D., I. Gaasland, R. Garcia and E. Vårdal (2009), 'How Effective are WTO Disciplines on Domestic Support and Market Access for Agriculture?' Working Paper No. 03-2009 (Bergen: Department of Economics, University of Bergen).

Blandford, D., D. Laborde and W. Martin (2008), 'Implications for the United States of the May 2008 Draft Agricultural Modalities', ICTSD Programme on Agricultural Trade and Sustainable Development, June 2008 (Geneva: International Centre for Trade and Sustainable Development).

Brink, L. (2008), 'Market Price Support in the WTO Aggregate Measure of Support', Presentation at the Annual Meeting of the International Agricultural Trade Research Consortium, December, Scottsdale, Arizona.

Brunstad, R. J., I. Gaasland and E. Vårdal (1995), 'A Model for the Agricultural Sector in Norway', Working Paper No. 25/95 (Bergen: Foundation for Research in Economics and Business Administration).

Brunstad, R. J., I. Gaasland and E. Vårdal (2005), 'Multifunctionality of Agriculture: An Inquiry into the Complementarity between Landscape Preservation and Food Security', European Journal of Agricultural Economics, 32, 469–88.

Gaasland, I., R. Garcia and E. Vårdal (2008), 'Norway: Shadow WTO Agricultural Domestic Support Notifications', IFPRI Discussion Paper No. 00812 (Washington, DC: International Food Policy Research Institute).

GATT (1994), The Results of the Uruguay Round of Multilateral Trade Negotiations: The Legal Texts (Geneva: GATT Secretariat).

Godo, Y. and D. Takahashi (2008), 'Japan: Shadow WTO Agricultural Domestic Support Notifications', IFPRI Discussion Paper No. 0822 (Washington, DC: International Food Policy Research Institute).

MAF (2005), Proposition to the Parliament, Nr. 69 (2004–2005) (Norway: Ministry of Agriculture and Food).

MAF (2006), Proposition to the Parliament, Nr. 68 (2005–2006) (Norway: Ministry of Agriculture and Food).

MAF (2009), 'Rapport fra Arbeidsgruppe om Markedsordningene for Kjøtt og egg' ('Report from Working Group on Market Arrangements for Meat and Eggs'). Available at http://www.regjeringen.no/upload/LMD/Vedlegg/brosjyrer_veiledere_rapporter/Rapport%20Markedsordninger%20kjøtt%20og%20egg.pdf (Norway: Ministry of Agriculture and Food).

Mjørlund, R. and E. Vårdal (2008), 'Kjerringa mot Strømmen: Om Norges Tilpasning til WTO-Regelverket' ('Swimming Against the Tide: On Norway's Adaptation to WTO Commitments'), Økonomisk Forum Nr. 9, 2007.

MLSI (2004), Proposition to the Parliament Nr. 66 (2003–2004) (Norway: Ministry of Labour and Social Inclusion).

MLSI (2005), *Proposition to the Parliament Nr. 69 (2004–2005)* (Norway: Ministry of Labour and Social Inclusion).

NILF (2007), *Norwegian Agriculture: Status and Trends, 2007* (Oslo: Norwegian Agricultural Economics Research Institute).

Normile, M. A. and M. Simone (2001), 'AoA Issues Series: Agriculture in the Uruguay Round'. Available at http://www.ers.usda.gov/briefing/WTO/uraa.htm (Washington, DC: Economic Research Service, U.S. Department of Agriculture).

OECD (2009), *Agricultural Policies in OECD Countries: Monitoring and Evaluation, 2009* (Paris: Organisation for Economic Co-operation and Development).

Orden, D. (2008), 'An Overview of WTO Domestic Support Notifications', IFPRI Conference Draft Paper, 14–15 March (Washington, DC: International Food Policy Research Institute).

WTO (2001), 'World Agriculture Negotiations: Proposal by Norway', Document No. G/AG/NG/W/101 (Geneva: World Trade Organization, WTO Secretariat, Committee on Agriculture, Special Session, 16 January).

WTO (2004), 'Trade Policy Review: Norway', Report by the WTO Secretariat, Document No. WT/TPR/S/138 (Geneva: World Trade Organization, Trade Policy Review Body, 13 September).

WTO (2008a), 'Norway: Notification of Export Subsidy Commitments for 2005, 2006 and 2007', Document No. G/AG/N/NOR/49 (Geneva: World Trade Organization, WTO Secretariat, Committee on Agriculture, 14 November).

WTO (2008b), 'Revised Draft Modalities for Agriculture', Document No. TN/AG/W/4/Rev.4 (Geneva: World Trade Organization, WTO Secretariat, Committee on Agriculture, Special Session, 6 December).

WTO (2008c), 'Norway: Notification of Domestic Support Commitments for 2002, 2003 and 2004', Document No. G/AG/N/NOR/47 (Geneva: World Trade Organization, WTO Secretariat, Committee on Agriculture, 22 February).

6

Why Is the Doha Development Agenda Failing? And What Can Be Done? A Computable General Equilibrium–Game Theoretical Approach

Antoine Bouët and David Laborde

1. INTRODUCTION

$\mathbb{T}$HE trade negotiations led under the banner of the Doha Development Agenda (DDA) is complex as highlighted by the Cancún summit on September 2003 and the Geneva meeting in July 2008. This last meeting largely confirmed the perception of the DDA as a failure.[1] During this meeting, Pascal Lamy tried to cut a deal amongst seven countries (European Union (EU), United States (US), China, India, Australia, Japan and Brazil). This initiative has been criticised (see Third World Network, 25 July 2008)[2] because of the fact that the World Trade Organization (WTO) rules call for consensus.[3]

The authors thank Jean-Christophe Bureau, Lionel Fontagné, Gaspar Frontini, Tom Hertel, Sébastien Jean, Will Martin, participants of the 2004 GTAP Conference in Washington DC and the September 2004 AFSE Congress in Paris and two anonymous referees who provided comments on an earlier version of this chapter. The usual disclaimer applies.

[1] *The Economist*, 2 August 2008.
[2] http://www.twnside.org.sg/title2/wto.info/twninfo20080737.htm.
[3] The July 2008 Geneva Group was supposed to identify a compromise representing interests well beyond those of group members.

Another distinctive feature of these negotiations is the emergence of countries' coalitions (like the G20, the G90 or the G10),[4] which play an active role in the bargaining process. A new characteristic also consists in the 'Aid for Trade' package, which, according to the WTO, means further assistance for developing countries 'to increase their capacity to take advantage of more open markets'[5]. Some observers, however, describe this initiative as a financial compensation for countries that are expected to suffer losses under the agreement (see Evenett, 2005b; Stiglitz and Charlton, 2006).

The objective of this chapter is to provide a strategic analysis of these negotiations. In particular, we examine whether these trade negotiations can reach a pro-liberalisation outcome, and if so, which packages may be approved. If no pro-liberalisation outcome is possible, we ask the following questions: Which countries are preventing the achievement of an agreement, and why? Is there any way to change the negotiation rules to achieve a pro-liberalisation outcome? How can we explain the creation of coalitions, and do they thwart the success of the negotiations?

Strategic analysis of international trade negotiations is common in the economic literature. Johnson (1953) studies a tariff equilibrium between two big countries. In a later work, he examines an international trade framework where trading partners exchange reduced production in import-competing sectors for increased production in exporting sectors (Johnson, 1965). Mayer (1981) shows that a domestic conflict of interests may prevent the negotiation of free trade between two big countries. The prisoners' dilemma is used by Riezman (1982) to show that the outcome of a non-cooperative game between big countries is tariff equilibrium. Baldwin and Clarke (1988) analyse the Tokyo Round as a bargaining process between the EU and the US where both trading partners try to minimise an overall welfare loss function. Tyers (1990) identifies policy preferences that are implicit in European and Japanese actual tariff patterns and uses these derived weights and associated objective function to assess which tariff reforms could be negotiated by both countries.

We think that the strategic context of the DDA is far different from that of previous rounds. The large number of players (from 23 in 1947 up to 153 today) and the diversity of economic situations are especially important considering that the WTO rules call for consensus. More importantly, while the outcomes of previous rounds were largely expected to be negotiated between the EU and the US,

---

[4] The G20 gathers 20 emerging countries and least developed countries (LDCs) and is led by Brazil and India and also comprises China and South Africa. It generally plays an active role in favour of agricultural liberalisation. The G90 is a set of 90 poor countries with more defensive pro-poor interests (most African countries are members of this group). The G10 includes 10 countries, mainly from the OECD; these include Japan, South Korea, Taiwan, Iceland, Norway and Switzerland. The G10 primarily seeks to impede agricultural liberalisation.

[5] http://www.wto.org/english/tratop_e/dda_e/background_e.htm.

the number of active participants (Brazil, India and Australia, for example) in the current bargaining process has increased. The immediate question that comes to mind, therefore, is whether these new features explain the stalemate in which these negotiations seem to be since the second half of 2008.

Recent methodological developments allow for a more systematic study of this bargaining process. Thanks to improvements in computation ability, the availability of databases on world macroeconomic variables (e.g. the GTAP database; Dimaranan and McDougall, 2005) and market access (e.g. the Mac-Map-HS6 database; Bouët et al., 2008) and the development of multi-country multi-sector computable general equilibrium (CGE) models, it is possible to simulate numerous scenarios of trade reform and evaluate their impacts on each WTO member. This may be done against the economic theories of negotiation developed by Nash (1953), Shapley (1953) and Kalai and Smorodinsky (1975). Hence, the combination of theoretical developments and modelling capacities allows us to model negotiations amongst numerous countries/regions with microeconomic foundations.

To analyse the potential outcome of the DDA, we use the MIRAGE (Modelling International Relations in Applied General Equilibrium)[6] model of the world economy and recent databases covering market access and domestic support. Unlike traditional studies that begin with a particular scenario, we herein study a set of agreements representative of discussions at the time the Cancún ministerial meeting failed. These include 143 trade shocks that are expected to represent the whole set of negotiations, and are studied with the help of the MIRAGE model. Inside the domain defined by all these potential outcomes, the Nash solution, as defined by the theory of axiomatic bargaining, is selected. The Nash solution defines an efficient and rational solution to any bargaining problem.

We find that a pro-liberalisation agreement is very difficult to achieve because of the heterogeneity of WTO members. There are, however, several possible solutions. For example, the exclusion of small countries improves the efficiency of the negotiation process, regardless of the governments' objectives. The creation of coalitions potentially allows developing countries to act against the solutions selected by rich countries. It may be possible and useful to expand the domain of trade negotiations. Finally, game theory indicates that side payments may be effective, in that actors can maximise the 'size of the cake' for their purposes by using side payments to compensate losers and buy the agreement of each player.

Section 2 presents our methodology. Section 3 broadly characterises the economic impacts of all scenarios. Section 4 applies the theory of cooperative games and introduces three mechanisms for improving the efficiency of the negotiations. Section 5 studies the possibility of coalitions. Section 6 concludes.

---

[6] The MIRAGE model was developed at the Centre d'Etudes Prospectives et d'Informations Internationales (CEPII) in Paris. A full description of the model is available in Decreux and Valin (2007).

2. METHODOLOGY

a. Model and Data

This study uses the MIRAGE model of the world economy to assess economic consequences of various trade reforms. The MIRAGE model is a multi-national multi-sector CGE model (see Decreux and Valin, 2007). In this study, the MIRAGE model is used under its static version, with a perfect competition hypothesis and without modelling foreign direct investment. The main purpose of this modelling scenario is to simulate many potential trade reforms and to represent as exhaustively as possible the entire domain of negotiation. We use perfect competition instead of imperfect competition as the latter framework necessitates supplementary data (number of firms, mark-up and magnitude of scale economies) for calibration purposes which are difficult to gather for many regions. At the same time, this theoretical option can deeply affect the impact of a trade reform (see Tongeren et al., 2001). The use of the static version is also justified by the fact that we are not interested in the dynamics of the reform, but only in the long-term impact on various regions.

The first source of data is GTAP6.1 (Dimaranan and McDougall, 2005), which provides world macroeconomic accounts and trade flows for the year 2001. Notably, we seek to describe the complexity of the negotiations at the beginning of the process. Of course, it would be worthwhile to study whether the current trade features have made the negotiations even more difficult than they were at the beginning of the process. However, we contend that the main reasons for the present stalemate are:

1. The large number of participants with heterogeneous economic and trade characteristics.
2. The dispersion of protection and other distortions across sectors.
3. The existence of trade preferences and regional agreements that generate preferential access.

When considering these three points, no major change has occurred in the world trading system since 2001, even where new policies have been put in place (e.g. the US Farm Bills implemented in 2002 and 2008, the Economic Partnership Agreements, the recent developments in the European Common Agricultural Policies, etc.).[7] On the contrary, the current negotiations focused on narrower issues. Starting with the 2004 July Package, the broad features of the modalities have been defined and the remaining controversial issues are more oriented on the flexibilities to be given to rich and developing countries, including sensitive and

---

[7] Our baseline takes into consideration the US Farm Bill in place in 2001 and the Everything But Arms (EBA) initiative.

special products and special safeguard mechanisms. As they address very particular political economy problems, introducing them in the analytical framework
presented here will bring limited insights.

The market access data come from the MAcMap-HS6 version 1 database
(Bouët et al., 2008), which measures protection in 2001 and includes all regional
agreements and trade preferences existing to this date. A database on bound duties
(Bchir et al., 2006) has been also developed to apply tariff formulae on bound
duties instead of applied duties. Accounting for the binding overhang effect is
particularly important in the case of developing countries for which binding overhang is often large. A database on domestic support has also been constructed from
the OECD's data on production subsidy equivalent as the traditional aggregated
measure of support relies upon old world prices data. This database takes into
account trends in agricultural policies established by the Farm Bill in place in
2001 and Agenda 2000. Existing databases on market access in services (Hoekman,
1996; Francois and Hoekman, 1999; Kalirajan et al., 2000; Trewin, 2000) are
incomplete and not enough reliable to be the basis of a systematic analysis of
WTO negotiation. In the GTAP database, protection in services is insufficiently
assessed. Frequency indices are very informative but do not fully account for the
complexity of trade barriers in this sector (see Chen and Schembri, 2002). To cope
with this lack of data, we impose a uniform *ad valorem* tax of 20 per cent in all
countries and in all business service activities. It is a transaction cost that generates
rents for economic agents in the importing country. As we acknowledge that using
a homogeneous 20 per cent tax on business services is a very crude modelling
approach, we present results with and without this modelling element to check
how it affects results.

Our initial expectation is that the heterogeneity of negotiating countries could
lead to a DDA failure. Therefore, when selecting the strategy of geographical
decomposition to be used for this work, we give priority to analysing the structural
diversity of the various WTO members. Of course, the geographic decomposition
is a key element of the methodological design of the study. We think that the main
elements that determine a country's stance in the negotiations are: (i) the average
level of tràde-related distortions that affect its imports and its exports; (ii) the
sector and partner dispersion of its protection; (iii) its economic size and dependence on trade; and (iv) its product and geographic concentration of imports and
exports.

On the basis of the GTAP6.1 database, we select countries which are specific
either in terms of trade specialisation (Brazil and Argentina, agriculture vs China
and Bangladesh, industry vs India, services), or in terms of preferential access
received (Bangladesh which is beneficiary of the EBA initiative vs China, India,
Indonesia and Thailand which are not; Mexico and Canada with their preferential
access to the US vs all other OECD countries), or preferential access given
(the EU vs Japan and Australia), or geographic structure of trade flows (all the

continents are represented). Another element is the structure of protection, in terms of average level (OECD vs middle-income countries vs low-income countries), of sector dispersion of protection (EU, Japan, Korea, Taiwan vs US). We also account for the diversity in economic size and dependence on trade (Bangladesh vs China and India, New Zealand and Chile vs US and EU).

Table 1 presents the geographic decomposition. Considering the inter-country/ region trade and protection, this decomposition captures 95.5 per cent of the world tariff revenue (which can be considered as a measure of the global distortion in play) and 71.3 per cent of world trade (which is the macroeconomic variable affected by the distortion).[8] It appears a solid basis for our modelling exercise.

The sector decomposition focuses on agriculture and identifies 23 sectors, 10 of which are agricultural (see Table 2). In agriculture, sectors where distortions are large are rice, sugar, cereals n.e.c. (not elsewhere classified), livestock and meat, meat products, milk and dairy products. In industry, these are mainly textile and wearing.

b. The Objective of Trade Negotiators

A strict definition of national objectives is necessary for analytical purposes. Those objectives have to represent the elements taken into account by negotiators. It leads us to consider four indicators in this study: (i) the Hicksian equivalent variation of the representative agent (this indicator has often been adopted in the literature and has robust microeconomic foundations; but it means that consumers' interests are as weighted in the government's objective as producers' interests and public receipts); (ii) real gross domestic product (GDP) is often cited as an objective by negotiators, but it lacks microeconomic foundations; (iii) maximisation of exports is a mercantilist objective, frequently quoted by negotiators; and (iv) the terms of trade is another mercantilist objective.

These objectives appear to be gross approximation but we will limit our analysis to these four objectives as it would be unviable to design a political model adapted to every WTO member. It could be argued that real GDP and welfare are very close objectives. In fact, if trade is initially balanced, we find that change in Hicksian variation as a share of initial expenditure is the change in nominal GDP deflated by the change in the cost of expenditure. However, trade is not initially balanced in our modelling exercise. Moreover, we define real GDP here by deflating nominal GDP by production prices, and not the cost of expenditure.

Optimising terms of trade is an important objective, and is considered politically important by authors such as Bagwell and Staiger (1999). Terms of trade are usually improved when trading partners liberalise. When only one country

---

[8] These calculations have been realised using the MAcMap-HS6 database.

TABLE 1
Geographic Decomposition

Region	GTAP Code	Coalition
Argentina	arg – Argentina	G22/Cairns
Australia	aus – Australia	Cairns
Bang	bgd – Bangladesh	G90
Brazil	bra – Brazil	G22/Cairns
Canada	can – Canada	Cairns
Chile	chl – Chile	G22/Cairns
China	chn – China	G22
CIS	rus – Russia, xsu – Rest of Former Soviet Union	
EFTA	che – Switzerland, xef – Rest of EFTA	G10
EU25	aut, bel, dnk, fin, fra, deu, gbr, grc, irl, ita, lux, nld, prt, esp, swe, cyp, cze, hun, mlt, pol, svk, svn, est, lva, ltu – 25 countries of the European Union	
India	ind – India	G22
Indonesia	idn – Indonesia	Cairns
Japan	jpn – Japan	G10
Korea_Tw	kor – South Korea, twn – Taiwan	G10
MeditCount/	tur – Turkey, xme – Rest of Middle East, mar – Morocco, xnf – Rest of North Africa	G90
Mexico	mex – Mexico	G22
NewZealand	nzl – New Zealand	Cairns
RoAsia	xea – Rest of East Asia, mys – Malaysia, phl – Philippines, vnm – Vietnam, xse – Rest of Southeast Asia, lka – Sri Lanka, xsa – Rest of Asia	
RoCentAm	Rest of Central America and of the Caribbean	G22
RoSouAm	Rest of South America	G22
ROW	xoc – Rest of Oceania, hkg – Hong Kong, sgp – Singapore, xna – Rest of North America, col – Colombia, per – Peru, ven – Venezuela, ury – Uruguay, xsm – Rest of South America, xer – Rest of Europe, alb – Albania, bgr – Bulgaria, hrv – Croatia, rom – Romania	
SouthAfrica	bwa – Botswana, zaf – South Africa, xsc –Rest of South Africa Customs Union	G90/G22/Cairns
SubSahAf	mwi – Malawi, moz – Mozambique, tza – Tanzania, zmb – Zambia, zwe – Zimbabwe, mdg – Madagascar, uga – Uganda, xss – Rest of Sub-Saharan Africa	G90
Thailand	tha – Thailand	G22/Cairns
US	usa – United States	

Notes:
'Bang', Bangladesh; 'CIS', Commonwealth of Independent States; 'EFTA', European Free Trade Association; 'EU25', European Union 25 countries; 'Korea-Tw', South Korea-Taiwan; 'MediterraneanCo.', Mediterranean countries; 'RoCentAm', Rest of Central America; 'RoAsia', Rest of Asia; 'RoSouAm', Rest of South America; 'ROW', Rest of the World; 'SouthAfrica', South Africa; 'SubSahAf', Sub-Saharan Africa.

TABLE 2
Sector Decomposition

Sector Code	Description	GTAP Code
Agri_ind	Food products, not elsewhere classified	ofd, vol
Bev_Tob	Beverages and tobacco	b_t
Bus_serv	Business services	isr, obs, ofi
Cereals nec	Cereals, not elsewhere classified	gro, wht
Chim_ind	Chemical industry	crp, p_c
Dairy_prod	Milk and dairy products	mil, rmk
Electronic	Electronic	ome
Lvst_Meat	Livestock and meat	ctl, oap
Mach_ind	Equipment goods	omf
Meat	Meat products	cmt, omt
Metal_ind	Metal industry	fmp, i_s, nfm
OthCrop	Other crops, not elsewhere classified	ocr, osd, pfb
OthInd	Other industries	ely, nmm
OthPrim	Other primary products	coa, frs, fsh, gas, oil, omn, wol
OthServ	Other services	cns, dwe, gdt, osg, ros, trd, wtr, ele
Rice	Rice	pcr, pdr
Sugar	Sugar	c_b, sgr
Textiles	Textile	tex
Tran_ind	Transportation industry	mvh, otn
Trans_com	Transportation and telecommunication	atp, cmn, otp, wtp
Veg_fruit	Vegetable and fruit	v_f
Wearing	Wearing apparel	lea, wap
Wood_paper	Wood and paper	lum, ppp

Note:
See the GTAP website for a full description of GTAP sectors and GTAP code.

liberalises and others do not, its terms of trade deteriorate, whereas a country that does not liberalise while others do may experience deterioration of its terms of trade because of its initial free access to foreign markets (this is the situation created by eroded preferences). In this sense, optimising terms of trade can accurately characterise the mercantilist spirit of trade negotiators. It is possible to consider a trade reform wherein all WTO members receive improved terms of trade, in that the WTO does not comprise all countries in the world. Of course, this case is less conceivable given an international organisation composed of 153 countries rather than the 23 present at the first negotiation.

c. Scenarios

A set of trade shocks is simulated to give a fairly correct representation of what could be negotiated under the DDA at the time of the launching of this negotiation and what the fundamental interests of WTO members are. From this point of view,

TABLE 3
Definition of Scenarios

Value	Domain			
	A	B	C	D
	Services	NAMA	AMA	Export Subsidies
0	Status quo	Status quo	Status quo	Status quo
1	Reduction by 50%	$a = 10\%$	$a = 25\%$	Reduction by 75%
2	n.a.	$a = 10\% + SDT$	$a = 25\% + SDT$	n.a.
3	n.a.	$a = 5\%$	$a = 15\%$	n.a.
4	n.a.	$a = 5\%þSDT$	$a = 15\% + SDT$	n.a.
5	n.a.	0-0	Linear formula + SDT	n.a.

Note:
'n.a.', not available.

it would not be correct to design numerous scenarios around the last modalities published in 2008, as that would not reflect the real problems associated with these negotiations since the beginning of the process. On the contrary, we have to design scenarios around the main dimensions that were discussed during the first years of the round. Five key dimensions of the negotiation are emphasised through the design of these shocks: (i) the extent to which import duties are cut; (ii) the degree of harmonisation (progressivity) adopted in the tariff reduction formulae; (iii) the provision of special and differential treatment (SDT); (iv) global- or sector-level negotiation; and (v) cut in export subsidies.

We consider services (A), industry (called NAMA for non-agricultural market access – B), agriculture (called AMA for agricultural market access – C) and reduction of export subsidies (D; see Table 3). We suppose that liberalisation in services takes the form of a reduction by 50 per cent in the transaction cost previously defined. As far as industry is concerned, on one hand, two Swiss formulae are simulated with coefficients $a = 5$ and 10 per cent. On the other hand, the agreement either includes an SDT or it does not. In case of SDT, the coefficient of the Swiss formula is doubled for developing countries, tripled for least developed countries (LDC), implying a reduced extent to which market access is improved in those countries. Finally, a complete liberalisation in the textile apparel sector is tested. This '0 for 0 option' is added to a scenario with a 5 per cent Swiss formula in other industrial sectors and without SDT. In agriculture, two Swiss formulae are also considered, with less harmonising coefficients ($a = 15$ and 30 per cent). SDT is also tested in the same way as for industry. As the EU proposed a linear reduction of import duties, by a 33 per cent coefficient, this non-harmonising formula is simulated. In this case, the coefficient is 25 per cent for developing countries and 15 per cent for LDC. Finally, concerning export subsidies, a cut by 75 per cent is considered.

In all trade shocks, duties less than 3 per cent are annulled. From a global point of view, 143 trade shocks are simulated. To facilitate identification, the following code is adopted (see Table 3). A trade shock is notified as sABCD with A, B, C and D being integers which belong to {0, 1, 2, 3, 4, 5}. For instance, the trade shock s0121 means (see Table 3): (i) the status quo in services; (ii) a Swiss formula in NAMA with a 10 per cent coefficient and no SDT; (iii) a Swiss formula in AMA with a 25 per cent coefficient and with SDT; and (iv) a reduction in export subsidies by 75 per cent.

3. ASSESSING ECONOMIC IMPACTS OF POTENTIAL REFORMS

The impact of the five modalities on protection applied is shown in Table 4 with the split between AMA and NAMA.

The trade reforms that maximise world gains in terms of Hicksian equivalent variation or GDP are presented in Table 5: s1531 is a liberalisation in services, a very harmonising Swiss formula without SDT in industry and agriculture, with a '0 for 0' option in textile and apparel and a 75 per cent reduction in export subsidies. It implies the largest increase in world welfare. This optimum is s0531, when excluding negotiation in services. If the criterion is the augmentation of exports, the best scenario is s1530 under which export subsidies are not cut. These gains are comparable with those obtained in similar studies (Bchir et al., 2005): US$105 billion as far as the most liberalising scenario is adopted.

The examination of results implied by each scenario leads to several conclusions.

- A major part of world gains come from agricultural liberalisation, because of the high level of initial protection. This confirms conclusions of other studies, like Van der Mensbrugghe and Beghin (2004), Francois et al. (2005) or Hertel and Keeney (2006).
- Gains coming from the liberalising industry are smaller. In the best-case scenario they add up to US$14 billion. It corresponds to a very harmonising Swiss formula, without SDT and with a '0 for 0' option in textile and apparel. A smaller initial protection explains these limited gains. Moreover, tariff peaks are less frequent.
- Gains are over-additive; the sum of gains coming from elementary shocks is inferior to that derived from the scenario in which all these shocks are combined.
- A cut in export subsidies is all the more fruitful as it is combined with a reduction in agricultural tariffs.

TABLE 4
Impact of Various Tariff Cuts on Applied Import Duties

Region	Per cent										
	Initial Level		Case 1		Case 2		Case 3		Case 4		Case 5
	AMA	NAMA	AMA	NAMA	AMA	NAMA	AMA	NAMA	AMA	NAMA	AMA
Argentina	11.8	12.7	10.6	6.9	11.7	10.0	8.8	4.3	11.0	6.9	11.8
Australia	3.1	5.4	2.2	3.0	2.2	3.0	1.9	2.1	1.9	2.1	2.2
Bangladesh	19.4	15.7	13.4	1.8	18.8	2.2	9.5	1.5	18.1	2.2	19.3
Brazil	11.1	12.5	9.6	6.5	10.9	9.4	7.8	4.0	10.1	6.5	11.1
Canada	23.2	2.9	6.0	1.7	6.0	1.7	4.3	1.3	4.3	1.3	15.7
Chile	7.0	6.8	7.0	6.8	7.0	6.8	7.0	4.3	7.0	6.8	7.0
China	23.5	7.4	9.9	3.7	12.9	4.8	7.7	2.7	10.7	3.7	18.5
CIS	16.9	8.8	16.8	8.8	16.9	8.8	16.8	8.8	16.9	8.8	16.9
EFTA	60.0	1.5	11.9	0.6	11.9	0.6	8.2	0.4	8.2	0.4	50.9
EU25	24.4	2.4	7.7	1.3	7.7	1.3	5.6	0.9	5.6	0.9	17.2
India	57.2	30.0	19.8	6.9	31.1	10.4	13.8	4.5	22.5	7.0	48.6
Indonesia	11.4	6.0	5.9	3.2	6.9	3.9	4.8	2.3	6.2	3.2	9.9
Japan	49.9	1.7	11.0	0.9	11.0	0.9	7.8	0.7	7.8	0.7	43.0
MediterraneanCo.	28.3	7.6	12.4	5.3	14.6	5.7	10.0	4.8	12.0	5.2	26.4
Mexico	41.1	10.4	14.2	5.3	19.5	7.6	10.7	3.5	15.6	5.3	34.3
New Zealand	2.3	2.8	1.9	2.5	1.9	2.5	1.9	1.9	1.9	1.9	2.1
Rest of Asia	16.0	9.6	8.2	3.4	9.3	4.1	7.5	2.9	8.6	3.5	15.4
RofWorld	5.2	1.9	3.7	1.2	3.9	1.4	3.2	1.0	3.5	1.2	4.9
RofCentAm	16.8	4.7	9.2	3.0	11.6	3.7	7.2	2.1	9.9	3.0	14.8
RofSouAm	15.7	11.0	11.7	8.6	13.5	9.7	9.7	7.4	12.0	8.5	15.2
SouthAfrica	21.8	7.3	7.9	3.1	10.1	4.3	6.2	2.0	8.6	3.1	21.6
S. Korea-Taiwan	41.8	7.8	11.2	3.3	11.2	3.3	8.2	2.3	8.2	2.3	29.7
SubSahAf	17.9	12.2	13.0	2.5	15.6	3.0	9.9	2.1	14.6	2.7	17.9
Thailand	27.1	11.5	14.0	3.8	19.1	5.2	10.4	2.6	15.4	3.8	23.4
United States	5.5	2.2	3.1	1.0	3.1	1.0	2.5	0.7	2.5	0.7	4.3

Notes:

Reference group weights. Please refer to notes in Table 1 for definition of abbreviations used.

Sources: MAcMap-HS6v1 and authors' calculations.

TABLE 5
World Optimum

	With Liberalisation in Services	Without Liberalisation in Services
Optimal scenario	s1531	s0531
Equivalent variation	US$105.05 billion or +0.33%	US$93.8 billion or 0.29%
Real GDP	US$127.21 billion or 0.41%	US$114.99 billion or 0.37%

Notes:

s1531 implies liberalisation in services, the strongest liberalisation ($a = 5$ per cent) in non-agricultural market access including the 0-0 in textile and wearing, the strongest liberalisation ($a = 15$ per cent) in agricultural market access and the reduction of export subsidies. s0531 is the same scenario without services liberalisation.

Source: Authors' calculation.

FIGURE 1

Distribution of Scenarios by Simple Average and Standard Deviation of Country Gains

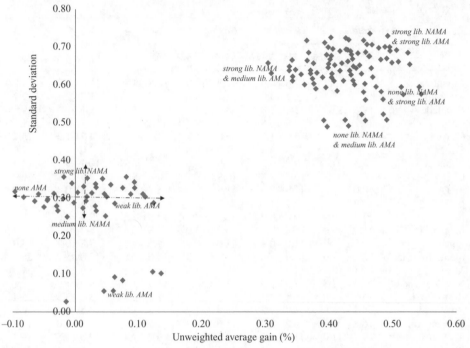

Notes:
'strong lib. NAMA', strong liberalisation in NAMA; 'none AMA', no liberalisation in AMA; 'medium lib. NAMA', medium liberalisation in NAMA; 'weak lib. AMA', weak liberalisation in AMA; 'none lib. NAMA & medium lib. AMA', no liberalisation in NAMA and medium liberalisation in AMA; 'none lib. NAMA & strong lib. AMA', no liberalisation in NAMA and strong liberalisation in AMA; 'strong lib. NAMA & medium lib. AMA', strong liberalisation in NAMA and medium liberalisation in AMA; 'strong lib. NAMA & strong lib. AMA', strong liberalisation in NAMA and strong liberalisation in AMA. 'NAMA' indicates non-agricultural market access and 'AMA' agricultural market access.

Source: Authors' calculation.

Figure 1 shows each scenario according to two characteristics: the unweighted average welfare gain in percentage of initial real income (horizontal axis), and the standard error of the welfare gains in the countries/regions (vertical axis). In the lower left corner of Figure 1, we see a set of 47 trade reforms characterised by negative or low unweighted average gains and low standard deviations. One common characteristic of these scenarios is that they yield a relatively small global gain for the world economy (the maximum is US$41.2 billion). In contrast, the minimum global gain predicted for the set of trade reforms located in the upper right corner is US$68.5 billion. Thus, we see that the larger the world gain, the more unequal its distribution.

All the trade reforms in the lower left corner of the graph are not only characterised by relatively low global gains for the world economy, but also relatively
small standard deviations and small unweighted average gains. Reforms leading
to negative unweighted average gains are projected to hurt many countries/regions
through losses and/or hurt some countries with large relative losses. All these
reforms lack liberalisation in agriculture or include a linear tariff reduction in this
sector. The distribution of welfare gains varies according to the modalities of each
liberalisation scenario. For instance, while generating the same increase in world
welfare (US$14 billion, i.e. a growth rate of 0.04 per cent), the scenarios of agri-
cultural liberalisation under a linear formula (s0050) or a large industrial liberalisation (s0500) give contrasting pictures in terms of distribution. In the first case,
total real income gain is more evenly shared out amongst players (whatever their
economic size), the per cent unweighted average gain is greater than the world
gain and the standard deviation is somewhat low. In the second case, industrial
liberalisation benefits the richest countries/regions, such that the percentage of
unweighted average gain is negative, whereas the world gain is positive. The
standard deviation is about four-fold higher.

Conversely, all reforms located in the upper right corner of the graph are characterised by a Swiss formula in agriculture, with or without SDT. For all scenarios
in the upper right corner of the graph where a Swiss formula is applied on agricultural tariffs, the standard deviation of gains is high, but the unweighted average
gain (in per cent) is greater than the global gain for the world economy, implying
that these reforms are supported by numerous countries/regions and large coun-
tries/regions do not capture most of the gains.

The uneven distribution of the gains is understandable if we consider that the
main effects are driven by agricultural liberalisation. First, the cost of protection
is quadratic for importing countries/regions. Therefore, we expect the gains to be
concentrated in regions where the distortions were initially high. Second, for
exporters, two complementary effects are in play, particularly for agricultural
liberalisation. (i) The elimination of tariff peaks creates strong losses for exporters
who initially enjoyed preferential access, but strong gains for non-preferred
exporters; in this sense, developing countries/regions have contrasting interests.
Furthermore, if agricultural liberalisation drives the majority of the gains, such
gains will be concentrated in countries/regions with stronger comparative advantages in this sector (e.g. the Cairns Group). (ii) In addition, the terms of trade will
affect food prices, thereby creating opposite effects on net importers and net
exporters of food products. Thus, liberalisation of industry alone yields an unfair
distribution of gains, whereas liberalisation of agriculture alone confers large gains
to numerous countries/regions, but these are more unequally distributed. Combining
the two options increases the size of the cake, but with an even more unequal
distribution (s1530). Therefore, agricultural liberalisation is crucial to make the
game politically acceptable.

4. MODELLING THE BARGAINING PROCESS

Based on game theory, this section describes trade negotiations as a cooperative bargaining process between players. The Nash solution is presented, according to several hypotheses about bargaining powers.

a. The Nash Solution

The Nash solution is characterised by the following features: the outcome is individually rational (no player is losing relatively to the pre-negotiation situation, called the 'threat point'); the outcome is Pareto-optimal (there is no negotiable outcome unanimously preferred); the outcome may be democratic or may reflect a given distribution of power between players (bargaining powers); unlike other axiomatic approaches (egalitarian solution, utilitarian solution, Kalai Smorodinsky solution), the Nash solution fulfils a set of other properties: independence of irrelevant alternatives, independence to a change of units, weak Pareto constraint and symmetry (Mas-Colell et al., 1995).

The Nash solution should not be confused with the concept of Nash equilibrium: (i) the *Nash equilibrium* applies to *non-cooperative games* and states that the outcome of a game where players do not cooperate is a situation where nobody has any interest to change his/her strategy as long as all other players do not change their own strategy; (ii) the *Nash solution* applies to *cooperative games* and states that the issue of a negotiation should be individually rational and Pareto-optimal, as just defined earlier.

Let us consider that the trade negotiation is a bargaining process between 25 zones on 143 potential outcomes. Let W_0^m be the region m's initial 'payment' in the case non-agreement is reached, $W^m(s)$ its payment when the outcome s is adopted and S the set of the 143 feasible outcomes. We assume that in case of failure of the bargaining game, the outcome (also called threat point) is the status quo, that is, $W^m(s) = W_0^m$, for all m. However, we can also imagine other cases, as follows:

1. Countries/regions start trade wars, increasing their applied duties to the maximum allowed by their bound duties (or even further). This alternative would require us to model and solve the Nash non-cooperative game across the 25 countries/regions.
2. Countries/regions decide to negotiate preferential agreements. In this case, we would have to define an optimal trade agreement for each of the 25 countries/regions with any combinations of the 24 other countries/regions, as well as potential agreements with third parties.

These two alternatives would require strenuous calculations that are beyond the scope of the current analysis. Here, we seek to understand, within a simple framework, the stalemate in which the trade negotiations have been stalled since 2001. Bouët and Laborde (2008) investigate the potential outcome of DDA failure, but the alternative scenarios they used are *ad hoc* and inconsistent with the game-theory approach discussed herein.

(i) The Nash solution without bargaining power

In a first stage, we consider that all regions participate in negotiations and have an identical bargaining power,[9] whatever their geographical, population and economic size are. The Nash solution is:

$$s* \in \arg_{s \in S} \max G(s) = \prod_m \left(W^m(s) - W_0^m \right), \tag{1}$$

with

$$W^m(s*) - W_0^m \geq 0, \quad \text{for all } m. \tag{2}$$

Condition (2) ensures that the solution will be individually rational.

Table 6 shows the different Nash solutions according to the objective adopted by governments and the negotiation rule defined by equations (1) and (2). The first row gives the Nash solutions when the 25 zones have identical bargaining

TABLE 6
Nash Solutions of the Cooperative Game

	Equivalent Variation	Real GDP	Exports	Terms of Trade
1 region, 1 voice	s1000	s1520	s1530	No solution
1 country, 1 voice	s1000	s1510	s1530	No solution
Economic weight	s1000	s1551	s1530	No solution

Notes:
s1000 is a status quo with only a liberalisation in services (a net gain for everyone in our modelling). s1510 implies liberalisation in services, the strongest liberalisation ($a = 5$ per cent) in non-agricultural market access (NAMA) including the 0-0 in textile, a moderate liberalisation ($a = 25$ per cent + SDT) in agricultural market access (AMA) and no export subsidies reduction. s1520 differs from s1510 by the introduction of special and differential treatment (SDT) in agriculture. On the contrary, s1530 is the same scenario but the AMA liberalisation is the strongest ($a = 15$ per cent, no SDT). s1551 implies liberalisation in services, the strongest liberalisation ($a = 5$ per cent) in NAMA including the 0-0 in textile and wearing, the weakest liberalisation (linear reduction) in AMA and the reduction of export subsidies. s0531 is the same scenario without services liberalisation.

Source: Authors' calculation.

---

[9] The objective function defined by equation (1) is a product of regions' changes in welfare; each element can be weighted either by the population of the region, the number of countries composing the region or economic size of the region (see next subsection). If we do not weigh these differences, regions have identical bargaining power.

power, the second row when each country has the same power (democratic weights – see next subsection) and the third row when zones have bargaining power (see next subsection) proportional to their economic size (GDP – CHELEM database,[10] 2001).

When maximising exports, the Nash solution represents a very ambitious degree of liberalisation (s1530) that benefits all players. Optimising terms of trade is not a sustainable objective, as this criterion features a purely mercantilist world where international liberalisation is a constant sum game and where no Paretian improvement is feasible. In our study, the only possible solution under this objective would be a situation in which all WTO members agree on a reform that improves their terms of trade while deteriorating those of non-WTO members. When maximising equivalent variation, the outcome is the status quo, except for liberalisation of services, which gives every player a welfare gain. Considering that our modelling of services is relatively limited, we can focus on the result without services. In this case, negotiation reaches a stalemate. If governments maximise GDP, it is likely that industry will be hugely liberalised but market access in agriculture will be only slightly improved.

As far as the objective of equivalent variation is concerned, Bangladesh clearly plays a key role in trade negotiations, as this country does not see improvement of its equivalent variation under numerous scenarios, because of deterioration of terms of trade and erosion of preferential margins. This illustrates the position of numerous developing countries/regions that have been granted significant preferences in rich and large markets and are highly specialised in a few products. Thus, our results suggest that the position of such countries forms the underlying basis for the stalemate of trade negotiations.

In the absence of bargaining power, each player has the same influence. However, our definition of a player follows the countries/regions modelled herein, meaning that our disaggregation scheme introduces a bias into the structure of the game. By introducing bargaining power based on measurable country/region features, we can correct for the arbitrary choices inherent in our disaggregation.

(ii) The Nash solution with bargaining power

The cooperative game theory allows for taking into account bargaining powers. It is possible to introduce differentiated bargaining powers in the Nash axiomatic approach. We modify equation (1) by weighting each player's surplus by α_m. The Nash solution is given by:

$$s^* \in \arg_{s \in S} \max G(s) = \prod_m \left(W^m(s) - W_0^m(s) \right)^{\alpha_m} \qquad (3)$$

under the same individual rationality constraint expressed by equation (2).

---

[10] http://www.cepii.fr/anglaisgraph/bdd/chelem.htm.

Two alternative weights are considered:

- α_m equals the number of voices at WTO for each zone (one voice for the US and the EU, two for the Korea/Taiwan zone, 11 for the Mediterranean countries, etc.). This weighting structure is qualified as a 'democratic'[11] system.
- α_m equals the share of the zone in the world GDP. This is the economic power.

Several elements justify giving larger countries a larger bargaining power: (i) multilateral trade negotiation is a bargaining process upon market access and opening the access to large and rich countries is a real priority for all players; (ii) big countries have a strong bargaining power as their threat of retaliation is potentially detrimental; (iii) big countries have a higher capacity to understand the impact of the various reforms and they can more easily influence other WTO members on non-trade issues.

The last two rows of Table 6 present the results when we use these weights. Only the Nash solution under real GDP criterion is modified when weights are included. In a democratic context, the same solution is adopted, except that it does not include SDT in agriculture. This option has a restrictive impact on South–South trade. When they have a greater decisional power, it is abandoned. On the contrary, when an economic weighting system is adopted, the s1551 is agreed. This is clearly a compromise between the EU, Japan and other industrialised countries. The US maximises GDP when s1500 is adopted; that is, large openness of industry and services.

If exports and GDP are not consistent objectives for trade negotiators, the main conclusion of this section is that a status quo is highly probable. In the following subsections, three ways out are considered: the exclusion of some players, the implementation of side payments and the extension of the domain of negotiation.

b. Excluding Some Players

A key reason for the Doha stalemate is obviously the number of negotiating members which adds constraints to the bargaining programme. As a consequence, a solution would be to exclude some members from the negotiating process. Several points support this view: (i) trade negotiation between more than 150 countries is an extremely difficult task as countries' preferences are quite different; (ii) trade negotiations require human and technical resources, which only rich countries have; (iii) an interpretation of the current situation, when considering the fact that neither LDCs nor small and vulnerable economies (SVEs) have to liberalise is that they are not officially excluded from the negotiation, but have no

---

[11] 'Democratic' must be interpreted as a relative concept, and not strictly.

TABLE 7
Cardinal of the Set of Feasible and Individually Rational (IR) Scenarios when Players'
Exclusion is Allowed

Exclusion Threshold	Equivalent Variation	Real GDP	Exports	Terms of Trade
None	1	31	39	0
<2% of world GDP	59	47	142	0
<3% of world GDP	60	47	142	0
<4% of world GDP	87	47	142	112

Notes:
The exclusion threshold is applied to the gross domestic product (GDP) of the player (region in the model) and not to each country belonging to the region. IR is the set of scenarios where all players have no negative payoff (individual rationality constraints).

Source: Authors' calculation.

obligations; so this situation is very close to an exclusion of these countries from the negotiation process; (iv) observers often describe past trade negotiations as a bargaining process between few rich countries (see e.g. the Blair House agreement between the EU and the US; Messerlin, 1995).

In order to go further, we examine how the exclusion of poor countries, that is, eliminating some of the m players of the optimisation programme, affects the negotiation. Until the end of this chapter we call IR-set the set of scenarios that respect the individual rationality constraint in each programme (see equation (2)). Table 7 indicates the number of solutions in the IR-set, according to various degrees of exclusion of poor countries (the criterion being a share in world GDP).

For example, when the equivalent variation is the objective of all negotiators, excluding countries the GDP of which is less than 2 per cent of the world GDP implies that the IR-set is 59 instead of 1. Excluding countries always expands the IR-set of the game. When terms of trade are the objective, exclusion has to be large: the 4 per cent threshold implies that India does not take part in the bargaining process such that some agreements may be reached: s1311 with economic weights and s1351 in other cases. When negotiators maximise equivalent variation, even the first threshold which excludes only small countries is efficient. The s1510 outcome is adopted under bargaining weights based on economic powers except when interests of all zones with less than 4 per cent of world GDP are precluded: the US, EU and Japan are the only negotiators (these are the Triad countries) and s1551 should be chosen (see above). With democratic weights, the outcome of trade negotiations is: (i) s1530 for a 2 per cent threshold; (ii) s1230 for a 3 per cent threshold; and (iii) s1511 for a 4 per cent threshold. Democracy undermines the influence of the US and EU, while improving the position of Mediterranean countries. From a global point of view, restricting negotiation to richer countries implies the adoption of a less harmonising tariff reduction formula in agriculture. Moreover, when only Bangladesh does not participate in the bargaining process, an outcome may be reached under the equivalent variation criterion.

Thus, we find that the exclusion of WTO members is efficient. However, this is quite opposite to the essence of multilateralism. Excluding poorer countries/ regions is particularly inconsistent with the developmental objective of this round. Therefore, the following subsection addresses a more cooperative solution: the inception of side payments among countries/regions.

c. Setting-up Side Payments

In a cooperative framework, a worldwide Pareto optimum should be agreed on when countries/regions are allowed to redistribute the benefits obtained from trade liberalisation. Setting side payments provides a supplementary degree of freedom, and all outcomes are then feasible as long as total welfare increases. The 'Aid for Trade' package cements this idea into a workable strategy (see Evenett, 2005a). From an institutional point of view, these international transfers may take several shapes: aid for development, financing of facilities, adjustment packages (see International Monetary Fund Anne Krueger's proposal[12] in Cancún). For example, various proposals have been put forth regarding the compensation of African–Caribbean–Pacific countries for preference erosion as part of the tentative banana deal reached between Latin American producers, the EU and the US. Equivalent variation is the criterion that best fits these international financial transfers; for this reason, we herein study the implementation of side payments under this objective function.

From a mathematical point of view, the programme of the cooperative game with side payments is defined by the equations:

$$s^* \in \arg_{s \in S} \max G(s) = \prod_m \left(W^m(s) + T^m - W_0^m \right)^{\alpha^m}, \tag{4}$$

with

$$W^m(s^*) + T^m \geq W_0^m, \quad \text{for all } m \tag{5}$$

and

$$\sum_m T^m = 0, \tag{6}$$

where T^m represents the payments received/paid by m. The objective function to be maximised (equation (4)) indicates that each country's real income variation,

---

[12] http://www.imf.org/external/np/speeches/2003/091003.htm.

thanks to the trade reform, is augmented by the side payment when it is positive, decreased when it is negative. Equation (5) expresses individual rationality and slightly differs from equation (2) as the side payment is included. Equation (6) means that the sum of the international transfers is balanced.

It can be shown that the optimal solution is defined by

$$W^m\left(s^*\right)+T^m-W_0^m = \alpha^m \times \sum_m \left(W^m\left(s^*\right)-W_0^m\right).$$

At the optimum, a player should get a share α^m – its bargaining power – of the total gain. If all players have the same power (the unweighted situation), the final distribution of gains has to be even. Otherwise, a player will use its veto power to block the outcome. Therefore, the more uneven the initial distribution, the larger will be the redistribution.

The Nash bargaining game set-up describes a redistribution process on absolute level of gains. Therefore, attributing the same bargaining power to different players will lead them to try to get the same share of the overall gain. But the same share represents very different outcomes in terms of relative gains. Adopting a weighting scheme that provides the same bargaining power to a big country and to a small one may be quite quixotic as an even distribution of absolute gains will lead to a very extreme distribution of relative gains. Using GDP weights allows us to correct for such a problem. However, a development-friendly outcome of the DDA may target the reduction of world inequalities which entails that developing countries' gains should be more than proportional to their initial GDP. The 'unweighted' and the 'democratic' weighting schemes have such properties.

When setting side payments, the first-best solution to be agreed is the one associated with the largest overall gain: s1531. It is the most ambitious scenario in terms of liberalisation. When services are excluded from negotiation, the solution is s0531.

The total amount of side payments is shown in Table 8. Notably, the international transfers are very large. As discussed in Section 3, the more efficient the reform, the larger the global gain and the higher its dispersion. So, in a sense these large transfers are because of the consensus rule and the right of veto given to

TABLE 8

Nash Solutions with Side Payments (US$ billion)

Global Transfers	Unweighted	Democratic	Economic Weights (GDP)
With liberalisation in services	66.4	80.7	44.0
Without liberalisation in services	63.2	78.8	44.1

Source: Authors' calculation.

each WTO member. They are much larger than the amount countries need to make up for their losses induced by the negotiated outcome: between 20 and 30 times larger. In fact, countries do not have to be compensated only for losses (difference between equivalent variation implied by reform and initial equivalent variation), but also for not getting the average gain. These transfers add up to between 40 and 80 per cent of total welfare gain and it represents a considerable financial payment. Moreover, the more power rich countries have, the smaller the transfers. For a similar reason, the 'democratic' weighting scheme induces large redistribution as most of the WTO members are small economies that have limited or no gains. The liberalisation of services, by increasing the size of the cake, leads to more redistribution except in the case of bargaining power based on economic size because of the specific situation of the US (see *infra*).

Figure 2 shows the distribution of transfers under side payments. Services are included in the liberalisation process and the Nash solution is defined with and without bargaining powers. This solution defines three net payers which are amongst the main beneficiaries from the liberalisation process: the EU, European Free Trade Association (EFTA) and Japan. It is obviously related to a tariff structure with numerous peaks. Japan pays US$40 billion to other countries upon a total gain of US$45 billion. For some LDCs, side payments obtained are the only source of gain (Bangladesh and Sub-Saharan Africa) and are quite significant (about 2.5 per cent of the Sub-Saharan Africa's income). The GDP-weighted case is obviously more advantageous for rich countries. For example, the EU does not pay anything and Japan's payment is reduced by about 25 per cent. The US benefits from large payments (US$34 billion). Previously, their gain did not reflect their economic size. When services are excluded, the profile of the distribution is similar. But larger side payments received by the US are noteworthy because of its gains related to trade liberalisation in services.

d. Extending the Domain of Negotiation

Another possible solution is to extend the domain of the negotiation. For example, the introduction of the Singapore issues, such as trade facilitation, or more generally, the inclusion of services in the negotiation might be viewed as an extension of the domain of negotiation: countries that lose because of the liberalisation of agriculture and industry could offset these losses by gains from the liberalisation of this sector. As it is not possible to extend the domain of negotiation from the situation depicted in the previous subsections, we consider a restriction of this domain and evaluate the IR-set of the game when the negotiation takes place either only in agriculture, or only in industry, or only in services, or only about export subsidies.

Results are illustrated in Table 9. For each criterion (equivalent variation/real GDP/terms of trade), we indicate the number of scenarios in the set of feasible

FIGURE 2
Distribution of Transfers among Players (Billions of US dollars)

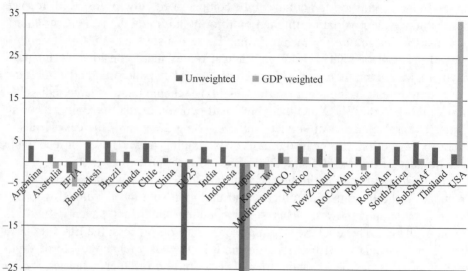

Notes:

'EFTA', European Free Trade Association; 'EU25', European Union 25 countries; 'Korea-Tw', South Korea-Taiwan; 'MediterraneanCo.', Mediterranean countries; 'RoCentAm', Rest of Central America; 'RoAsia', Rest of Asia; 'RoSouAm', Rest of South America; 'SouthAfrica', South Africa; 'SubSahAf', Sub-Saharan Africa; 'USA', United States of America. The most ambitious scenario is the optimal outcome with transfers (s1531) when transfers are allowed. A negative transfer is a payment done and a positive one is a payment received.

Source: Authors' calculation.

issues (column 'Domain'), then the number of scenarios in the IR-set (column 'IR-set'). As a negotiation between all players gives birth to a quasistalemate when players maximise equivalent variation (the IR-set only consists in the liberalisation of services), and complete stalemate in case of an objective of terms of trade, we also consider an exclusion of countries/zones representing less than 2 per cent of the world GDP, then a situation where countries / zones of which GDP is less than 4 per cent of the world GDP are excluded.

For example, when the objective is equivalent variation and in case of an exclusion of countries/zones of less than 2 per cent of world GDP, a negotiation in all dimensions is especially beneficial as the IR-set consists of 59 potential agreements instead of 0 if the negotiation takes place only in agriculture or industry.

TABLE 9
Impact of an Extension of the Negotiation Domain (IR)

Criteria	Dimension	Domain	IR-Set		
			All Players	Exclusion at 2% of World GDP	Exclusion at 4% of World GDP
Equivalent variation	Services	1	1	1	1
	Industry	5	0	0	5
	Agriculture	5	0	0	0
	Export subsidies	1	0	0	1
	All dimensions	143	1	59	87
Real GDP	Services	1	1	1	1
	Industry	5	5	5	5
	Agriculture	5	0	0	0
	Export subsidies	1	1	1	1
	All dimensions	143	47	47	47
Terms of trade	Services	1	0	0	0
	Industry	5	0	0	2
	Agriculture	5	0	0	0
	Export subsidies	1	0	0	1
	All dimensions	143	0	0	112

Notes:
The results for the 'all dimensions' rows mimic the information of Table 8. IR is the set of scenarios where all players have non-negative payoff (individual rationality constraints).

Source: Authors' calculation.

It appears from Table 9 that an extension of the domain of negotiation systematically increases the number of trade reforms which countries can potentially agree on. The agricultural sector appears once again at the cornerstone of the trade negotiations. Whatever the negotiators' objective is and in any scheme of country participation (all players/exclusion at 2 per cent of world GDP/exclusion at 4 per cent of world GDP), it is impossible to find out a solution other than the status quo if a negotiation takes place only in agriculture: the IR-set of the game is systematically empty.

5. ANALYSING COALITIONS

Since 1995, the functioning of the WTO is clearly affected by coalitions whose life span is more or less long and the *raison d'être* is not evident. The G20 case clearly illustrates this point. This coalition gathers heterogeneous countries in terms of trade characteristics. In this context, it is useful to examine the role and the impact of such coalitions.

We suppose that a coalition is justified when small players have been excluded from a negotiation, and see the formation of a coalition as a means to continue

participating. The presence of small countries/regions in a negotiation that is sup-
posedly taking place only amongst large countries deeply affects the cooperative
game. To exemplify this, we examine the situation in which a 4 per cent threshold
has been applied; in this case, if no coalition is introduced, the Nash solution is
determined by taking into account only gains for the Triad countries (i.e. the US,
EU and Japan).

Numerous coalitions of countries appeared during the eight years of the Doha
negotiations. Among them, the G90, G20 and G10 have been especially effective,
and are studied herein. Assuming that each WTO country has veto power under
the principle of unanimity, it is difficult to justify the appearance of coalitions.
However, we feel that coalitions allow small countries to gather so as to participate
in negotiations from which they would otherwise be excluded.

As far as the consequences of a coalition formation, we compare the gain
obtained by each country/region in the presence and absence of a coalition. For a
country/region, participation in the coalition implies that its interests are taken
into account, whereas such interests are not accounted for in the absence of the
coalition, and/or because the formation of this coalition entails a change in the set
of agreeable reforms and in the solution of the cooperative game. Moreover, we
assume that the bargaining power of a coalition equals the sum of its members'
bargaining powers.[13] Tables 10–13 show these comparisons for different countries/
regions in different game configurations (with or without other coalitions, with or
without bargaining power).

Table 10 provides the results for the G10 coalition, which provides gains to all
its members. The situation of Japan is strongly improved (+US$44 billion) when
the other G10 members' participation constraints are introduced, especially, in the

TABLE 10
Effects of the Apparition of the G10 Coalition on its Members (US$ billion)

Country	Unweighted	GDP Weights	Democratic Weights
EFTA	0	4.6	0.3
Japan	0	44.4	1.2
Korea-Taiwan	0	4.2	0.2

Notes:
This table represents the change in real income for the different members of the G10 if this coalition appears.
The exclusion threshold is set to 4 per cent of world gross domestic product (GDP), thus the reference situation
is the case where only the US, the EU and Japan participate in the negotiations. The presence of the G90 and/
or G20 does not allow the G10 to modify the outcome of the game and these cases are not represented here.
'EFTA', European Free Trade Association.

Source: Authors' calculation.

[13] An existing coalition larger than the fixed threshold keeps its right of veto when individual rationality is not satisfied.

TABLE 11

Effects of the Apparition of the G20 Coalition on its Members (US$ billion)

Country	G20 Facing the Triad (US, EU and Japan)			G20 Facing the Triad and the G10		
	Unweighted	GDP Weights	Democratic Weights	Unweighted	GDP Weights	Democratic Weights
Argentina	0.6	**1.0**	0.6	0.6	0.4	0.4
Brazil	**0.9**	**0.8**	**0.9**	**0.9**	**0.9**	**0.9**
Chile	**0.1**	**0.1**	**0.1**	**0.1**	**0.1**	**0.1**
China	1.1	3.9	1.1	1.1	0.8	0.8
India	1.6	**3.6**	1.6	1.6	1.0	1.1
Mexico	1.4	**2.5**	1.4	1.4	1.0	1.0
RoCentAm	0.1	**0.3**	0.1	0.1	0.1	0.1
RoSouthAm	0.2	**0.5**	0.2	0.2	0.1	0.2
South Africa	0.1	0.3	0.1	0.1	0.1	0.1
Thailand	0.1	0.3	0.1	0.1	0.1	0.1

Notes:
This table represents the change in real income for the different members of the G20 if this coalition appears. The exclusion threshold is set to 4 per cent of world gross domestic product (GDP). The presence of the G90 does not allow the G20 to modify the outcome of the game and this case is not represented here. Figures in bold indicate countries that move from losses to positive gains with the implementation of the coalition. 'RoCentAm', Rest of Central America; 'RoSouthAm', Rest of South America.

Source: Authors' calculation.

TABLE 12

Effects of the Apparition of the G90 Coalition on its Members (US$ billion)

G90 Facing. . .		Bangladesh	MediterraneanCo.	SubSahAf
Triad	Unweighted	**0.3**	−1.3	**1.1**
	GDP weighted	**0.3**	0.8	**1.5**
	Democratic weights	**0.3**	−1.3	**1.1**
Triad + G10	Unweighted	**0.3**	−1.3	**1.1**
	GDP weighted	**0.3**	−1.7	**0.9**
	Democratic weights	**0.3**	−1.6	**1.0**
Triad + G20	Unweighted	**0.2**	−2.5	**0.6**
	GDP weighted	**0.3**	−2.3	**0.7**
	Democratic weights	**0.2**	−2.5	**0.6**
Triad + G10 + G20	Unweighted	**0.2**	−2.5	**0.6**
	GDP weighted	**0.3**	−2.3	**0.7**
	Democratic weights	**0.2**	−2.5	**0.6**

Notes:
This table represents the change in real income for the different members of the G90 if this coalition appears. The exclusion threshold is set to 4 per cent of world gross domestic product (GDP). South Africa is not represented here but the existence of the G90 always reduces its gains. Figures in bold indicate countries that move from losses to positive gains with the implementation of the coalition. 'MediterraneanCo.', Mediterranean countries; 'SubSahAf', Sub-Saharan Africa.

Source: Authors' calculation.

TABLE 13
Effects of the Coalitions on the EU and US Gains (US$ billion)

Game Configuration	Unweighted		GDP Weights		Democratic Weights	
	EU25	US	EU25	US	EU25	US
Triad + G10	0.0	0.0	1.9	−2.8	1.4	−0.4
Triad + G20	−11.4	−2.0	−3.0	−5.1	−11.4	−2.0
Triad + G90	−27.5	0.1	−18.3	−3.3	−27.5	0.1
Triad + G10 + G20	−11.4	−2.0	−3.0	−5.1	−11.4	−2.0
Triad + G10 + G90	−27.5	0.1	−18.3	−3.3	−27.5	0.1
Triad + G20 + G90	−27.5	0.1	−18.3	−3.3	−27.5	0.1
Triad + G10 + G20 + G90	−27.5	0.1	−18.3	−3.3	−27.5	0.1

Notes:
'EU25', European Union 25 countries; the Triad is composed of the EU, the US and Japan the three countries in which gross domestic product (GDP) is above 4 per cent of world GDP, the threshold we have chosen for participating in the negotiations. The reference situation is the scenario chosen when only the Triad participates in the negotiations.

Source: Authors' calculation.

case of GDP weights. The G10 is worthwhile for its members only if they have to face the US and the EU. In the presence of other coalitions (G20 and G90), the G10 does not manage to influence the final outcome of the game.

The situation for G20 members is displayed in Table 11. This coalition improves the welfare of all its members, especially when bargaining powers are based on GDP size. In this case, seven of the 10 G20 countries/regions modelled herein move from net losses to net gains when we switch from the s1551[14] (weighted case) outcome selected by the Triad to the s1210 situation, in which NAMA liberalisation is limited, SDT is introduced and the AMA tariff reduction is deepened with a moderate Swiss formula coefficient instead of the linear formula chosen by the Triad. In the presence of the G10, the G20 still has incentives to appear. However, the presence of the G90 eliminates the incentives for the G20 to appear. Indeed, the G90 allows small economies to step back in the arena and enforce their participation constraints; they empty the core of the game, meaning that there is only one possible outcome (i.e. s1000, which is the status quo or the unique liberalisation of services, depending on the possibility of negotiating in this sector). The presence or absence of other players cannot modify the outcome. In all configurations, India benefits the most from the G20 implementation.

The G90 (Table 12) is the most interesting coalition. By allowing Bangladesh to re-enter the negotiation, the presence of this coalition empties the core of the

---

[14] We consider that s1551 is the scenario closest to the US–EU agreement that preceded the Cancún meeting.

game. The G90 allows both Sub-Saharan countries and Bangladesh to avoid the losses from the outcomes that would be negotiated by the other players if these small and vulnerable countries were excluded. Therefore, the G90 always improves the situation of both Sub-Saharan countries and Bangladesh. For the Mediterranean countries, in contrast, status quo in AMA and NAMA is not the best outcome. These countries would prefer a liberalisation scheme that is agreed upon by the largest players. For this reason, the G90 brings them net losses. Finally, the G90 is never useful for South Africa; this country is always better off when playing with the G20. These two last remarks illustrate the heterogeneity of the interests inside the G90 coalition.

We conclude by looking at the consequences on the EU and US gains of the implementation of these different coalitions (Table 13). As expected, in most situations, the gains of the two major players are negatively impacted by the apparition of counter-powers.

6. CONCLUDING REMARKS

In this chapter, the simultaneous use of CGE analysis and game theory allows us to explain some strategic features of the DDA trade negotiations. In particular, we see that agricultural market access talks play a crucial role: they increase the overall gain but also reduce the inequalities driven by NAMA liberalisation. Simultaneously, trade negotiation cannot take place if only liberalisation in agriculture is negotiated, as the core of the game would be empty. Moreover, the adoption of tariff-harmonising formulae (more cuts in higher import tariffs) leads to greatly increased global gains. Finally, the dramatic complexity in the current structure of protection and market access convincingly explains why trade negotiations are so difficult today. Thus, it does not seem surprising that our game-theoretic CGE approach concludes with a rather pessimistic statement: status quo is often the Nash solution.

Obviously, the number of negotiating members adds constraints to the bargaining programme. We show that the exclusion of countries/regions with GDPs below a certain threshold drastically improves the efficiency of the negotiation process, regardless of the governments' objective. We also demonstrate that the formation of coalitions is a potential means through which developing countries/regions may block solutions imposed by rich countries/regions. The G20 coalition is successful with the inclusion of the SDT clause and with less liberalisation of the industrial sector. Moreover, the G10 is always beneficial for its members. We also consider the expansion of the domain of trade negotiation. Negotiating in services, industry and agriculture is more efficient than negotiating in only industry and agriculture, which is itself more efficient than negotiating in agriculture alone. Side payments may also be a workable solution, as they allow large agents to maximise the size of the cake, while compensating losers. When we implement a cooperative solution of the game with side payments, we find that these international payments represent a significant share of global income gain. Notably, however, in one solution, side payments are used to remunerate very rich countries/regions (e.g. the US). Both characteristics of this cooperative solution make it implausible.

An illustration of the realistic aspect of our conclusions is that WTO Director-General Pascal Lamy is currently combining the three solutions that we propose herein, in the hopes of breaking the stalemate. (i) He has sought to expand the coverage of the negotiations. We feel that more could be done in this regard, especially with the inclusion of the Singapore issues. (ii) He has tried to reach an agreement between a limited number of WTO members (most of the WTO Geneva meetings in July 2008 took place amongst seven countries). (iii) He has sought to implement side payments ('Aid for Trade' can be interpreted along these lines). Let us note that there may be other means to compensate for losses related to erosion of preferences, such as granting new preferences (e.g. see the Duty Free Quota Free regime given by rich countries to LDCs at the Hong Kong Ministerial). Given the complexity of the current trade and protection structures, negotiators must be highly creative when designing a final trade agreement that could be accepted by all WTO members.

REFERENCES

Bagwell, K. and R. Staiger (1999), 'An Economic Theory of GATT', *American Economic Review*, **89**, 1, 215–48.
Baldwin, R. E. and R. Clarke (1988), 'Game Modeling Multilateral Trade Negotiations', *Journal of Policy Modeling*, **9**, 2, 257–84.
Bchir, M., L. Fontagné and S. Jean (2005), 'From Bound Duties to Actual Protection: Industrial Liberalisation in the Doha Round', CEPII Working Paper No. 2005-12 (Paris).
Bchir, M., S. Jean and D. Laborde (2006), 'Binding Overhang and Tariff-cutting Formulas', *Review of World Economics*, **142**, 2, 207–32.
Bouët, A. and D. Laborde (2008), 'The Cost of a Failed Doha Round', *International Food Policy Research Institute Issue Brief*, **56**, 1–8.
Bouët, A., Y. Decreux, L. Fontagné, S. Jean and D. Laborde (2008), 'Assessing Applied Protection across the World', *Review of International Economics*, **16**, 5, 850–63.
Chen, Z. and L. Schembri (2002), *Measuring the Barriers to Trade in Services: Literature and Methodologies* (Canada: Trade Policy Research, Development of Foreign Affairs and International Trade).
Decreux, Y. and H. Valin (2007), 'MIRAGE, Updated Version of the Model for Trade Policy Analysis Focus on Agriculture and Dynamics', CEPII Working Paper No. 2007-15 (Paris).
Dimaranan, B. V. and R. A. McDougall (2005), *Global Trade, Assistance, and Production: The GTAP 6 DataBase* (West Lafayette, IN: Center for Global Trade Analysis, Purdue University).
Evenett, S. J. (2005a), 'Some Tough Love on "Aid for Trade"', *Intereconomics*, **40**, 6, 326–29.
Evenett, S. J. (2005b), 'From "Trade versus Aid" to "Aid for Trade?"', Public Policy Papers, September (University of St. Gallen).
Francois, J. and B. Hoekman (1999), 'Market Access in the Service Sectors manuscript', (Rotterdam: Tinbergen Institute).

Francois, J., H. van Meijl and F. van Tongeren (2005), 'Trade Liberalization in the Doha Development Round', *Economic Policy*, **20**, 42, 349–91.

Hertel, T. W. and R. Keeney (2006), 'Assessing the Impact of WTO Reforms on World Agricultural Markets: A New Approach', in A. Sarris and D. Hallam (eds.), *Agricultural Commodity Markets and Trade. New Approaches to Analyzing Market Structure and Instability* (Rome: FAO/Edward Elgar), 402–28.

Hoekman, B. (1996), 'Assessing the General Agreement on Trade in Services', in W. Martin and L. A. Winters (eds.), *The Uruguay Round and the Developing Countries* (Cambridge: Cambridge University Press).

Johnson, H. (1953), 'Optimum Tariffs and Retaliation', *Review of Economic Studies*, **21**, 2, 142–53.

Johnson, H. (1965), 'An Economic Theory of Protectionism, Tariff Bargaining, and the Formation of Customs Unions', *Journal of Political Economy*, **73**, 3, 256–83.

Kalai, E. and M. Smorodinsky (1975), 'Other Solutions to Nash's Bargaining Problem', *Econometrica*, **43**, 3, 513–18.

Kalirajan, K., G. McGuire, D. Nguyen-Hong and M. Schuele (2000), *The Price Impact of Restrictions on Banking Services. Impediments to Trade in Services: Measurement and Policy Implications* (London and New York: Routledge), 215–30.

Mas-Colell, A., M. Whinston and J. Green (1995), *Microeconomic Theory* (New York: Oxford University Press).

Mayer, W. (1981), 'Theoretical Considerations on Negotiated Tariff Adjustments', *Oxford Economic Papers*, **33**, 1, 135–53.

Messerlin, P. (1995), *La Nouvelle Organisation Mondiale du Commerce* (Paris: IFRI/Dunod).

Nash, J. (1953), 'Two-person Cooperative Games', *Econometrica*, **21**, 1, 128–40.

Riezman, R. (1982), 'Tariff Retaliation from a Strategic Viewpoint', *Southern Economic Journal*, **48**, 3, 583–93.

Shapley, L. S. (1953), 'A Value for *n*-Person Games', in *Contributions to the Theory of Games*, Vol. II, by H. W. Kuhn and A. W. Tucker (eds.), Annals of Mathematical Studies, 28 (Princeton, NJ: Princeton University Press).

Stiglitz, J. and A. Charlton (2006), *Aid for Trade. Report for the Commonwealth Secretariat*, Initiative for Policy Dialogue (New York: Columbia University Press).

Tongeren, F., H. Meijl and Y. Surry (2001), 'Global Models Applied to Agricultural and Trade Policies: A Review and Assessment', *Agricultural Economics*, **26**, 2, 149–72.

Trewin, R. (2000), *A Price-impact Measure of Impediments to Trade in Telecommunications Services. Impediments to Trade in Services: Measurement and Policy Implications* (London: Routledge).

Tyers, R. (1990), 'Implicit Policy Preferences and the Assessment of Negotiable Trade Policy Reforms', *European Economic Review*, **34**, 7, 1399–426.

Van der Mensbrugghe, D. and J. Beghin (2004), *Global Agricultural Liberalization: An In-depth Assessment of What Is At Stake*, M. A. Aksoy and J. C. Beghin (eds.), (Washington, DC: The World Bank).

7

Does International Trade Cause Economic Growth? A Survey

Tarlok Singh

1. INTRODUCTION

THE effects of international trade on economic growth remain an area of protracted controversy in both theoretical and empirical research. The contemporary paradigms of theory have been characterised by a lack of consensus: the 'neoclassical trade' theory supports, while the 'neoclassical growth' theory does not recognise; and the 'new trade' theory is dubious, while the 'new growth' theory supports the positive effects of trade on output and growth. Mixed support is reinforced by mixed empirical evidence. The time-series models testing non-causality, and cross-section and panel data models examining the macroeconomic cross-country and microeconomic firm (industry) level effects commonly support positive and significant effects of trade on output and growth; the evidence is, however, not unambiguous. Rodriguez and Rodrik (2000) raise sceptical concerns on the strength of the argument for the beneficial effects of trade. An archival analysis and the historical evidence suggest that trade openness and growth were not correlated during the interwar period; were negatively correlated a century ago (Foreman-Peck, 1995; O'Rourke and Williamson, 1999; Vamvakidis, 2002); and became significantly correlated only in recent decades (Vamvakidis, 2002; Clemens and Williamson, 2004).

Emerging evidence pioneered by Rose (2004a, 2004b; 2005a, 2005b), casts a dubious note on the efficacy of GATT/WTO in promoting world trade and

I am grateful to Glenn Otto of The University of New South Wales, Sydney, Australia, for his valuable comments and incisive suggestions. I am also grateful to two anonymous referees of the original journal for very useful comments and suggestions; however, I am solely responsible for any error and omissions that may remain in the chapter.

The World Economy: Global Trade Policy 2010, First Edition. Edited by David Greenaway.

reducing trade volatility. It suggests that the insiders trade at no higher levels than the outsiders. Such evidence in the wake of avowed recognition for the contributions of GATT/WTO in spurring multilateral free trade marks a puzzle in open economy macroeconomics. While a few studies have attempted to resolve the 'Rose Paradox' and support the significant role of GATT/WTO in spurring world trade (Subramanian and Shang-Jin, 2007; Tomz et al., 2007), the controversy remains unsettled. Rose (2007) argues that the preferential trade agreements and protectionist tariffs still hamper any real progress by the WTO to foster free trade. The GATT/WTO remains surrounded by a multitude of preferential trade agreements (PTAs) that are non-discriminatory for members, but discriminatory against non-members. The PTAs have proliferated exponentially and spurred several studies evaluating binary choices and examining their effects on the trade and welfare of non-members of the bloc, level of Pareto-efficient multilateral free trade and welfare, and the enforcement of WTO agreements. An issue that remains centre stage is whether the PTAs supplement or supplant the multilateral trading system and, thus, have the 'trade creation' and 'building block' or the 'trade diversion' and 'stumbling block' effects. While several studies support the 'trade creation' and 'building block' effects (Baldwin, 1993, 1995; Ethier, 1998; Laird, 1999; Clausing, 2001; Glick and Rose, 2002; Lee et al., 2008), a parallel counterstrand raises apprehensive concerns and contrarily postulates the 'trade diversion' and 'stumbling block' effects of PTAs (Bhagwati, 1991; Panagariya, 1996; Bagwell and Staiger, 1998; Bhagwati et al., 1998; Karacaovali and Limão, 2008).

Several factors seem catalytic to the variance in empirical findings and unresolved controversies on the gains of trade, the role of GATT/WTO in world trade, and the effects of PTAs on multilateral cooperation and trade, such as the differences in the sample periods and sample countries covered, frequency of data used, measures of trade openness employed, model specifications estimated, and the test statistics used for testing the null. The estimating econometric methodology has itself been evolving and so have been the conclusions of empirical research. A number of studies have reviewed the trade–growth empirics and assessed the associated methodological and measurement issues (Edwards, 1993, 1998; Girma et al., 2004; Lopez, 2005; Greenaway and Kneller, 2007a; Wagner, 2007). While the studies by Edwards (1993, 1998) asymmetrically focus on the macroeconomic aspects of the trade–growth nexus and pre-date the microeconomic research that spurted since the mid-1990s, the studies by Girma et al. (2004), Greenaway and Kneller (2007a) and Wagner (2007) provide a distinctively exclusive focus on the microeconomic aspects of the effects of trade on firm-level efficiency and productivity. The study by Lopez (2005) attempts to reconcile the microeconomic and macroeconomic evidence, but it bypasses the analysis of several methodological issues concerning the trade–growth relationship. Temple (1999) provides a more generic review of the macroeconomic sources of growth, and dwells very sparsely on the specific issues surrounding the trade–growth empirics.

This study surveys the literature on the relationship between trade and growth and differs from previous research on two counts. First, it provides an extensive account of the macroeconomic and microeconomic evidence, and distils the debate on the gains of trade from a comprehensively wider and diverse domain. The review of empirical evidence is juxtaposed with the policy issues concerning protectionism versus trade liberalisation, and an analytical account is undertaken of the role of GATT/WTO in spurring multilateral trade. Second, the study undertakes an in-depth analysis of the methodological and measurement issues. Such an analysis is particularly essential to gauge the depth of empirical support and determine the strength of the argument for the gains of trade. The study is organised as follows. Section 2 reviews the macroeconomic and microeconomic evidence. Section 3 dwells on the policy debate on protectionism versus trade liberalisation, and examines the role of the GATT/WTO in fostering free trade. Section 4 presents a critical account of the methodological and measurement issues surrounding the trade–growth empirics. Section 5 sums up the conclusions emerging from the study.

2. TRADE AND GROWTH: THE EMPIRICAL EVIDENCE

The empirical literature on trade–growth relationships can be classified into two broad strands of studies: one using time-series models and assessing mainly the demand-driven effects, and the second estimating cross-section and panel data models and examining mostly the supply-induced investment and productivity effects of trade on output and economic growth.

a. Trade–Growth Non-causality: The Time-series Models

The testing of non-causality and the implied 'export-led growth' versus 'growth-led export' hypothesis marks one of the major areas of time-series research on trade and growth. Most studies conducted in the 1960s and 1970s performed unconditional correlation and static regression analyses (Emery, 1967; Maizels, 1968; Kravis, 1970; Voivodas, 1973), and examined the demand-driven role of trade in affecting income and growth. Nurkse (1961) postulated that trade served as the 'engine of growth' for a number of developed countries in the nineteenth century, but he was pessimistic about its similar role for the developing countries in the twentieth century. Kravis (1970) examines growth in the nineteenth century and for the 1950s and the 1960s for the developing countries, and raises concerns about Nurkse's argument. He instead asserts that growth was mainly the consequence of favourable internal factors, and the external demand represented an added stimulus, which varied in importance from country to country and period to period.[1] Kravis (1970) postulates that a more generally applicable metaphor would be to describe trade expansion as the 'handmaiden' of successful growth, rather than as an autonomous 'engine of growth'. The unconditional correlation and static regression analyses of the 1950s and 1960s are beset with several snags and limitations. The correlation does not imply causality and it does not control for the effects of several conditioning factors on growth. Similarly, the standard regression models assume all regressors to be exogenous, and predict unidirectional causality from trade to income and growth. These models, *a priori*, preclude the possibility of feedback effects and do not provide any information on the plausible reverse-causation from growth to trade. The development of noncausality tests since the late 1960s (Granger, 1969; Sims, 1980) facilitated the analysis of feedback effects, and spurred several studies testing non-causality and assessing the 'export-led growth' versus 'growth-led export' hypothesis.

The conventional strand of research estimating static models in levels, and the dynamic models in (normally) first-differences remained dominant until the late 1980s (Michaely, 1977; Balassa, 1978; Heller and Porter, 1978; Jung and Marshall, 1985; Chow, 1987). The *ex post* recognition of the limitations of time-series econometric models (since the 1980s) suggests that the studies estimating the long-run models in levels did not test stationarity and I(d), where $d > 0$, properties of the model series, while those estimating the dynamic models in first-differences ignored the possible long-run relationship among the level variables. It is likely that some or all of the variables in a model are individually I(d) and, in such cases, regressing an I(d) variable on one or more I(d) variables leads to a 'spurious regression' problem and complicates the statistical inference.[2] The strand of

---

[1] Kravis (1970) argues that trade is one among many factors affecting growth and, as such, it is unlikely to be a dominant variable in many instances. The exaggeration of the past role of trade has often served to heighten the contrast drawn with allegedly less favourable world markets, and, thus, to minimise the potential role of trade for the developing countries. The term 'engine of growth' is not generally descriptive and involves expectations which cannot be fulfilled by trade alone (Kravis, 1970).

[2] The classical econometrics indeed suggests differencing the I(d) variables d times to make them I(0) and stationary. The difference-stationary variables can be used to estimate the model and the standard asymptotic distribution can be used to draw statistical inferences. The differencing of data, however, results in a loss of long-run information and it precludes the possibility of estimating a steady-state relationship among the level variables. While the models estimated on I(0) series did resolve the problem of non-stationarity, these models could capture only the short-run and ignored the possible long-run relationship relevant for the steady-state analysis of economic growth. The causality in these models could arise from purely short-run dynamics. Granger (1988) shows that in a cointegrated I(1) process, the simple dynamic model suffers from a misspecification problem and the standard causality tests are not valid. The exclusion of error correction terms from the dynamic model results in a model misspecification. The failure of classical methodology to provide statistical inference in the models estimated on non-stationary data in levels and that to model long-run relationship in the models estimated on stationary data in differences, led to a paradigm shift in estimating methodology marked by the development of cointegration estimators and error correction models (ECMs) since the late 1980s.

studies testing non-causality based on dynamic models with I(0) series did not unequivocally differentiate between the 'short'- and 'long'-run relationship and thus ended-up assessing mainly the short-run business cycle, rather than the long-run steady-state, relationship between trade and growth.

The late 1980s marked the development of more efficient cointegration estimators and error correction models (ECMs), which fashioned a new approach to the analysis of the trade–growth nexus. The ECMs resolve the 'spurious regression' problem without losing long-run information, and are useful for distinguishing between the steady-state equilibrium and short-run dynamic relationship between trade and growth. Most studies conducted since the 1990s have used the cointegration estimators and estimated ECMs to re-assess the relationship between trade and growth (Table 1). The methodological evolution and the shifting paradigms of econometric modelling have been two of the key factors catalytic to the variance in empirical findings and unresolved controversies: some studies support the 'export-led growth' hypothesis (Emery, 1967; Maizels, 1968; Voivodas, 1973; Michaely, 1977; Balassa, 1978; Heller and Porter, 1978; Williamson, 1978; Fajana, 1979; Tyler, 1981; Feder, 1982; Balassa, 1984; Kavoussi, 1984; Jung and Marshall, 1985; Ram, 1987; Moschos, 1989; Greenaway and Sapsford, 1994; Bodman, 1996; Henriques and Sadorsky, 1996); some provide only limited support to the 'export-led growth' hypothesis (Chow, 1987; Chen, 1990; Kugler, 1991; Boltho, 1996); and yet some others yield mixed results (Nishimizu and Robinson, 1984; Kunst and Marin, 1989; Tybout, 1992; Oxley, 1993).

b. Productivity Effects of Trade on Growth: The Cross-section and Panel Data Models

(i) Macroeconomic cross-country models

The time-series studies testing non-causality mainly focus on the Keynesian demand-driven role of trade in affecting income and growth. A parallel strand of studies using a cross-section, and more recently panel data (since the 1990s), approach examines the productivity and supply-side effects of trade on output and growth, traversing through the accumulation of capital and TFP parameter of production technology. Krueger (1978) and Bhagwati (1978, 1988) postulate the productivity effects of trade and argue that the liberal trade regimes encourage specialisation in industries having scale economies and lead to an increase in efficiency and productivity in the long run. In the case of non-OPEC and middle-income developing countries, Tyler (1981) shows that an increase in manufacturing exports leads to the increase in technological progress. Feder (1982) estimates separate production functions for the export and non-export sectors and finds a significant externality effect and high factor productivity differentials. He argues that the productivity differentials across sectors can be due to various factors including a more competitive environment in which the export sector operates.

TABLE 1

Effects of International Trade on Productivity and Economic Growth: Macroeconomic Evidence

Author (Year)	Data and Sample	Economic Growth	Openness	Other Variables	Methodology and Estimators	Main Results and Conclusions
Emery (1967)	Cross-section, 50 countries (average of 1953–63).	GNP.	Exports.	Current account.	OLS.	Support for export growth hypothesis.
Maizels (1968)	Time-series, 1950–62, 9 countries.	GDP.	Exports.	None.	OLS.	Support for export growth hypothesis.
Voivodas (1973)	Cross-section, 22 countries; 1956–67.	GDP growth.	Export share.	Country dummies.	OLS.	Support for export growth hypothesis.
Michaely (1977)	Cross-section, 41 countries (average of 1950–73).	Per capita GNP growth.	Growth in export share.	None.	Rank correlation.	Support for export growth hypothesis. Threshold effect.
Balassa (1978)	Cross-section, 11 countries; (average of 1960–66 and 1966–73).	GNP growth.	Export growth, Real export growth.	Labour force, Domestic investment and Foreign investment/ output.	Rank correlation, OLS, Production function.	Support for export growth hypothesis.
Heller and Porter (1978)	Cross-section, 41 countries (average of 1950–73).	Per capita GNP growth.	Growth in export share.	None.	Rank correlation.	Support for export growth hypothesis. Threshold effect.
Williamson (1978)	Cross-section, 22 countries (average of 1960–74).	Change in GDP.	Lagged exports.	Country dummies, Direct investment, Other foreign capital.	OLS, Linear models.	Support for export growth hypothesis.
Fajana (1979)	Time-series, 1954–74, 1 country.	GDP growth.	Export share, Export change /output.	Trade balance, Current account.	OLS.	Support for export growth hypothesis.
Tyler (1981)	Cross-section, 55 countries.	GDP growth.	Export growth.	Labour force, Investment growth.	OLS, Production function.	Support for export growth hypothesis. Threshold effect.
Feder (1982)	Cross-section, 31 semi-industrialised countries; 1964–73 (average).	GDP growth.	Export growth, Export change/ output.	Labour force, Investment/ Output.	OLS.	Support for export growth hypothesis. Positive externality from export sector to non-export sector.
Balassa (1984)	Cross-section, 10 countries.	GNP growth.	Export growth.	Labour force growth, Ratio of output to domestic investment.	OLS, Production function.	Support for export growth hypothesis.
Kavoussi (1984)	Cross-section, 73 countries.	GDP growth.	Export growth.	Labour growth rate, Capital growth rate.	Rank correlation, OLS, Production function.	Support for export growth hypothesis. Threshold effect.

(Continued)

TABLE 1 (*Continued*)

Author (Year)	Data and Sample	Economic Growth	Openness	Other Variables	Methodology and Estimators	Main Results and Conclusions
Nishimizu and Robinson (1984)	4 countries, Annual data; Korea (1960–77); Turkey (1963–76); Yugoslavia (1965–78); Japan (1955–73). Industry-based analysis.	TFP growth by industry (manufacturing industries).	Output growth allocated to export expansion; Output growth allocated to import substitution.	–	OLS.	Import substitution regimes seem to be negatively correlated with TFP change, whereas export expansion regimes are positively correlated with TFP change.
Balassa (1985)	Cross-section, 43 developing countries; Annual data: 1973–79 (after oil shock).	GNP growth.	Export growth, Ratio of exports to GNP, Share of manufactured goods in total exports (all in real terms).	Labour force growth, Saving rate, GNP per capita, Current account balances as a percentage of GNP, Investment.	OLS.	Significant positive effects of trade orientation on economic growth.
Jung and Marshall (1985)	Time-series, 1950–81, 37 countries.	Real GNP (or GDP) growth.	Lagged real export growth.	Lagged GNP (GDP) growth.	Maximum-likelihood simultaneous linear functions, granger-causality test.	Limited support for export growth causing economic growth.
Chow (1987)	Cross-section and Time series, Annual data: 1960–84, 8 Asian NICs.	Growth rate of manufacturing output.	Growth rate of manufacturing exports.	None.	Sims-causality test.	No causality for Argentina, uni-directional causality for Mexico, and bidirectional causality for remaining sample.
Ram (1987)	Time-series and Cross-section, 73 countries, 1960–72 (before oil shock) and 1973–82 (after oil shock).	Real GDP growth.	Real export growth.	Labour force growth, Investment growth.	Production function, OLS, Test for hetero-scedasticity and specification bias.	Support for export growth hypothesis. Threshold effect.
Kohli and Singh (1989)	30 countries (same sample as in Feder (1982) excluding Taiwan), 1960–70 and 1970–81 (averages).	Growth rate of GDP.	Growth rate of exports, Growth rate of exports multiplied by the share of exports in GDP.	Share of Investment in GDP, Growth rate of labour.	OLS.	Support for positive and significant effects of exports on growth.
Kunst and Marin (1989)	Time-series, 1965.2–85.4, 1 country (Austria).	GDP of OECD.	Manufactured exports.	Productivity (output per employee in manufacturing sector), Terms of trade.	Unrestricted VAR and Subset Model Autoregression.	Support for productivity growth causes exports.
Moschos (1989)	Cross-section.	Real GDP growth.	Real export growth.	Labour force growth, Real domestic investment growth.	OLS, Production function.	Support for export growth hypothesis. Threshold effect.

TABLE 1 (*Continued*)

Author (Year)	Data and Sample	Economic Growth	Openness	Other Variables	Methodology and Estimators	Main Results and Conclusions
Chen (1990)	Time-series, 1968–82, 1 country (Taiwan).	Growth in TFP and growth in output in manufacturing sector.	Growth in exports in manufacturing sector.	None.	Correlation, Rank correlation, OLS regression.	Limited support for the effect of export growth on productivity growth.
Kugler (1991)	Time-series, quarterly data: 1970–1987; 6 countries.	Real GDP.	Real exports.	Total private consumption, Gross fixed business investment.	Johansen Cointegration test.	Weak support for export-led growth hypothesis: in two countries. In remaining four, no cointegrating relationship.
Bonelli (1992)	1 country, Cross-section, 1975–85; Sectoral annual data for 22 industries.	Total factor productivity.	Export, Import.	None.	Cross-section regressions, OLS, Demand-side decomposition of growth.	Positive association between export expansion and TFP growth. TFP growth is explained by variables related to export expansion and import change.
Dollar (1992)	95 LDCs, 1976–85.	Per capita GDP growth.	Index of openness based on weighted average of distortions and variability of real exchange rate.	Investment rate, Real exchange rate variability, Index of real exchange rate distortion.	OLS, Cross-section regressions.	Trade increases per capita GDP growth. Outward-orientation is highly correlated with per capita GDP growth. Significant, negative relationship between distortion in real exchange rate and growth of per capita GDP.
Edwards (1992)	Cross-section, developing countries and developed and developing countries; 1960–82.	Growth of real GDP per capita.	Deviation from predicted trade. Nine indicators of trade orientation.	Ratio of gross investment to GDP, Proxies for knowledge gap, Human capital, Government expenditure, Political instability.	OLS, Production function.	Significant positive effects of trade on growth. More open economies tend to grow faster than economies with trade distortions.
Marin (1992)	4 OECD industrialised countries; Time series: 1960:1 to 1987:2.	Labour productivity (manufacturing output per employee).	Export of manufacturing goods.	Terms of trade for manufacturing goods, OECD output at constant prices.	VAR model, Cointegration tests, Error correction model; Granger-causality tests.	Support for export-led growth hypothesis. Exports Granger-cause productivity in all four countries.
Tybout (1992)	4 countries; 1976–88.	TFP.	Import substitution.	–	Cross-section, Production function.	Trade orientation affects productivity. No clear link between trade policies and patterns of entry and exit.

(*Continued*)

TABLE 1 (*Continued*)

Author (Year)	Data and Sample	Economic Growth	Openness	Other Variables	Methodology and Estimators	Main Results and Conclusions
Knight et al. (1993)	Panel data: 98 countries comprising 22 industrial OECD countries and 76 developing countries; 1960–85.	Real GDP per worker.	'Closedness' proxied by weighted average of tariff rates.	Real GDP per worker, Average growth rate of working-age population. Technological progress and real investment to real GDP, Human capital investment to GDP, Public infrastructure.	Panel data estimation, Seemingly Unrelated Regressions estimator.	A high tariff structure discourages imports of capital goods and leads to less technology transfer. Coefficient on 'Closedness' is negative and highly significant.
Lee (1993)	Cross-section: 1960–85 and 81 countries, 21 industrial and 60 developing.	Growth of real GDP per capita.	Import-weighted average tariff rate, Black market exchange rate premium, Share of total imports in GDP and estimate of openness.	Secondary school enrolment rate, Ratio of real domestic investment to real GDP.	OLS, Neoclassical model, Cross-country regressions.	Trade distortions generate cross-country divergences in growth rates and per capita income. Tariff rates and black market premia interacting with estimated share of imports, have significant negative effects on the growth rate of per capita income.
Oxley (1993)	Time-series, Annual data: 1833–85, 1 country: Portugal.	Real GDP (at 1914 prices).	Real exports (at 1914 prices).	None.	Granger-causality tests, Johansen Cointegration tests and Error correction model.	No support for export-led growth hypothesis. Evidence of reverse causality.
Greenaway and Sapsford (1994)	Time-series (1957–85) and Cross-section (1960–88), 104 countries, 1960–88.	Real GDP growth, Real GDP per capita and Real GDP per worker.	Growth rates of export shares in GDP, i.e. Ratio of exports to GDP.	None.	OLS regression, DF and ADF Unit root tests, White test, CUSUM and CUSUMSQ.	Statistically significant effect of export share growth on real per capita GDP growth. Threshold effect.
Harrison (1994)	Côte d'Ivoire. Time-series and Cross-section, Annual data: Sample firms aggregated into 9 sectors; 1979–87.	Firm-level capital productivity and Total factor productivity.	Tariff rates, Import penetration, and TFP comparison before and after trade reforms (1985).	Market power across sector as measured by price–cost margins.	OLS, Instrumental variable (IV) estimator; Generalised Least Squares, TFP growth.	Positive association between trade policies and higher productivity growth. Productivity growth four times higher in less protected sectors.
Harrison and Revenga (1995)	United States; Four-digit manufacturing sub-sector; Annual data: 1958 and 1984.	Sector-specific real output.	Import competition, Export shares.	Labour, Material inputs, Energy consumption, Capital stock, R&D expenditure, Rate of Unionisation.	Modified production function.	Higher import competition associated with productivity increases. Export activity positively associated with productivity growth. No significant association between import competition and productivity growth.

TABLE 1 (*Continued*)

Author (Year)	Data and Sample	Economic Growth	Openness	Other Variables	Methodology and Estimators	Main Results and Conclusions
Sachs and Warner (1995)	135 countries, 1970–89; Subsample: 117, 81, 79, 78 and 33 countries.	Real annual per capita growth in GDP over 1970–89.	Openness dummies; using: Average tariff, Non-tariff barriers, State monopoly on major exports, and Black market premiums.	Real GDP per capita, School enrolment rate, Ratio of government consumption to GDP, Deviation of investment price level from cross-country mean, and political and social factors.	Cross-section regressions, OLS.	High and robust coefficient on openness dummy in growth regression. Protectionist trade policies reduce overall growth. Openness raises investment to GDP ratio.
Bodman (1996)	Time-series: Quarterly data: 1960:1–1995:4; 2 countries: Australia and Canada.	Labour productivity.	Exports.	None.	Cointegration and Granger-causality tests.	Support for export-led growth hypothesis. Reverse causality from productivity to exports is rejected for both countries.
Boltho (1996)	Time-series: Japan, Annual data, 1885–1913: (i) 1913–37; (ii) 1952–73; and (iii) 1973–1990. Macroeconomic and Microeconomic analysis.	GDP growth and Output growth.	Export growth and Shares of import and export.	None.	Granger-causality, OLS regression.	No support for export-led growth hypothesis. Support for growth-led export hypothesis.
Eaton and Kortum (1996)	Cross-section, 19 OECD countries; 1986–88 (average).	Technology diffusion: Productivity measured in terms of real GDP per worker.	Share of imports in GDP.	Human capital, Distance between countries, Dummy to capture country differences, Research efforts.	OLS, 2SLS, NLLS and Generalised Non-linear Least Squares.	Each country will grow at the same rate, with relative productivity determined by ability to adopt new inventions. Ability to tap into the sources of invention depends on human capital, trade relationships and proximity to sources of innovation.
Frankel and Romer (1996)	Cross-country, 150 countries and a subsample of 98 countries; 1985.	Per capita income.	Exports plus Imports as a ratio to GDP.	Population, Area, Real investment to GDP; Working-age population in secondary school, Initial per capita income.	Cross-country income regressions; OLS, IV estimator.	Significant effect of trade on income. Openness to trade raises income.

(*Continued*)

TABLE 1 (*Continued*)

Author (Year)	Data and Sample	Economic Growth	Openness	Other Variables	Methodology and Estimators	Main Results and Conclusions
Harrison (1996)	Cross-section and Panel data. Countries vary from 17 to 51. 1960–87 and 1978–88. Annual data.	Real GDP growth, Share of investment in GDP.	Seven different proxies for trade openness and policy.	Capital stock, Years of primary and secondary education, Labour, Human capital, Land.	General production function, Spearman rank correlation, OLS, Cross-section and Panel data models.	Half of the measures do exhibit a robust relationship with GDP growth. The choice of time period is critical. A generally positive association between growth and different measures of openness. Bidirectional causality between openness and growth.
Henriques and Sadorsky (1996)	Time-series, (i) 1877–1945; (ii) 1946–91; and (iii) 1877–1991; Canada.	Real GDP.	Real exports.	Real terms of trade.	VAR, Cointegration and Granger-causality tests.	Support for growthled export hypothesis. No evidence for export-led growth hypothesis.
Riezman et al. (1996)	Time-series, 126 countries; 1950–90.	Real GDP.	Exports, Imports.	Human capital growth, Investment growth.	Granger-causality, Forecast Error Variance Decomposition.	Unidirectional causality from exports growth to income growth in 30 countries and from income growth to exports growth in 25 countries. Bidirectional causality in 65 countries.
Edwards (1998)	Panel data for 1960–90; 93 advanced and developing countries.	Total factor productivity growth.	Nine indices of trade policy.	Initial GDP per capita, Initial human capital.	Weighted least squares, Instrumental weighted least squares.	More open countries experience faster productivity growth.
Frankel and Romer (1999)	Cross-section: 150 countries. 1985. Sub-sample: 98 countries (averages).	Income per person.	Actual trade share, Constructed trade share. Distance, Relative country size, Dummies for a common border and being landlocked.	Two country size measures: Population and Land area.	OLS, IV estimator.	Statistically and economically significant relationship between trade and income.
O'Rourke (2000)	10 developed countries, 1875–1914.	Growth of real GDP per capita.	Average tariff rate.	Saving rate, School enrolment. Population. Change of capital–labour and land–labour ratios. Deviation of output. Country and time dummies.	Conditional and Unconditional convergence models, Factor accumulation models, Panel data estimation.	Tariffs were positively correlated with growth during 1875–1914. Tariffs boosted late nineteenth century growth.

TABLE 1 (*Continued*)

Author (Year)	Data and Sample	Economic Growth	Openness	Other Variables	Methodology and Estimators	Main Results and Conclusions
Rodriguez and Rodrik (2000)	Review of Key studies	Growth of real GDP per capita: 1970–89 and 1976–85; TFP growth: 1980–90; Income per person in 1985.	Openness indicators with alternative definitions and weighting.	Same as used in the reviewed studies and some additional variables.	OLS, 2SLS, Weighted least squares, IV estimator, Sensitivity analysis.	Sceptical concerns on the strength of beneficial effects of trade on growth, and contend the view that integration into the world economy is such a potent force for economic growth.
Easterly and Levine (2001)	Panel data: 73 countries; 1960–95.	Real per capita GDP growth.	Ratio of exports plus imports to GDP.	Initial income per capita, Years of schooling, Inflation, Government consumption, Black market exchange rate premium, Financial intermediary credit.	Generalised Method of Moments (GMM) Dynamic panel estimator.	TFP residual, rather than factor accumulation, accounts for most of the cross-country and cross-time variations in income and growth. Openness and black market exchange rate premium significantly correlated with economic growth.
Lane (2001)	Cross-section: 71 low- and middle-income debtor countries; 1970–95.	Net resource inflows, to GDP.	Trade ratio adjusted for cross-country differences in trade policies; geography-based measure of natural openness.	Initial GDP per capita, Government consumption, Country size (population), Trade shocks, Inflation rate.	Numerical simulations and Empirical estimates. Cross-section regressions, OLS.	Open economies exhibit greater debt to output ratios. External liabilities to output positively associated with trade openness. Trade not only has direct effects on allocation and growth, but also promotes convergence.
Wacziarg (2001; 1998)	Panel data: 57 countries; 1970–89.	Per capita GDP growth.	Two trade policy indices.	Price distortions, Government consumption, Manufactured exports, Investment rate, FDI, Macro policy quality.	Correlation, Simultaneous equation model, 3SLS, Seemingly Unrelated Regressions estimator.	Positive impact of openness on growth. Enhanced technology transmission and improvements in macroeconomic policy account for smaller effects.
Irwin and Terviö (2002)	Pre-World War I, Inter-war, Great Depression, Early Post-war, Later Post-war. Countries vary each year.	GDP per capita.	Trade to GDP ratio. Bilateral trade.	Distance, Population, Area.	OLS, 2SLS, IV estimator.	Positive effects of trade on growth. Countries that trade more as a proportion of their GDP have higher incomes even after controlling for the endogeneity of trade.
Vamvakidis (2002)	Historical data: Countries vary in different time periods.	Growth of GDP per capita.	Six proxies for openness to trade.	Investment to GDP, School enrolment, Population, Inflation, Black market premium, Illiteracy rate.	Cross-country growth regressions, OLS, Spearman rank correlation.	No correlation between openness and growth between 1870 and 1970, with the exception of the interwar period. Positive correlation between openness and growth during 1970–90.

(*Continued*)

TABLE 1 (*Continued*)

Author (Year)	Data and Sample	Economic Growth	Openness	Other Variables	Methodology and Estimators	Main Results and Conclusions
Awokuse (2003)	Time-series, Canada; Quarterly data: 1960:1 to 2000:4.	Real GDP.	Real exports.	Real terms of trade, manufacturing employment, capital formation, industrial production.	Johansen Cointegration test, Granger-causality with VECM.	Long-run relationship among model variables, and unidirectional Granger-causality from exports to GDP. Support for export-led growth hypothesis in both short run and long run.
Dollar and Kraay (2003)	Cross-country: Number of countries vary; 1970s to the 1990s.	Growth of real GDP per capita.	Share of trade in GDP, Decadal changes in trade volume.	Measures of institutional quality and market size.	Cross-section regressions, OLS, IV estimator.	Joint role of trade and institutions in the long run, larger role for trade over shorter horizons. Both trade and institutions are important in differences in growth rates in the very long run.
Alcala and Ciccone (2004)	Cross-section: 138 countries.	GDP per worker in PPP US$; TFP.	Imports plus exports relative to purchasing power parity GDP.	Population, Area, Institutional quality.	OLS, 2SLS.	Trade has a significant and robust positive effect on productivity.
Clemens and Williamson (2004)	35 countries, 1865–1996. Sample sizes vary depending on the years.	Growth in real GDP per capita.	Average tariff rate.	School enrolment, Railway density, Primary products exports, Energy consumption, Average trading partner tariff and real GDP growth, Distance to trading partners.	Panel data estimation, Cross-section regressions, OLS, IV estimator.	High tariffs associated with fast growth before World War II, and associated with slow growth thereafter. Increase in own tariffs after 1950 hurt or at least did not help growth.
Dollar and Kraay (2004)	Approximately 100 countries; 1980s and 1990s.	Per capita income in bottom quintile, Annual growth of per capita GDP (average).	Ratio of exports plus imports to GDP.	Initial income, Contract-intensive money, Government consumption, Inflation, Revolutions, Commercial bank assets, Rule of law.	Panel data estimation, OLS, IV estimator.	No relationship between changes in trade volumes and changes in inequality. Increase in growth rates that accompanies expanded trade, translates into proportionate increases in income of the poor. Open trade regimes lead to faster growth and poverty reduction.
Lee et al. (2004)	Approximately 100 countries; 1961–2000.	Growth of real GDP per capita.	Imports and exports to GDP, Tariff index, Black market premium.	Initial GDP per capita, Investment to GDP, Inflation, M2 to GDP, Population, Education, Age dependency.	Panel data estimation, Identification through hetero-scedasticity, GMM, OLS.	Openness has a positive effect on growth, even when controlling for the effect from growth to openness.

TABLE 1 (*Continued*)

Author (Year)	Data and Sample	Economic Growth	Openness	Other Variables	Methodology and Estimators	Main Results and Conclusions
Rodrik et al. (2004)	Cross-section, 137 countries.	GDP per capita in 1995 on PPP basis.	Integration, Predicted trade share.	Geography, Settler mortality, Institutions, English and any European language, Regional dummies. Land area, Population.	OLS, IV estimator, Sensitivity analysis.	Quality of institutions 'trumps' everything. Once institutions are controlled for, conventional measures of geography have at best weak direct effects: trade is almost always insignificant.
Felbermayr (2005)	Panel data: 108 countries; 1960–99 (five-year averages).	Per capita output.	Trade share.	Lagged output, Secondary schooling, Investment, Population.	OLS, IV estimator, Pooled 2SLS regression, System-GMM estimator.	Support for strong effect of trade on income.
Kónya (2006)	24 OECD countries; Annual data: 1960–97.	Real GDP.	Real exports of goods and services, Openness.	None.	Panel-data based on SUR systems, Bivariate and Trivariate Granger-causality tests.	Support for: one-way causality from exports to GDP in some; one-way causality from GDP to exports in others; two-way causality between exports and growth in a few; and no causality in either direction for a few.
Awokuse (2007)	Time-series, Three Transition economies; Quarterly data.	Real GDP, Real GDP growth.	Real exports, Real imports.	Gross capital formation, Labour force.	Johansen Cointegration test, ECM, Granger-causality test.	Support for both export-led growth and growth-led export.
Awokuse and Christopoulos (2009)	Time series, 5 industrialised countries.	Real GDP growth.	Real exports.	Real terms of trade, manufacturing employment, gross capital formation, and industrial production index.	Causality tests Linear VAR model and Non-linear multivariate STAR (LSTAR and ESTAR) estimations.	Non-linear Granger-causality tests provide support for the validity of 'export-led growth' in some, and growth-led export hypothesis in others.

Notes:
GDP stands for Gross Domestic Product; GNP: Gross National Product; Govt.: Government; TFP: Total Factor Productivity; R&D: Research and Development expenditure; FDI: Foreign Direct Investment; PPP: Purchasing Power Parity; DCs: Developed Countries; LDCs: Less Developed Countries; SICs: Semi-industrialised Countries; NICs: Newly Industrialised Countries; OECD: Organisation for Economic Co-operation and Development; EC: European Community; OLS: Ordinary Least Squares; 2SLS: Two-stage Least Squares; IV: Instrumental Variables; 3SLS: Three-stage Least Squares; NLLS: Non-linear Least Squares; SUR: Seemingly Unrelated Regressions; DF: Dickey–Fuller; ADF: Augmented Dickey–Fuller; VAR: Vector Autoregression; ECM: Error Correction Model; VECM: Vector Error Correction Model; GMM: Generalised Method of Moments; STAR: Smooth Transition Autoregression; ESTAR: Exponential Smooth Transition Autoregression; and LSTAR: and Logistic Smooth Transition Autoregression.

The studies using Feder's model show the positive and significant relationship between exports and growth (Balassa, 1985; Ram, 1987). Chenery (1983) conducts a comprehensive study covering Western European and North American countries with high growth of TFP relative to growth of factor inputs, East Asian semi-industrialised countries with outward-orientation and high growth of both productivity and factor inputs, and middle-income developing countries with more inward-orientation and low growth of productivity relative to growth of factor inputs. He finds that the higher productivity growth observed in the East Asian semi-industrialised countries reinforces the favourable effects of outward orientation on productivity. Nishimizu and Robinson (1984) find similar evidence for Japan, Korea, Turkey and Yugoslavia, and suggest that export expansion leads to higher TFP growth through economies of scale and competitive incentives, while import substitution leads to lower TFP growth.

The post-neoclassical endogenous theory of economic growth (Romer, 1986, 1990; Lucas, 1988) provided a more nuanced focus on the productivity effects of trade, and added an additional dimension examining trade-induced convergence in income per capita and growth across countries. Several studies have since suggested positive and significant effects of trade on productivity and growth, and shown that openness to trade induces convergence in income per capita and TFP across countries (Dollar, 1992; Ben-David, 1993, 1996; Sachs and Warner, 1995; Harrison, 1996; Edwards, 1998; Vamvakidis, 1999; Alcala and Ciccone, 2004). Ben-David (1996) shows that trade reduces the income gaps among countries; a majority of trade-based country groups witness significant convergence. The trade leads to an increase in productivity and growth by providing a wider range of intermediate inputs (Grossman and Helpman, 1991; Rivera-Batiz and Romer, 1991a, 1991b) and facilitating an international diffusion of technology (Benhabib and Spiegel, 1994; Parente and Prescott, 1994; Coe and Helpman, 1995; Eaton and Kortum, 1994, 1996). Alcala and Ciccone (2004) show the economically significant and statistically robust positive effects of trade on TFP. The technology is developed and produced in the inventing country and is then exported and diffused for use as an intermediate input in other countries (Coe and Helpman, 1995). Eaton and Kortum (1996) develop a model of innovations and international diffusion of technology to explain the relative productivity and growth among the OECD countries. Relative productivity depends on the ability of a country to innovate or adopt a new technology, and they predict that each country will eventually grow at the same rate.

TFP in developed countries is higher than that in the developing countries, and the barriers to trade reduce TFP (Parente and Prescott, 1999; Schor, 2004; Berthold and Teixeira, 2005; Schmitz, 2005). Parente and Prescott (1999) argue that insider groups in developing countries have stronger monopoly rights than those in developed countries, and these reduce TFP. Schor (2004) shows that tariffs on inputs have a negative marginal effect on productivity and that, along with higher competition, new access to better inputs contributes to productivity gains after liber-alisation. Berthold and Teixeira (2005) examine the effects of trade barriers on TFP in the presence of insider groups and monopoly rights in import-competing industries, and show that these industries use inefficient technology which adversely affects efficiency and productivity. Low productivity in developing countries affects product quality and reduces competitiveness in international markets. Frankel and Romer (1996) show significant effects of trade on income and argue that openness raises income both by inducing factor accumulation and increasing output. Landlocked countries and regions are geographically disadvan-taged and likely to trade less, compared to countries and regions with their own seaports. Frankel and Romer (1999) re-assess the issue and examine the effects of geography using a gravity model. They find a statistically and economically significant relationship between trade and income.

Empirical evidence could be sensitive to the measures of openness. Some studies use multi-measures of openness (Levine and Renelt, 1992; Lee, 1993, 1995; Sachs and Warner, 1995; Baldwin and Seghezza, 1996; Harrison, 1996; Edwards, 1998; Wacziarg, 2001; Vamvakidis, 2002; Lee et al., 2004; Rodrik et al., 2004) (Table 1). Levine and Renelt (1992) use trade volumes, black market premium, real exchange rate index and the Leamer index, and find no robust and consistent evidence for the positive relationship between openness and long-run growth. They instead find a positive and robust correlation between growth and share of investment in GDP, and between investment share and ratio of trade to GDP. This implies that the favourable effects of trade traverse through capital accumulation, rather than a more efficient allocation of resources. Trade policies are important insofar as these policies facilitate the access to investment goods and encourage the accumulation of capital.

Several studies have shown that trade fosters growth through its favourable effects on investment and capital stock (Lee, 1995; Baldwin and Seghezza, 1996; Frankel and Romer, 1996; Wacziarg, 2001). Baldwin and Seghezza (1996) argue that trade induces investment, as the traded goods sector is relatively more capital intensive than the non-traded sector, investment goods require imported interme-diate inputs, and competition in international markets lowers the price of capital. Wacziarg (2001) finds that the rate of physical capital accumulation explains 46 to 63 per cent of the impact of trade policy on growth, and openness affects growth mainly by raising the ratio of domestic investment to GDP. Harrison and Revenga (1995) use three measures of trade orientation – export plus import as a share of GDP, average level of tariffs, and adjusted dollar index – to capture the extent of distortions in a country's relative prices of tradables. They examine the link between trade policies and foreign investment flows, and argue that trade reforms have been accompanied by significant increases in investment inflows. Harrison (1996) uses seven measures of openness and finds that only one posi-tively affects growth when cross-section data are employed; three reveal a positive association with growth when data are averaged over five-year periods; and six measures are significant. Greenaway et al. (1998) use several measures of liberalisation and find liberalisation and openness do impact favourably on growth of GDP per capita. Edwards (1998) uses a set of nine indices of trade policy and finds that more open countries experience faster productivity growth; the results are robust to the use of openness indicator, estimation technique, time period, and functional form.

An archival analysis and historical evidence suggest that openness and growth were not correlated during the interwar period; were negatively correlated a century ago (Foreman-Peck, 1995; O'Rourke and Williamson, 1999; Vamvakidis, 2002); and became significantly correlated only in recent decades (Vamvakidis, 2002; Clemens and Williamson, 2004). Foreman-Peck (1995) examines the effect of tariffs on the level of output per capita for 18 European countries (1860–1910), and finds that tariffs were negatively related to output per capita. O'Rourke (2000) uses a different sample and shows tariffs were instead positively correlated with growth during 1875–1914. Clemens and Williamson (2001) find that the positive relationship between openness and growth was reversed for a number of countries in the period prior to 1950. Irwin (2002) examines the correlation between tariffs and growth in the late nineteenth century and argues that correlation does not establish a causal relationship. Vamvakidis (2002) uses data from 1870 onwards and employs six proxies of openness, and finds no support for a positive growth–openness connection before 1970; in fact, the correlation is negative for the period 1920–40. He argues that the positive correlation between openness and growth is only a recent phenomenon.

(ii) Microeconomic firm-level models

The strand of studies following the microeconomic approach examine the effects of trade on the firm- or industry-level X-efficiency and productivity. While a number of studies show favourable effects (Condon et al., 1985; Chen, 1990), some find little or no correlation between openness measures (exports, imports, tariffs and quotas) and productivity (Tybout and Westbrook, 1995). Katrak (1997) finds a positive, though weak, relationship between technology imports and firm-level R&D. The degree and extent to which foreign technology imports encourage domestic R&D depends on the availability of technological skills and infrastructure in the domestic economy. Keller (2000) uses industrylevel data for machinery goods imports and productivity for eight OECD countries (1970–91), and finds that countries benefit more from domestic R&D than from the R&D of the average foreign country.[3] Keller (2002) further reinforces these results and shows strong

---

[3] The import composition of a country matters only if it is strongly biased toward or away from technological leaders. The differences in technology inflows related to the pattern of imports explain about 20 per cent of the total variations in productivity growth.

productivity effects from both own R&D spending and R&D conducted elsewhere. The R&D in industry itself contributes about 50 per cent, R&D in other domestic industries about 30 per cent, and R&D in foreign industries about 20 per cent of the increase in productivity. Singh (2003) examines the effects of exports on productivity and growth and tests the exportinduced convergence in 10 manufacturing industries in India. The effects of exports on TFP are significant in half of the sample industries, while in the remaining half these are statistically insignificant.

The mid-1990s marked the development of a distinct strand of research based on micro-theoretic models, and provided new dimensions to the transmission channels. These models draw on the industry dynamics models, which show a systematic relationship between 'entry and exit' and firm-level productivity differentials (Jovanovic, 1982; Hopenhayn, 1992; Ericson and Pakes, 1995). The micro-theoretic models disregard the assumption of representative firms underlying most traditional models based on the Heckscher–Ohlin framework, and instead consider intra-sectoral heterogeneity in productivity and export behaviour as arising from the 'entry and exit' decisions of firms in the export market. The plant-level heterogeneity within the same industry potentially induces the reshuffling of resources and reallocation of market shares from less efficient to more efficient firms, and leads to the improvements in productivity. These studies use longitudinal data and test two mutually-reinforcing hypotheses to explain the higher productivity and X-efficiency of exporters as compared to non-exporters: *self-selection* or *market-selection* hypothesis and the *learning-by-exporting* hypothesis. The *self-selection* hypothesis suggests the causal effects of firm-level productivity on exports, while the *learning-by-exporting* hypothesis shows the feedback and learning effects of exports on firm-level productivity.

The *self-selection* hypothesis postulates that the firms with exogenously determined high levels of productivity self-select themselves into the export markets, and this hypothesis builds on two propositions. First, the firms entering the export market incur higher irreversible sunk costs as compared to firms operating in the domestic market and, therefore, the initial productivity levels for the export-oriented firms need to be higher than the domestic-oriented firms (Roberts and Tybout, 1997; Bernard and Jensen, 1999; Bernard and Wagner, 1997, 2001; Isgut, 2001; Delgado et al., 2002; Melitz, 2003).[4] Second, firms entering a foreign market are exposed to more intense competition than firms in a domestic market. Such

---

[4] Tybout (2000) argues that in developing countries: (i) markets tolerate inefficient firms, so the cross-firm productivity dispersion is high; (ii) small groups of entrenched oligopolists exploit monopoly power in product markets; and (iii) many small firms are unable or unwilling to grow, so important scale economies go unexploited. He draws on firm-level studies to assess these conjectures and finds none to be systematically supported.

competition in export markets provides fewer opportunities to inefficient firms (Aw and Hwang, 1995; Delgado et al., 2002).[5] The export markets, thus, select the most productive and efficient firms from among potential entrants. It is only the productive and above-average firms that are likely to cope with sunk costs and face fierce competition abroad, and self-select themselves into the foreign export market. The patterns of entry, survival and exit in the export market are related to the firm-level productivity differentials. Melitz (2003) uses a dynamic industry model with heterogeneous firms and shows that the exposure to trade will induce only more productive firms to enter export markets (while some less productive firms continue to produce only for domestic markets) and will simultaneously force the least productive firms to exit.[6] Feenstra (2006) argues that the gains from trade in monopolistic competition models arise from three sources: (i) price reductions due to increasing returns to scale; (ii) increased product variety available to consumers; and (iii) self-selection of firms with only the most efficient firms surviving after liberalisation.

The *learning-by-exporting* hypothesis, which is analogous to the *learning-by-doing* model of Arrow (1962), suggests that internationalisation is a catalytic source of technological innovations and managerial inputs for the exporting firms.[7] Several studies find support for the learning effects of exports, such as Clerides et al. (1998) for Colombia, Mexico and Morocco; Kraay (1999) for China; Aw et al. (2000) for Taiwan (but not for South Korea); Castellani (2002) for Italy; Delgado et al. (2002) for Spain; Mengistae and Patillo (2004) for Kenya, Ghana and Ethiopia; Bigsten et al. (2004) for four Sub-Saharan African countries; and Girma et al. (2004) for Great Britain. Clerides et al. (1998) find strong evidence for the self-selection mechanism, but no evidence for learning effects from exporting in Colombia, Mexico and Morocco. Aw et al. (2000) find support for learning-by-exporting in Taiwan, but not in South Korea. The newly exporting firms in Taiwan outperform the non-exporting firms before entry into the export market and, in some industries, the exporting firms show productivity improvements after

---

[5] Even if the competitive pressures in domestic and export markets are similar, the differences in sunk entry costs explain the productivity differentials between exporters and domestic-oriented firms (Delgado et al., 2002).

[6] Melitz (2003) argues that the firms with different productivity levels co-exist in an industry because each firm faces an initial uncertainty concerning its productivity before making an irreversible investment to enter the industry. Entry into export markets is also costly, but the firm's decision to export occurs after it gains the knowledge of its productivity.

[7] The interaction of export-oriented domestic firms with foreign clients and competitors engenders positive learning effects. The exporting firms accumulate experience and knowledge and are systematically more productive and close to the efficiency frontier than the domestic-oriented non-exporting firms. The exporting is viewed as a learning process and it improves the productivity premium of exporting firms.

their entry into the export market. In the case of Korea, the correlation between exporting and firm productivity is somewhat weak. Delgado et al. (2002) examine the TFP differences between exporting and non-exporting Spanish manufacturing firms (1991–96).[8] They find significant evidence for self-selection, but insignificant evidence for learning effects; the learning effects become significant only when the sample is restricted to young firms. For German manufacturing firms, Arnold and Hussinger (2005) show Granger-causality from TFP to exporting and not vice versa. Castellani (2002) observes that only the firms with very high exposure to export markets experience learning effects and not the firms below this threshold export intensity. Van Biesebroeck (2005) supports both self-selection and learning-by-exporting hypotheses in nine African countries. A study conducted by the International Study Group on Exports and Productivity (2008) for 14 countries finds that the exporters are more productive than non-exporters when observed and unobserved heterogeneity is controlled for, and these exporter productivity premia tend to increase with the share of exports in total sales.

The learning effects are likely to be more pronounced in trade between countries with wider technological gaps (such as trade between developed and developing countries), rather than in trade between countries with similar technologies (such as trade among developed countries or among developing countries). In self-selection hypothesis, the exporting firms are exogenously more productive from the outset, and exporting contributes to productivity only when the productivity premium of already productive firms improves after their entry into the export market. The studies supporting the *self-selection* hypothesis numerically overwhelm the studies supporting the *learning-by-exporting* hypothesis, and this implicitly provides a stronger support for the effects of productivity and growth on trade as compared to the effects of trade on productivity and growth (Table 2). Rodriguez and Rodrik (2000) review the studies by Dollar (1992), Ben-David (1993), Lee (1993), Sachs and Warner (1995), Harrison (1996), Edwards (1998), Frankel and Romer (1999) and Wacziarg (2001; 1998), and raise sceptical concerns on the strength of the argument for the beneficial effects of trade. They argue that 'these papers . . . find little evidence that firms derive technological or other benefits from exporting per se; the more common pattern is that efficient producers tend to self-select into export markets. In other words, causality seems to go from productivity to exports, not vice versa' (Rodriguez and Rodrik, 2000, p. 317).

---

[8] Delgado et al. (2002) argue that the productivity distribution of exporters should stochastically dominate the productivity distribution of non-exporters in the period prior to their entry into the export market. On the exit side of the export market, the productivity distribution of continuing exporters stochastically dominates the distribution of exiting exporters. In the presence of learning-by-exporting effects, the differences between productivity levels for exporting and non-exporting firms should increase after the entry of exporters in the export market.

TABLE 2
Effects of International Trade on Productivity and Economic Growth: Microeconomic Evidence

Author (Year)	Country	Sample	Methodology and Estimators	Main Results and Conclusions
Aw and Hwang (1995)	Taiwan	2,832 Firms, 1986.	Translog production function, Cross-section.	Support for SS; Higher productivity of exporters; No support for LE.
Bernard and Wagner (1997)	Germany	7,624 Firms, 1978–92.	Panel data.	Support for SS. Exporting firms have higher productivity.
Roberts and Tybout (1997)	Colombia	Manufacturing plants in four major exporting industries.	Panel data, Dynamic Probit Model, Method of Simulated Moments and Maximum-Likelihood.	Sunk costs are significant, and prior export experience increases the probability of exporting. Plants that are large, old and owned by corporations are all more likely to export.
Clerides et al. (1998)	Colombia, Mexico and Morocco	2,800 Firms; 1981–91, 1986–90 and 1984–91.	FIML of cost function; Panel data.	Exporting firms are more efficient; Quitters are less productive; No support for LE in Colombia and Mexico; Support for SS and LE in some Moroccan industries; Spillover effects from exporters to non-exporters.
Bernard and Jensen (1999)	USA	50,000–60,000 Firms; 1984–92. Subsamples: 1984–88 and 1989–92.	Panel data.	Support for SS. Exporting firms have higher productivity. No support for LE.
Kraay (1999)	China	2,105 Firms; 1988–92.	Dynamic panel data.	Exporting firms have higher productivity; Support for LE in established exporters.
Aw et al. (2000)	Korea, Taiwan (China)	Korea: 39,022 to 88,864 Firms. Taiwan: 88,000 to 100,000 Firms.	Cross-section.	Support for SS; No support for LE in Korea. LE in some Taiwanese industries. Productivity is correlated less strongly with export market participation in Korea than in Taiwan.
Aw et al. (2001)	Taiwan	80,000 to 100,000 Firms; Sample period: 1981, 1986 and 1991.	Panel data.	More productive firms, on average, survive and, in many cases, their productivity converges to older incumbents. Exiting firms are less productive than survivors. Productivity differential between entering and exiting firms is an important source of industry-level productivity growth.
Isgut (2001)	Colombia	6,454 Plants; 1981–91.	Panel data.	Support for SS. Does not rule out possibility that successful exporters learn from participation in export markets.
Castellani (2002)	Italy	2,898 Firms; 1989–94.	Cross-section.	Support for SS; LE in plants with high export orientation. Exporting firms have higher productivity.
Delgado et al. (2002)	Spain	1,766 Firms; 1991–96.	Non-parametric method.	Support for self-selection. Higher levels of productivity of exporting firms than non-exporting firms; Inconclusive evidence on LE.
Pavcnik (2002)	Chile	4,379 Plants; 1979–86.	Semi-parametric method; Panel data.	Within-plant productivity improvements can be attributed to liberalised trade in import-competing sector. In many cases, aggregate productivity improvements stem from reshuffling of resources from less to more efficient producers.
Wagner (2002)	Germany	353 Firms; 1978–89.	Panel data; Matching approach.	No support for LE. Support for positive effects of starting to export on growth of employment and wages; weaker evidence for a positive effect on labour productivity.

TABLE 2 (*Continued*)

Author (Year)	Country	Sample	Methodology and Estimators	Main Results and Conclusions
Baldwin and Gu (2003)	Canada	236 Manufacturing industries (at four-digit 1980 SIC level); Four periods: 1974–79; 1979–84; 1984–90; and 1990–96.	Panel data, GMM; System GMM estimator.	Support for SS and LE. Among non-exporters, more productive ones and those whose productivity has recently been growing more rapidly expand into export markets and less productive remain non-exporters.
Girma et al. (2003)	UK	2,989 Firms; 1991–97.	Difference-in-Differences based on Matched Firms.	Temporary negative contemporaneous impact of exit on TFP, but more persistent and sizeable negative effects on output and employment trajectories.
Head and Ries (2003)	Japan	1,070 Firms; 1977–89.	Ordered regression.	Firms that invest abroad and export are more productive than firms that just export. Firms that export are larger than firms that serve domestic market, but both are smaller than firms that invest abroad as well as export.
Baldwin and Gu (2004)	Canada	19,142 Plants; 1984–90 and 1990–96.	Survey data and Difference regressions.	Support for SS and LE. Exporters tend to be the more innovative firms. Plants that enter into export markets increase investments in R&D and training. Entry into export market leads to an increase in number of advanced technologies, increases in foreign sourcing, and improvements in information available.
Bernard and Jensen (2004a)	USA	50,000–60,000 Plants; 1983–92.	Panel data: Unbalanced panel.	Support for SS. Exporting is associated with reallocation of resources from less to more efficient plants. Reallocation effects account for over 40 per cent of total TFP growth.
Bernard and Jensen (2004b)	USA	13,550 Plants; 1984–92.	Panel data; GMM estimator.	Entry and exit in export market is substantial, past exporters are apt to reenter, and plants are likely to export in consecutive years. Entry costs are significant and spillovers from export activity negligible.
Bigsten et al. (2004)	Cameroon, Ghana, Kenya and Zimbabwe	289 Firms: (1991/93–1994/95).	Panel data; Maximum-likelihood and GMM.	Support for LE. Significant efficiency gains from exporting. Little direct evidence for self-selection.
Criscuolo et al. (2004)	UK	1980–2000.	Cross-section.	Productivity growth increased due to entry and exit. Share of productivity growth accounted for by entry and exit increased considerably from 1980s to 1990s. Globalisation and increased information and communication technology contribute to productivity growth.
Girma et al. (2004)	UK	8,992 Firms; 1988–99.	Panel data; Matching approach.	Support for SS and LE; Exporting involves sunk costs. Exporters are more productive and exporting further increases firm productivity.
Greenaway and Kneller (2004)	UK	11,225 Firms; 1989–2002.	Probit model.	Support for SS. Sunk costs are important, and firms have to become more productive to enter the export market. LE only in unmatched and not in matched sample.

(*Continued*)

TABLE 2 (*Continued*)

Author (Year)	Country	Sample	Methodology and Estimators	Main Results and Conclusions
Greenaway et al. (2004)	UK	3,662 Firms; 1992–96.	Panel data.	Positive spillover effects from multinational enterprises on the decision to export and export propensity. Probability of domestic firms exporting positively influenced by intensity of foreign R&D expenditure, and relative importance of production and export activities of multinational enterprises.
Hansson and Lundin (2004)	Sweden	3,275 Firms; 1990–99.	Matching and Difference-in-Differences Analysis.	No TFP growth differentials for entrants into the export market.
Schor (2004)	Brazil	4,484 Firms; 1986–98.	Panel data.	Tariffs on inputs have negative effect on productivity. Higher competition, access to better inputs contributes to productivity gains.
Alvarez and López (2005)	Chile	Manufacturing Plants with 10 or more workers; 1990–96.	Probit Model, Panel data Model.	Plants that enter international markets show superior initial performance, consistent with self-selection. Existence of learning-by-exporting for entrants, but not for those that export continuously.
Arnold and Hussinger (2005)	Germany	389 Firms; 1999–2000.	Panel data, Probit model, Granger-causality, Matching.	Support for SS. No support for LE.
Greenaway et al. (2005)	Sweden	3,570 Firms; 1980–97.	Matching and Difference-in-Differences; Panel data.	No evidence of pre- or post-entry differences in firm-level productivity. Performance characteristics of exporters and non-exporters remarkably similar.
Ruane and Sutherland (2005)	Ireland	2,854 Firms; 1991–98.	Panel data.	Support for SS. Superior characteristics of exporters relative to non-exporters. No evidence that enterprises improve their performance after entry.
Van Biesebroeck (2005)	9 African countries	1,916 Firms, with approximately 200 in each country; 1992–96.	Panel data; GMM estimator.	Support for SS and LE. Exporting firms have higher productivity.
Bernard et al. (2006)	USA	Approximately 210,000 Plants in 337 manufacturing industries; 1987–97.	Panel data; OLS and Logistic Regressions.	Reallocation of economic activity towards high-productivity firms as trade costs fall. Evidence for productivity growth within firms in response to decreases in industry-level trade costs.
Fernandes (2007)	Colombia	Average of 6,474 Plants per year; 1977–91.	Panel data; OLS; GMM.	Liberalisation has positive impact on plant productivity. Impact is stronger for large plants and for plants in industries with less domestic competition.
Greenaway and Kneller (2007b)	UK	12,875 observations on domestic manufacturing firms.	Probit Model, Panel Difference-in-Differences.	Post-entry productivity growth of new export firms faster than non-export firms. Potential for learning varies across industries, depending upon the extent to which they are already exposed to international competition and where R&D intensity is already high.
Greenaway et al. (2007c)	UK	9,292 manufacturing firms (total 51,668 annual observations); Of the 9,292 firms, 5,461 are continuous exporters (58.77 per cent) and 2,798 never exported (30.11 per cent); and 434 are starters (4.67 per cent); 1993–2003.	Pooled Probit Model, Random-effects Probit, Fixed effects, GMM, Dynamic Random-effects Probit and Dynamic GMM.	Exporters exhibit better financial health than non-exporters. Starters generally display low liquidity and high leverage. No evidence that firms enjoying better *ex ante* financial health are more likely to export, and strong evidence that participation in export markets improves firms' *ex post* financial health.

TABLE 2 (*Continued*)

Author (Year)	Country	Sample	Methodology and Estimators	Main Results and Conclusions
Alvarez and López (2008)	Chile	Manufacturing plants with 10 or more workers; 1990–99.	Olley and Pakes (1996) method to estimate productivity. Pooled regressions with OLS and IV estimators.	Domestic as well as foreign-owned exporting plants improve productivity of local suppliers. Higher exporting activity increases productivity of plants in domestic sector. No evidence of spillovers from exporters. Foreign-owned exporters generate positive productivity spillovers. Support for backward spillover effects from domestic exporters.
Andersson et al. (2008)	Sweden	Manufacturing firms with at least 10 employees. 56,957 firm-level observations; 1997–2004.	Panel data Model; GLS, IV and GMM estimations.	Support for selection operating from market to market. Productivity premiums increase in number of markets and number of products. Firms that both export and import are more productive.
Bellone et al. (2008)	France	23,000 Manufacturing firms with at least 20 employees; 1990–2002.	Non-parametric methodology to compute TFP, Pooled Regression.	Support for U-shaped productivity dynamics of new exporters. Pattern more pronounced for intensively exporting firms and firms operating in capital-intensive or high-technology sectors. Both self-selection and learning-to-export mechanisms prevail during the pre-entry period.
Fryges and Wagner (2008)	Germany	All establishments from mining and manufacturing industries that employ at least 20 persons or in company that owns the unit; 1995–2005.	Propensity Score, Dose–Response functions and Fractional Logit model; Pooled Regressions.	Support for causal effect exports on labour productivity growth, but only within a sub-interval of the range of firms' export–sales ratios. Evidence for time-varying causal relationship between labour productivity growth and the export–sales ratio.
Girma et al. (2008)	Great Britain and the Republic of Ireland	UK firms with fixed or current assets in excess of £150,000; 1996–2003. Irish Manufacturing plants with at least 10 employees; 2000–03.	Bivariate Probit Model; Maximum-likelihood and 3SLS estimators.	Previous exporting experience enhances innovative capacity of Irish firms and positive LE effects. No strong evidence for such direct effects for British firms.
Greenaway and Kneller (2008a)	UK	11,225 manufacturing firms. Taking 1995 as representative, 66 per cent of firms exported; 1989–2002.	Probit Model, Propensity Score-matching and Difference-in-Differences.	Spillovers associated with agglomeration raise probability of export entry. Survival is driven partly by size and TFP and partly by industry characteristics. Exporters larger and have higher productivity. Regional and industry agglomeration relevant to successful entry. Firms receive a significant boost to productivity in the year they enter. Firms that exit are more likely to do so due to loss of market share than loss of productivity. Having a sales mix with a larger share of exports and being in activities with differentiated products offer some protection against exit.

(*Continued*)

TABLE 2 (*Continued*)

Author (Year)	Country	Sample	Methodology and Estimators	Main Results and Conclusions
Greenaway et al. (2008b)	Sweden	3,570 manufacturing firms with more than 50 employees; 1980–96.	TFP estimated using Olley and Pakes and Levinsohn and Petrin methodology, Multinominal Logit Regression.	Higher levels of international competition increase probability of exit by merger and closedown. If trade is more intra-industry in character, effect of import penetration on exit is less. Probability of exit by switching is higher in revealed comparative disadvantage industries. The geographical source of international competition is important. Structure of international competition matters indirectly as well directly.
International Study Group on Exports and Productivity (ISGEP) (2008)	14 countries	Sample varies across countries.	Country-by-Country Analysis using identically specified and estimated models; Pooled Regressions; Meta-Regression Analysis.	Exporters are more productive than non-exporters and exporter productivity premia tend to increase with the share of exports in total sales. Support for SS for less developed countries and for all European Union countries. Support for LE for only one out of 14 countries.
Serti and Tomasi (2008)	Italy	38,771 Manufacturing firms with employment of 20 units or more; 1989–97.	Semi-parametric technique to estimate productivity; Panel data model, OLS, Propensity Score Matching and Difference-in-Differences.	Support for self-selection and exporters outperform non-exporters. Firms serving foreign markets have higher productivity and are larger, more capital and skilled labour intensive, and more (labour) cost competitive. Heterogeneous post-entry effects with respect to characteristics.

Notes:
SS stands for self-selection or market-selection hypothesis; LE: learning-by-exporting hypothesis; R&D: Research and Development; SIC: Standard Industrial Classification; TFP: Total Factor Productivity; OLS: Ordinary Least Squares; 3SLS: Three-stage Least Squares; GLS: Generalised Least Squares; IV: Instrumental Variables; GMM: Generalised Method of Moments; and FIML: Full Information Maximum-likelihood.

3. PROTECTIONISM VERSUS TRADE LIBERALISATION:
A TALE OF TWO PARADIGMS

a. Protectionism and Barriers to Trade

Recognition for the 'gains of trade' paradoxically co-exists with the preferences for 'barriers to trade' and passion for protectionism. Developing countries, until the 1980s, have been sceptical about the gains of free trade, and many pursued protectionist and import-substituting industrialisation policies. Several factors seem catalytic to the support for trade barriers, such as: (i) infant-industry protection; (ii) export-pessimism arising from the apprehensions of adverse terms of trade in the developing countries (Singer, 1950; Nurkse, 1958; Prebisch, 1959);[9]

---

[9] Singer (1950), Nurkse (1958) and Prebisch (1959) provide a theoretical and generalised argument for the poor export performance of the developing countries, and suggest that, as a result of the low income and price elasticities of demand for primary commodities, the developing countries specialising in the production and export of these commodities have experienced steady and long-run deterioration in terms of trade. In conjunction with low demand elasticities, the increased supplies lead

(iii) disbelief in the market mechanism that stemmed from the Great Depression and failure of the *laissez-faire* system; (iv) concerns regarding the decline in real wages and displacement of workers from jobs due to the increased foreign competition engendered by trade liberalisation (Krueger, 2004); and (v) the plausible adverse effects of trade on environmental quality.

A parallel counter-strand postulates protectionism as a myopically short-term development strategy in that it encourages X-inefficiency and leads to reduction in productivity and growth and rise in costs and prices. The *immiserising growth* model (Bhagwati, 1958, 1968) shows the possibilities of immiserising tariffs, where import protection leads to negative real growth. Krueger (2004) asserts that the job protection case for protectionism comes at the cost of increased inefficiency and higher prices for consumers, arising from the tariff and non-tariff barriers. In contrast, trade liberalisation and free trade lead to the rapid and sustainable growth, rise in living standards and reduction in poverty (Krueger, 2004). Greenaway (2004) postulates that infrastructure investment and trade liberalisation, which reduce natural and man-made barriers, respectively, are good for growth. Copeland and Taylor (2004) review the literature on the effects of trade and growth on environment, and assert there is now a great deal of evidence supporting the view that rising incomes affect environmental quality in a positive way. The 'Environmental Kuznets Curve' hypothesises an inverse-U-shaped relationship between a country's per capita income and its level of environmental quality: increased incomes are associated with an increase in pollution in poor countries, but a decline in pollution in rich countries. If environmental quality is a normal good, then the increases in income brought about by trade or growth will both increase the demand for environmental quality and increase the ability of the governments to afford costly investments in environmental protection (Copeland and Taylor, 2004). Frankel and Rose (2005) examine the effects of trade on environment, and assert that there is little evidence that trade has a detrimental effect on environment.

b. Multilateral Trade Liberalisation and the Preferential Trade Agreements

The protectionism of the 1920s and 1930s and failure of multilateral attempts to foster a cooperative trade-policy environment led to the formation of the GATT in 1947, which was subsequently transformed into the WTO in January 1995. GATT/WTO emphasises the reduction or removal of tariff and non-tariff barriers

---

to the reduction in prices of primary commodities relative to the prices of manufactured goods imported by the developing countries. Nurkse (1958) argues that, as a result of both relatively low income elasticities of demand and the increased substitution of synthetic material for raw material in the production of manufactured goods in the developed countries, the primary exports are confronted with a stagnant world demand.

to foster multilateral free trade in goods, services and capital. The World Bank and the IMF have the lending powers and, thus, are in a position to enforce liberalisation in (developing) countries seeking financial assistance, as compared to GATT/WTO that works on the principles of most favoured nations (MFNs) and reciprocal liberalisation. Irwin (1995) argues that the World Bank and IMF are the autonomous institutions that use lending power to affect economic policies of the member countries, as compared to GATT that has no autonomous power, independent leverage or financial sanction. Trade liberalisation remains a characteristic feature of the IMF loan conditionality for (developing) countries seeking financial assistance.

(i) GATT/WTO and the world trading system

The GATT/WTO prescribes the rules that govern the trade policy of the member countries and help foster multilateral free trade by: (i) facilitating the reduction or removal of trade restrictions;[10] (ii) resolving the *prisoners' dilemma* that may arise in unilateral trade (tariff) policy in response to the adverse terms-of-trade (Bagwell and Staiger, 1999, 2002; Tomz et al., 2007), (iii) eliminating tariff wars and protectionism; (iv) resolving hegemonic and power asymmetries across negotiating partners; and (v) helping countries to coordinate on efficient outcomes. In Nash equilibrium, tariffs too high and trade volumes too low, and hence a trade agreement that facilitates a reciprocal reduction in Nash tariffs would be mutually beneficial (Bagwell and Staiger, 2002). The reciprocal reduction in trade barriers spurs higher trade, and MFN principle forbids member countries from pursuing discriminatory trade policies against one another (Panagariya, 1999). The rules-based approach reduces uncertainty and provides a guaranteed market access. It also helps alleviate *time-inconsistency* problems and policy reversals (Staiger and Tabellini, 1987; Maggi and Rodriguez-Clare, 1998; Tomz et al., 2007). Irwin (1995) argues that in spite of its small size and uncertain place as an economic institution, GATT's long-run impact on the world economy has been more significant than either that of the World Bank or the IMF.

While there has been a long-standing recognition and widely-held consensus on the substantive contributions of GATT/WTO to the promotion of world trade, the emerging evidence pioneered by Rose (2004a, 2004b; 2005a, 2005b) casts a sceptical note. It suggests that insiders trade at no higher levels than outsiders.[11] Rose (2004a) uses a gravity model of bilateral merchandise trade and a large panel dataset covering over 50 years and 175 countries, and estimates the effects of

---

[10] The 'prisoners' dilemma' problem in repeated Nash games on tariff agreements suggests that it is individually rational to impose and collectively rational to remove the tariffs.

[11] The GATT conducted eight 'rounds' of multilateral trade negotiations before it was subsumed by the World Trade Organization in 1995: Geneva (concluded in 1947), Annecy (1949), Torquay (1951), Geneva (1956), Dillon (1961), Kennedy (1967), Tokyo (1979), and Uruguay (1994) (Rose, 2004a).

multilateral trade agreements – GATT/WTO and Generalised System of Preferences – on trade. He finds little evidence that the countries joining or belonging to GATT/ WTO have different trade patterns from the outsiders. Using a comprehensive set of over 60 measures of trade policy, Rose (2004b) finds no support for the significant differentials in terms of tariff rates and other measures of trade policy between members and outsiders. Rose (2005a) then compares the effects of three multilateral organisations on trade: GATT/WTO, IMF and the Organisation for Economic Co-operation and Development (OECD) and its predecessor, the Organisation for European Economic Co-operation (OEEC). He finds that the membership in the OECD is consistently associated with a strong positive effect on trade, while the comparable evidence is weaker for GATT/WTO and especially the IMF.[12] Rose (2005b) further examines the effects of GATT/WTO on the stability and predictability of trade flows, and finds little evidence that membership in GATT/WTO has a significant dampening effect on the volatility.

The Rose evidence marks a puzzle in open economy macroeconomics. A few studies have attempted to resolve the 'Rose Paradox' and support the significant role of GATT/WTO in spurring world trade (Subramanian and Shang-Jin, 2007; Tomz et al., 2007). Subramanian and Shang-Jin (2007) argue that the GATT/WTO has served to increase world imports substantially, possibly by about 120 per cent of world trade. Tomz et al. (2007) suggest that grouping nonmember participants with non-participants causes a substantial downward bias in the estimated effects of GATT membership. They argue that, when this misclassification is corrected, the agreement proved beneficial for both formal members and non-member participants, which traded at higher levels than the countries outside GATT. The GATT exerted a positive effect on trade in nearly all time periods and for most groups of countries (Tomz et al., 2007).

(ii) Preferential trade agreements (PTAs)

The system of GATT/WTO remains surrounded by a multitude of economic integration and preferential trade agreements that are non-discriminatory for members, but discriminatory against non-members.[13] The formation of economic

---

[12] The effects of both IMF and GATT/WTO membership on trade are usually quite small (indeed, often negative). The exception is that the effects of GATT/WTO membership are positive when a fixed-effects estimator is employed: that is, *joining* the GATT/WTO is associated with a trade-creating effect, though simply *belonging* to it is not. The OECD, on the other hand, has a robustly positive effect on trade that is both economically and statistically significant (Rose, 2005a).

[13] The GATT's Article XXIV permits preferential agreements, provided that member countries eliminate tariffs on substantially all trade between them in a reasonable period of time (Bagwell and Staiger, 1998). This exception to the principle of non-discrimination was controversial in its inception and has met with renewed controversy recently, as many GATT members have increasingly exercised their rights under this article to negotiate preferential trading agreements. These agreements may take either of two forms. When countries form a *free trade area*, they eliminate barriers

unions and PTAs has proliferated exponentially in that these have come to constitute a numerically massive magnitude and encompass a predominant proportion
of the globe.[14]

Panagariya (1999) argues that the aggressive race between the European Union
and United States on the promotion of Free Trade Areas (Agreements) led to the
renewal of efforts for PTAs by and among smaller countries of Africa, Latin
America, South and Central Asia, Central and Eastern Europe and the Baltic
Republic. The only region which has, so far, remained firmly committed to the
MFN approach to liberalisation is East Asia (Panagariya, 1999).[15]

The proliferation of PTAs has spurred several concerns and numerous studies
evaluating binary choices and the effects of PTAs on the trade and welfare of
non-members of the bloc, level of multilateral free trade and welfare, and the
enforcement of WTO agreements. An issue that remains centre stage is whether
PTAs supplement or supplant the multilateral trading system and, thus, have the
'trade creation' and 'building block' or 'trade diversion' and 'stumbling block'
effects.[16] A number of studies have supported the 'building block' effects (Baldwin,
1993, 1995; Ethier, 1998; Laird, 1999; Clausing, 2001; Glick and Rose, 2002; Lee
et al., 2008). Krugman (1991, 1993) envisions that the PTAs among the 'natural'
trading partners are likely to generate positive effects, as the gains from trade
creation would outweigh the losses from trade diversion.[17] The process of coalition
formation and PTA configuration could lead to two possible outcomes: First, as
per the Vinerian static analysis, the expansion of existing PTAs would raise intra-
bloc, but reduce inter-bloc trade, and also trade with non-members. The emergence
of several PTAs would lead to inter-bloc trade discrimination and tariff barriers

---

to internal trade, but maintain independent external trade policies. Under a *customs union*, member
countries also agree to harmonise their external trade policies, and create a common external-tariff-
setting authority (Bagwell and Staiger, 1998).

[14] A common characteristic of Free Trade Agreements (FTAs), Preferential Trade Agreements (PTAs)
and the Regional Trade Agreements (RTAs) is that these Agreements (Areas) are non-discriminatory
for members, but discriminatory against non-members. The terms FTAs, PTAs and RTAs are, therefore, used interchangeably throughout the study.

[15] Panagariya (1999) provides a description of the three key concepts used by the academic and
policy literature: Preferential Trade Area (PTA), Free Trade Area (FTA) and the Customs Union
(CU). A PTA is a union between two or more countries in which goods produced within the union
are subject to lower trade barriers than the goods produced outside the union. An FTA is a PTA in
which member countries do not impose *any* trade barriers on the goods produced within the union,
but do so on those produced outside the union. A CU is an FTA in which member countries apply
a common external tariff (CET) on a good imported from outside countries. The CET can differ
across goods, but not across union partners. In policy documents and debates, the acronym FTA is
often used to refer to a Free Trade *Agreement* or Free Trade *Arrangement*, rather than Free Trade
Area (Panagariya, 1999). For a review of literature on the preferential trade liberalisation, see
Panagariya (2000).

[16] Bhagwati (1991) coins the 'building block' and 'stumbling block' effects of PTAs.

[17] The countries that trade substantially and disproportionately more with each other are termed as
the 'natural' trading partners.

and, thus, would cripple multilateral cooperation and impede global free trade. Second, as per the post-Vinerian dynamic analysis, higher intra-bloc trade would lead to higher income and growth of the member countries, which, in turn, would lead to expansion of market size and creation of trade and investment opportunities for non-member countries. These growth externalities and spillover effects would transform PTAs into the 'building blocks' of global free trade (Baldwin, 1993, 1995; Laird, 1999; Lee, 2008).

The domino theory of Baldwin (1993, 1995, 1997) postulates that increased integration among a subset of countries would provide incentives for outsiders to seek accession, thereby expanding the trading blocs and fostering trade liberalisation. Baldwin (1997) asserts that the 'idiosyncratic incidents of regionalism triggered a multiplier effect that knocked down bilateral import barriers like a row of dominos' (Baldwin, 1997, p. 877). He asserts that almost all empirical studies of the European and North American arrangements find the positive impacts of PTA's on the living standards of members. Egger et al. (2008) postulate that the likelihood of new RTA membership is influenced by economic fundamentals, such as the country size, factor endowments, and trade and investment costs. They find strong effects of endogenous PTAs on intra-industry trade in a sample of country-pairs covering mainly the OECD countries. They argue that the PTA-induced increase in trade volumes can be mainly attributed to an associated growth in intra-industry trade, at least in developed economies. Ethier (1998) suggests that the new regionalism is a direct result of the success of multilateral liberalisation, as well as being the means by which new countries trying to enter the multilateral system compete among themselves for direct investment. By internalising an important externality, regionalism plays an important role in expanding and preserving liberal trading order (Ethier, 1998). Laird (1999) argues that the quantitative estimates tend to show that trade creation effects outweigh trade diversion effects and hence are overall welfare-enhancing. Clausing (2001) finds that the Canada–United States FTA had substantial trade creation effects, with little evidence of trade diversion. Glick and Rose (2002) examine the effects of currency union on trade, using a comprehensive panel dataset of over 200 countries (1948–97). They find that a pair of countries which joined (left) a currency union experienced near-doubling (halving) of bilateral trade. Lee et al. (2008) use a panel dataset of 175 countries (1948–99) and examine the effects of regional trading blocs on global trade. They conclude that on average, they increase global trade by raising intra-bloc trade, without damaging the extra-bloc trade.

While several studies support the 'building block' effects, a parallel counter-strand raises concerns and postulates 'stumbling block' effects (Bhagwati, 1991; Panagariya, 1996; Bhagwati et al., 1998; Romalis, 2007). These arrangements not only reduce the incentives for MTL, but could also lead to retaliatory and periodic tariff wars. While an infinite extension of a trading bloc in that it would encompass the globe and map multilateral free trade seems a theoretical possibility and is unlikely to materialise, the finite extensions are as likely to strengthen the retaliatory power of a trading bloc against non-bloc members and lead to higher bloc-lateral trade barriers, as could induce the removal of bilateral trade barriers and incite the liberalisation of trade as envisioned in the domino theory. Krugman (1991) asserts that the enlargement of trading blocs leads to more retaliatory power for each, which, in a non-cooperative environment, could lead to higher inter-bloc trade barriers; the welfare reaches the minimum in a world with two or three CUs. Bhagwati et al. (1998) assert that the formation of PTAs multiplies by imitation; one PTA leads to another and so on and so forth, and eventually Gresham's Law takes over. Panagariya (1996) argues that when trade liberalisation is discriminatory, as in FTA, within the Vinerian framework, the effects of freer trade have a strong mercantilist bias: a country gains from the liberalisation by the partner, but loses from its own liberalisation.[18] Romalis (2007) finds that the North American Free Trade Agreement (NAFTA) had a substantial impact on international trade volumes, but a modest effect on prices and welfare. The NAFTA increased North American output and prices in many highly protected sectors by driving out imports from non-member countries.

4. METHODOLOGICAL AND MEASUREMENT ISSUES

The above discussion suggests the evidence is not unambiguous. Several factors, such as differences in sample periods and countries, estimators and econometric methodologies employed, frequency of data used, measures of trade openness employed, model specifications estimated, and test statistics used for testing the null have a bearing on this. This section explores methodological and measurement issues that surround the trade–growth empirics.

a. Solow and Stochastic Residuals: A Generated Regressand

The findings of the studies examining the productivity effects of trade are contingent on the quality of data on productivity, commonly represented by TFP and is computed as the residual difference between output and weighted contribution of factor inputs to output or as the ratio of output to (weighted) factor inputs as,

---

[18] Panagariya (1996) argues that a country benefits from *receiving* a preferential (or discriminatory) access to the partner's market and is hurt by *giving* the partner a similar access to its own market. When the country gives access to the partner on a preferential basis, it loses the tariff revenue collected on the imports from the partner. The revenue goes to boost the terms of trade of the latter. The reverse happens when the country receives a preferential access from the partner. On balance, the country which liberalises the most, is likely to lose (Panagariya, 1996).

$$TFP(t) = A(t) = \left[\frac{Y(t)}{K(t)^\alpha L(t)^\beta}\right]; \quad t \in [1, \ldots, T]. \tag{1}$$

A major problem in computing *TFP* in (1) is that the aggregate data on the incomes accruing to capital, $K(t)$, and labour, $L(t)$, are commonly beset with measurement problems in developing economies with large informal sectors. Consistent time-series data are, in fact, not available in many cases. In the absence of actual data on factor income shares, α and β, a commonly used alternative is to use a regression analogue of growth accounting, and estimate the Cobb–Douglas production technology with unity restriction, $\alpha + \beta = 1$, imposed on its parameters,

$$\ln Y(t) = \ln A(t) = \alpha \ln K(t) + \beta \ln L(t) + \varepsilon(t). \tag{2}$$

In (2), $\varepsilon(t) = \mu(t) + v(t)$ with $\text{cov}[\mu(t), v(t)] = 0$. The estimated parameters, α and β, from (2) are used to mimic the income shares of capital and labour in output, and derive the TFP in levels as,

$$\ln TFP(t) = [\ln A(t) + \varepsilon(t)] = \ln Y(t) - \hat{\alpha} \ln K(t) - \hat{\beta} \ln L(t). \tag{3}$$

Some of the limitations of computing TFP based on production technology are as follows. First, since the intercept term in (3) is constant, productivity is virtually represented by the stochastic residual term of the production technology. All the estimation problems (such as omitted variables bias, functional-form misspecification bias, sample-selection bias and simultaneity bias) and the errors-in-variables bias (such as measurement of capital stock and total employment in the economy) get reflected in the residuals, $\varepsilon(t)$, and, thus, embodied in the TFP.

Second, the TFP derived using parameter estimates obtained from the production technology is apparently a 'generated' series with the possibility of itself containing the standard errors. The use of TFP as a regressand or regressor in the model is likely to compound the standard errors of the estimated parameters, and provide a misleading statistical inference. It is likely to commit a Type I (Type II) error and erroneously overstate (understate) the relationship between trade and TFP.

Third, the regression or TFP residuals in (3) represent a linear combination of (normally) non-stationary series of factor inputs, $K(t)$ and $L(t)$, and the output $Y(t)$. If the TFP residuals are non-stationary and I(d), then it implies a lack of cointegrating and equilibrium relationship between factor inputs and output and, thus, 'spurious estimates' of the production technology parameters used to proxy the factor income shares and estimate the TFP. In contrast, if the TFP residuals are stationary and I(0), then it is difficult to regress TFP on its possibly I(d) determinants such as trade. A first-difference transformation of the I(d) determinants of TFP (such as trade) to make them synchronous with I(0) TFP would result in a loss of long-run information. The short-run model, based on I(0) variables, loses its relevance for the long-run analysis of economic growth.

Fourth, the OLS parameters, $\hat{\alpha}$ and $\hat{\beta}$, are by definition constants and thus, do not account for possible yearly (quarterly) variations that may occur in the actual income shares of capital and labour. Besides, the OLS estimates of α and β and implied TFP are likely to be biased and inconsistent, given simultaneity between inputs and unobserved productivity.[19]

b. Estimates of GDP and Measures of Trade Openness

The estimates of GDP in developing countries with a large unorganised sector are beset with numerous measurement problems (Heston, 1994).[20] The differences in the magnitudes of the informal sector, definitions and coverage of items, and the timings of revisions commonly characterise the cross-country dispersion in GDP. Such differentials weaken the conclusions drawn from cross-country growth models that use a heterogeneous mix of GDP estimates. As regards the measures of trade openness, the most commonly used measures based on trade volumes and trade ratios are not perfect proxies for trade policy and access to international markets. The developed countries with higher trade volumes generally have smaller trade shares, and the trade ratios in these countries may not differ discern-ibly from those in the developing countries with lower trade volumes.[21] Measures of openness based on trade policy have been used relatively sparsely, possibly due to the lack of consistent time-series and cross-section data. Leamer (1988) argues that in the absence of direct measures of trade barriers, it is impossible to deter-mine the degree of openness for most countries, as does Edwards (1997, 1998). Temple (1999) argues that the measures which are most defensible on theoretical grounds, such as the effective rates of protection, can be difficult to calculate for a sufficiently large number of countries. Typically, researchers fall back on simple proxies, such as trade shares in GDP or a black market exchange rate premium, meant to give some indication of openness (Temple, 1999).

A major problem concerns the aggregation of tariff and non-tariff barriers into a single trade policy index (Harrison, 1996; Edwards, 1998; Dollar and Kraay,

---

[19] Van Biesebroeck (2007) asserts that estimating a production function by ordinary least squares (OLS) is generally not advisable. He argues that the GMM system estimator provides the most robust productivity level and growth estimates. The disadvantages of OLS are, however, less acute for productivity growth than for productivity levels. For a review and discussion on the econometric estimators to estimate productivity, see Van Biesebroeck (2007).

[20] Heston (1994) argues that the data on per capita GDP are prone to fewer errors as compared to the data on aggregate GDP, as some of the errors in the estimates of GDP are counterbalanced by the errors in the estimates of population.

[21] Harrison and Revenga (1995) suggest that the large countries generally have smaller trade shares, and no independent measure of openness is free of methodological problems.

2003). Rodriguez and Rodrik (2000) argue that the simple trade-weighted tariff averages or non-tariff coverage ratios – which I believe to be the most direct indicators of trade restrictions – are misleading as indicators of the stance of trade policy. Dollar and Kraay (2003) argue that the most immediate candidates of trade policy (average tariff rates and non-tariff barrier coverage ratios) have obvious drawbacks, and it is not possible to construct very convincing measures of overall trade policy. Rose (2004b) asserts that all tariff measures are affected by the well-known fact that tariff revenues divided by total imports is a downward-biased measure of tariff rates, since highly taxed imports tend not to be imported. The coverage of non-tariff barriers (NTBs) in terms of total imports is another measure of trade policy. It is, however, widely recognised that the presence of NTBs is a potentially poor substitute for the importance or intensity of the NTBs; hence this measure of trade policy is certainly measured with error (Rose, 2004b).[22] Different measures reflect different aspects of trade policy and have differential effects on growth. Pritchett (1996) argues that different measures could be uncorrelated or weakly correlated among themselves and, thus, different dimensions of trade policy would have different effects on growth.[23] Historically, many tariffs were raised for revenue purposes and were not necessarily directly protective, though even these revenue tariffs could have some general equilibrium impact on the economy (O'Rourke, 2000).

Another commonly used measure has been the deviations of actual from predicted trade flows (Balassa, 1985; Leamer, 1988; Syrquin and Chenery, 1989; Edwards, 1992, 1998; Wacziarg, 2001). This, however, basically represents the stochastic residual term of the model estimated for trade flows, and is likely to contain omitted variables model misspecification bias. It not only measures restrictiveness, but also encompasses the unobserved effects of all the factors omitted from the model for trade flows. Some studies use a black market premium on foreign exchange to surrogate the efficiency of price system and capture the effects of economic and policy distortions on growth (Lee, 1993; Barro and Sala-i-Martin, 1995; Sachs and Warner, 1995; Rodriguez and Rodrik, 2000; Wacziarg, 2001; Vamvakidis, 2002; Lee et al., 2004). Such a premium reflects the controlled market for foreign exchange and measures the expectations for the depreciation of exchange rate (Fischer, 1993). The black market premium, however, captures only

---

[22] Rodriguez and Rodrik (2000) argue that no papers that document the existence of serious biases in these direct indicators, much less establish that an alternative indicator performs better (in the relevant sense of calibrating the restrictiveness of trade regimes).

[23] Irwin (2002) argues that high tariff measures are imperfect indicators of trade-policy orientation and may not always reflect protectionist policies. Winters (2004) suggests that the fiscal consequences of tariff revenue losses are far from inevitable, especially if non-tariff barriers are converted into tariffs (exemptions are reduced and collections improved); but they can pose a problem for poorer countries in which trade taxes account for large proportions of total revenue.

a narrow (foreign exchange) dimension of the macroeconomic and policy distortions, as compared to the distortions inflicted by tariff and non-tariff barriers to trade.

It is also difficult to disentangle the effects of trade policies from those of other macroeconomic policies and unequivocally interpret the observed correlations between trade policies and economic growth. IMF-supported structural adjustment programmes commonly begin with a devaluation, which results in high, albeit exceptional, performance of domestic exports. These programmes are closely followed by stabilisation programmes and the adoption of several macroeconomic measures to sustain the effects and avoid policy reversals. The improvements in productivity and growth that are commonly ascribed to trade liberalisation, in fact, arise from the conglomerate effects of comprehensive and wide-ranging economic reforms undertaken in almost all the real and financial sectors of the economy; trade liberalisation is only one segment in the whole spectrum of reforms. Rodrik (1995) argues that the trade-regime indicators are measured very badly, and trade openness in the sense of a lack of trade restrictions is often confused with the macroeconomic aspects of policy regimes.

c. Model Specification, Estimators and Endogeneity

The problem of endogeneity and non-orthogonality of regressors remains unresolved in the time-series models and least addressed in the cross-section and panel data models (Trefler, 1993; Rodrik, 1995; Harrison, 1996; Edwards, 1993, 1998; Frankel and Romer, 1999; Temple, 1999; Pritchett, 2000; Wacziarg, 2001; Irwin and Terviö , 2002; Lee et al., 2004; Winters, 2004; Felbermayr, 2005; Frankel and Rose, 2005; Alvarez and López, 2008). The openness to trade and trade policies may not be determined exogenously, and these may themselves be a function of productivity and growth. Exports and imports vary with the level of production and are determined jointly within the system. The endogeneity between trade (exports) and productivity is reinforced more conspicuously in the microeconomic self-selection models, which suggest that the firms with exogenously determined high levels of productivity self-select themselves into the export market. The trade policy-based measures of openness, such as tariffs, could be affected by growth and are not completely immune from simultaneity. In a low growth and recessionary phase, tariff rates may be raised to export domestic recession and revive economic growth. Since most studies perform partial equilibrium analysis and use single-equation models, the problem of endogeneity remains a serious concern for the conclusions drawn from these studies. The non-orthogonality of regressors to the residual process makes the least squares estimates biased and inconsistent. Trefler (1993) shows that the US import flows are 10 times higher than previously estimated, partly because the previous studies have ignored the simultaneity of trade policy and import flows.

A commonly used measure to alleviate reverse-causation and possible sources of endogeneity has been to use some of the lagged regressors as instruments and estimate the model using an instrumental variables (IV) estimator. The efficiency of an IV estimator, however, hinges heavily on the quality and validity of instruments. Besides, when several regressors in a model are instrumented, then validity requirements for instruments (used for endogenous regressors) become even more stringent (Staiger and Stock, 1997). It is difficult to find appropriate instruments that are strongly correlated with endogenous regressors, but uncorrelated with Gaussian disturbances. Temple (1999) argues that some studies use initial values, such as regressing growth over 1960–85 on the 1960 secondary school enrolment rate, to avoid simultaneity. This is not quite as watertight as the researchers seem to think: even if the endogeneity problem is solved, perhaps some omitted variables affect both growth and initial level of the variables like schooling.

The microeconomic firm-level models commonly use matching and semiparametric estimators, such as the estimator developed by Olley and Pakes (1996), to alleviate endogeneity (Pavcnik, 2002; Bernard and Jensen, 2004a; Schor, 2004; Van Biesebroeck, 2005; Fernandes, 2007). These account for unobserved plant heterogeneity by using observable firm characteristics, and are robust to endogeneity and simultaneity-bias arising from endogenous input and exit choices.[24] Greenaway and Kneller (2007a), however, argue that matching attempts to reduce heterogeneity have the disadvantage of removing observations from the dataset and requiring specific assumptions about the nonobservable factors, such as managerial ability. These estimators, by design, have remained restricted to only the microeconomic models estimating productivity in the manufacturing sector, and have not been extended to the economy-wide macroeconomic models. Temple (1991) argues that the micro studies often miss the economy-wide resource allocation effects that may be central to understanding the effects of trade policy.

Model misspecification bias impinges on the robustness of results and yields misleading statistical inference. The commonly used bivariate models testing 'export-led growth' versus 'growth-led export' hypotheses do not control for the effects of various other conditioning factors on growth. The studies testing 'export-led growth' hypotheses commonly provide a solo focus on the role of exports and erroneously ignore the role of imports (and other factors such as investment). The goods embody technical know-how, and the imports play a catalytic role in the transfer and diffusion of foreign technology. An incomplete analysis aside, this leads not only to omitted variables model misspecification bias and serial correlation problems, but also to the endogeneity of trade, as the unobserved factors and

---

[24] Pavcnik (2002) argues that the selection-bias induced by plant closings and the simultaneity-bias induced by plant dynamics significantly affect the magnitude of the capital coefficient in the production function, and that Olley and Pakes's semi-parametric methodology provides a useful alternative to the techniques used in previous studies.

several unknowns that affect economic growth could also contemporaneously affect the orientation to trade. The use of simultaneous-equation models has recently been uncommon, albeit virtually abandoned, possibly due to the identification and estimational problems associated with a large system. The commonly used single-equation models (which assume all regressors as exogenous) need to be appropriately specified and instrumented, so as to draw statistically robust and economically meaningful interpretations.

Most studies do not perform model misspecification tests and examine robustness to the inclusion of additional regressors. Levine and Renelt (1992) use a variant of extreme bounds analysis from Leamer (1988) and conduct a sensitivity analysis. The statistical significance of a majority of regressors is shown to be sensitive to model specification, and it disappears if the set of regressors is altered; they find that almost all results are fragile. They suggest that it is important to provide a formal sensitivity test by systematically varying the right-hand variables to ensure the robustness of results to variations in the model specification. Harrison (1996) finds that when three macro variables are included in the model, the statistical significance of openness measures disappears in half the cases. Rodriguez and Rodrik (2000) and Irwin and Terviö (2002) examine the sensitivity of the Frankel and Romer (1999) results. The effect of trade disappears with the inclusion of geographical latitude (distance from equator) in the model (Rodriguez and Rodrik, 2000), and the sensitivity of results holds for different sets of historical data (Irwin and Terviö, 2002).

5. CONCLUSIONS

This study has surveyed the literature on the relationship between international trade and economic growth, and reviewed the role of GATT/WTO in fostering free trade. Most studies support the gains of trade and recognise the substantive contributions of GATT/WTO in fostering free trade; the evidence is, however, not ubiquitously unambiguous. The macroeconomic evidence provides dominant support for the positive and significant effects of trade on output and growth, while the microeconomic evidence lends larger support to the exogenous effects of productivity on trade, as compared to the effects of trade on productivity. The studies supporting the self-selection hypothesis overwhelm the studies supporting the learning-by-exporting hypothesis. The rounds of the GATT/WTO trade negotiations could not vanquish the support for trade barriers and passion for protectionism. The globally Pareto-efficient multilateral free trade system of GATT/WTO remains surrounded by locally-efficient preferential (free and regional) trade agreements (areas). The strength of the argument for the gains of trade needs to be evaluated in juxtaposition with several methodological and measurement issues surrounding the trade–growth empirics, such as the estimation of TFP, measurement of trade openness, quality of data, frequency of data, possible structural breaks and regime-switches in the model series, construction of trade policy indices, specification of an econometric model, endogeneity of trade, netting of exports and imports from GDP, disentanglement of the effects of trade policy from those of other macroeconomic policies, and the decomposition of the effects of trade into short-run transitory and long-run permanent components. The econometric methodology that is central to the empirical evidence has itself been evolving and so have been the estimates and statistical evidence on the relationship between trade and growth.

The most commonly used measures of trade openness based on trade volumes are highly endogenous, while those based on trade policy are characterised by several measurement problems and have been used relatively sparsely. The different measures represent different aspects of trade openness, and have differential effects on growth. Most studies focus on the partial equilibrium analysis of trade policy, and ignore the general equilibrium aspects of macroeconomic policy. It is difficult to disentangle the effects of trade policies from those of other macroeconomic policies and unequivocally interpret the observed correlations between trade policies and economic growth. The productivity improvements that are commonly ascribed to trade liberalisation in the developing countries, in fact, arise from the conglomerate effects of comprehensive and wide-ranging economic reforms undertaken in almost all the real and financial sectors of the economy. Trade is one of the several catalysts of productivity and growth and hence its contribution is contingent on its weight in the aggregate economic activity. The hitherto unresolved methodological and measurement issues characterise a challenging agenda for future research. Future research needs to resolve these issues and unambiguously determine and crystallise the strength and robustness of the argument for the gains of trade.

REFERENCES

Alcala, F. and A. Ciccone (2004), 'Trade and Productivity', *Quarterly Journal of Economics*, **119**, 2, 613–46.

Alvarez, R. and R. A. López (2005), 'Exporting and Performance: Evidence from Chilean Plants', *Canadian Journal of Economics*, **38**, 4, 1384–400.

Alvarez, R. and R. A. López (2008), 'Is Exporting a Source of Productivity Spillovers?' *Review of World Economics*, **144**, 4, 723–49.

Andersson, M., H. Lööf and S. Johansson (2008), 'Productivity and International Trade: Firm Level Evidence from a Small Open Economy', *Review of World Economics*, **144**, 4, 774–801.

Arnold, J. M. and K. Hussinger (2005), 'Export Behaviour and Firm Productivity in German Manufacturing: A Firm-level Analysis', *Review of World Economics*, **141**, 2, 219–43.

Arrow, K. J. (1962), 'The Economic Implications of Learning by Doing', *Review of Economic Studies*, **29**, 3, 155–73.

Aw, B. Y. and A. R. Hwang (1995), 'Productivity and the Export Market: A Firm-level Analysis', *Journal of Development Economics*, **47**, 2, 313–32.

Aw, B. Y., S. Chung and M. J. Roberts (2000), 'Productivity and Turnover in the Export Market: Micro-level Evidence from the Republic of Korea and Taiwan (China)', *World Bank Economic Review*, **14**, 1, 65–90.

Aw, B. Y., X. Chen and M. J. Roberts (2001), 'Firm-level Evidence on Productivity Differentials and Turnover in Taiwanese Manufacturing', *Journal of Development Economics*, **66**, 1, 51–86.

Awokuse, T. O. (2003), 'Is the Export-led Growth Hypothesis Valid for Canada?' *Canadian Journal of Economics*, **36**, 1, 126–36.

Awokuse, T. O. (2007), 'Causality between Exports, Imports, and Economic Growth: Evidence from Transition Economies', *Economics Letters*, **94**, 3, 389–95.

Awokuse, T. O. and D. K. Christopoulos (2009), 'Nonlinear Dynamics and the Exports–Output Growth Nexus', *Economic Modelling*, **26**, 1, 184–90.

Bagwell, K. and R. W. Staiger (1998), 'Will Preferential Agreements Undermine the Multilateral Trading System?' *Economic Journal*, **108**, 449, 1162–82.

Bagwell, K. and R. W. Staiger (1999), 'An Economic Theory of GATT', *American Economic Review*, **89**, 1, 214–48.

Bagwell, K. and R. W. Staiger (2002), 'Economic Theory and the Interpretation of GATT/WTO', *American Economist*, **46**, 2, 3–19.

Balassa, B. (1978), 'Exports and Economic Growth: Further Evidence', *Journal of Development Economics*, **5**, 2, 181–89.

Balassa, B. (1984), 'Adjustment to External Shocks in Developing Economies', World Bank Staff Working Paper No. 472 (Washington, DC: World Bank).

Balassa, B. (1985), 'Exports, Policy Choices, and Economic Growth in Developing Countries After the 1973 Oil Shock', *Journal of Development Economics*, **18**, 1, 23–35.

Baldwin, J. R. and W. Gu (2003), 'Export-market Participation and Productivity Performance in Canadian Manufacturing', *Canadian Journal of Economics*, **36**, 3, 634–57.

Baldwin, J. R. and W. Gu (2004), 'Trade Liberalization, Export-market Participation, Productivity Growth and Innovation', *Oxford Review of Economic Policy*, **20**, 3, 372–92.

Baldwin, R. E. (1993), 'A Domino Theory of Regionalism', National Bureau of Economic Research Working Paper No. 4465, Cambridge, MA: NBER.

Baldwin, R. E. (1995), 'A Domino Theory of Regionalism', in R. E. Baldwin, P. Haarparanta and J. Kianden (eds.), *Expanding Membership of the European Union* (Cambridge: Cambridge University Press).

Baldwin, R. E. (1997), 'The Causes of Regionalism', *The World Economy*, **20**, 7, 865–88.

Baldwin, R. E. and E. Seghezza (1996), 'Trade-induced Investment-led Growth', Working Paper No. 5582, Cambridge, MA: National Bureau of Economic Research.

Barro, R. J. and X. Sala-i-Martin (1995), *Economic Growth* (New York: McGraw-Hill).

Bellone, F., P. Musso, L. Nesta and M. Quere (2008), 'The U-Shaped Productivity Dynamics of French Exporters', *Review of World Economics*, **144**, 4, 636–59.

Ben-David, D. (1993), 'Equalizing Exchange: Trade Liberalization and Income Convergence', *Quarterly Journal of Economics*, **108**, 3, 653–79.

Ben-David, D. (1996), 'Trade and Convergence among Countries', *Journal of International Economics*, **40**, 3/4, 279–98.

Ben-David, D. and D. H. Papell (1997), 'International Trade and Structural Change', *Journal of International Economics*, **43**, 3/4, 513–23.

Benhabib, J. and M. M. Spiegel (1994), 'The Role of Human Capital in Economic Development: Evidence from Aggregate Cross-country Data', *Journal of Monetary Economics*, **34**, 2, 143–73.

Bernard, A. B. and J. Wagner (1997), 'Exports and Success in German Manufacturing', *Weltwirtschaftliches Archiv*, **133**, 1, 134–57.

Bernard, A. B. and J. Wagner (2001), 'Export Entry and Exit by German Firms', *Review of World Economics/Weltwirtschaftliches Archiv*, **137**, 1, 105–23.

Bernard, A. B. and J. B. Jensen (1999), 'Exceptional Exporter Performance: Cause, Effect, or Both?' *Journal of International Economics*, **47**, 1, 1–25.

Bernard, A. B. and J. B. Jensen (2004a), 'Exporting and Productivity in the USA', *Oxford Review of Economic Policy*, **20**, 3, 343–57.

Bernard, A. B. and J. B. Jensen (2004b), 'Why Some Firms Export', *Review of Economics and Statistics*, **86**, 2, 561–69.

Bernard, A. B., J. B. Jensen and P. K. Schott (2006), 'Trade Costs, Firms and Productivity', *Journal of Monetary Economics*, **53**, 5, 917–37.

Berthold, H. and A. Teixeira (2005), 'How Barriers to International Trade affect TFP', *Review of Economic Dynamics*, **8**, 4, 866–76.

Bhagwati, J. N. (1958), 'Immiserizing Growth: A Geometrical Note', *Review of Economic Studies*, **25**, 3, 201–05.

Bhagwati, J. N. (1991), *The World Trading System at Risk* (Princeton, NJ: Princeton University Press).

Bhagwati, J. N., D. Greenaway and A. Panagariya (1998), 'Trading Preferentially: Theory and Policy', *Economic Journal*, **108**, 449, 1128–48.

Bhagwati, J. N. (1968), 'Distortions and Immiserizing Growth: A Generalization', *Review of Economic Studies*, **35**, 4, 481–85.

Bhagwati, J. N. (1978), *Foreign Trade Regimes and Economic Development: Anatomy and Consequences of Exchange Control Regimes* (Cambridge, MA: Ballinger).

Bhagwati, J. N. (1988), 'Export-promoting Trade Strategy: Issues and Evidence', *World Bank Research Observer*, **3**, 1, 27–57.

Bigsten, A., P. Collier, S. Dercon, M. Fafchamps, B. Gauthier, J. W. Gunning, A. Oduro, R. Oostendorp, C. Pattillo, M. Söderbom, F. Teal and A. Zeufack (2004), 'Do African Manufacturing Firms Learn from Exporting?' *Journal of Development Studies*, **40**, 3, 115–41.

Bodman, P. M. (1996), 'On Export-led Growth in Australia and Canada: Cointegration, Causality and Structural Stability', *Australian Economic Papers*, **35**, 67, 282–99.

Boltho, A. (1996), 'Was Japanese Growth Export-led?' *Oxford Economic Papers*, **48**, 3, 415–32.

Bonelli, R. (1992), 'Growth and Productivity in Brazilian Industries: Impacts of Trade Orientation', *Journal of Development Economics*, **39**, 1, 85–109.

Bound, J., D. Jaeger and R. Baker (1995), 'Problems with Instrumental Variables Estimation when the Correlation between the Instruments and the Endogenous Explanatory Variable is Weak', *Journal of the American Statistical Association*, **90**, 430, 443–50.

Castellani, D. (2002), 'Export Behaviour and Productivity Growth: Evidence from Italian Manufacturing Firms', *Review of World Economics/Weltwirtschaftliches Archiv*, **138**, 4, 605–28.

Chen, T. J. (1990), 'Export Performance and Productivity Growth: The Case of Taiwan', *Economic Development and Cultural Change*, **38**, 3, 577–85.

Chenery, H. B. (1983), 'Interaction between Theory and Observation in Development', *World Development*, **11**, 10, 853–61.

Chow, P. C. Y. (1987), 'Causality between Export Growth and Industrial Development: Empirical Evidence from the NICs', *Journal of Development Economics*, **26**, 1, 55–63.

Clausing, K. A. (2001), 'Trade Creation and Trade Diversion in the Canada–United States Free Trade Agreement', *Canadian Journal of Economics*, **34**, 3, 677–96.

Clemens, M. A. and J. G. Williamson (2001), 'A Tariff–Growth Paradox? Protection's Impact the World Around 1875–1997', Working Paper No. 8459, Cambridge, MA: National Bureau of Economic Research.

Clemens, M. A. and J. G. Williamson (2004), 'Why Did the Tariff–Growth Correlation Change After 1950?' *Journal of Economic Growth*, **9**, 1, 5–46.

Clerides, S. K., S. Lach and J. R. Tybout (1998), 'Is Learning by Exporting Important? Microdynamic Evidence from Colombia, Mexico, and Morocco', *Quarterly Journal of Economics*, **113**, 3, 903–47.

Coe, D. T. and E. Helpman (1995), 'International R&D Spillovers', *European Economic Review*, **39**, 5, 859–87.

Condon, T., V. Corbo and J. de Melo (1985), 'Productivity Growth, External Shocks, and Capital Inflows in Chile: A General Equilibrium Analysis', *Journal of Policy Modeling*, **7**, 3, 379–405.

Copeland, B. R. and M. S. Taylor (2004), 'Trade, Growth, and the Environment', *Journal of Economic Literature*, **42**, 1, 7–71.

Criscuolo, C., J. Haskel and R. Martin (2004), 'Import Competition, Productivity, and Restructuring in UK Manufacturing', *Oxford Review of Economic Policy*, **20**, 3, 393–408.

Delgado, M., J. C. Farinas and S. Ruano (2002), 'Firm Productivity and Export Markets: A Non-parametric Approach', *Journal of International Economics*, **57**, 2, 397–422.

Dollar, D. (1992), 'Outward-oriented Developing Economies Really Do Grow More Rapidly: Evidence from 95 LDCs, 1976–1985', *Economic Development and Cultural Change*, **40**, 3, 523–44.

Dollar, D. and A. Kraay (2003), 'Institutions, Trade, and Growth', *Journal of Monetary Economics*, **50**, 1, 133–62.

Dollar, D. and A. Kraay (2004), 'Trade, Growth, and Poverty', *Economic Journal*, **114**, 493, F42–49.

Easterly, W. and R. Levine (2001), 'What Have We Learned from a Decade of Empirical Research on Growth? It's Not Factor Accumulation: Stylized Facts and Growth Models', *World Bank Economic Review*, **15**, 2, 177–219.

Eaton, J. and S. Kortum (1994), 'International Patenting and Technology Diffusion', Working Paper No. 4931, Cambridge, MA: National Bureau of Economic Research.

Eaton, J. and S. Kortum (1996), 'Trade in Ideas: Patenting and Productivity in the OECD', *Journal of International Economics*, **40**, 3/4, 251–78.

Edwards, S. (1992), 'Trade Orientation, Distortions and Growth in Developing Countries', *Journal of Development Economics*, **39**, 1, 31–57.

Edwards, S. (1993), 'Openness, Trade Liberalization, and Growth in Developing Countries', *Journal of Economic Literature*, **31**, 3, 1358–93.

Edwards, S. (1997), 'Trade Policy, Growth, and Income Distribution', *American Economic Review*, **87**, 2, 205–10.

Edwards, S. (1998), 'Openness, Productivity and Growth: What Do We Really Know?' *Economic Journal*, **108**, 447, 383–98.

Egger, H., P. Egger and D. Greenaway (2008), 'The Trade Structure Effects of Endogenous Regional Trade Agreements', *Journal of International Economics*, **74**, 2, 278–98.

Emery, R. F. (1967), 'The Relation of Exports and Economic Growth', *KYKLOS*, **20**, 470–86.

Ericson, R. and A. Pakes (1995), 'Markov-perfect Industry Dynamics: A Framework for Empirical Work', *Review of Economic Studies*, **62**, 1, 53–82.

Ethier, W. J. (1998), 'The New Regionalism', *Economic Journal*, **108**, 449, 1149–61.

Fajana, O. (1979), 'Trade and Growth: The Nigerian Experience', *World Development*, **7**, 1, 73–78.

Feder, G. (1982), 'On Exports and Economic Growth', *Journal of Development Economics*, **12**, 1/2, 59–73.

Feenstra, R. C. (2006), 'New Evidence on the Gains from Trade', *Review of World Economics*, **142**, 4, 617–41.

Felbermayr, G. J. (2005), 'Dynamic Panel Data Evidence on the Trade–Income Relation', *Review of World Economics*, **141**, 4, 583–611.

Fernandes, A. M. (2007), 'Trade Policy, Trade Volumes and Plant-level Productivity in Colombian Manufacturing Industries', *Journal of International Economics*, **71**, 1, 52–71.

Fischer, S. (1993), 'The Role of Macroeconomic Factors in Growth', *Journal of Monetary Economics*, **32**, 3, 485–512.

Foreman-Peck, J. (1995), 'A Model of Later Nineteenth Century European Economic Development', *Revista de Historia Economica*, **13**, 3, 441–71.

Frankel, J. A. and A. K. Rose (2005), 'Is Trade Good or Bad for the Environment? Sorting Out the Causality', *Review of Economics and Statistics*, **87**, 1, 85–913.

Frankel, J. A. and D. Romer (1996), 'Trade and Growth: An Empirical Investigation', Working Paper No. 5476, Cambridge, MA: National Bureau of Economic Research.

Frankel, J. A. and D. Romer (1999), 'Does Trade Cause Growth?' *American Economic Review*, **89**, 3, 379–99.

Fryges, H. and J. Wagner (2008), 'Exports and Productivity Growth: First Evidence from a Continuous Treatment Approach', *Review of World Economics*, **144**, 4, 695–722.

Girma, S., D. Greenaway and R. Kneller (2003), 'Export Market Exit and Performance Dynamics: A Causality Analysis of Matched Firms', *Economics Letters*, **80**, 2, 181–87.

Girma, S., D. Greenaway and R. Kneller (2004), 'Does Exporting Increase Productivity? A Microeconometric Analysis of Matched Firms', *Review of International Economics*, **12**, 5, 855–66.

Girma, S., H. Görg and A. Hanley (2008), 'R&D and Exporting: A Comparison of British and Irish Firms', *Review of World Economics*, **144**, 4, 750–73.

Glick, R. and A. K. Rose (2002), 'Does a Currency Union Affect Trade? The Time-series Evidence', *European Economic Review*, **46**, 6, 1125–51.

Granger, C. W. J. (1969), 'Investigating Causal Relations by Econometric Models and Cross-spectral Methods', *Econometrica*, **37**, 3, 424–38.

Granger, C. W. J. (1988), 'Some Recent Development in a Concept of Causality', *Journal of Econometrics*, **39**, 1/2, 199–211.

Greenaway, D. (2004), 'The Assessment: Firm-level Adjustment to Globalization', *Oxford Review of Economic Policy*, **20**, 3, 335–42.

Greenaway, D. and D. Sapsford (1994), 'Exports, Growth, and Liberalization: An Evaluation', *Journal of Policy Modeling*, **16**, 2, 165–86.

Greenaway, D. and R. Kneller (2004), 'Exporting and Productivity in the United Kingdom', *Oxford Review of Economic Policy*, **20**, 3, 358–71.

Greenaway, D. and R. Kneller (2007a), 'Firm Heterogeneity, Exporting and Foreign Direct Investment', *Economic Journal*, **117**, 517, F134–61.

Greenaway, D. and R. Kneller (2007b), 'Industry Differences in the Effect of Export Market Entry: Learning by Exporting?' *Review of World Economics*, **143**, 3, 416–32.

Greenaway, D. and R. Kneller (2008), 'Exporting, Productivity and Agglomeration', *European Economic Review*, **52**, 5, 919–39.

Greenaway, D., A. Guariglia and R. Kneller (2007), 'Financial Factors and Exporting Decisions', *Journal of International Economics*, **73**, 2, 377–95.

Greenaway, D., J. Gullstrand and R. Kneller (2005), 'Exporting May Not Always Boost Firm Productivity', *Review of World Economics*, **141**, 4, 561–82.

Greenaway, D., J. Gullstrand and R. Kneller (2008), 'Surviving Globalisation', *Journal of International Economics*, **74**, 2, 264–77.

Greenaway, D., N. Sousa and K. Wakelin (2004), 'Do Domestic Firms Learn to Export from Multinationals?' *European Journal of Political Economy*, **20**, 4, 1027–43.

Greenaway, D., W. Morgan and P. Wright (1998), 'Trade Reform, Adjustment and Growth: What Does the Evidence Tell Us?' *Economic Journal*, **108**, 450, 1547–61.

Grossman, G. M. and E. Helpman (1991), *Innovation and Growth in the Global Economy* (Cambridge, MA: MIT Press).

Hansson, P. and N. Lundin (2004), 'Exports as an Indicator on or Promoter of Successful Swedish Manufacturing Firms in the 1990s', *Review of World Economics*, **140**, 3, 415–45.

Harrison, A. E. (1994), 'Productivity, Imperfect Competition and Trade Reform: Theory and Evidence', *Journal of International Economics*, **36**, 1/2, 53–73.

Harrison, A. E. (1996), 'Openness and Growth: A Time-series, Cross-country Analysis for Developing Countries', *Journal of Development Economics*, **48**, 2, 419–47.

Harrison, A. E. and A. Revenga (1995), 'The Effects of Trade Policy Reform: What Do We Really Know?' Working Paper No. 5225, Cambridge, MA: National Bureau of Economic Research.

Head, K. and J. Ries (2003), 'Heterogeneity and the FDI versus Export Decision of Japanese Manufacturers', *Journal of the Japanese and International Economies*, **17**, 4, 448–67.

Heller, P. S. and R. C. Porter (1978), 'Exports and Growth: An Empirical Re-investigation', *Journal of Development Economics*, **5**, 2, 191–93.

Henriques, I. and P. Sadorsky (1996), 'Export-led Growth or Growth Driven Exports? The Canadian Case', *Canadian Journal of Economics*, **29**, 3, 541–55.

Heston, A. (1994), 'A Brief Review of Some Problems in Using National Accounts Data in Level of Output Comparisons and Growth Studies', *Journal of Development Economics*, **44**, 1, 29–52.

Hopenhayn, H. A. (1992), 'Entry, Exit, and Firm Dynamics in Long Run Equilibrium', *Econometrica*, **60**, 5, 1127–50.

Hwa, E. C. (1988), 'The Contribution of Agriculture to Economic Growth: Some Empirical Evidence', *World Development*, **16**, 11, 1329–39.

International Study Group on Exports and Productivity (2008), 'Understanding Cross-country Differences in Exporter Premia: Comparable Evidence for 14 Countries', *Review of World Economics*, **144**, 4, 596–635.

Irwin, D. (1995), 'The GATT in Historical Perspective', *American Economic Review*, **85**, 2, 323–28.

Irwin, D. A. (2002), 'Interpreting the Tariff–Growth Correlation of the Late 19th Century', *American Economic Review*, **92**, 2, 165–69.

Irwin, D. A. and M. Terviö (2002), 'Does Trade Raise Income? Evidence from the Twentieth Century', *Journal of International Economics*, **58**, 1, 1–18.

Isgut, A. E. (2001), 'What's Different about Exporters? Evidence from Colombian Manufacturing', *Journal of Development Studies*, **37**, 5, 57–82.

Jovanovic, B. (1982), 'Selection and the Evolution of Industry', *Econometrica*, **50**, 3, 649–70.

Jung, W. S. and P. J. Marshall (1985), 'Exports, Growth and Causality in Developing Countries', *Journal of Development Economics*, **18**, 1, 1–12.

Karacaovali, B. and N. Limão (2008), 'The Clash of Liberalizations: Preferential vs. Multilateral Trade Liberalization in the European Union', *Journal of International Economics*, **74**, 2, 299– 327.

Katrak, H. (1997), 'Developing Countries' Imports of Technology, In-house Technological Capabilities and Efforts: An Analysis of the Indian Experience', *Journal of Development Economics*, **53**, 1, 67–83.

Kavoussi, R. M. (1984), 'Export Expansion and Economic Growth: Further Empirical Evidence', *Journal of Development Economics*, **14**, 1/2, 241–50.

Keller, W. (2000), 'Do Trade Patterns and Technology Flows Affect Productivity Growth?' *World Bank Economic Review*, **14**, 1, 17–47.

Keller, W. (2002), 'Trade and the Transmission of Technology', *Journal of Economic Growth*, **7**, 1, 5–24.

Knight, M., N. Loayza and D. Villanueva (1993), 'Testing the Neoclassical Theory of Economic Growth: A Panel Data Approach', *International Monetary Fund Staff Papers*, **40**, 3, 512–41.

Kohli, I. and N. Singh (1989), 'Exports and Growth: Critical Minimum Effort and Diminishing Returns', *Journal of Development Economics*, **30**, 2, 391–400.

Kónya, L. (2006), 'Exports and Growth: Granger Causality Analysis on OECD Countries with a Panel Data Approach', *Economic Modelling*, **23**, 6, 978–92.

Kraay, A. (1999), 'Exportations et performances economiques: etude d'un panel d'entreprises chinoises', *Revue d'Economie du Developpement*, **7**, 1/2, 183–207.

Kravis, I. B. (1970), 'Trade as a Handmaiden of Growth: Similarities between the Nineteenth and Twentieth Centuries', *Economic Journal*, **80**, 320, 850–72.

Krueger, A. O. (1978), *Foreign Trade Regimes and Economic Development: Liberalization Attempts and Consequences* (Cambridge, MA: Ballinger).

Krueger, A. O. (2004), 'Wilful Ignorance: The Struggle to Convince the Free Trade Skeptics', *World Trade Review*, **3**, 3, 483–93.

Krugman, P. (1993), Regionalism versus Multilateralism: Analytic Notes', in J. de Melo and A. Panagariya (eds.), *New Dimensions in Regional Integration* (Cambridge: Cambridge University Press for CEPR).

Krugman, P. R. (1991), 'Is Bilateralism Bad?' in E. Helpman and A. Razin (eds.), *International Trade and Trade Policy* (Cambridge, MA: MIT Press), 9–23.

Kugler, P. (1991), 'Growth, Exports and Cointegration: An Empirical Investigation', *Weltwirtschaftliches Archiv*, **127**, 1, 73–82.

Kunst, R. M. and D. Marin (1989), 'On Exports and Productivity: A Causal Analysis', *Review of Economics and Statistics*, **71**, 4, 699–703.

Laird, S. (1999), 'Regional Trade Agreements: Dangerous Liaisons?' *The World Economy*, **22**, 9, 1179–200.

Lane, P. R. (2001), 'International Trade and Economic Convergence: The Credit Channel', *Oxford Economic Papers*, **53**, 2, 221–40.

Leamer, E. (1988), 'Measures of Openness', in R. E. Baldwin (ed.), *Trade Policy and Empirical Analysis* (Chicago: University of Chicago Press).

Lee, H. Y., L. A. Ricci and R. Rigobon (2004), 'Once Again, Is Openness Good for Growth?' *Journal of Development Economics*, **75**, 2, 451–72.

Lee, J. W. (1993), 'International Trade, Distortions, and Long-run Economic Growth', *International Monetary Fund Staff Papers*, **40**, 2, 299–328.

Lee, J. W. (1995), 'Capital Goods Imports and Long-run Growth', *Journal of Development Economics*, **48**, 1, 91–110.

Lee, J. W., I. Park and K. Shin (2008), 'Proliferating Regional Trade Arrangements: Why and Whither?' *The World Economy*, **31**, 12, 1525–57.

Levine, R. and D. Renelt (1992), 'A Sensitivity Analysis of Cross-country Growth Regressions', *American Economic Review*, **82**, 4, 942–63.

Levinsohn, J. and A. Petrin (2003), 'Estimating Production Functions using Inputs to Control for Unobservables', *Review of Economic Studies*, **70**, 243, 317–41.

Lopez, R. A. (2005), 'Trade and Growth: Reconciling the Macroeconomic and Microeconomic Evidence', *Journal of Economic Surveys*, **19**, 4, 623–48.

Lucas Jr., R. E. (1988), 'On the Mechanics of Economic Development', *Journal of Monetary Economics*, **22**, 1, 3–42.

Maggi, G. and A. Rodriguez-Clare (1998), 'The Value of Trade Agreements in the Presence of Political Pressures', *Journal of Political Economy*, **106**, 3, 574–601.

Maizels, A. (1968), *Exports and Growth in Developing Countries* (London: Cambridge University Press).

Marin, D. (1992), 'Is the Export-led Growth Hypothesis Valid for Industrialized Countries?' *Review of Economics and Statistics*, **74**, 4, 678–88.

Melitz, M. J. (2003), 'The Impact of Trade on Intra-industry Reallocations and Aggregate Industry Productivity', *Econometrica*, **71**, 6, 1695–725.

Mengistae, T. and C. Pattillo (2004), 'Export Orientation and Productivity in Sub-Saharan Africa', *International Monetary Fund Staff Papers*, **51**, 2, 327–53.

Michaely, M. (1977), 'Exports and Growth: An Empirical Investigation', *Journal of Development Economics*, **4**, 1, 49–53.

Michaely, M. (1979), 'Exports and Growth: A Reply', *Journal of Development Economics*, **6**, 1, 141–43.

Moschos, D. (1989), 'Export Expansion, Growth and the Level of Economic Development: An Empirical Analysis', *Journal of Development Economics*, **30**, 1, 93–102.

Nishimizu, M. and S. Robinson (1984), 'Trade Policies and Productivity Change in Semi-industrialized Countries', *Journal of Development Economics*, **16**, 1/2, 177–206.

Nurkse, R. (1958), 'Trade Fluctuations and Buffer Policies of Low-income Countries', *KYKLOS*, **11**, 2, 141–54.

Nurkse, R. (1961), 'Patterns of Trade and Development', in G. Haberler and R. M. Stern (eds.), *Equilibrium and Growth in the World Economy* (Cambridge, MA: Harvard University Press), 282–304.

O'Rourke, K. H. (2000), 'Tariffs and Growth in the Late 19th Century', *The Economic Journal*, **110**, 463, 456–83.

O'Rourke, K. H. and J. G. Williamson (1999), *Globalization and History: The Evolution of a 19th Century Atlantic Economy* (Cambridge, MA: MIT Press).

Olley, G. S. and A. Pakes (1996), 'The Dynamics of Productivity in the Telecommunications Equipment Industry', *Econometrica*, **64**, 6, 1263–97.

Oxley, L. (1993), 'Cointegration, Causality and Export-led Growth in Portugal, 1865–1985', *Economics Letters*, **43**, 2, 163–66.

Pagan, A. (1984), 'Econometric Issues in the Analysis of Regressions with Generated Regressors', *International Economic Review*, **25**, 1, 221–47.

Panagariya, A. (1996), 'The Free Trade Area of the Americas: Good for Latin America?' *The World Economy*, **19**, 5, 485–515.

Panagariya, A. (1999), 'The Regionalism Debate: An Overview', *The World Economy*, **22**, 4, 455–76.

Panagariya, A. (2000), 'Preferential Trade Liberalization: The Traditional Theory and New Developments', *Journal of Economic Literature*, **38**, 2, 287–331.

Parente, S. L. and E. C. Prescott (1994), 'Barriers to Technology Adoption and Development', *Journal of Political Economy*, **102**, 2, 298–321.

Parente, S. L. and E. C. Prescott (1999), 'Monopoly Rights: A Barrier to Riches', *American Economic Review*, **89**, 5, 1216–33.

Pavcnik, N. (2002), 'Trade Liberalization, Exit, and Productivity Improvements: Evidence from Chilean Plants', *Review of Economic Studies*, **69**, 1, 245–76.

Prebisch, R. (1959), 'Commercial Policy in the Underdeveloped Countries', *American Economic Review*, **49**, 2, 251–73.

Pritchett, L. (1996), 'Measuring Outward Orientation in LDCs: Can It Be Done?' *Journal of Development Economics*, **49**, 2, 307–35.

Pritchett, L. (2000), 'Understanding Patterns of Economic Growth: Searching for Hills among Plateaus, Mountains, and Plains', *World Bank Economic Review*, **14**, 2, 221–50.

Ram, R. (1987), 'Exports and Economic Growth in Developing Countries: Evidence from Time Series and Cross-section Data', *Economic Development and Cultural Change*, **36**, 1, 50–72.

Riezman, R. G., C. H. Whiteman and P. M. Summers (1996), 'The Engine of Growth or Its Handmaiden? A Time-series Assessment of Export-led Growth', *Empirical Economics*, **21**, 77–110.

Rivera-Batiz, L. A. and P. M. Romer (1991a), 'International Trade with Endogenous Technological Change', *European Economic Review*, **35**, 4, 971–1001.

Rivera-Batiz, L. A. and P. M. Romer (1991b), 'Economic Integration and Endogenous Growth', *Quarterly Journal of Economics*, **106**, 2, 531–55.

Roberts, M. J. and J. R. Tybout (1997), 'The Decision to Export in Columbia: An Empirical Model of Entry with Sunk Costs', *American Economic Review*, **87**, 4, 545–64.

Rodriguez, C. A. and D. Rodrik (2000), 'Trade Policy and Economic Growth: A Skeptic's Guide to the Cross-national Evidence', in B. S. Bernanke and K. Rogoff (eds.), *NBER Macroeconomics Annual 2000* (Cambridge, MA: National Bureau of Economic Research).

Rodrik, D. (1995), 'Trade Policy and Industrial Policy Reform', in J. Behrman and T. N. Srinivasan (eds.), *Handbook of Development Economics*, Vol. 3B (Amsterdam: North-Holland).

Rodrik, D., A. Subramanian and F. Trebbi (2004), 'Institutions Rule: The Primacy of Institutions Over Geography and Integration in Economic Development', *Journal of Economic Growth*, **9**, 2, 131–65.

Romalis, J. (2007), 'NAFTA's and CUSFTA's Impact on International Trade', *Review of Economics and Statistics*, **89**, 3, 416–35.

Romer, P. M. (1986), 'Increasing Returns and Long-run Growth', *Journal of Political Economy*, **94**, 5, 1002–37.

Romer, P. M. (1990), 'Endogenous Technical Change', *Journal of Political Economy*, **98**, 5, S71–102.

Rose, A. K. (2004a), 'Do We Really Know that the WTO Increases Trade?' *American Economic Review*, **94**, 1, 98–114.

Rose, A. K. (2004b), 'Do WTO Members Have More Liberal Trade Policy?' *Journal of International Economics*, **63**, 2, 209–35.

Rose, A. K. (2005a), 'Which International Institutions Promote International Trade?' *Review of International Economics*, **13**, 4, 682–98.

Rose, A. K. (2005b), 'Does the WTO Make Trade More Stable?' *Open Economies Review*, **16**, 1, 7–22.

Rose, A. K. (2007), 'Do We Really Know that the WTO Increases Trade? Reply', *American Economic Review*, **97**, 5, 2019–25.

Ruane, F. and J. Sutherland (2005), 'Export Performance and Destination Characteristics of Irish Manufacturing Industry', *Review of World Economics*, **141**, 3, 442–59.

Sachs, J. D. and A. Warner (1995), 'Economic Reform and the Process of Global Integration', *Brookings Papers on Economic Activity*, **1**, 1–118.

Schmitz Jr., J. A. (2005), 'What Determines Labor Productivity? Lessons from the Dramatic Recovery of US and Canadian Iron-ore Industries Following Their Early 1980s Crisis', *Journal of Political Economy*, **113**, 3, 582–625.

Schor, A. (2004), 'Heterogeneous Productivity Response to Tariff Reduction: Evidence from Brazilian Manufacturing Firms', *Journal of Development Economics*, **75**, 2, 373–96.

Serti, F. and C. Tomasi (2008), 'Self-selection and Post-entry Effects of Exports: Evidence from Italian Manufacturing Firms', *Review of World Economics*, **144**, 4, 660–94.

Sims, C. A. (1980), 'Macroeconomics and Reality', *Econometrica*, **48**, 1, 1–48.

Singer, H. W. (1950), 'The Distribution of Gains between Investing and Borrowing Countries', *American Economic Review*, **40**, 2, 473–85.

Singh, T. (2003), 'Effects of Exports on Productivity and Growth in India: An Industry-based Analysis', *Applied Economics*, **35**, 7, 741–49.

Solow, R. M. (2001), 'What Have We Learned from a Decade of Empirical Research on Growth? Applying Growth Theory across Countries', *World Bank Economic Review*, **15**, 2, 283–88.

Staiger, D. and J. H. Stock (1997), 'Instrumental Variables Regression with Weak Instruments', *Econometrica*, **65**, 3, 557–86.

Staiger, R. W. and G. Tabellini (1987), 'Discretionary Trade Policy and Excessive Pretection', *American Economic Review*, **77**, 5, 823–37.

Subramanian, A. and W. Shang-Jin (2007), 'The WTO Promotes Trade, Strongly but Unevenly', *Journal of International Economics*, **72**, 1, 151–75.

Syrquin, M. and H. Chenery (1989), 'Three Decades of Industrialization', *World Bank Economic Review*, **3**, 2, 145–81.

Temple, J. (1999), 'The New Growth Evidence', *Journal of Economic Literature*, **37**, 1, 112–56.

Tinbergen, J. (1962), *Shaping the World Economy* (New York: Twentieth Century Fund).

Tomz, M., J. Goldstein and D. Rivers (2007), 'Do We Really Know that the WTO Increases Trade? Comment', *American Economic Review*, **97**, 5, 2005–18.

Trefler, D. (1993), 'Trade Liberalization and the Theory of Endogenous Protection: An Econometric Study of U.S. Import Policy', *Journal of Political Economy*, **101**, 1, 138–60.

Tybout, J. R. (1992), 'Linking Trade and Productivity: New Research Directions', *World Bank Economic Review*, **6**, 2, 189–211.

Tybout, J. (2000), 'Manufacturing Firms in Developing Countries: How Well Do They Do, and Why?' *Journal of Economic Literature*, **38**, 1, 11–44.

Tybout, J., J. de Melo and V. Corbo (1991), 'The Effects of Trade Reforms on Scale and Technical Efficiency: New Evidence from Chile', *Journal of International Economics*, **31**, 3/4, 231–50.

Tybout, J. R. and M. D. Westbrook (1995), 'Trade Liberalization and the Dimensions of Efficiency change in Mexican Manufacturing Industries', *Journal of International Economics*, **39**, 1/2, 53–78.

Tyler, W. G. (1981), 'Growth and Export Expansion in Developing Countries: Some Empirical Evidence', *Journal of Development Economics*, **9**, 1, 121–30.

Vamvakidis, A. (1999), 'Regional Trade Agreements or Broad Liberalization: Which Path Leads to Faster Growth?' *International Monetary Fund Staff Papers*, **46**, 1, 42–68.

Vamvakidis, A. (2002), 'How Robust is the Growth–Openness Connection? Historical Evidence', *Journal of Economic Growth*, **7**, 1, 57–80.

Van Biesebroeck, J. (2005), 'Exporting Raises Productivity in Sub-Saharan African Manufacturing Firms', *Journal of International Economics*, **67**, 2, 373–91.

Van Biesebroeck, J. (2007), 'Robustness of Productivity Estimates', *Journal of Industrial Economics*, **55**, 3, 529–69.

Viner, J. (1950), *The Customs Union Issue* (New York: Carnegie Endowment for International Peace).

Voivodas, C. S. (1973), 'Exports, Foreign Capital Inflow and Economic Growth', *Journal of International Economics*, **3**, 4, 337–49.

Wacziarg, R. (1998), 'Measuring the Dynamic Gains from Trade', *World Bank Policy Research Working Paper No. WPS200I* (Washington, DC: World Bank).

Wacziarg, R. (2001), 'Measuring the Dynamic Gains from Trade', *World Bank Economic Review*, **15**, 3, 393–429.

Wagner, J. (2002), 'The Causal Effects of Exports on Firm Size and Labor Productivity: First Evidence from a Matching Approach', *Economics Letters*, **77**, 2, 287–92.

Wagner, J. (2007), 'Exports and Productivity: A Survey of the Evidence from Firm-level Data', *The World Economy*, **30**, 1, 60–82.

Williamson, R. (1978), 'The Role of Exports and Foreign Capital in Latin American Economic Growth', *Southern Economic Journal*, **45**, 2, 410–20.

Winters, L. A. (2004), 'Trade Liberalisation and Economic Performance: An Overview', *Economic Journal*, **114**, 493, F4–21.

8

Beyond the WTO? An Anatomy of EU and US Preferential Trade Agreements

Henrik Horn, Petros C. Mavroidis and André Sapir

1. INTRODUCTION

THERE is growing concern about preferential trade agreements (PTAs) and the role they should play within the multilateral trading system. This concern stems both from their increasing number and their ever-broader scope.

During the period 1948–94, the General Agreement on Tariffs and Trade (GATT) received 124 notifications of PTAs, of which about 50 were active at the creation of the World Trade Organization (WTO) in 1995. Since then, more than 250 new arrangements have been notified to the WTO, and the number of arrangements active in 2008 was about 200. A large part of this expansion involves agreements where the European Community (EC) or the United States (US) is a partner.[1] As a result, the EC and the US have become the two main 'hubs' in the

This chapter draws substantially on a study prepared for Bruegel, a European think tank, to whom we are grateful for financial support. A longer version of the chapter can be found on Bruegel's website at http://www.bruegel.org. An earlier version was presented at a seminar held at the Columbia Law School in New York in October 2008. We are grateful for constructive comments to our discussants, Gary Horlick and Nuno Limão, and to Kyle Bagwell, Jagdish Bhagwati and Bernard Hoekman. We are also grateful to participants at seminars held at the European Commission in Brussels and at the WTO in Geneva in February 2009. Comments and helpful criticism from an anonymous referee are gratefully acknowledged. Finally, we are especially indebted for research assistance to Malwina Mejer and also to Vera Squaratti and Anna Wolf.

[1] We will generally use the term European Community (EC), which is the legally correct expression in the WTO context. However, we will also sometimes use the term European Union (EU) where appropriate.

pattern of PTAs, with the 'spokes' represented by agreements with the various partner countries.

Modern PTAs exhibit features that earlier PTAs did not possess. In particular, PTAs formed before 1995 concerned only trade in goods and took the form of (mostly) free-trade areas (FTAs) or (more rarely) customs unions (CUs), involving mainly tariff liberalisation. Since the creation of the WTO and the extension of multilateral trade agreements to trade in services and trade-related aspects of intellectual property rights, new PTAs also tend to cover these two subjects, which revolve chiefly around regulatory issues. Besides, there are claims that the new preferential agreements signed by the EC or the US go even further in the coverage of regulatory issues, by including provisions in areas that are not currently covered by the WTO agreements at all, such as investment protection, competition policy, labour standards and protection of the environment.

This claim has potential systemic implications because, although they jointly account for no more than 40 per cent of world GDP (at PPP) and world trade, the EC and the US are sometimes viewed as the 'regulators of the world'. It is estimated indeed that, together, they account for around 80 per cent of the rules that regulate the functioning of world markets.[2]

The relatively broad scope of PTAs involving the EC and the US is reflected in the policy debate, and to a lesser extent in the academic literature. Economic scholars have been arguing for some time about the relationship between PTAs and the multilateral trading system, with a clear division into two camps. On one hand, there are those who argue that PTAs, especially those of the 'new generation', constitute a dangerous threat to the system.[3] On the other, there are those who feel that such concern is overstated, and that there are potential solutions to reconcile the two, providing the political will exists.[4]

There is now also an institutional acknowledgement that PTAs should be regarded as a serious concern for the multilateral trading system. Thus, in opening the conference entitled 'Multilateralising Regionalism', held in Geneva in September 2007, WTO Director-General Pascal Lamy reflected 'that it would be fair to say that proliferation [of PTAs] is breeding concern – concern about incoherence, confusion, exponential increase of costs for business, unpredictability and even unfairness in trade relations'. Yet no concrete action has been taken so far by the policy community to address this multifaceted concern.

This chapter serves as a building block in this discussion. We believe that, before embarking upon a discussion as to whether (new) PTAs should be viewed with concern, one needs to examine the facts in greater detail than is typically done in the debate. Our primary purpose, therefore, is to analyse the precise content of the

---

[2] See Sapir (2007).
[3] See, in particular, Bhagwati (2008).
[4] See, for instance, Baldwin (2006).

EC and US preferential trade agreements. In order to do this, we divide the subjects covered by these agreements into two categories: 'WTO-plus' (WTO+), and 'WTO-extra' (WTO-X). The first category corresponds to those provisions of PTAs which come under the current mandate of the WTO, where the parties undertake bilateral commitments going beyond those they have accepted at the multilateral level. An example would be a reduction in tariffs. By contrast, the WTO-X category comprises those PTA provisions that deal with issues lying outside the current WTO mandate. An example would be a commitment on labour standards.

At the outset it should be emphasised, however, that our aim is not to answer the question of why WTO members – and in particular the EC and the US – include WTO-X obligations in their PTAs. At one end of the spectrum, one might suppose that PTAs serve as a kind of preparation for setting tomorrow's multilateral agenda. According to this argument, assuming consistency in the subject-matter across PTAs, it will be easier to interconnect them and multilateralise them in the future, or at least use their subject-matter as a basis for negotiating tomorrow's WTO rules.[5] But one could also argue that the very existence of WTO-X provisions is evidence that the preferential partners do not wish to include certain items in the WTO, and that is why they consistently maintain them in their PTAs.

The study covers all the 14 EC and 14 US agreements with WTO partners signed by the parties and, generally, notified to the WTO as of October 2008. In order to fully map these agreements, we proceed in two steps.

The first step consists of listing all the policy areas contained in the 28 agreements. For each of the 52 areas identified, we then record whether each agreement specifies obligations.

As a second step, we determine whether each obligation contained in the agreements is *legally enforceable*. We describe more precisely below why we believe that this is an important feature and how we evaluate whether a provision is enforceable or not. Let us simply say for the moment that the general idea is that texts that specify clear legal obligations are more likely to be implemented than less hard-edged ones.[6]

In order to shed light on the validity of the claim that the EC and US agreements go substantially beyond the WTO agreements, we divide the (52) identified

---

[5] This view can be found, for instance, in Baldwin (2006).

[6] Our work bears some resemblance to the study by Bourgeois et al. (2007) which characterises the form, content and implementation of certain provisions contained in 27 PTAs. Nevertheless, the two differ in several respects. First, we cover all EC and US PTAs with WTO members, whereas Bourgeois et al. cover only one EC PTA and 10 US PTAs, plus 16 other PTAs. Second, we cover all the provisions contained in EC and US PTAs, whereas Bourgeois et al. focus on five types of provisions: social and labour standards, environmental policies, government procurement, five specific non-tariff barriers, and competition and state aid policies.

policy areas into two groups as already indicated. The first, labelled WTO+, contains 14 areas, whereas the second, labelled WTO-X contains 38 areas.

Applying the WTO+/WTO-X distinction to the EC and the US sets of agreements, our main findings are as follows.

First, we observe that while both sets cover both WTO+ and WTO-X types of provisions, the 14 EC agreements contain almost four times as many instances of WTO-X provisions as the 14 US agreements do. This would suggest that EC PTAs extend much more frequently beyond the WTO agreements than US PTAs.

Second, however, the picture changes dramatically once the nature of the obligations is taken into account. The EC agreements evidence a very significant amount of 'legal inflation', in particular in the parts dealing with development policy. US agreements actually contain more legally enforceable WTO-X provisions than the EC agreements. Hence the latter contain many obligations that have no legal standing.

Third, we also find that both the EC and the US PTAs contain a significant number of legally enforceable, substantive undertakings in WTO+ areas. Fewer obligations contained in EC agreements tend to be enforceable than those of US agreements, but the difference is not as pronounced as for the WTO-X areas.

Finally, we find that there is a difference in the nature of the legally enforceable obligations contained in EC and US agreements, with the latter putting more emphasis on regulatory areas.

The general conclusion emerging from our study is that the implementation of PTAs should not be taken for granted. There is very little systematic evidence on the actual implementation of PTAs, as already pointed out by Hoekman and Winters (2007). An exception is the recent study by Hoekman and Zarrouk (2009) on the Pan-Arab Free Trade Area, which entered into force in 1997. Although this PTA involves neither the EC nor the US, it is still of some interest to the present study, since it contains obligations expressed with varying degrees of precision. Hoekman and Zarrouk (2009) find that clearly expressed obligations, such as removal of tariffs, are implemented to a much larger degree than more loosely worded obligations, such as those concerning e.g. technical barriers to trade. This picture is also consistent with the general view of Hoekman and Winters (2007, p. 30), who, with regard to the 'deep integration' parts of developing country PTAs, claim that '. . . there is very little direct evidence that PTAs do a lot more than unilateralism or drive reform'.

The plan of the remainder of the chapter is as follows. Section 2 deals with methodological issues related to the agreements being studied, the classification of policies into either WTO+ or WTO-X areas, and the definition of 'legally enforceable' obligations. Section 3 presents our initial findings concerning the coverage, the legal enforceability, and the 'depth' of obligations for WTO+ areas. Section 4 contains similar findings for WTO-X areas. These two sections prepare the ground for Section 5, which contains our main analyses. Section 6 briefly summarises the results.

2. METHODOLOGICAL ISSUES

The purpose of this section is to describe the set of PTAs under study, to set out how we classify the coverage of these agreements, and how we evaluate whether a covered policy contains legally enforceable obligations.

a. PTAs and the WTO

According to WTO rules, members may enter into PTAs with other WTO members either concerning trade in goods, or trade in services, or both. With respect to trade in goods, WTO members that satisfy the requirements included in Article XXIV GATT can legally treat products originating in some WTO Members (those with which they have formed a PTA) more favourably than like products originating in the other WTO member countries. Article XXIV GATT distinguishes between two forms of PTA: free-trade areas (FTAs) and customs unions (CUs). For an FTA to be GATT-consistent, its members must liberalise trade between them; for a CU to be GATT-consistent, its members must, beyond liberalising trade between them, agree on a common trade policy vis-à-vis the rest of the WTO membership. All the PTAs that will be considered here are FTAs, with the exception of the EC–Turkey agreement, which is a CU.

In the WTO, it is also possible to form PTAs under a separate legal instrument – the 'Enabling Clause'. But since this possibility is only available where *all* members of the PTA are developing countries, such agreements are not relevant to this study.

The specific conditions for satisfying consistency with the multilateral rules concerning goods trade are laid down in Article XXIV.5–8 GATT. Apart from requesting the PTA to encompass substantially all trade between its members, and not to raise the overall level of protection vis-à-vis the rest of the WTO member-ship, these provisions oblige WTO members wishing to enter into a PTA to show that they have complied with the relevant multilateral rules.

With respect to trade in services, Article V GATS mentions only one form of preferential scheme, entitled economic integration. It is akin to a GATT FTA since its members are entitled to retain their own trade policies vis-à-vis third countries, although there are also some differences between the two schemes. The disciplines of economic integration echo those preferential schemes which apply to trade in goods: Article V.1 GATS requires that a PTA has substantial sectoral coverage, and Article V.4 GATS requires PTA members not to raise the overall level of bar-riers against non-participants.

b. The Agreements under Study

Table 1 lists the set of agreements that are scrutinised in this study, which consists of all PTAs signed between the EC and the US, respectively, and other WTO members as of October 2008. The list includes agreements signed before and after the creation of the WTO, but excludes those where the partner is not a WTO member. It also includes agreements signed by the parties but not yet ratified, and therefore not yet notified to the WTO or actually in force. Of the 28 listed agreements 14 are EC PTAs and 14 are US PTAs, counting the EC agreements with individual EFTA partners (Liechtenstein and Switzerland counting as one owing to their economic union) and the European Economic Area agreement (between the EC and the EFTA countries, except Switzerland) as one PTA.

TABLE 1
EC and US PTAs with Other WTO Members, Signed as of October 2008[a]

EC Agreements	Date of Signature by Parties	US Agreements	Date of Signature by Parties
Norway	11/11/1970		
Iceland	22/07/1972		
Switzerland	22/07/1972		
EEA[b]	02/05/1992	Israel	22/04/1985
Turkey	06/03/1995	NAFTA	17/12/1992
Tunisia	17/07/1995	Jordan	24/10/2000
Israel	20/11/1995	Singapore	06/05/2003
Morocco	26/02/1996	Chile	06/06/2003
Jordan	24/11/1997	Australia	18/05/2004
South Africa	11/10/1999	Morocco	15/06/2004
Mexico	23/03/2000	CAFTA-DR	05/08/2004
FYRoM	09/04/2001	Bahrain	14/09/2004
Egypt	25/06/2001	Oman	19/01/2006
Croatia	29/10/2001	Peru	12/04/2006
Chile	18/10/2002	Colombia	22/11/2006
Albania	12/06/2006	Panama	28/06/2007
CARIFORUM	15/10/2008	South Korea	30/06/2007

Notes:
[a]The EC also has reciprocal PTAs with several non-WTO members: Algeria, Andorra, Faroe Islands, Lebanon, Overseas Countries and Territories (OTCs), the Palestinian Authority, San Marino, and Syria.
[b]The EEA was signed between the European Community and the EFTA countries, except Switzerland. Some EFTA countries later joined the European Community (now Union). The remaining EFTA countries which belong to the EEA are Iceland, Lichtenstein and Norway. Switzerland has signed separate bilateral agreements with the European Community that also cover both trade in goods and in services. When we refer to the EEA, we will use the term loosely to cover all agreements that have been concluded between EFTA countries, excluding Switzerland, and the EC.

Source: World Trade Organization (WTO), European Commission (DG External Relations) and Office of the United States Trade Representative.

c. The Coverage of the Agreements

A basic aim of this study is to identify, more precisely than has been done in the literature so far, the legal obligations imposed by PTAs involving the EU and the US, and to compare the nature of these two sets of agreements. To this end, we have gone through the 28 agreements in their entirety, and characterised the obligations which they impose. The contents of these agreements have been divided into 52 policy 'areas'. This characterisation is intended to be exhaustive, in the sense that all the provisions contained in the 28 agreements fall under one or other of the areas, except for those that concern the administration of the agreement, which we disregard. The classification is largely based on the article headings in the case of the EC agreements, and on the chapter headings in the case of the US agreements.

In order to shed light on our central issue – whether the EC and US agreements provide for 'more of the same' relative to the WTO agreements, or impose obligations in areas *other* than those already covered in the WTO agreements – we classify the 52 policy areas into two broad groups: 'WTO-plus' (WTO+) and 'WTO-extra' (WTO-X). The former is meant to include obligations relating to policy areas that are already subject to some form of commitment in the WTO agreements. The PTA can here either reconfirm existing commitments, or provide for further obligations. The archetypal obligation here would be the formation of an FTA, since this would be a reduction in tariffs going beyond what is already committed to in the WTO context. Examples of other areas we have classified as WTO+ include obligations concerning SPS (sanitary and phytosanitary) measures, TBT (technical barriers to trade) measures, antidumping, state aid and obligations covered by the GATS. We have also included those intellectual property rights provisions which address issues falling under the TRIPs agreement. Finally, we have also included export taxes, although the WTO contains no precise commitment in this area. Nonetheless, WTO members could negotiate commitments on export taxes under Article II GATT, so it can be argued that a WTO instrument already exists in this area.

A WTO-X designation is, on the other hand, meant to capture an obligation in an area that is 'qualitatively new', relating to a policy instrument that has not previously been regulated by the WTO. For instance, there are no undertakings with regard to environmental protection in the WTO. We thus classify an environmental obligation as WTO-X. Other such clear examples are obligations concerning labour laws or movement of capital.

d. The Legal Enforceability of Identified Areas

In order to determine the impact of the EC and US preferential trade agreements, it is important not only to identify the areas in which the agreements contain provisions, but also to determine the extent to which these provisions are legally enforceable. Unclearly specified undertakings, and undertakings that parties are only weakly committed to undertake, and that can be seemingly fulfilled with some token measure, are not likely to be successfully invoked by a complainant in a dispute settlement proceeding, and would presumably therefore also have little impact. In order to shed light on the extent to which this is an issue in practice, we have evaluated each provision in each agreement for the extent to which it specifies at least some obligation that is clearly defined, and that is likely effectively to bind the parties.

With a view to maintaining some degree of objectivity, we have classified certain terms as either implying enforceable or non-enforceable obligations. The following are some examples of terms that we interpret as creating legally enforceable obligations:

- 'The parties shall allow the free movement of capital . . .'
- 'Neither party may expropriate or nationalise a covered investment . . .'
- 'If a party does not accept the technical regulation that is equivalent of its own it shall, at the request of the other party, explain the reasons . . .'
- 'By the end of (exact date) a party shall accede to the following international conventions: . . .'
- 'Neither party may impose performance requirements or enforce any commitment or undertaking, in connection with the establishment, acquisition, expansion, management, conduct, operation or sale . . .'
- 'Each party shall not fail effectively to enforce labour (environmental) laws . . .'

As can be seen, the word 'shall' appears in many of these examples.

The following examples illustrate formulations that we define to be in the opposite category, not meeting the test of effectively binding the parties:

- 'The parties shall cooperate . . .'. It is likely to be very difficult to prove that a party has not 'cooperated'.
- 'Dialogue shall be established . . .'. It would require almost complete silence from the respondent for the complainant successfully to argue that no dialogue has been established.
- 'Special attention shall be paid to . . .'. How could it be verified that special attention has not been devoted to an issue?
- 'Measures necessary for development and promotion of . . .'. It is likely to be very hard for a complainant in a dispute to prove either that a measure is necessary or that it is not necessary for development.
- 'Parties may conclude . . .'. This phrase does not impose any restriction on the parties.
- 'Parties shall strive (aim) to . . .'. It would be difficult to prove absence of best endeavours.

Distinguishing the degree of legal enforceability in this way cannot only be defended from the point of view of practical experience, but also from the point of view of the principles of international law. One of the requirements in Article 2 of the Vienna Convention on the Law of Treaties for an agreement to be a treaty is that it is 'governed by international law'. This is normally interpreted to require the parties to intend that the agreement has legal effect under international law. The terminology of an agreement may indicate the extent to which such intent exists.

3. WTO+ AREAS

This section discusses the extent to which the various WTO+ areas we have identified are covered in the 28 EC and US agreements, whether existing obligations are legally binding, and the extent to which they entail substantive undertakings.[7]

a. Coverage of WTO+ Areas

The coverage of WTO+ areas in the EC and US agreements is displayed under the heading 'AC' (for Area Covered) in, respectively, Tables 2 and 3, where a dark box indicates that a particular agreement contains an obligation in a particular area.

As can be seen, there is generally speaking a very high degree of coverage in both EC and US agreements. There are three areas for which all EC and all US agreements contain obligations: Industrial Products, Agricultural Products, and TRIPs. All the EC agreements also include obligations concerning Customs Administration, TBT, Antidumping and Countervailing Measures. Most (but not all) of the US agreements also cover these areas. All the US agreements include obligations concerning Public Procurement and Export Taxes, and so do all but one or two of the EC agreements. Also, most EC and US agreements include provisions concerning State Trading Enterprises and State Aid. There is thus a fairly high degree of similarity between the two sets of agreements when it comes to the coverage of WTO+ areas. Both contain obligations in more or less the same areas.

There are, however, a few important differences between the two sets of agreements in terms of coverage. First, GATS obligations are included in all US agreements, but only in four EC ones. Second, most US agreements include TRIMs obligations, while none of the EC ones has anything explicit on this.[8]

---

[7] Section 4 will undertake a parallel analysis of WTO-X areas. While we will discuss some findings in the respective sections, we will save the broader discussion to Section 5.

[8] Note, however, that by reaffirming the Articles III and XI GATT rights and obligations in its PTAs, the EC effectively introduces obligations with respect to the two forms of TRIMs currently sanctioned by the multilateral system, that is, export performance- and local content-type of investment measures.

b. The Enforceability of WTO+ Obligations

So far we have discussed the areas that appear in the two sets of agreements. We next seek to identify those obligations that are legally enforceable. The 'LE' in Tables 2 and 3 shows the areas where undertakings are legally enforceable.

A dark box indicates that the language is sufficiently precise or committing to provide a legally enforceable obligation. A cross-hatched box indicates that the language is sufficiently precise or committing, but that it is non-enforceable due to an explicit statement that dispute settlement is not available.

Let us start by pointing to the areas that are exempt from dispute settlement. As can be seen, the EC agreement with Mexico has four such exemptions, for SPS, Antidumping, Countervailing Measures, and TRIPs; the EC agreement with CARIFORUM has exemptions for the latter two areas, and the EC–Chile agreement has exemptions for State Trading Enterprises and State Aid. The US agreements contain exemptions from dispute settlement only in the context of SPS, but do so for 10 agreements, allowing dispute settlement regarding SPS measures only in the agreement with Israel and in NAFTA.

In areas that are non-enforceable due to imprecise language, we note that, with respect to the EC agreements, in seven of the 14 agreements Public Procurement undertakings are not enforceable; in nine out of the 14 agreements TBT undertakings are not enforceable; and in 10 out of 12 agreements SPS undertakings are not enforceable. The US agreements, on the other hand, contain relatively speaking substantially fewer areas where legally non-enforceable language has been included, both in absolute numbers and relative to the number of covered areas.

Turning to the areas with enforceable obligations, we observe that both sets of agreements include such obligations for all their agreements with regard to tariff liberalisation (FTAs) for both industrial and agricultural products, and with respect to 12 out of the 14 agreements in the areas of Customs Administration, Export Taxes, Antidumping, Countervailing Measures, State Aid, and TRIPs.

c. Main Observations Concerning WTO+ Undertakings

Our initial conclusions concerning the WTO+ parts of the agreements are the following:

1. Both the EC and US sets of agreements have a large number of legally enforceable obligations with significant undertakings in areas covered by the current WTO mandate, such as tariff cuts in goods, Customs Administration, Export Taxes, Antidumping, Countervailing Measures, Agriculture, and TRIPs.
2. Commitments in the 'new WTO areas' (GATS, TRIPs) figure prominently in both sets of agreements, although more so in US PTAs as far as services are concerned.

TABLE 2
Classification of WTO+ Areas in EC Agreements

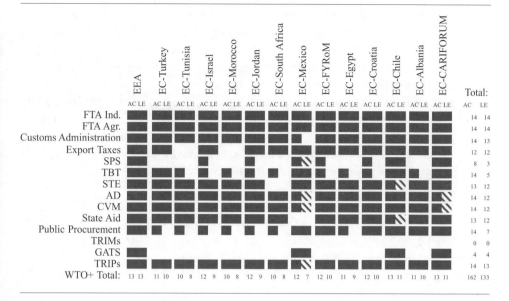

TABLE 3
Classification of WTO+ Areas in US Agreements

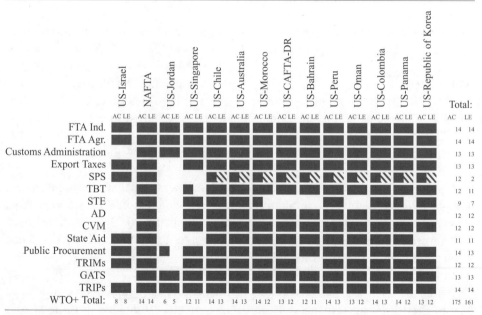

Notes:
The GATS area covers commitments related to services liberalisation. AC: Area covered; LE: Legally enforceable.

Source: Authors.

3. The extent of the overlap between the two sets of agreements notwithstanding, we still observe some notable differences: the US agreements have
   substantial, legally enforceable obligations concerning TRIMS, TBT and
   GATS, while the EC agreements contain significantly more obligations of
   this kind concerning State Trading Enterprises.
4. Both sets of agreements opt for staged tariff liberalisation with respect to
   both industrial and farm goods. Still, it is very difficult to pronounce on their
   consistency with the WTO rules in light of the confusion surrounding the
   meaning of the terms appearing in Article XXIV GATT, and the lack of
   practice regarding the interpretation of Article V GATS.[9]

4. WTO-X AREAS

We now turn our attention to the WTO-X areas, which refer to provisions
regarding commitments in policy areas not covered by the current mandate of the
WTO.

a. The Coverage of WTO-X Areas

Tables 4 and 5 provide information about the coverage of the two sets of agreements for WTO-X areas.

We will start by describing the overlap between the two sets of agreements, and
then revert to the differences among them. We should note at the outset however
that, for the most part, the two sets of agreements differ significantly in their
WTO-X subject-matter. Four areas – Environment, Intellectual Property,
Investment, and Movement of Capital – appear in both sets of agreements; 12 of
the 14 EC agreements include commitments in these areas, and so do 11 of the
14 US agreements. There is also some overlap with regard to Competition: all EC
agreements include such a commitment, while seven of the US agreements
also do.

US agreements typically also include commitments in two additional areas:
Labour Market Regulation, an item that has been included in 13 US agreements,
and Anti-Corruption, where the corresponding number is 10. Besides these areas,
US agreements contain commitments in two additional WTO-X areas – Data
Protection, which has been included in two agreements, and Energy, which has
been included in one.

All of the 38 WTO-X areas – except Anti-Corruption – are covered in at least
one of the 14 EC agreements. Of the 14 agreements, 10 include provisions con-

---

[9] See Mavroidis (2007).

TABLE 4
WTO-X Areas Covered in EC Agreements

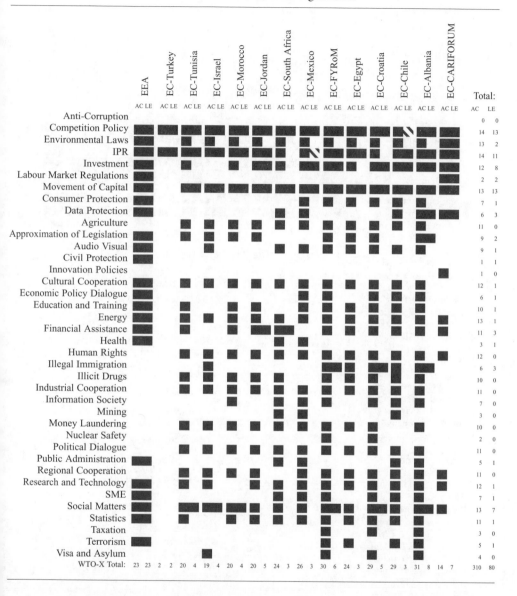

	EEA	EC-Turkey	EC-Tunisia	EC-Israel	EC-Morocco	EC-Jordan	EC-South Africa	EC-Mexico	EC-FYRoM	EC-Egypt	EC-Croatia	EC-Chile	EC-Albania	EC-CARIFORUM	Total: AC	LE
	AC LE	AC LE	AC LE	AC LE	AC LE	AC LE	AC LE	AC LE	AC LE	AC LE	AC LE	AC LE	AC LE	AC LE	AC	LE
Anti-Corruption															0	0
Competition Policy															14	13
Environmental Laws															13	2
IPR															14	11
Investment															12	8
Labour Market Regulations															2	2
Movement of Capital															13	13
Consumer Protection															7	1
Data Protection															6	3
Agriculture															11	0
Approximation of Legislation															9	2
Audio Visual															9	1
Civil Protection															1	1
Innovation Policies															1	0
Cultural Cooperation															12	1
Economic Policy Dialogue															6	1
Education and Training															10	1
Energy															13	1
Financial Assistance															11	3
Health															3	1
Human Rights															12	0
Illegal Immigration															6	3
Illicit Drugs															10	0
Industrial Cooperation															11	0
Information Society															7	0
Mining															3	0
Money Laundering															10	0
Nuclear Safety															2	0
Political Dialogue															11	0
Public Administration															5	1
Regional Cooperation															11	0
Research and Technology															12	1
SME															7	1
Social Matters															13	7
Statistics															11	1
Taxation															3	0
Terrorism															5	1
Visa and Asylum															4	0
WTO-X Total:	23 23	2 2	20 4	19 4	20 4	20 5	24 3	26 3	30 6	24 3	29 5	29 3	31 8	14 7	310	80

cerning Agriculture,[10] Cultural Cooperation, Education and Training, Energy, Financial Assistance, Human Rights, Illicit Drugs, Industrial Cooperation, Money Laundering, Political Dialogue, Regional Cooperation, Research and Technology, Social Matters, and Statistics. The only agreement that stands out in terms of

---

[10] We refer to commitments which lie outside the current WTO mandate.

TABLE 5
WTO-X Areas Covered in US Agreements

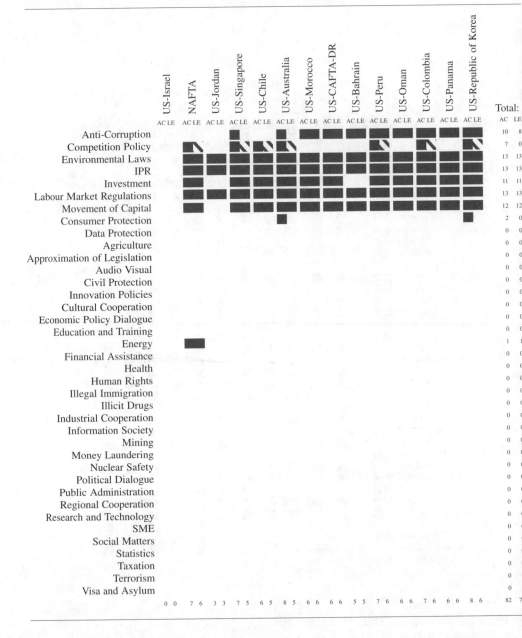

coverage is the one with Turkey, which contains commitments in only two areas: Competition and Intellectual Property Rights.

b. The Enforceability of WTO-X Obligations

While the EC agreements contain a larger number of WTO-X areas, it is the US agreements that contain the (proportionately speaking) higher number of legally enforceable obligations in these areas.

The US agreements contain few areas with non-enforceable provisions:

1. The main source of non-enforceability is the exemption of Competition-related disciplines from dispute settlement (illustrated by a cross-hatched box under the heading LE in Table 4); all seven agreements that include a Competition provision explicitly exclude the commitments from dispute settlement.
2. There are four further instances of non-enforceability: two regarding Anti-Corruption and two concerning Consumer Protection. In total, only 13 per cent (11 out of 82) of the covered provisions are deemed to be non-enforceable.

By contrast, nearly 75 per cent (230 out of 310) of the provisions included in the EC agreements are non-enforceable. The EC agreements contain enforceable obligations in only five WTO-X areas in a significant number of agreements:

1. Competition (in 13 out of the 14 agreements that contain commitments in this area);
2. IPR (11 out of 14);
3. Movement of Capital (13 out of 13);
4. Investment (8 out of 12); and
5. Social Matters (7 out of 13).

For each of the remaining 33 areas, there are no legally enforceable obligations in more than three agreements signed by the EC. Most obligations are not enforceable at all. One agreement represents an outlier, the EEA, an agreement that involves the EC and some of its Western European trading partners with whom there is a long tradition of multi-level cooperation.

c. Main Observations Concerning WTO-X Undertakings

Our initial conclusions concerning the WTO-X parts of the agreements are as follows:

1. Whereas the US agreements typically contain few areas where enforceable obligations have been agreed, the EC agreements contain a smaller

(proportional to the overall) number of areas with enforceable obligations, and a much larger number of areas where exhortatory language has been agreed. It thus seems that, whereas the US has adopted a rather 'functionalist' approach (ensuring legal enforceability of the selected areas), the EC has opted for 'legal inflation', whereby a large number of areas are included in the agreement, but very few of them are coupled with legally enforceable obligations.

2. Altogether, only eight of the 38 WTO-X areas involve legally enforceable obligations in a significant number of agreements.
3. Three of these eight areas concern both EC and US agreements: Intellectual Property Rights, Investment, and Movement of Capital.
4. Three areas concern mostly or solely US agreements: Anti-Corruption, Environment and Labour.
5. Two areas involve EC agreements only: Competition, and Social Matters.
6. Finally, provisions concerning Terrorism, Illegal Immigration, Visa and Migration, and Illicit Drugs appear in some of the EC agreements (in respectively five, six, three and 10 agreements), but typically the obligations are not enforceable. Contrary to what may have been expected, these national security-related areas are not present in US agreements.

5. PTAS AND THE WTO – MORE OF THE SAME OR NEW TERRITORIES?

A central issue in the policy debate concerning PTAs has been whether they support or hinder multilateral trade liberalisation. This issue has received a new twist during the last decade, because of the common claim that these agreements are no longer about deeper integration in areas where the multilateral system already provides a degree of integration but are instead mainly to be seen as ventures into new policy areas. Having so far analysed the WTO+ and the WTO-X areas separately, we will in this section discuss the balance in the EC and US PTAs between the WTO+ and the WTO-X areas. Our purpose is to distil an overall picture of where the *centre of gravity* of these agreements lies. Are they essentially about further integration along the same lines as in the GATT/WTO, or are they mainly about providing integration in new policy areas? As before, we will put particular emphasis on the extent to which identified obligations are likely to be legally enforceable, and we will seek to characterise the areas where legal inflation is most pervasive, and also whether it is likely to be an intentional feature of certain areas.

a. Differences in Coverage of EC and US PTAs

In order to detect the centre of gravity of the EC and US agreements in terms of coverage, Figure 1 plots the number of covered WTO+ areas (measured on the

FIGURE 1
The Balance between WTO+ and WTO-X Undertakings in Terms of Coverage

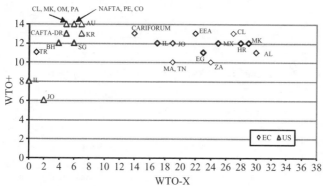

Source: Own calculations based on Tables 2, 3, 4 and 5.

vertical axis) against the number of covered WTO-X areas (measured on the horizontal axis) for each of the 28 agreements. As can be seen, a very pronounced pattern emerges: all the EC agreements (with one exception) are positioned to the southeast of the US agreements. That is, in terms of coverage, the EC agreements have more WTO-X and fewer WTO+ areas than the US agreements. Hence, while both the EC and the US agreements cover a large proportion of WTO+ areas (between 10 and 12 for the EC and between 12 and 14 for the US, out of a maximum of 14), the EC PTAs cover a much greater proportion of WTO-X areas (reaching around 30 in recent agreements, out of a maximum of 38) than US agreements (with fewer than 10 areas covered, even in the most recent agreements).

b. Centre of Gravity of EC and US PTAs Adjusted for Legal Enforceability

If one discards non-enforceable obligations, the previous picture changes dramatically. As shown in Figure 2, while the number of WTO+ areas remains slightly larger for US agreements (ranging between 11 and 13) compared to EC agreements (ranging between 8 and 10), the number of WTO-X areas with legally enforceable provisions is now slightly higher for US (ranging between 5 and 6) compared to EC (ranging mostly between 3 and 5) agreements.[11] The EC agreements thus evidence a very considerable degree of 'legal inflation' in WTO-X areas, a phenomenon which is much less prevalent in the EC agreements for WTO+ areas or in the WTO+ and WTO-X areas of the US PTAs.

---

[11] One agreement stands out in each set: the EEA agreement on the EC side, with 23 legally binding provisions, and the US–Israel agreement, with zero.

FIGURE 2

The Balance between WTO+ and WTO-X Undertakings, Discounting for the Lack of Legal Enforceability

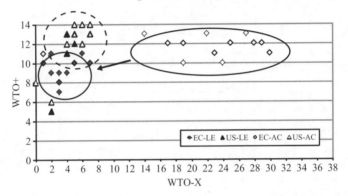

Note:

LE: Legally enforceable; AC: Areas covered.

Source: Own calculations based on Tables 2, 3, 4 and 5.

It should be noted that the two latest EC agreements, with Albania and the CARIFORUM, contain slightly more legally enforceable WTO-X provisions than do the US agreements. In this respect, the EC–CARIFORUM agreement resembles more the US PTAs than any other EC PTA: it covers relatively few WTO-X areas, of which many contain legally enforceable provisions.[12] Still, only half of the 14 WTO-X areas that are covered contain enforceable obligations. And the EC–Albania agreement, while having eight areas with enforceable obligations, features the same degree of legal inflation – 23 out of the 31 areas in the EC–Albania agreement are classified as non-enforceable – as the other EC agreements.

c. In Which Areas Is Legal Inflation Most Pervasive?

Table 6 reorganises somewhat the data on coverage and legally enforceability in order to highlight the type of areas where legal inflation is most pervasive. The table divides all areas (i.e. both WTO+ and WTO-X areas) into five broad groups, along different lines than the WTO+/WTO-X distinction, which was designed to capture the nature of each area relative to the WTO agreements. Here the intention is instead to capture the content of each area in terms of policy objectives or instruments. Group 1, Trade- and Investment-related Obligations, is meant to capture obligations that address policy instruments affecting goods trade and

---

[12] The EC–Albania PTA is a more traditional EC agreement in this respect: it covers 31 WTO-X areas, of which only eight contain legally binding provisions.

TABLE 6
Legal Inflation by Groups of Areas

	EU PTAs			US PTAs		
	AC	LE	Legal Inflation	AC	LE	Legal Inflation
1. Trade- and Investment-related Obligations	107	98	8%	113	113	0%
2. GATS/TRIPs/IPR	32	28	13%	40	40	0%
3. Migration-related Regulations	23	10	57%	–	–	–
4. Domestic Trade-related Regulations	104	60	42%	103	78	24%
Total Trade and Regulations:	266	196	26%	256	231	10%
5. Other	206	17	92%	1	1	0%
Total all areas:	472	213	55%	257	232	10%

Source: Authors' own calculations.

investment, and which are applied at the border. Group 2, GATS/TRIPs/IPR, and Group 3, Migration-related Regulations, are self-explanatory. Group 4, Domestic Trade-related Regulations, is intended to include obligations concerning domestic (behind-the-border) regulations. Finally, Group 5, labelled 'Other', includes all remaining areas and mainly contains development-related provisions from EC agreements. Although this grouping of areas is heuristic, we believe that it is informative in that it reflects sharp differences in legal inflation across groups as the discussion below indicates.

Table 6 gives, group by group, the number of times each area within the group occurs in EU or US agreements; it then gives, group by group, the number of instances each area within that group occurs with enforceable obligations. In addition, it calculates an Index of Legal Inflation, which is defined as the number of instances of legally non-enforceable obligations in a group of areas relative to the total number of times that group of areas occurs.

There are two main findings that emerge from the table. First, and once again, there is a striking difference between the EC and the US agreements. Taking all areas together, the inflation rate is 55 per cent for the EC PTAs compared to only 10 per cent for the US agreements. Second, there are significant differences across areas. Distinguishing between the 'Trade and Regulations' areas (i.e. groups 1–4) and the 'Other' areas, one observes a second striking difference. For the EC the inflation rate is only 26 per cent in the former grouping as opposed to 92 per cent in the latter. Moreover, the difference in inflation rates between the EC and the US is much less for Trade and Regulations (26 versus 10 per cent) than it is for the total of all areas.

One may wonder whether the difference of legal inflation between EC and US agreements is not simply the reflection of a unique feature of some EC agreements, which is that they are not simply trade agreements, but instead constitute a first step towards EU membership. In order to check for this possibility, we have computed the legal inflation rates for the nine EC agreements with non-European countries,[13] which can be regarded as trade agreements comparable to those between the US and its partners. Taking all areas together, the inflation rate for these nine EC agreements is 61 per cent, which is six percentage points more than the inflation rate for all the 14 EC agreements. Moreover, the inflation rate for the EC RTAs with non-European partners is larger than the inflation rate for the EC RTAs with all partners for every one of the five broad groups shown in Table 6. One can, therefore, safely conclude that the difference of legal inflation between EC and US RTAs is not caused by the presence of agreements with potential future EU members amongst the EC RTAs.

We now detail these differences across the five groups. As can be seen from Table 6, there are clearly systematic differences in the extent of legal inflation in the different groups. At one end we have the Trade and Investment group, which displays literally zero legal inflation for the US agreements, and only 9 per cent for the EC agreements, with most of the latter explained by obligations in the WTO-X Investment area. Furthermore, not only is there little or no inflation, these areas are also covered in almost all agreements of both the EC and the US (with the exception of Export Taxes, and TRIMs in EC agreements), and they very often involve substantial undertakings. The GATS/TRIPs/IPR group displays a very similar pattern.

At the other end of the spectrum in terms of legal inflation is the 'Other' group, which largely consists of development-related undertakings appearing in the cooperation parts of the EC agreements. The US agreements effectively have no instances of this group of areas, and are therefore irrelevant here. For this group, which contains a large number of areas which are covered in a large number of EC agreements, the legal inflation rate is 92 per cent! This average is higher than the inflation rate for any of the other groups, and is even higher than each individual area in all other groups, with the exception of two areas: the Visa, Border Control and Asylum area, and the Human Rights area. Based on this observation, we would argue that, to the extent that these agreements promote development, it is not because of the enforceability of their legal commitments.

Provisions related to domestic regulations, in the broad sense of the term, can be found in both WTO+ and WTO-X areas. In the group Domestic Trade-related Regulations we have tried to distinguish regulations which have more obvious potential to be used as legal arguments in a trade dispute from those that do not seem to have such potential. It is for this reason that, for instance, Labour and Environment areas are grouped together with the SPS and TBT areas, while areas such as Nuclear Safety and Money Laundering – which can also be said to address

---

[13] Five of the 14 EC PTAs are with European partners: EEA, Turkey, FYRoM, Croatia and Albania.

domestic regulation – are kept under the 'Other' label. It is also for this reason that the Environment and Labour areas are classified as potentially affecting trade.

Turning to the numbers, we see that this group reveals a more complicated pattern than the other groups. However, there is a significant difference in legal inflation in the group for the EC and the US agreements, with 42 per cent of the areas covered in EC agreements being non-enforceable, compared to only 24 per cent for the US.

An issue of particular interest with regard to EC and US PTAs is the extent to which they can be seen as a means of transferring the regulatory regimes of the EC and the US to other countries. The scattered pattern that emerges for this group makes it difficult to draw unambiguous conclusions in this regard, and may also indicate that the groups need to be redefined to answer this question properly. But it is noteworthy that in almost all the areas in this group, the PTAs extend either international or EU/US domestic regulatory standards to partner countries. Since the EU and the US already broadly meet the international or domestic regulatory standards contained in the PTAs, these agreements could indeed potentially be vehicles for transferring regulatory rules of the EC and the US to their PTA partners. One might imagine various ways in which such a transfer occurs. For instance, the formation of the PTAs may affect domestic policy discussions concerning the choice of regulatory regime. However, for these agreements to effect such a transfer by legally binding the partner countries to a hub's regulatory regime, they must contain enforceable provisions. As we have seen, the picture seems to be mixed in this regard.

d. Closing Remarks

The general picture that emerges from comparing the undertakings in the WTO+ and WTO-X areas for the two sets of PTAs is the following:

1. The EC agreements go much further than the US agreements in covering areas outside the scope of the WTO agreements. There has also been an increasing tendency to this effect.
2. When adjusting for non-enforceable language, one observes significant 'legal inflation' in non-WTO parts of the EC agreements. In fact, the EC agreements are similar to the US agreements in that much of the emphasis of enforceable language is on existing WTO areas.
3. Both EC and US PTAs contain non-WTO areas with substantial undertakings. An important aspect of both sets of agreements is thus that they combine substantial undertakings in WTO areas and in non-WTO areas.
4. A significant proportion of the substantial, legally enforceable obligations is in areas where domestic or international regulations are important, but the specific regulatory areas differ for the two hubs.

6. CONCLUSIONS

There is growing concern about preferential trading agreements and the role they should play in the multilateral trading system. Not only are they becoming increasingly prevalent, there is also a perception that many recent PTAs, especially those centred on the EC and the US, go far beyond the scope of the current WTO agreements.

With a view to shedding light on whether the above perception corresponds to reality, this study has assessed in some detail all the PTAs signed by the EC or the US and other WTO members by dividing all the areas they include into two categories: WTO+ obligations, which are areas already covered by the present WTO agreements, and WTO-X obligations, which are areas currently falling outside these agreements.

Our examination of the two sets of PTAs yields two main findings.

First, both EC and US agreements contain a significant number of WTO+ and WTO-X obligations. However, EC agreements go much further in terms of WTO-X coverage than US agreements. When discounting for 'legal inflation' the picture remains largely the same for US agreements, but it changes dramatically for EC agreements. Adjusting for 'legal inflation', US agreements actually contain more legally binding provisions, both in WTO+ and WTO-X areas, than EC agreements.

It is thus clear that the EU and the US have chosen markedly different strategies for including provisions in their PTAs that go beyond the WTO agreements. In particular, EC agreements display a fair deal of 'legal inflation', a phenomenon almost totally absent in US agreements. The study does not permit us to draw precise conclusions about this asymmetry of behaviour between the EU and the US, but the fact that much of the 'legal inflation' occurs in development-related provisions, which are unique to the EC agreements, suggests that the EU has a greater need than the US to portray its PTAs as not driven solely by commercial interests. Our feeling is that this may reflect a lack of consensus on the part of EU member states about the ultimate purpose of these PTAs, the wide variety of provisions of weak legal value representing a compromise between various interests among EU members.

Second, although EC and US preferential trade agreements do go significantly beyond the WTO agreements, the number of legally enforceable WTO-X provisions contained in EC and US PTAs is still in fact quite small. Provisions that can be regarded as really breaking new ground compared to existing WTO agreements are few and far between: environment and labour standards for US agreements, and competition policy for EC agreements. These provisions clearly all deal with regulatory issues. The other enforceable WTO-X provisions found in EC and US PTAs concern domains that relate to existing WTO provisions in areas such as investment, capital movement and intellectual property, which are also mainly regulatory.

The fact that the new, legally enforceable WTO-X provisions all deal with regulatory issues suggests that EC and US agreements effectively serve as a means for the two hubs to export their own regulatory approaches to their PTA partners. The study does not permit us to draw conclusions about the respective costs and benefits of this situation for the hubs and the spokes, but our feeling is that it serves primarily the interests of the two 'regulators of the world'. This feeling is based on the fact that the legally enforceable WTO-X provisions included in EC and US agreements have all been the subject of earlier, but failed, attempts by the EU and/or the US to incorporate them in WTO rules, against the wishes of developing countries. To the extent that our conclusion is correct, it supports the view expressed *inter alia* by WTO Director-General Pascal Lamy that PTAs might be breeding concern about unfairness in trade relations.

The implications of our findings for the 'regionalism-versus-multilateralism' issue are beyond the scope of this chapter. Our sentiment, however, is that there is no substantial difference between EC and US PTAs in this respect. It is striking that the EC and the US quite often sign PTAs with the same partners, with five of the nine non-European partners of the EC having also signed PTAs with the US, and several other US partners that are currently negotiating PTAs with the EC. This seems to suggest the presence of a 'domino effect' between the EC, the US and their PTA partners. Hence, contrary to the stumbling-block view, the formation of a PTA between the EC or the US hub and a partner country does not seem to lock the latter into an exclusive relationship with one of the two hubs. However, the evidence presented in this study does not suffice to conclude unambiguously whether the formation of PTAs by the EC and the US serves as a building block toward multilateral integration. Further research would be needed to reach a firmer conclusion on this conceptually difficult issue. It is our belief, however, that a central aspect of this issue is the extent to which PTAs are legally binding and more generally to which they are implemented.

REFERENCES

Baldwin, R. E. (2006), 'Multilateralising Regionalism: Spaghetti Bowls as Building Blocks on the Path to Global Free Trade', *The World Economy*, **29**, 1451–518.

Bhagwati, J. N. (2008), *Termites in the Trading System: How Preferential Agreements Undermine Free Trade* (Oxford: Oxford University Press).

Bourgeois, J., K. Dawar and S. J. Evenett (2007), *A Comparative Analysis of Selected Provisions in Free Trade Agreements*, Study Commissioned by DG Trade (Brussels: European Commission).

Hoekman, B. and L. A. Winters (2007), 'Multilateralising Preferential Trade Agreements: A Developing Country Perspective', mimeo (Washington, DC: The World Bank).

Hoekman, B. and J. Zarrouk (2009), 'Changes in Cross-border Trade Costs in the Pan-Arab Free Trade Area, 2001–2008', Policy Research Working Paper No. 5031 (August), International Trade Department (Washington, DC: The World Bank).

Mavroidis, P. C. (2007), *Trade in Goods* (Oxford: Oxford University Press).

Sapir, A. (2007), 'Europe and the Global Economy', in A. Sapir (ed.), *Fragmented Power: Europe and the Global Economy* (Brussels: Bruegel).

9

Third-country Effects of Regional Trade Agreements

Caroline Freund

1. INTRODUCTION

There are over 200 regional trade agreements (RTAs) currently in force. More than half of these agreements have been implemented following the conclusion of the Uruguay Round in 1995, and many new agreements are currently under negotiation. In contrast, multilateral liberalisation through the World Trade Organization has stalled: after seven years of negotiation, agreement among members on further multilateral trade liberalisation remains unattainable. These facts speak for themselves; regionalism has been the dominant force for negotiated trade liberalisation in recent years. This has led economists to re-examine the implications of regionalism for trade, welfare and the world trade system both theoretically and empirically. A number of concerns have arisen, leading many prominent trade economists to oppose regionalism as a means of trade liberalisation.

At issue is the discriminatory nature of RTAs.[1] Although tariff preferences stimulate trade among bloc members, they can have deleterious effects on non-members, potentially even on members and on the political economy of trade policy formation.[2] There are three main concerns. The first is trade diversion:

I am grateful for comments from Kyle Bagwell, Petros Mavroidis, Kamal Saggi, an anonymous referee and participants in the WTO seminar at Columbia Law School. The views presented in this chapter are the views of the author and do not reflect the views of the World Bank.

[1] We use RTA to refer to all types of discriminatory reciprocal trade agreements.
[2] Bhagwati and Panagariya (1996) provide in-depth discussions of these concerns. Frankel (1997) summarises theoretical and empirical issues; Pomfret (2003) presents the literature on the theory of RTAs; and Schiff and Winters (2003) extend the literature to focus on developing countries.

regional trade agreements may lead to diversion of imports away from the most efficient global producers to regional partners. This means that the formation of trade blocs can be welfare reducing, even for the member countries if little new trade is created. The second concern is that regionalism may hinder unilateral and multilateral tariff reduction, leading to a bad equilibrium, with several trade blocs maintaining high external trade barriers. This would happen if trade bloc members have less incentive to lower external tariffs than individual countries. Alternatively, regionalism could hinder multilateralism simply by detracting from the multilateral process, especially in countries where government resources for trade initiatives are limited. Third, the creation of regional agreements may result in cumbersome new trade barriers being erected against non-regional members. One oft-cited example of this is rules of origin, which abound in RTA countries to prevent imports of goods into a high-tariff country via a low-tariff member.

A more sanguine view maintains that, as a form of trade liberalisation, regionalism should generate growth effects commonly associated with increased trade. By providing competition to the multilateral system, expanding regional- ism may also lead to a redoubling of multilateral efforts. To the extent that trade diversion costs arise, these costs are likely to be small, as agreements tend to be formed among natural trade partners, or will push countries to lower external tariffs to minimise them. General Agreement on Tariffs and Trade (GATT) founders clearly saw regionalism and multilateralism as complementary, or rules for creating free trade agreements and customs unions would not have been formalised in Article XXIV. Indeed, Snape (1993) discusses the history of Article XXIV and argues that this exception to non-discrimination is vital to maintaining the multilateral club. Some members might opt out of the multilateral agreements if RTAs were not permitted.

In this chapter, I focus on the effects of regionalism on trade with third countries. In particular, have regional agreements led to significant trade diversion – sharp drops in trade with non-members? And, how have regional agreements affected the members' external tariffs that non-members face? Much of the existing work on the effects of regional agreements on trade is theoretical – this literature is discussed in the next section. A few empirical papers have begun analysing in-depth the consequences of regional agreements. These are discussed in Section 3. Section 4 provides some new evidence on these questions and finally Section 5 concludes.

2. THEORETICAL FOUNDATIONS FOR TRADE DIVERSION
AND TRADE POLICY

Two key questions raised by the formation of a regional agreement are: Will it make the member countries better off? And, will non-members be severely damaged? It turns out that these two questions are related. In seminal work, Viner

(1950) shows that the preferential removal of tariffs can lead to trade diversion – where goods that formerly were imported from a low-cost producer outside the agreement are now sourced from the high-cost member of the trade agreement. If there is a significant trade diversion, both member countries and non-member countries will be made worse off.

To see how trade diversion affects members and non-members, and the conditions under which diversion is more likely to occur, let us consider three hypothetical cases involving trade discrimination in a particular product, say shoes. In particular, we examine how trade patterns change, following the initiation of a free trade agreement between Mexico and the United States.

Case I: The United States is a price taker and importer of shoes. When there are no regional agreements, Brazil is the lowest-cost producer and all shoes are imported from Brazil for $10 a pair. Shoes face a 10 per cent tariff in the United States, implying that US consumers pay $11 for a pair of shoes. Now, the United States signs a free trade agreement with Mexico, and eliminates the tariff on Mexican shoes. Assume Mexican shoes cost $11 a pair to produce. After the agreement is implemented, the United States imports some shoes from Mexico. US consumers still pay $11 for a pair of shoes. In this case, the United States loses because it formerly received tariff revenue of $1 for each pair of imported shoes, which is now lost for all Mexican imports. At the same time, the price to consumers has remained unchanged, meaning there is no gain in consumer surplus. Thus, the United States loses significant tariff revenue, without any substantial offsetting gains. Similarly, Brazil loses because of lost exports to the United States. The more trade diversion there is, the greater will be the loss (or smaller the gain) to both the United States and Brazil, i.e. the member and the non-member.

Case II: Everything is the same as in Case I, except the US tariff, which is 5 per cent. Now, consumers initially pay $10.50 for shoes and all shoes are imported from Brazil. The agreement does not affect this relationship because Brazilian shoes *cum* tariff remain cheaper than Mexican shoes when the tariff is eliminated. There is no trade diversion, and the relationship between Brazil and the United States is unaffected by the RTA between Mexico and the United States.

Case III: Mexico is the low-cost provider. Mexico exports shoes to the United States at $10 before the agreement, the tariff is 10 per cent and consumers pay $11 for a pair of shoes. After the agreement, the price of shoes falls to $10, leading to a large consumer gain, more than offsetting the tariff loss since consumers can afford more shoes at the lower price. This is a case of pure trade creation by the agreement. Again, there is no effect on Brazil.

These stark cases highlight three important implications of regional liberalisation. First, trade diversion is costly to members and non-members alike. Trade diversion is costly to members because imports are shifted from efficient third-country producers to less efficient regional producers – this leads to relatively small gains in consumer surplus coupled with large losses in tariff revenue. Second, trade diversion is more likely if the external tariff is high. When the external tariff is high, preferential tariff elimination puts a bigger wedge between the members and non-members, providing a large scope for trade diversion. Third, trade diversion is absent when the members are low-cost providers. In the extreme case, when all exports come from the members then preferential tariff elimination is akin to free trade.

We have seen that when external tariffs are low, trade diversion is unlikely. This means that how regionalism affects member countries' incentives to alter their external (most-favoured-nation, MFN) trade barriers is extremely important in determining whether regionalism is harmful. The effects on incentives can also be seen in the example above. In Case I, there is a large cost to the United States from trade diversion. This implies there is an incentive for the United States to reduce its external tariff. Following implementation of the trade agreement, if the US external tariff is reduced from 10 per cent to 5 per cent then the situation changes from Case I to Case II and there is a real welfare gain. Moreover, if the agreement facilitates this reduction, it implies that the preferential trade agreement was a building block to freer trade.

If the formation of a preferential trading bloc is accompanied by reductions in external tariffs, the arrangement is more likely to enhance aggregate world welfare without harming excluded countries. In contrast, if the trading bloc raises trade barriers against the excluded countries (or fails to reduce them deeply enough), diversion of external trade to bloc members is more likely, harming countries in the bloc as well as those in the rest of the world. The welfare consequences of an RTA therefore depend heavily on the member countries' tariff response.

There is a considerable theoretical literature that explores the optimal tariff response of countries. In a standard model, with a welfare-maximising government, optimal tariffs are likely fall in a free trade area precisely because of the welfare costs outlined in Case I above (Bagwell and Staiger, 1999; Freund, 2000; Bond et al., 2002; Ornelas, 2005). The intuition is that the welfare cost of trade diversion leads countries to lower external tariffs to recapture tariff revenue and improve efficiency. Put another way, losses to non-members are limited precisely because trade diversion lowers welfare for *both* the non-members and the members. This means that the members' optimal tariff response will limit trade diversion and potential losses to non-members.

However, when political-economy effects are incorporated, the results are ambiguous. For example, Richardson (1993) and Cadot et al. (2001) find that, following the initiation of a free trade area, lobbying will decline and external tariffs will fall, as the import-competing sector contracts. However, in a different model, Panagariya and Findlay (1996) find that countries in a free trade area will raise tariffs because lobbying in favour of tariffs against the partner will be diverted to lobbying for a greater external tariff.[3]

Incentives are also different in a customs union, where members set a common external tariff. Members of a customs union maximise welfare jointly, and if the union is relatively large, optimal tariffs are likely to rise as a result of enhanced market power (Kennan and Riezman, 1990; Syropoulos, 1999; Freund, 2000; Bond et al., 2001). The basic intuition is that the trade agreement expands the market for goods produced in the bloc, resulting in a decline in demand for third-country goods, which will cause an improvement in the bloc's terms of trade if it is large enough. Moreover, it is not just *existing* trade blocs that matter; Bagwell and Staiger (2005) show that the mere potential for a future trade agreement may affect the extent of current tariff reduction that can be negotiated multilaterally. The threat of 'bilateral opportunism' will reduce the extent of multilateral tariff reduction since current global trade agreements can be diluted by bilateral preferences.

3. EMPIRICAL EVIDENCE ON TRADE DIVERSION AND TRADE POLICY

There is some evidence that trade diversion may be of concern in high-tariff countries, but obtaining reliable estimates of diversion is difficult. The problem is that to estimate diversion, trade flows both in the absence and presence of a RTA are required. Since this is not possible, trade diversion is estimated from comparisons between predicted and actual trades.

Most studies use a gravity equation, which predicts bilateral trade based on income and other characteristics, and focus on variables that capture the extent to which RTA partners trade more or less than would otherwise be expected. The key trade creation variable is a dummy that is one if both countries are members of a common RTA; the key trade diversion variable is a dummy that is one if one country belongs to an RTA and the other does not (see e.g. Frankel et al., 1995). A positive coefficient on the former offers evidence of trade creation; a negative coefficient on the latter offers evidence of diversion. Overall, the message from such studies is of a predominance of trade creation. In fact, a concern is that the estimates of the creation effect may be implausibly large, as well as too dependent on the sample of countries and variables included (Haveman and Hummels, 1998).

Magee (2008) expands on the traditional approach, with insights from the literature on the proper estimation of gravity models. He uses panel data for 133

---

[3] A large literature addresses the related question of whether allowing countries to form RTAs helps or hinders the viability of a multilateral free trade agreement (Grossman and Helpman, 1995; Levy, 1997; Krishna, 1998; Ornelas, 2005; Aghion et al., 2007; Saggi and Yildiz, 2007).

countries from 1980 to 1998, and includes country–pair fixed effects, exporter–year fixed effects and importer–year fixed effects to capture the counterfactual more accurately than standard gravity specifications would. The dyad effects pick up what is natural about the trade partners, the exporter– and importer–year effects pick up country-specific dynamics. Magee finds that the average impact of agreements on trade flows is small – 3 per cent. Moreover, on average trade creation dominates trade diversion by about one order of magnitude.

Another strand of the literature uses more disaggregated data to examine specific agreements. Clausing (2001) presents a product-level analysis of the Canada–United States free trade agreement (CUSFTA) of 1988. Using variation in liberalisation across industries to identify trade creation and diversion, she finds that trade creation tends to be the rule, and trade diversion the exception, in most sectors. Using a similar approach, Trefler (2004) finds both trade creation and trade diversion in CUSFTA but calculates positive welfare effects to the average Canadian. In contrast, Romalis (2007) finds that the expansion of CUSFTA to Mexico (North American Free Trade Agreement, NAFTA) has been trade-diverting. Romalis's exercise is similar to Clausing's and Trefler's, but he uses changes in European Union trade over the period to capture what would have happened in the absence of the agreement. While this might create a better counterfactual if the NAFTA countries were very similar to the European Union, it could lead to overestimates of trade diversion in NAFTA if the European Union was increasing trade more rapidly with its own new and existing trade agreement partners. Even so, Romalis's results suggest that the welfare costs of the agreement are tiny.

The empirical literature on the effect of RTA formation on external tariffs is in its infancy. Foroutan (1998) provides a general account of how countries forming regional trade blocs have adjusted their external tariffs. Using data on trade and trade policy in 50 countries, she finds that both integrating and non-integrating countries have reduced their trade barriers, suggesting that regionalism is relatively benign. Bohara et al. (2004) examine tariff adjustment in Argentina following the formation of Mercosur and find some support for Richardson's (1993) hypothesis that the decline of some industries will lead to a reduction in their lobbying and lower tariffs. Similarly, Estevadeordal et al. (2008) examine changes in preferential tariffs and MFN tariffs in 10 Latin American countries and 100 industries over 12 years. Using a number of empirical techniques to determine causality, they find that free trade areas lead to a decline in external tariffs; however, these results are much weaker in customs unions. In related work, Calvo-Pardo et al. (2010) examine the relationship between preferential tariffs and MFN tariffs in the Association of Southeast Asian Nations (ASEAN). They also find strong evidence of a complementary relationship. In contrast, Limão (2006) finds that the United States was more reluctant to lower tariffs in the Uruguay Round for products that offered preferences. His results imply that trade preferences lead to less multilateral tariff reduction. Karacaovali and Limão (2008) find similar results for the European Union.

The findings of Foroutan (1998), Bohara et al. (2004), Estevadeordal et al. (2008) and Calvo-Pardo et al. (2010), which imply that regionalism is a building bloc to external liberalisation in developing countries, contrast sharply with those of Limão (2006) and Karacaovali and Limão (2008), which find that the United States and the European Union liberalised less during the Uruguay Round in sectors where preferences were granted. One reason that the results may differ is because the countries analysed are very different. Since the multi- lateral system has not enforced much tariff reduction on developing countries, tariffs are relatively high there, creating a large potential for trade diversion. Lower external tariffs moderate that loss. The first set of studies suggest that this force is important in explaining changes in MFN tariffs of developing countries involved in free trade areas. In contrast, the work of Limão focuses on the industrial countries. Tariffs were already quite low in the United States and the European Union at the onset of the Uruguay Round, which reduces the importance of this channel. In addition, the theoretical underpinnings in Limão's work used to justify the importance of preferences in North–South agreements, rely on RTAs being formed for non-economic reasons – preferential treatment is given in exchange for non-economic benefits, such as cooperation on migration, on drug trafficking or a global political agenda. This is not the case in South–South RTAs, where the goal is exchanging market access and improving regional economic cooperation.

Even if trade barriers are not altered when a trade bloc is formed, Chang and Winters (2002) show that non-members can be negatively affected because of price competition with member countries. Non-members may reduce prices to compete with member producers that face a lower tariff. Although this is good for the members, who face lower import prices, this negatively impacts welfare of non-members.

4. NEW EVIDENCE ON DIVERSION AND LIBERALISATION IN RTAS

In this section, we use trade data for three regional accords and three accessions to existing agreements to examine how trade patterns change following the implementation of trade preferences. The regional agreements are NAFTA (Canada, Mexico and the United States, 1994), Mercosur (Argentina, Brazil, Paraguay and Uruguay, 1991) and the Andean Community (Bolivia, Colombia, Ecuador, Peru, Venezuela, 1991).[4] We also examine three accessions to the European Union, including the first wave: Denmark, Great Britain and Ireland (1973); the second

---

[4] Peru left the group in 1992, but it maintained bilateral agreements with all other Andean Community members.

wave: Portugal and Spain (1986);[5] and the third wave: Austria, Finland and Sweden (1995). All data for this part are from Comtrade and are recorded in US dollars. The purpose is to identify whether and how trade growth with members and non-members changed subsequent to the agreement.

We also want to look at the effect of regional agreements on external tariffs. We use detailed industry data on preferential tariffs and MFN tariffs over 12 years for Mercosur, the Andean Community and NAFTA to examine how preferences affect trade with members and non-members and also the path of the external tariff.

Figures 1 and 2 show import growth by member countries from both other members and non-members, 10 years before and after the six agreements (or accessions) were implemented. There is no evidence that trend import growth with non-members fell sharply following the implementation of the agreements. Moreover, internal import growth and import growth with non-members are highly correlated, following very similar paths, implying that other factors besides the RTA are the main drivers of aggregate trade growth.

Table 1 shows the mean growth rates of external and internal imports before and after the regional agreements were implemented. A couple of things are interesting. First, the RTA does not always lead to higher internal trade growth. In half of the RTAs, internal trade growth declines, while external import growth slows in only two of the episodes. Second, in the post-RTA period, internal trade grows faster than external trade only half of the time. In contrast, in the pre-RTA period internal trade growth was faster than external import growth in five of six cases. This consistent with the argument that trade agreements are formed naturally among partners whose trade is large and growing, where there is much to be gained from freeing trade.[6] Thus, looking at import growth there is little evidence that the trade agreement led to higher trade growth among members at the expense of non-members.

Although the sample is small, to more rigorously test whether import growth from non-members was retarded, we perform t-tests on the difference in the means of the pre-union and post-union growth rates and also between the growth rate of internal trade and trade with non-members. Results are reported in Table 1. The t-tests of the difference in the mean growth rates show that growth rates of members and non-members are never significantly different from each other. In addition, only in one case is mean growth after the agreement significantly different (at the 10 per cent level) for non-members, and that is in Mercosur, but growth

---

[5] Greece also joined in 1981 and is sometimes considered with Portugal and Spain as part of the second wave.
[6] Wonnacott and Lutz (1989) were the first to argue that trade agreements among natural partners are likely to be welfare enhancing. Krugman (1991) shows the relationship theoretically. Baier and Bergstrand (2004) find empirical evidence in favour of the natural trade partners hypothesis.

FIGURE 1
Internal and External Import Growth

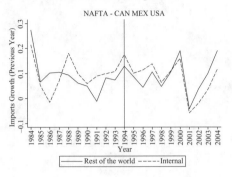

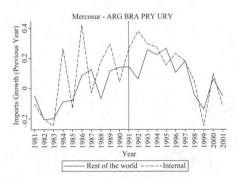

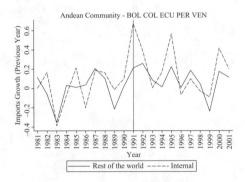

is significantly *higher* in the period after the agreement was formed. This was largely due to large (unilateral) external trade liberalisation that accompanied the agreement.

Finally, if increased trade with bloc members was displacing imports from third countries, we would expect to see a decline in the correlation between internal and external trade growths subsequent to the formation of the RTA. However, as shown in the last column of Table 1, the correlation between external trade growth

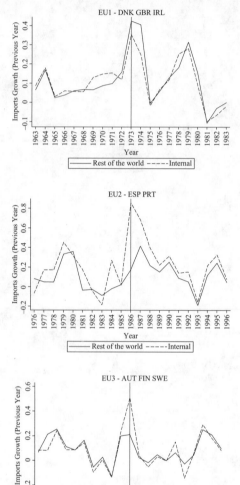

FIGURE 2
Internal and External Import Growth in the European Union

and internal trade goes up in four of the six agreements – and by a large amount for Mercosur and the Andean Community. In the two episodes where the correlations fell, NAFTA and EU1, the changes were marginal. Overall, the results suggest that regional agreements do not have large diversionary effects on trade patterns.

Next, we examine in more detail the relationship between third-country imports, and preferential and MFN tariffs. In particular, we examine how MFN and preferential tariffs affect import growth, using detailed industry data on tariffs in nine

TABLE 1
Growth Rates of Imports

	Internal	External	t-Test	p-Value	Correlation
NAFTA					
Before RTA	0.096	0.089	0.199	0.844	0.958
After RTA	0.076	0.087	−0.338	0.739	0.943
t-Test	0.654	0.093			
p-Value	0.522	0.927			
Mercosur					
Before RTA	0.049	−0.021	0.845	0.409	0.338
After RTA	0.131	0.093	0.497	0.625	0.980
t-Test	−0.855	−1.889			
p-Value	0.404	0.075			
Andean Community					
Before RTA	0.016	−0.010	0.327	0.748	0.754
After RTA	0.166	0.088	0.917	0.371	0.858
t-Test	−1.592	−1.423			
p-Value	0.129	0.172			
EU1					
Before RTA	0.103	0.084	0.860	0.401	0.994
After RTA	0.086	0.110	−0.358	0.724	0.991
t-Test	0.352	−0.500			
p-Value	0.729	0.623			
EU2					
Before RTA	0.129	0.073	0.711	0.486	0.924
After RTA	0.237	0.139	1.140	0.269	0.969
t-Test	−1.172	−0.948			
p-Value	0.256	0.356			
EU3					
Before RTA	0.072	0.093	−0.382	0.707	0.983
After RTA	0.064	0.070	−0.109	0.915	0.990
t-Test	0.148	0.490			
p-Value	0.884	0.630			

Note:
Own calculations based on bilateral import data (CIF $US) using the DOT-IMF database.

Latin American countries from Estevadeordal et al. (2008). The dataset includes Argentina, Brazil, Colombia, Ecuador, Mexico, Paraguay, Peru, Uruguay and Venezuela.[7] The data are reported at the ISIC four-digit level (96 industries) and include data on preferential tariffs and MFN tariffs from 1990 to 2001.

---

[7] Estevadeordal et al. (2008) present a detailed discussion of the data. There are 10 countries in the full dataset. In the results presented here, Chile is excluded because it is not part of a major trade bloc and external tariffs are uniform across sectors. Each of the nine countries has preferences to Bolivia, but data for Bolivia's preferences were not available.

TABLE 2
Correlation between Tariffs and Trade in Latin America

	ln(*Internal Imports*)	ln(*External Imports*)	*Margin*
ln(*External Imports*)	0.57 (0.00) 10,752		
Margin	0.20 (0.00) 7,790	0.14 (0.00) 8,199	
MFN	0.04 (0.00) 7,925	0.04 (0.00) 8,353	0.42 (0.00) 10,168

Notes:
p-Value in parentheses. Number of observations below.

   Table 2 shows correlations between MFN tariffs, preference margins, internal trade and imports from the rest of the world. Imports from regional members are positively correlated with imports from non-members. This is not too surprising since some categories of imports are much larger. Preference mar- gins and MFN tariffs are positively correlated; in part, this is because preference margins can only be large when MFN tariffs are high. Finally, tariffs and margins are positively correlated with imports from both members and non- members. This suggests that tariffs tend to be set slightly higher on large imported goods. The correlation between member trade and preference margins is higher than the correlation between non-member trade and margins, suggesting that margins are larger on goods that are more important to members, or that because of margins these goods have become more important to members.
   To control for other factors which might affect trade patterns, we use regression analysis. First, we examine the effect of trade preferences and MFN tariffs on internal imports and imports from third countries. Specifically, we run the follow- ing regression:

$$\ln M_{ijtg} = \gamma_{ijg} + \gamma_{jtg} + \beta_1 margin_{ijt} + \beta_2 MFN_{ijt} + \varepsilon_{ijt}, \qquad (1)$$

where M_{ijtg} are imports in industry i, country j, year t, from group g (members or non-members); γ_{ijg} is a country–industry fixed effect for group g and γ_{ijg} is a country–year fixed effect for group g. The country–industry effects will control for average demand for products from that group in the country industry, and the country–year effects will control for general liberalisation and business cycle effects. A positive and significant β_1 implies that a higher preference margin leads to more imports from the group. We expect β_1 to be positive for members, who can take advantage of the preferential treatment. The coefficient, β_1, will be nega-

TABLE 3
The Effect of Tariffs and Preference Margins on Imports

	Dependent Variable					
	ln(*Internal Imports*)			ln(*External Imports*)		
	(1)	(2)	(3)	(4)	(5)	(6)
Margin	0.02***		0.03***	0.00		0.01***
	(0.01)		(0.01)	(0.00)		(0.00)
MFN		−0.01***	−0.03***		−0.02***	−0.02***
		(0.00)	(0.01)		(0.00)	(0.00)
Observations	7,790	7,790	7,790	8,199	8,199	8,199
R^2	0.918	0.918	0.919	0.932	0.932	0.932

Notes:
Country–industry and country–year fixed effects in all regressions. Robust standard errors in parentheses.
*** $p < 0.01$.

tive and significant for non-members if trade is being diverted and insignificant if there is mostly trade creation from the RTA. The coefficient on the applied MFN tariff, β_2, is likely to be negative for both groups, implying that a higher tariff leads to lower imports.

Table 3 reports the results. As expected, preference margins are correlated with higher internal trade (column 1) and MFN tariffs with lower internal trade (column 2). When we include both variables in the regression (column 3), we find a stronger effect of MFN on internal trade than when it is included alone. This makes sense since some high MFN sectors will have low preferential tariffs, which is especially good for internal trade. The results suggest that a one percentage point higher preference margin leads to 3 per cent more internal trade. In addition, a one percentage point higher MFN tariff, controlling for preference margins, leads to 3 per cent less internal trade.

With respect to non-members, we see no significant effect of preference margins on imports (column 4) and a more negative effect of MFN tariffs (column 5). Surprisingly, when we include both variables in the regression (column 6), the preference margin has a small but significant *positive* effect on imports from non-members. This suggests that controlling for the MFN tariff level, preference margins tend to stimulate imports from non-members. One potential explanation is that more trade with members could lead to more imports from non-members if goods are complements in production. For example, if goods produced by members use inputs from non-members then more regional trade (and production of tradables) will lead to more imported inputs from non-members. At the level of aggregation of the data, many of the inputs will be in the same industry, so a greater preference margin could stimulate imports from non-members through this

TABLE 4
The Effect of Preferential Tariff Reduction on MFN Tariff Reduction

	Dependent Variable: dMFN			
	(1)	(2)	(3)	(4)
L.dmargin	−0.28***			
	(0.03)			
L2.dmargin		−0.13***		
		(0.02)		
L.dpref			0.15***	
			(0.02)	
L2.dpref				0.06***
				(0.01)
Observations	8,349	7,445	8,349	7,445
R^2	0.555	0.45	0.532	0.439

Notes:
Country–industry and country–year fixed effects in all regressions. Robust standard errors in parentheses.
*** $p < 0.01$.

channel. Alternatively, there may be improvements in the general trade environment – such as harmonising product standards or improving customs procedures for some sectors – that coincide with the preferential tariff reduction. Overall, the results imply that greater preference margins do not negatively impact imports from non-members. As expected, applied MFN tariffs do restrict imports from non-members. Specifically, results suggest that a one percentage point higher MFN tariff leads to 2 per cent less trade.

In Table 4, we examine the effect of preference margins on MFN tariffs. The regression we estimate is:

$$dMFN_{ijt} = \gamma_{ij} + \gamma_{jt} + \beta_0 L.dmargin_{ijt} + \varepsilon_{ijt}, \qquad (2)$$

where MFN_{ijt} is the MFN tariff in industry i, of country j and year t; $L.dmargin$ is the lagged change in the preference margin; γ_{ij} is a country–industry fixed effect and γ_{jtg} is a country–year fixed effect. A positive coefficient on the lagged change in margin, β_0, implies that increases in the preference margin are followed by increases in the MFN tariff – a stumbling block effect. A negative coefficient points to a building block effect. The change in margin is lagged (we also report results with two lags) to control for unobserved factors that might affect all tariffs, both preferential and MFN, simultaneously. For example, assume preferential tariffs and MFN tariffs are reduced together because some industries are easier to liberalise. In this case, the change in the margin and the change in the MFN tariff will be negatively correlated, provided preferential tariffs are cut more sharply, but the relationship may not be a causal one. Since the change in the margin

(*margin = MFN − preferential tariff*) is a function of the change in the MFN tariff (the dependent variable), which may cause econometric problems, we also report results using the lagged (and twice lagged) change in the preferential tariff as the independent variable of interest. In this case, the coefficient on the change in the preferential tariff will have a positive sign for a building block effect and negative for a stumbling block effect. These regressions are similar to the regressions reported in Estevadeordal et al. (2008).[8]

Table 4 reports results for the effect of lagged changes in preference margins on MFN tariffs. The table shows complementarity between preferential liberalisation and unilateral tariff reduction. A past increase in the preference margin, or a decline in the preferential tariff, precedes a decline in the MFN tariff. In particular, the results from column 1 suggest that a one percentage point increase in the preference margin is associated with about a 0.3 percentage point cut in the MFN tariff in the following year.

The findings of no significant trade diversion and external liberalisation following preferential liberalisation are likely to be related. Countries that lower both preferential tariffs and MFN applied tariffs will experience less diversion. Moreover, if they are setting external tariffs optimally, it may be the potential cost of diversion that encourages them to lower MFN tariffs subsequent to pref- erential liberalisation. In this case, preferential liberalisation generates external trade liberalisation to prevent trade diversion, and regionalism serves as a mechanism for freer trade with the world.

5. CONCLUSION

This chapter explores third-country effects of regional integration. Concerns have been raised that regional integration will harm outsiders through trade diversion and potentially less external liberalisation by members. In the six agreements that we examine, there is no evidence of trade diversion. We also find no evidence that trade preferences have reduced imports from non-members in Latin America. Finally, we present evidence that preferential tariff reduction tends to be followed by MFN tariff reduction in Latin America. These findings may be related: preferential liberalisation enhances the incentives for external trade liberalisation to prevent trade diversion. Thus, in products where pre-regional agreement tariffs were high, the regional agreement creates incentives to reduce them and observed

---

[8] These results draw on Estevadeordal et al. (2008). In that article, we also focus on effects in customs unions vs free trade areas. In particular, we show that the complementary effect of preferential tariff reduction does not extend to customs unions. We use theoretical underpinnings and econometric techniques to provide strong evidence that the relationship is causal – preferential tariff reduction leads to a reduction of the applied MFN tariff in free trade areas.

diversion is limited. As a result, regionalism serves as a mechanism for freer trade with the world.

Considering the frailty of the Doha Round, the move to regionalism may be beneficial. Regional trade agreements offer an alternative forum for negotiation to further trade liberalisation. Although there are sure to be some costs, the costs associated with trade diversion and potential stumbling block effects are absent in the data presented here. In most other areas of economics we focus on first-order effects, with only a few words for second-order concerns – it appears as if regionalism may not be the exception that people once thought. If trade liberalisation does not happen through multilateral negotiation, regional agreements do not appear to be so worrisome so as to be avoided.

REFERENCES

Aghion, P., P. Antràs and E. Helpman (2007), 'Negotiating Free Trade', *Journal of International Economics*, **73**, 1, 1–30.
Bagwell, K. and R. Staiger (1999), 'Regionalism and Multilateral Tariff Cooperation', in J. Piggott and A. Woodland (eds.), *International Trade Policy and the Pacific Rim* (London: Macmillan), 157–85.
Bagwell, K. and R. Staiger (2005), 'Multilateral Trade Negotiations, Bilateral Opportunism and the Rules of GATT/WTO', *Journal of International Economics*, **67**, 2, 268–94.
Baier, S. L. and J. H. Bergstrand (2004), 'Economic Determinants of Free Trade Agreements', *Journal of International Economics*, **64**, 1, 29–63.
Bhagwati, J. N. and A. Panagariya (1996), 'Preferential Trading Areas and Multilateralism: Strangers, Friends or Foes?', in J. N. Bhagwati and A. Panagariya (eds.), *The Economics of Preferential Trade Agreements* (Washington, DC: AEI Press), 1–78.
Bohara, A., K. Gawande and P. Sanguinetti (2004), 'Trade Diversion and Declining Tariffs: Evidence from Mercosur', *Journal of International Economics*, **64**, 1, 65–88.
Bond, E., R. Riezman and C. Syropoulos (2002), 'A Strategic and Welfare Theoretic Analysis of Free Trade Areas', mimeo.
Bond, E., C. Syropoulos and L. A. Winters (2001), 'Deepening of Regional Integration and Multilateral Trade Agreements', *Journal of International Economics*, **53**, 2, 335–61.
Cadot, O., J. de Melo and M. Olarreaga (2001), 'Can Bilateralism Ease the Pains of Multilateral Trade Liberalization?', *European Economic Review*, **45**, 1, 27–44.
Calvo-Pardo, H., C., Freund and E. Ornelas (2010), 'The ASEAN Free Trade Agreement: Impact on Trade Flows and External Trade Barriers', in R. Barro and J. Lee (eds.), *Costs and Benefits of Regional Economic Integration* (Oxford: Oxford University Press), forthcoming.
Chang, W. and L. A. Winters (2002), 'How Regional Blocs Affect Excluded Countries: The Price Effects of Mercosur', *American Economic Review*, **92**, 4, 889–904.
Clausing, K. (2001), 'Trade Creation and Trade Diversion in the Canada–United States Free Trade Agreement', *Canadian Journal of Economics*, **34**, 3, 678–96.
Estevadeordal, A., C. Freund and E. Ornelas (2008), 'Does Regionalism Affect Trade Liberalization Towards Nonmembers?', *Quarterly Journal of Economics*, **123**, 4, 1531–75.
Foroutan, F. (1998), 'Does Membership in a Regional Preferential Trade Arrangement Make a Country More or Less Protectionist?', *The World Economy*, **21**, 3, 305–35.
Frankel, J. (1997), *Regional Trade Blocs in the World Economic System* (Washington, DC: Institute for International Economics).
Frankel, J., E. Stein and S. Wei (1995), 'Trading Blocs and the Americas: The Natural, the Unnatural and the Supernatural', *Journal of Development Economics*, **47**, 10, 61–95.

Freund, C. (2000), 'Multilateralism and the Endogenous Formation of Free Trade Agreements', *Journal of International Economics*, **52**, 2, 359–76.

Grossman, G. and E. Helpman (1995), 'The Politics of Free-trade Agreements', *American Economic Review*, **85**, 4, 667–90.

Haveman, J. and D. Hummels (1998), 'Trade Creation and Trade Diversion: New Empirical Results', *Journal of Transnational Management Development*, **3**, 2, 47–72.

Karacaovali, B. and N. Limão (2008), 'The Clash of Liberalizations: Preferential vs. Multilateral Trade Liberalization in the European Union', *Journal of International Economics*, **74**, 2, 299–327.

Kennan, J. and R. Riezman (1990), 'Optimal Tariff Equilibria with Customs Unions', *Canadian Journal of Economics*, **23**, 1, 70–83.

Krishna, P. (1998), 'Regionalism and Multilateralism: A Political Economy Approach', *Quarterly Journal of Economics*, **113**, 1, 227–52.

Krugman, P. (1991), 'Is Bilateralism Bad?', in E. Helpman and A. Razin (eds.), *International Trade and Trade Policy* (Cambridge, MA: MIT Press), 9–23.

Levy, P. (1997), 'A Political–Economic Analysis of Free Trade Agreements', *American Economic Review*, **87**, 4, 506–19.

Limão, N. (2006), 'Preferential Trade Agreements as Stumbling Blocks for Multilateral Trade Liberalization: Evidence for the U.S.', *American Economic Review*, **96**, 3, 896–914.

Magee, C. (2008), 'New Measures of Trade Creation and Trade Diversion', *Journal of International Economics*, **75**, 2, 340–62.

Ornelas, E. (2005), 'Rent Destruction and the Political Viability of Free Trade Agreements', *Quarterly Journal of Economics*, **120**, 4, 1475–506.

Panagariya, A. and R. Findlay (1996), 'A Political-economy Analysis of Free-trade Areas and Customs Unions', in R. Feenstra, G. Grossman and D. Irwin (eds.), *The Political Economy of Trade Reform: Essays in Honor of J. Bhagwati* (Cambridge, MA: MIT Press), 265–87.

Pomfret, R. (2003), *Economic Analysis of Regional Trading Arrangements* (Cheltenham: Elgar Reference Collection).

Richardson, M. (1993), 'Endogenous Protection and Trade Diversion', *Journal of International Economics*, **34**, 3–4, 309–24.

Romalis, J. (2007), 'NAFTA's and CUSFTA's Impact on International Trade', *Review of Economics and Statistics*, **89**, 3, 416–35.

Saggi, K. and H. M. Yildiz (2007), 'Bilateral Trade Agreements and the Feasibility of Multilateral Free Trade', mimeo.

Schiff, M. and L. A. Winters (2003), *Regional Integration and Development* (Washington, DC, and Oxford: The World Bank and Oxford University Press).

Snape, R. (1993), 'The History and Economics of GATT's Article XXIV', in K. Anderson and R. Blackhurst (eds.), *Regional Integration and the Global Trading System* (New York: St. Martin's Press), 273–91.

Syropoulos, C. (1999), 'Customs Unions and Comparative Advantage', *Oxford Economic Papers*, **51**, 2, 239–66.

Trefler, D. (2004), 'The Long and Short of the Canada–U.S. Free Trade Agreement', *American Economic Review*, **94**, 4, 870–95.

Viner, J. (1950), *The Customs Union Issue*, Chapter 4 (New York: Carnegie Endowment for International Peace).

Wonnacott, P. and M. Lutz (1989), 'Is There a Case for Free Trade Areas?', in J. Schott (ed.), *Free Trade Areas and U.S. Trade Policy* (Washington, DC: Institute for International Economics), 59–84.

10

Dispensing with NAFTA Rules of
Origin? Some Policy Options

Patrick Georges

1. INTRODUCTION

*F*OR pragmatic trade policymakers, preferential rules of origin (ROO), the
gatekeepers of preferential commerce, represent a sort of pact with the devil.
The backing of their supporters is often needed for a free trade agreement (FTA)
to become law. But, as aptly pointed out by Destler (2006), 'if ROO seem politically necessary in the short run, they are pernicious in the longer run. So the
question for pragmatic trade-expanders is the ancient one: Can one dicker with
the devil without joining him in Hell?' ROO are of Byzantine complexity, inconsistent across several FTAs, opaque and costly. And although the potential distortions created by ROO have been recognised, they warrant greater analyses in order
to better understand and, eventually, better regulate them. Furthermore, as long as
the cost of ROO is not made transparent in models, there is little hope for generating much policy interest in proposals for 'loosening' or 'liberalising' them in the
context of alternatives to FTAs, such as customs unions (CUs) or MFN tariff
liberalisation at the WTO, which would make ROO lacking relevance and impact
even if they remained on 'the books'.

Since the work of Estevadeordal (2000), the econometric literature has typically
coded the *ex ante* restrictiveness of ROO as an independent variable in order to
estimate the economic impact of these rules on, for example, trade flows (Cadot
et al., 2006a; Estevadeordal and Suominen, 2008), investment flows (Estevadeordal
et al., 2008b), and tariff preference utilisation rates (Carrère and de Melo, 2004;

I thank, without implicating, Yazid Dissou, Marcel Mérette, Aylin Seçkin and an anonymous referee
for helpful comments.

Kunimoto and Sawchuk, 2005).[1] However, ROO imply complex interconnections between the use of primary factors of production, intermediaries and final goods, and the current econometric studies do not seem able to deal appropriately with all these complexities, nor to gauge the impact that these rules, or their liberalisation under specific trade scenarios, might have on economic welfare or GDP.

Given these limitations, the objective of this chapter is to use a computable general equilibrium (CGE) methodology to estimate the economic gains, for both Canada and Mexico, of: (1) adopting a North American CU that would also liberalise ROO; and (2) reviving the WTO scenario of multilateral free trade, thereby eliminating preferential commerce and thus the need for preferential ROO across FTAs. Such a CGE methodology is useful as it would take into account interactions between agents and repercussions on goods, primary factors, intermediaries and investment decisions at different stages of the production process and across different countries. Furthermore, the approach permits computation of an efficiency (or *ex post*) cost of ROO that might, in some context, be more relevant than Estevadeordal's *ex ante* index of ROO restrictiveness, which is unable to account for the fact that the use of preferential access in an FTA (and the concomitant ROO compliance) is an option, not an obligation.

Despite the general equilibrium dimension of ROO, there has been scant attempt to model ROO, or their liberalisation, in CGE studies that analyse alternatives to FTAs. For example, Brown et al. (2001) measure the impact of moving from NAFTA to a North American CU but typically limit their CGE experiment to the adoption of a common external tariff (CET). Although Ghosh and Rao (2005) stress the relevance of estimating the cost of ROO when measuring the economic effect of a potential North American CU, their impact is not captured adequately in their CGE analysis because they do not model ROO explicitly nor do they calibrate their model to reflect the presence of ROO distortions in the benchmark dataset.

Georges (2008b), however, has studied the general equilibrium impact, on the Canadian economy, of a counterfactual policy of moving away from NAFTA and into a CU that would have explicitly liberalised NAFTA ROO. Four extensions are addressed in this new chapter. First, the analysis is fully extended to Mexico, and the substantial impact that a North American CU would bring to Mexico strengthens the case for establishing a 'good neighbour' policy as recently pointed out by Pastor (2008). Second, we examine how NAFTA tariff preference erosion since 1997, which *unintentionally* resulted from the phasing-in of both NAFTA and Uruguay Round measures, has reduced the efficiency costs of NAFTA ROO, somewhat limiting the gains that might be expected from establishing a North American CU in the 2000s versus the 1990s. Third, we study the impact of an

---

[1] For a recent collection of papers analysing different aspects of ROO, see Cadot et al. (2006b).

active policy of NAFTA preference erosion through MFN tariff liberalisation at the WTO, which, by eliminating preferential commerce, would also make ROO lacking relevance. Finally, we propose a new graphical representation of a simplified calibration procedure in order to highlight some key ingredients needed to capture the essence of ROO in a CGE model.

The rest of the chapter is as follows. Section 2 briefly reviews some key features of FTAs, CUs and ROO, and gives some reasons behind the recent backlash on ROO. Section 3 illustrates the general equilibrium impacts of respectively moving to a CU which also liberalises ROO, and moving towards a multilateral free trade world that makes preferential ROO obsolete. We also examine the technical and political economy problems of adopting a CU that also liberalises ROO. Section 4 concludes by reviewing the policy options for Canada and Mexico. An Appendix offers a graphical approach to the challenge of capturing the impact of ROO liberalisation in a CGE model.

2. FTAs, CUs AND ROO

In economic literature, a CU is the second level of regional integration following an FTA and involves (as in an FTA) the eventual elimination of all tariffs between member countries but, unlike an FTA, also establishes a common external trade policy, in particular by adjusting all tariffs external to the CU to a common level. In an FTA, however, the members maintain their individual MFN tariffs that they impose on countries outside the agreement. As a result, a CU requires members to negotiate a common trade policy and a CET with respect to non-member countries, while an FTA requires negotiating measures such as preferential ROO, to avoid trade deflection. Trade deflection – a modification of trade flows between the rest of the world and the members of the FTA – occurs when a non-member agent transits goods through the FTA member country with the lowest-external tariff and then tranships duty-free (or with preferential treatment) to the final destination. To eliminate the incentive for trade deflection, preferential ROO are negotiated among members of the FTA. These rules determine which goods have 'origin' in member countries and thus are eligible for duty-free (or preferential) treatment when crossing partners' borders, and which goods are not as they are simply being transhipped through, or undergoing only minor transformations in a member country.

However, FTAs also generate distortionary effects that lead member countries to purchase less from the rest of the world and more from other members in order to fulfil the ROO and obtain the tariff preference (Krishna and Krueger, 1995). Therefore, as suggested long ago by Krueger (1995), CUs are Pareto superior to FTAs because the establishment of a CET in a CU would also remove the incentives for trade deflection and therefore eliminates both the need for preferential

ROO and their distortionary impact on the economy and competitiveness of firms.[2] Thus, preferential ROO are typically absent from a CU arrangement, and movements of goods within a CU are not based on their 'originating status' but on the principle of 'free circulation'.

For a variety of reasons reviewed in Bhagwati (2008), US trade negotiators started to pursue extensive FTA negotiations in the 1980s and 1990s and they looked for particularised benefits they could offer important industries in exchange for their support.[3] Industries looked for ways to gain advantage within the new economics of globalisation.[4] ROO was the ideal instrument to meet the needs of both. The 'success' of this strategy can be measured by the overwhelming positive response of foreign leaders, which resulted, as illustrated in Figure 1, in a pandemic of overlapping FTAs in America, and across the world. In fact several countries went beyond forming single PTAs and joined several.[5] The 'spaghetti bowl' of regional FTAs is by now a well-established culinary analogy to the visual effect of Figure 1 and of other figures drawn for different regions in the world. One outcome of these overlapping FTAs, however, is the ensuing proliferation of ROO. And even if ROO, the gatekeepers of preferential commerce, are required in FTAs, some of their unpleasant consequences have also been discussed in the literature, generating a recent backlash on these rules.

First, in a study which measures the restrictiveness of preferential ROO across the world, Estevadeordal and Suominen (2006) show that NAFTA ROO and the

---

[2] Starting at any FTA, the theorem of Kemp and Wan (1976) ensures that there is a CU that is Pareto superior (to the FTA) if ROO are eliminated, but this requires the choice of a CET that does not affect the terms of trade of the union with respect to outside countries and that member countries implement lump-sum transfers so that no individual member is worse off.

[3] Bhagwati (2008) gives three motivations underlying the extensive US FTA negotiations that started in the 1980s. One argument is imitation of the European Union hub which increasingly had a number of spokes through regional FTAs. Some of the US trade negotiators had in mind the spectacle of the spokes voting on GATT issues with the hub, and this might have led to the US abandoning its exclusive embrace of multilateralism in free trade. A second argument is that in order to respond to growing pressures from South America for debt relief, the US responded by offering trade instead and the US became a hub for some spokes. Finally, the over-appreciation of the US dollar in the 1980s led to protectionism voices there, and the only way to countervail and contain the protectionists was to mobilise exporting interests by offering them markets abroad. However, the Europeans and the developing countries would not agree to declaring a new multilateral Round when the US tried hard to start one in the early 1980s. This led the US to conclude that it was left with no option except to take the bilateral route.

[4] Krueger (1993) points out that ROO can effectively extend the protection that the US intermediary industry receives within the US, to Canada and Mexico, so that the ROO can be used by the US to secure its NAFTA intermediary market for the exports of its own intermediate products.

[5] According to Pomfret (2007), this positive response reflects the fact that many foreign political leaders appear to take a talk-is-cheap attitude to trade agreements, happy to sign them at summit meetings and leave the details to lower officials who might bury the agreement when unpleasant consequences seem likely or political alliances shift.

FIGURE 1
North America's Hub and Spoke Trade System

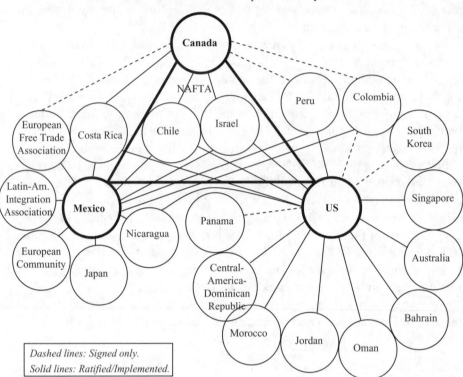

Note:
Central-America includes: Costa Rica, El Salvador, Guatemala, Honduras and Nicaragua. Latin-American Integration Association includes: Argentina, Bolivia, Brazil, Chile, Colombia, Ecuador, Paraguay, Peru, Uruguay and Venezuela. European Free Trade Association includes: Iceland, Liechtenstein, Norway and Switzerland.

Sources: Chart based on Robson (2007) and updated on the basis of: World Trade Law.Net, Office of US Trade Representative, and Department of Foreign Affairs and International Trade Canada.

(external) ROO of the EU are highly restrictive.[6] However, these two regimes have often been used as a blueprint for new inter-regional agreements, therefore transmitting their overall high ROO restrictiveness (Garay and De Lombaerde, 2004). Second, Krishna (2005) argues that beyond their economic justification to prevent trade deflection, ROO have been increasingly used for protectionist purposes. Given that these rules are negotiated industry by industry, there is enormous scope for well-organised industries to insulate themselves from the effects of the FTA

---

[6] Although the European Union (EU), in principle, does not impose preferential ROO among its members (as it is also a CU), it does have ROO regimes with countries external to the union and which have signed FTAs with the EU.

by devising suitable ROO. Thirdly, and somewhat complementary to the previous point, preferential ROO have a distortionary impact when they induce firms to substitute cheaper non-originating materials for intermediary goods originating from the zone (Krueger, 1995). Fourthly, because ROO favour FTA intermediary producers relative to more efficient world producers, they will constitute an additional opposition to any moves towards globally freer trade. Therefore, the political economy of FTAs is likely to lead, in Bhagwati's (1993) terminology, to a stumbling-block to (future) multilateral trade liberalisation. Finally, the international segmentation of production in which intermediate inputs are traded and transformed into more processed intermediate inputs, which are then moved across borders to the next stage of production, has led to a growing share of parts and components in total exports (World Bank, 2005). Restrictive ROO in downstream sectors may therefore impede FTA firms in taking advantage of the global production chains. This might also generate a ROO-jumping FDI that is diverted to the FTA member country with the largest market size.

Despite these concerns, as long as the cost of ROO is not made transparent, there is little hope for generating much interest in proposals for liberalising ROO in the context of viable trade alternatives to FTAs. Furthermore, the debate on ROO *per se* has often been obscured by the level of technicalities of these rules and it might be useful to develop a framework highlighting key ingredients needed in order to shed some light on the 'forest' behind the 'tree' of legal and technical details. Georges (2008a) provides a framework to capture the essence of ROO in the benchmark of a CGE model and to gauge the economic impact of liberalising ROO in a counterfactual experiment. The objective of the Appendix is to make this procedure more accessible, using a graphical representation of a simplified calibration exercise. In particular, the Appendix shows that the impact of ROO is not adequately taken into account in typical CGE models because ROO are not modelled nor do authors calibrate their model to reflect the presence of ROO distortions in the benchmark dataset.[7] The proposed approach is to capture the distortionary impact of ROO within the benchmark and is based on the fact that a ROO acts as an implicit tax to NAFTA firms for the use of non-originating intermediaries but an implicit subsidy for the use of capital, labour and intermediaries purchased within NAFTA.[8] This way of proceeding, which eventually leads to an (*ex post*) efficiency cost of ROO, is a much sounder approach that any attempt to directly compute a tariff equivalent of a ROO. Indeed, as shown in

---

[7] Indeed, unless CGE modellers re-calibrate their models appropriately, there is no 'room' for the ROO distortion (that is only implicitly present in the initial database) and thus there is no way to remove it.

[8] In this context, complying with ROO leads to a country- and sector-specific efficiency cost that has been estimated using the 'participation constraint' approach formulated by Cadot et al. (2002) and Anson et al. (2005).

Falvey and Reed (2002), ROOs are complementary to, rather than substitutes for, tariffs on final outputs. And if ROO were 'equivalent' in their economic effects to some level of intra-FTA tariffs, then liberalising ROO among members of the FTA would be trade creating among members while possibly trade diverting between members and non-members even if, on the contrary, members should now be able to source cheaper intermediaries from the rest of the world.[9]

3. SIMULATION RESULTS: CU VERSUS MULTILATERAL FREE TRADE LIBERALISATION

The calibration method outlined in the Appendix has been introduced in a CGE model, described in Georges (2008b), in which the world economy consists of seven countries/regions composing two blocks: NAFTA countries (Canada, USA and Mexico), and non-NAFTA countries (Latin America, Mercosur, Europe, and the Rest of the World). All seven countries/regions are fully modelled.[10] In this section, we use the model to evaluate and compare several new counterfactual experiments: (1) the benefit that Canada and Mexico would have obtained if they had moved away from NAFTA and into a CU with the US at the end of the 1990s; (2) the impact of moving to a CU in the 2000s; (3) the impact of a multilateral free trade world in the 1990s (instead of the spaghetti bowl of PTAs); and (4) the impact of a multilateral free trade world in the 2000s.

a. A North American CU in the 1990s versus NAFTA

As said in Section 2, had North American countries negotiated a CU in the 1990s instead of NAFTA, then a North American CET would have been established while a NAFTA preferential ROO would be virtually absent. Therefore, in order to simulate the impact of the counterfactual policy scenario of moving away from NAFTA into a CU, we need to model both the adoption of a CET and the removal of the existing NAFTA ROO.

---

[9] This is indeed what Ghosh and Rao (2005) generated in their CGE study of the impact of a North American CU–deeper trade integration between Canada and the US at the expense of trade with countries from the rest of the world. This results from the conjecture that the (upper bound) effects of ROO might be gauged by assuming that ROO are equivalent to an intra-NAFTA tariff equal to the difference between pre-NAFTA and preferential tariffs (so that the tariff equivalent of the ROO is set at a level that completely offsets the gains occurring from tariff preferences).

[10] Each country has eight sectors of production, all perfectly competitive. These sectors are agriculture, resource sectors, food processing, textiles and clothing, manufactures excluding machinery and equipment, machinery and equipment, automotives, and services. Each of these industries is assumed to produce a single commodity. Trade flows among countries are organised through an Armington system.

As discussed in the Appendix, a ROO is an implicit subsidy on capital, labour and NAFTA intermediary goods, but an implicit tax on intermediary goods from the rest of the world. Hence, the main impact of removing ROO is the elimination of the implicit subsidies and taxes.[11] This shock would reallocate efficiently the demand for factors of production in each sector of NAFTA countries, lowering NAFTA firms' demand for capital, labour and NAFTA intermediary goods, but increasing the demand for non-NAFTA intermediary goods. The efficient realloca-tion of factors of production within NAFTA countries would lower the unit cost of production while real GDP would also increase because resources would be used more efficiently.

From a modelling perspective, establishing a CET among North American countries is a much simpler exercise than modelling ROO liberalisation, although clearly it might be a political nightmare. In our simulation experiments, the CET has been set equal to the US MFN tariff in order to avoid protracted negotiations with the US on the CET itself.[12] This implies that the Canadian and Mexican MFN tariffs would have to be reduced, in most sectors, to the lower US MFN tariffs. This typically should increase GDP and welfare in Canada and Mexico through reduced trade diversion effects and more efficient resource allocations.

In the first simulation experiment, we calibrate our CGE model to the GTAP5 database (2002 release of 1997 data) so that NAFTA and MFN tariffs are those observed about three years after the 1994 implementation of NAFTA. Figure 2 illustrates the gains in terms of GDP that Canada and Mexico could have reaped if they had moved away from NAFTA into a CU with the US, *circa* 1997. Canada would have gained a permanent (yearly) additional increase in GDP of 0.9 per cent of which 0.7 per cent would be due to the fact that a CU does not require ROO, and 0.1 per cent would be due to the adoption of a North American CET equal to the US MFN tariff. Observe that the full impact of a CU includes second-order or 'cross-effects' (0.92–0.70–0.14 per cent): the removal of NAFTA ROO *per se* modifies trade patterns between North American countries and the rest of the world. Therefore, second-order effects measure the impact that the adoption of a CET might also have on this new pattern of trade due to the ROO removal.

For Canada, the basic insight of Figure 2 is that the impact on GDP, of liberalis-ing ROO, largely dominates the small impact of adopting a CET. This can also

---

[11] The documentation and administrative costs of ROO are not taken into account in this analysis so that our results underestimate the true benefits of removing ROO.

[12] Even a CET set equal to the US MFN is likely to generate much lobbying, negotiation and opposi-tion. Industries where Canadian or Mexican MFN tariffs have to be reduced to US levels are likely to oppose such a move. Furthermore, foreigners are likely to oppose the (less common) cases of upward adjustment of Canadian or Mexican external tariffs to US levels, which would violate Article 24 of the WTO (in cases *actual* external tariffs are at their WTO *bound* levels) and trigger retaliation or require compensation.

FIGURE 2
Percentage Increase in Real GDP if North America had Negotiated a Customs Union instead of
NAFTA in the 1990s (GTAP5 data, 2002 release of 1997 data)

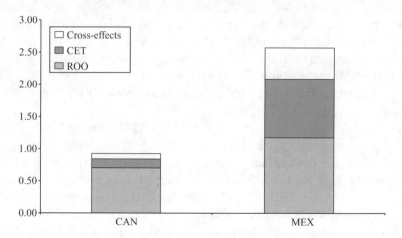

Source: Author's simulations.

be seen in Table 1(a) by observing the relative contribution of the two CU components, ROO removal versus CET adoption, on Canada's trade (real export and
import), real consumption, real investment and real GDP. The dominating effect
of ROO liberalisation when moving to a CU should be expected given the convergence of Canadian and US MFN tariffs in the 1990s. However, this shows that
typical CGE studies that assume away the ROO liberalising effect when gauging
the economic impact of moving away from NAFTA to a CU, must be far off the
true estimate and Figure 2 provides a magnitude of the misestimation in the existing literature. Although a CU negotiation process with the US would have taken
more time and would have been, perhaps, more difficult to achieve than an FTA,
it would have resulted in a net overall benefit, not through the adoption of a CET,
but because Canadian exporters to the US would not have had to comply with
NAFTA ROO in order to obtain tariff preference.

The opportunity cost in terms of foregone GDP, for not moving to a CU with
the US, is even more significant for Mexico. A CU *circa* 1997 would have resulted
in a permanent increase of real GDP by 2.6 per cent, of which 1.2 per cent would
be due to the elimination of ROO in a CU, and 0.9 per cent due to the adoption
of a CET. ROO have resulted in a severe resource misallocation in Mexico which
prevented Mexicans from fully benefiting from NAFTA. Furthermore, and unlike
Canada, the adoption of a North American CET would have led to a significant
increase in Mexican GDP because of the large Mexico–US MFN tariff spread in
the 1990s.

TABLE 1(a–b)
CU and WTO Counterfactual Scenarios Implemented circa 2001 and 1997:
Long-term Impacts on Selected Variables
(Per cent change from benchmark)

(a) Canada		Real Export	Real Import	Real Consumption	Real Investment	Real GDP
CU *circa 1997* of which:		**13.8**	**12.7**	**0.3**	**−0.7**	**0.9**
	ROO only	10.6	9.8	0.3	−0.7	0.7
	CET only	2.2	2.1	0.1	−0.1	0.1
CU *circa 2001* of which:		**10.2**	**9.9**	**0.0**	**−0.6**	**0.5**
	ROO only	9.1	8.7	0.1	−0.6	0.4
	CET only	0.8	0.8	0.0	−0.1	0.0
WTO *circa 1997* of which:		**27.0**	**27.2**	**1.5**	**1.7**	**2.3**
	ROO only	10.6	9.8	0.3	−0.7	0.7
	MFN = 0 only	12.1	13.5	1.2	2.0	1.2
WTO *circa 2001* of which:		**15.9**	**16.2**	**0.3**	**−0.1**	**0.8**
	ROO only	9.1	8.7	0.1	−0.6	0.4
	MFN = 0 only	5.0	5.7	0.3	0.5	0.3

(b) Mexico		Real Export	Real Import	Real Consumption	Real Investment	Real GDP
CU *circa 1997* of which:		**20.0**	**17.2**	**0.9**	**1.6**	**2.6**
	ROO only	9.8	9.3	0.9	0.0	1.2
	CET only	5.9	4.4	0.1	1.1	0.9
CU *circa 2001* of which:		**24.9**	**20.5**	**0.8**	**2.2**	**2.9**
	ROO only	7.4	7.1	0.6	−0.2	0.8
	CET only	12.0	9.1	0.2	1.9	1.6
WTO *circa 1997* of which:		**30.0**	**28.6**	**1.3**	**1.7**	**2.9**
	ROO only	9.8	9.3	0.9	0.0	1.2
	MFN = 0 only	13.5	13.7	0.4	0.9	1.0
WTO *circa 2001* of which:		**30.7**	**26.8**	**0.9**	**2.3**	**3.1**
	ROO only	7.4	7.1	0.6	−0.2	0.8
	MFN = 0 only	16.7	14.4	0.3	1.9	1.6

Note:
Numbers rounded to one decimal.

Source: Author's simulations.

TABLE 2
US MFN and US NAFTA Tariff Rates circa 1997 and 2001 (Selected sectors)

	US MFN circa 1997	US NAFTA circa 1997		US MFN circa 2001	US NAFTA circa 2001	
	MFN Countries	CAN	MEX	MFN Countries	CAN	MEX
agri	13.8	4.4	8.5	1.8	0.0	0.2
reso	0.4	0.0	0.0	0.0	0.0	0.0
food	11.9	8.8	8.8	4.1	1.7	0.4
text	12.9	0.0	0.0	11.4	0.0	0.1
manu	2.9	0.0	0.0	1.8	0.0	0.1
tech	1.9	0.0	0.0	0.9	0.0	0.0
auto	2.3	0.0	0.0	1.8	0.0	0.0
serv	0.0	0.0	0.0	0.0	0.0	0.0

Note on abbreviations:
agri = agriculture; reso = resource sector; food = food processing; text = textiles and clothing; manu = manufactures excluding machinery and equipment; tech = machinery and equipment; auto = automotives; serv = services.
CAN = Canada; US = United States of America; MEX = Mexico.

Source: Author's calculations based on GTAP5 and GTAP6 databases.

b. A North American CU in the 2000s versus NAFTA

In the second simulation experiment, we calibrate our CGE model to the GTAP6 database (2006 release of 2001 data) so that NAFTA and MFN tariffs are those observed at least seven years after the 1994 implementation of NAFTA. The main reason for doing this is that while NAFTA duty-free tariffs have been progressively phased-in since 1994 (and since 1989 for the Canada–US FTA), MFN tariffs have also been lowered since 1995 as a result of the phasing-in of the Uruguay Round (1986–94) measures. The ensuing phasing-in differential might have led to tariff preference erosion, ultimately lowering the *ex post* (effective) distortionary cost of NAFTA ROO and therefore the potential benefit of adopting a CU in the 2000s versus the 1990s.[13]

Based on two GTAP databases (GTAP5 and GTAP6), Tables 2 and 3 illustrate the erosion of NAFTA preferences. Table 2 provides the magnitude of the US MFN and US NAFTA tariff rates in selected sectors *circa* 2001 (GTAP6, 2006 release of 2001 data) and *circa* 1997 (GTAP5, 2002 release of 1997 data). From these data we compute in Table 3 the tariff preference level that Canadian and Mexican exporters received in specific sectors *circa* 1997 and 2001. A faster reduc-

---

[13] Table A1 in the Appendix illustrates that the distortionary factors due to sectoral ROO decreased over the period.

TABLE 3

Tariff Preference and Preference Erosion for Canadian and Mexican Exporters to the US
(Selected sectors)

	Tariff Preference circa 1997		Tariff Preference circa 2001		Tariff Preference Erosion 1997–2001	
	CAN	MEX	CAN	MEX	CAN	MEX
agri	9.4	5.2	1.8	1.6	7.6	3.6
reso	0.4	0.4	0.0	0.0	0.4	0.4
food	3.2	3.1	2.4	3.7	0.8	−0.5
text	12.9	12.9	11.4	11.3	1.5	1.6
manu	2.9	2.9	1.8	1.7	1.1	1.2
tech	1.9	1.9	0.9	0.9	1.0	1.0
auto	2.3	2.3	1.8	1.8	0.5	0.5
serv	0.0	0.0	0.0	0.0	0.0	0.0

Source: Author's calculations based on GTAP5 and GTAP6 databases.

tion in US MFN versus US NAFTA tariffs over the period 1997–2001 implies an erosion of NAFTA tariff preferences for Canada and Mexico, which both countries likely experienced as shown in Table 3, with the possible exception of a preference deepening for the Mexican food sector.

A fall in trade-weighted tariff rates across the two GTAP databases may reflect a fall in tariff rates or a fall in trade weights, so that, through a composition effect, we might erroneously attribute the results in Table 3 to preferential erosion. However, other studies have documented the phasing-in of NAFTA and MFN measures and the resulting NAFTA preference erosion. For example, Kunimoto and Sawchuk (2005) show that in 1998, 68 per cent of total US imports from Canada entered under the NAFTA regime and 32 per cent entered at MFN rates. When they disaggregate US imports from Canada under NAFTA preference, into dutiable and duty-free imports, they find that although the NAFTA duty-free component was initially the smaller, the duty-free component has risen quickly, so that, by 1997, US imports from Canada under NAFTA preference were almost exclusively duty free. This pattern of NAFTA dutiable and duty-free imports is thus a reflection of the phasing-in of the NAFTA tariff reductions between Canada and the United States (that actually started in 1989 with the Canada–US FTA). However, the authors also report that the year 1998 witnessed the start of the accelerated growth in US imports from Canada under MFN tariffs while imports under NAFTA preferences started to decline. In fact, NAFTA utilisation rates fell from 68 per cent in 1998, to 62 per cent in 1999, and to 54 per cent in 2002 after which it stabilised around that level. This pattern of MFN/NAFTA utilisation rates between 1998 and 2002 suggests that while most NAFTA tariffs were already duty free by 1997, MFN tariff rates continued to be reduced in accordance with the phasing calendar of the Uruguay Round measures, supporting the assumption that the results in Table 3 reflect NAFTA preferences erosion after 1997.[14]

What is the economic impact of tariff preference erosion? Together with a ROO index of *ex ante* restrictiveness based on Estevadeordal (2000), tariff preferences have been introduced as an independent variable to explain tariff preference utilisation rates (Carrère and de Melo, 2004; Kunimoto and Sawchuk, 2005). With respect to Mexican exports, Carrère and de Melo find that NAFTA utilisation rates are positively influenced by the tariff preference margins while Kunimoto and Sawchuk show that reducing tariff preferences by one percentage point would decrease NAFTA utilisation rates by 3.4 per cent. Of particular importance for our study is that intra-North America trade outside the NAFTA regime may reflect exporters taking advantage of the prevailing zero or low MFN rates since the NAFTA margin of preference is not sufficiently attractive to offset the cost of complying with ROO requirements. Therefore, the fall in the NAFTA utilisation rates due to preference erosion tends to reduce the *ex post* efficiency cost of ROO (discussed in the Appendix) even if the (*ex ante*) restrictiveness of the ROO has not changed. Eventually, the *ex post* efficiency costs of ROO would virtually disappear if tariff preferences collapsed to zero, even if ROO remained 'on the books', because NAFTA utilisation rates would in this case tend to zero.[15]

We have used our CGE modelling framework to estimate the economic impact of moving away from NAFTA into a North American CU in the lower tariff preferences environment of the early 2000s (i.e. based on the 2006 GTAP6 release of 2001 data). Figure 3 and Table 1(a) illustrate that the gain of this policy amounts to a (permanent) 0.5 per cent increase in real Canadian GDP, most of it originating in the elimination of ROO. This is a significantly smaller impact than what Canadians would have obtained from the same policy shift in the 1990s (Figure 2). As discussed above, tariff preference erosion has led to lower NAFTA utilisation rates which reduced the *ex post* efficiency cost of NAFTA ROO and, therefore, concomitantly reduced the potential gains of a CU that would eliminate ROO. For example, the gains resulting from the prospect to remove ROO have fallen from 0.7 per cent of GDP in 1997 to 0.4 per cent of GDP by 2001.

---

[14] Tariff preference erosion has also occurred in a more subtle way, as the US has signed a large number of FTAs since 1994. Although this does not affect NAFTA utilisation rates of Canadian or Mexican exporters, this negatively affects the volume of trade between US and its NAFTA partners.

[15] Indeed, Canadian or Mexican firms exporting to the US would not bother with modifying the production process (input mix) to fulfil ROO (and pay the documentation cost), if the resulting gain (the tariff preference) was zero. In this case, the *ex post* efficiency cost of ROO would necessarily be zero.

FIGURE 3
Percentage Increase in Real GDP if North America had Negotiated a
Customs Union instead of NAFTA in the 2000s
(GTAP6 data, 2006 release of 2001 data)

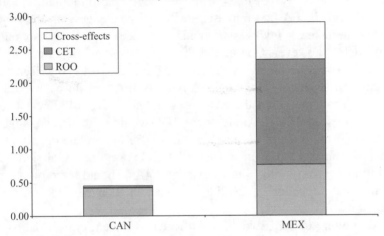

Source: Author's simulations.

For Mexico, however, the economic impact of moving away from NAFTA into a North American CU remains an impressive permanent increase in real GDP by 2.9 per cent (Figure 3) and an increase in real consumption by 0.8 per cent (Table 1(b)). Two factors may explain the strong and sustained economic impact on Mexico of a potential CU. First, as shown in Table 3, preference erosion might have been less important for Mexico than for Canada during the 1997–2001 period, in particular in the agriculture sector, and in the food sector which actually benefited from preference deepening. Therefore, NAFTA utilisation rates for US imports from Mexico and the *ex post* efficiency cost of ROO (from the Mexican point of view) probably did not decline in these sectors and the economy-wide impact of liberalising NAFTA ROO through a CU should remain substantial, albeit smaller than in 1997 (compare Figures 2 and 3). Second, harmonising the CET at the US MFN tariffs in the early 2000s would have had a stronger positive effect on real GDP and other variables than in the 1990s, as shown in Table 1(b). This reflects that the period 1997–2001 saw an increase in the average Mexican–US MFN tariff gap, which accentuated the potential benefit for Mexico of adopting a North American CET set at the US MFN levels.[16]

---

[16] This might reflect that US MFN tariffs were reduced faster than the Mexican MFN tariffs. Furthermore, according to Bhagwati (2008), the external tariffs of Mexico were raised in the mid to end 1990s on 502 items from 20 per cent or less to as much as 35 per cent. This did not constitute a violation of the GATT/WTO Article 24 because members of an FTA are free to raise their external MFN tariffs from the *applied* levels to the higher *bound* levels.

Of course North American countries did not move to a CU either in the 1990s or the early 2000s but our simulation experiments shed some light on whether engaging the US on the CU path at the end of the 2000s, if the option was at all technically or politically feasible, would be worth the diplomatic efforts from Mexico and Canada.[17] A first important technical challenge with the negotiation of a North American CU involves harmonising trade policy. This is not only about selecting a CET, however. One of the thornier issues, as mentioned by Meilke et al. (2008), would be the many different FTAs that North American countries have negotiated separately (Figure 1). A *full* North American CU would require the eventual reconciliation of the ROO used in *each* FTA in Figure 1 (excluding NAFTA, of course, as NAFTA preferential ROO would, in theory, no longer exist). Research along the lines of Gasiorek et al. (2007) on cumulating ROO, and of Cornejo and Harris (2007) on a General Origin Regime as an indispensable minimum to effectively interconnect existing FTAs, should therefore be pursued and encouraged to better gauge the technical challenge of doing this ROO reconciliation.

Second, moving to a CU would make ROO redundant only if their objective was truly to eliminate trade deflection. But that interpretation, however common, is somewhat inconsistent with the observation that the 'Northern' partner (e.g. the US) in 'North–South' FTAs is typically the side that insists on strict ROO whereas it is also typically the partner with the lowest MFN tariffs (so that trade deflection would actually benefit the US, not Mexico nor Canada, in terms of tariff revenues).[18] This suggests that the real reason for having ROO in an FTA might be a capture by interest groups (for example, the US intermediary goods' producers in the automobile and in textiles and clothing sectors) instead of a genuine concern with trade deflection. These groups will inevitably lobby against any North American CU agenda, and this also implies that even the adoption of a CET which would automatically eliminate trade deflection might not lead to the automatic abolition of NAFTA ROO.

Against that backdrop of technical and political economy challenges, several points merit stress from an economic point of view. First, the economic gains of a CU, especially from the Mexican perspective, remain substantial, and recalling that a good neighbour policy within North America is also a vision based on the premise that each country benefits from its neighbours' success and each is diminished by their problems, then these gains should also be taken into account by the

---

[17] The GTAP7 database (2008 release of 2004 data) released after the completion of our modelling exercise could be used to provide a more recent update. However, it is unlikely that the economic impact of a CU implemented at the end of the 2000s would substantially differ from our results for the early 2000s. Indeed, the phasing of the NAFTA and Uruguay Round measures was largely completed by 2002 while the Doha Round derailed, putting a stop to any new reductions in MFN tariffs since then.

[18] I thank an anonymous referee for making this comment.

US. Second, however, comparing the simulation results for Canada for both periods illustrates that tariff preference erosion, which unintentionally resulted from a different phasing of NAFTA and the Uruguay Round measures, has led to a significant reduction in the gains of a prospective CU. Indeed, the ensuing fall in NAFTA utilisation rates has reduced the *ex post* efficiency cost of NAFTA ROO, making NAFTA ROO economically less relevant, and therefore seriously limiting any gains from removing them through a CU.

This, in fact, leads us to the second (indirect) policy option with regard to ROO – to actively pursue multilateral trade negotiations within the WTO and reduce MFN tariffs towards zero. Indeed, if a renewed WTO agenda for multilateral MFN liberalisation at the Doha Round was implemented, erosion of NAFTA tariff preferences would continue and, in this context, the additional economic gains that could be captured (essentially due to ROO elimination) for moving away from NAFTA to a CU would continue to plummet. In the next section, we report the benefits for Canada and Mexico of the 'WTO' scenario and compare them with the benefits resulting from a CU scenario.

c. Multilateral Tariff Liberalisation versus the FTA Spaghetti Bowl

Preferences are relative to MFN tariffs. So, if countries cannot do much about the existing FTAs to directly remove the tariff preferences, they can virtually eliminate FTAs by reducing the MFN tariff itself to zero. And, as argued by Bhagwati (2008), because MFN tariffs are more likely to be cut under reciprocity than through unilateral liberalisation, the Doha Round remains a key element of a strategy to successively eliminate the negative influence of FTAs and their ROO. What then would be the gains for Canada and Mexico of a multilateral free trade world? Although most CGE modelling studies, in this context, typically examine the impact of setting MFN rates to zero in a counterfactual experiment, we argue that this is incomplete because the beneficial impact of dismantling ROO in existing FTAs should also be captured. In this perspective, our model is uniquely positioned because the distortionary impacts of ROO are included in the benchmark and we can eliminate them together with the establishment of zero MFN tariffs.[19]

Table 1(a–b) provides a summary of the long-term impacts of the 'WTO' multilateral free trade scenario implemented at two different times (*circa* 1997 and *circa* 2001). Our simulations illustrate that if all countries in the world had been pursuing MFN tariff liberalisation by multilaterally pushing their MFN tariffs to

---

[19] Our benchmark model only takes into account the distortions due to NAFTA ROO because its multi-country dimension (seven regions) is not detailed enough to include ROO distorting effects from other PTAs across the world. At this stage this is better left as a future extension. The fact that ROO of other PTAs are not modelled in the benchmark implies that our results, in general, underestimate the true gains of moving to a multilateral free trade world.

zero *circa* 2001, then Canada (Mexico) could have reaped an additional yearly gain of 0.8 per cent (3.1 per cent) of GDP of which 0.4 per cent (0.8 per cent) would have originated from the dismantling of ROO in a free trade world and 0.3 per cent (1.6 per cent) would have come from setting MFN tariffs to zero.

The results in Table 1(a–b) suggest two comments. First, Canada and Mexico stand to gain more by reviving multilateral free trade than by moving to a CU with the US. In theory, a CU is a second best choice and our simulation results show that for both periods and both countries, the WTO scenario dominates the North American CU scenario, generating a higher impact on GDP and real consumption. Second, a country like Canada has already captured most of the gains of living in a freer trade world by lowering MFN tariffs for manufactured goods to negligible levels after seven successive multilateral trade negotiations under the auspices of the GATT. For example, with respect to the 2001 benchmark, the pure GDP gains for Canada resulting from setting MFN tariffs to zero amount to a somewhat modest 0.3 per cent of GDP, slightly less than the pure gains from ROO dismantling (0.4 per cent of GDP), for an overall permanent increase of 0.8 per cent of GDP. But other countries achieved substantially less tariff liberalisation, especially developing countries, including Mexico. For Mexico, a full MFN tariff liberalisation in the 2000s could still bring an additional yearly gain of 3.1 per cent of GDP of which 1.6 per cent would originate from setting MFN tariffs to zero and 0.8 per cent would come from the dismantling of NAFTA ROO. Therefore, Mexico stands to benefit greatly from a multilateral free trade world.

Table 1 shows another interesting result: real investment and with it the stock of capital in Canada (and to a lesser extent in Mexico) tends to fall as a result of ROO liberalisation, whereas the pure impact of setting MFN tariffs to zero is more likely to increase investment.[20] This shows that NAFTA tends to inflate, in an inefficient way, the capital-value added in North America in order to satisfy ROO. Capital rents increase as a result of excess demand for capital, which also attracts foreign investment into the FTA, a channel described by Rodriguez (2001). The elimination of ROO under a CU would lead firms to purchase intermediaries from the rest of the world (which embody the services of foreign capital), reducing the need for domestic capital formation.[21]

Table 4(a–d) illustrates the impacts of the North American CU and WTO scenarios, on the sectors of the seven regions in the model, while Figure 4(a–d)

---

[20] Table 1 reports steady-state (long-term) results. In our model, steady-state investment is equal to the depreciation of the stock of capital. Therefore, a decline in real investment translates into a lower steady-state stock of capital for the country.

[21] By generating an excess demand for capital and labour, the rents of the factors of production tend to increase due to ROO in an FTA and they would fall if ROO are removed. However, the elimination of ROO also makes North American firms more efficient, resulting in an increased demand for their cheaper goods which, assuming full employment, implies an increased demand for primary factors of production, potentially offsetting the initial fall in rents.

TABLE 4(a–d)
CU and WTO Counterfactual Scenarios Implemented circa 2001 and 1997:
Long-term Sectoral Impacts (Per cent change from benchmark)

(a) CU 2001	CAN	USA	MEX	MER	LAT	EUR	ROW
agri	0.1	0.3	−1.2	−0.2	0.2	0.2	0.1
reso	−6.1	0.5	2.5	−0.3	0.4	1.8	0.0
food	−2.1	0.0	−0.5	0.1	0.1	0.4	0.2
text	−1.0	−1.0	8.1	0.1	−1.6	0.5	0.2
manu	0.8	−0.1	0.7	0.1	0.6	0.2	0.1
tech	3.1	−0.2	14.6	−0.2	0.3	−0.2	−0.3
auto	15.6	−3.5	29.6	5.7	6.1	0.3	0.2
serv	−0.2	0.1	0.9	0.1	0.1	0.0	0.0

(b) WTO 2001	CAN	USA	MEX	MER	LAT	EUR	ROW
agri	24.1	22.9	−1.8	46.7	17.6	−5.3	−4.3
reso	−6.9	−0.1	6.2	−2.8	13.0	0.8	1.2
food	2.4	5.2	1.5	15.7	9.0	−1.6	0.5
text	−11.8	−21.0	−2.5	−3.9	17.7	1.8	13.3
manu	1.0	0.7	1.7	−1.0	3.2	1.9	1.7
tech	4.0	−0.1	16.7	−10.3	0.9	2.3	1.9
auto	20.0	−5.5	37.9	−4.6	−3.7	3.7	4.5
serv	−0.2	0.3	0.8	1.3	1.4	0.0	0.4

(c) CU 1997	CAN	USA	MEX	MER	LAT	EUR	ROW
agri	2.6	0.4	0.2	0.0	−0.3	0.3	−0.1
reso	−6.8	0.1	1.5	0.4	1.1	2.0	0.1
food	−6.7	0.0	−0.6	0.0	0.2	0.8	0.1
text	−2.7	−0.8	10.7	0.1	−0.9	0.2	0.1
manu	1.7	−0.2	0.0	0.2	1.1	0.2	0.1
tech	6.4	0.0	16.3	−0.2	−0.3	−0.3	−0.2
auto	20.5	−3.6	21.3	0.4	0.0	0.2	0.9
serv	−0.1	0.1	0.6	0.0	0.2	0.0	0.0

(d) WTO 1997	CAN	USA	MEX	MER	LAT	EUR	ROW
agri	103.1	27.7	2.2	15.3	22.8	−5.1	−5.4
reso	−12.0	−1.3	2.0	2.2	9.6	2.3	2.4
food	5.2	8.8	3.5	14.4	25.0	−2.4	1.9
text	−16.8	−21.4	−0.5	−0.9	16.3	−2.2	16.7
manu	0.1	0.2	2.0	1.0	5.7	2.9	2.1
tech	4.5	0.2	18.2	−6.7	−2.4	2.8	3.6
auto	22.6	−6.2	34.3	−9.6	−20.8	5.6	6.6
serv	0.0	0.4	0.3	1.3	2.5	0.1	0.6

Note on abbreviations:
MER = Mercosur; LAT = Latin America; EUR = Europe; ROW = Rest of the World.

Source: Author's simulations.

FIGURE 4(a–d)
Sectoral impacts of CU and WTO scenarios for Canada and Mexico,
decomposed by ROO, CET, and cross effects, circa 2001

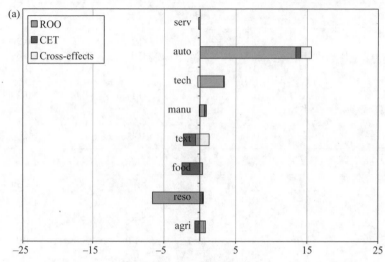

Percentage change from benchmark

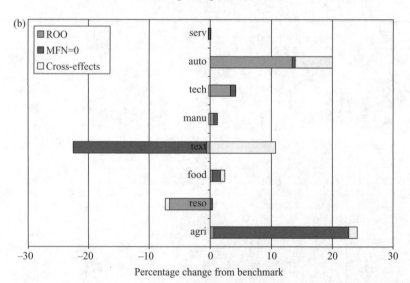

Percentage change from benchmark

FIGURE 4(a–d) (*Continued*)

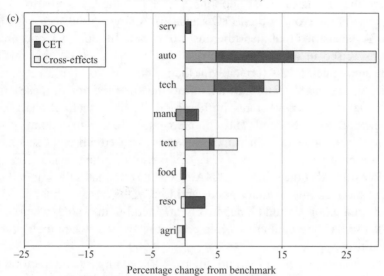

(c)

Percentage change from benchmark

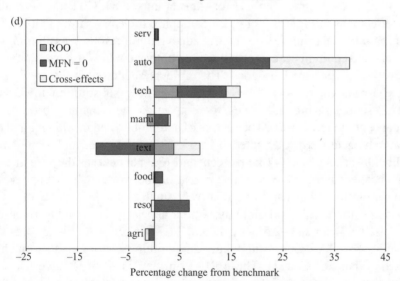

(d)

Percentage change from benchmark

Notes:
(a) CU impact on Canadian sectors, decomposed by ROO, CET and cross-effects, *circa* 2001. (b) Multilateral free trade impact, on Canadian sectors, decomposed by ROO, MFN = 0, and cross-effects, *circa* 2001. (c) CU impact on Mexican sectors, decomposed by ROO, CET and cross-effects, *circa* 2001. (d) Multilateral free trade impact on Mexican sectors, decomposed by ROO, MFN = 0, and cross-effects, *circa* 2001.

Source: Author's simulations.

decomposes, for Canada and Mexico, sectoral impacts into ROO dismantling effects and the effects of either adopting a CET (for the CU scenario) or setting the MFN tariffs to zero (for the WTO scenario). Analysing the sectoral impact of CU or WTO scenarios that also liberalise ROO is a difficult task and great care must be exercised in interpreting the results. First, most ROO are legislated at highly disaggregated levels (typically at the HS-4 or HS-6 digit levels), whereas our model has just eight sectors, which makes the interpretation of these aggregate results challenging. This warrants further, more detailed, sectoral analyses using a CGE methodology. Second, and complementary to the first point, given the input–output principles on which CGE analysis is based, all eight sectors in our analysis are both *final* goods and *intermediaries* used in the production of other sectors. Recalling that the removal of NAFTA ROO eliminates the implicit subsidy on North American intermediary goods and lowers the costs of final goods, then, sectors of production should be negatively affected by this shock when their production is used as intermediaries while positively affected when their production is for final uses.

With this word of caution in mind, Figure 4(a) decomposes the sectoral impact of adopting a North American CU for Canada into ROO, CET and secondary or 'cross' effects (as in Figures 2 or 3, for example). It clearly shows that ROO have had strong dominant impacts on the Canadian natural resources, automobile, and machinery and equipment sectors. All sectors of the economy use natural resources intensively as an intermediary good. Therefore, as suggested in the previous paragraph, the removal of ROO *per se* induces strong substitution towards non-NAFTA resources, which has a negative impact on the Canadian resource sector (−6.6 per cent in Figure 4(a)). The sectors of automobile and machinery and equipment are characterised by an intensive use of intermediaries and they gain from ROO liberalisation *per se* (+13.4 per cent and +3.3 per cent) as they are in position to buy cheaper intermediaries from the rest of the world, which improves their efficiency. On the other hand, the relatively small negative impacts of a CU on the food and the textile and clothing sectors appear to be mainly driven by the setting of a CET *per se* (−2.5 per cent and −1.7 per cent). As Figure 4(c) shows, eliminating NAFTA ROO in the textile and clothing sectors matters much more for Mexico than for Canada. These ROO on textiles seem to have had a large negative impact in Mexico, of a magnitude similar to ROO in the automobile and the machinery and equipment sectors, and the adoption of a North American CU that would establish a CET and also remove ROO would strongly benefit this sector (+8.1 per cent). Unlike for Canada, the Mexican resource sector would benefit from a CU, and this mainly through the adoption of a CET. Finally, as is expected, the setting of a CET has, in general, a much stronger impact on Mexican sectors than is the case in Canada.

The sectoral impacts of the WTO scenario are given in Figures 4(b) and 4(d). This scenario leads to a strong negative impact on the Canadian and Mexican textile and clothing industry and, at the same time, a strong positive impact on Canadian agriculture. These results can intuitively be explained on the basis of the existing structure of MFN tariffs which shows that both Canada and Mexico still have high tariffs on textile and clothing, while Europe, the Rest of the World (ROW) and Mexico still have high trade barriers in agriculture. The setting of MFN tariffs to zero is therefore likely to hurt the Canadian and Mexican textile and clothing sectors while there should be an expansion of Canadian agriculture at the expense of Europe, the ROW and Mexico.

A key message that we also want to emphasise from the analysis is the often large discrepancy in sectoral results between ROO liberalisation and tariff liberalisation. This shows that ROO liberalisation has not much to do with tariff liberalisation *per se* and that analyses trying to capture the impacts of ROO by using a 'tariff-equivalent' methodology to such rules are likely to be misguided.[22]

4. CONCLUSION: POLICY OPTIONS

What, thus, are the options for Canadian and Mexican policymakers? The analysis above suggests two alternatives. They should either focus on establishing a CU with the US, or concentrate their efforts at the WTO table and pursue MFN tariff liberalisation. According to our simulations, however, a CU is a second best solution and the WTO scenario remains the approach that would deliver the largest economic gains in terms of GDP and welfare. Furthermore, our analysis shows that there are technical and political economy problems that suggest that a North American CU scenario which sets a CET but also liberalises NAFTA ROO will be difficult to achieve given the lobbying that is to be expected in Washington from interest groups against any loss of protection that ROO have provided. Keeping up with our previous culinary image, liberalising ROO in this political economy context is not unlike removing the sauce from the FTA spaghetti bowl – an arguably difficult task!

It remains nevertheless true that a North American CU that would remove ROO would bring substantial economic gain to US partners, in particular to Mexico. A possible path for North American political leaders could be to focus discussions, under the WTO auspice, to outlaw preferential trade agreements (PTAs) that are not CUs. This would require a revision of Article 24 of the GATT which is the legal loophole through which the malign genie escaped the 'PTAs bottle' to fulfil

---

[22] Although there is a rationale in the quest for a 'tariff equivalent' of a ROO, the end of Section 2 mentions some reasons why we believe that an approach based on the fact that a ROO acts as an implicit tax to NAFTA firms for the use of non-originating intermediaries but an implicit subsidy for the use of capital, labour and intermediaries purchased within NAFTA is sounder.

the wishes of the EU and the US.[23] Had a CET requirement been initially imposed in Article 24, as a condition to the formation of any PTAs, then preferential ROO would not currently pervade the international trade system. This proposal, however, is a utopia because the 'FTA horse' has left the barn, and it appears difficult to imagine a systemic transformation of FTAs into ROO-free CUs under some form of legal pressures.

Couldn't we find a solution within the existing FTAs spaghetti bowl? ROO are often presented as the necessary gatekeepers of preferential commerce, assumed to be a building block of multilateral free trade. However, it is generally acknowledged that the diversity of ROO across PTAs strongly limits inter-regional trade flows, and that the restrictiveness of some ROO is beyond the levels that would be justified to prevent trade deflection, suggesting a capture by special interest groups and which might have several perverse effects on intra-PTA trade flows (Cadot and de Melo, 2007). Some calls exist with regard to simplification or harmonisation of NAFTA ROO between *sectors* or across *preferential trade agreements*.[24] Some economists have proposed to 'tame' ROO, by, for example, binding or capping their restrictiveness, and then by progressively reducing their restrictiveness to the appropriate level required for ROO to continue their essential role of gatekeepers of preferential commerce (Estevadeordal et al., 2008a). To help in this process, there are proposals to harmonise the methods that determine the origin of goods by converting tariff shift and technical tests into a local content percentage rate, a technique somewhat equivalent to the process of 'tariffication' of non-tariff barriers at the WTO (Hirsch, 2002). Other authors (e.g. Cornejo and Harris, 2007; Gasiorek et al., 2007) advocate some variants of a ROO cumulation process across FTAs, first at a regional level through 'diagonal' and 'triangular' cumulation (in a process similar to the 1997 pan-European cumulation system), and then at a more global level through 'multilateralising cumulation'. Although these research efforts are certainly valuable, it remains to be seen whether trade negotiators will be able to pursue this route in a significant manner. In fact, it is difficult not to sense unease among these authors for their own proposals and that, eventually, very little is likely to emerge due to technical and political difficulties. All things considered, aren't these proposals likely to generate an even more formidable stalemate than the current one at the WTO?

---

[23] This would require a stricter mandate for the WTO Committee on Regional Trade Agreements which is charged to examine whether preferential trade agreements are compatible with Article 24.
[24] It seems reasonable enough to suggest an across-the-board standard instead of the current heterogeneous rules across sectors (e.g. NAFTA triple transformation test in the textile/apparel sectors or the 62.5 per cent test in the automobile sector). In practice, however, as argued by Destler (2006), harmonisation across sectors would be difficult to achieve on a large scale simply because these rules resulted from hardly-disputed sector-specific negotiations and that their current settings matter a great deal to producers. ROO should not be viewed as a deal between nations but instead as a deal between private business interests and governments that needed to obtain their support in the legislative battle.

Furthermore, any forms of PTAs, either FTAs or CUs, have serious problems, beyond the systemic proliferation of ROO associated to FTAs. The Vinerian trade diversion concern is the traditional objection to PTAs, but a more recent objection, compellingly expressed by Bhagwati, is that these arrangements have become a way for the US and the EU to impose all sorts of 'trade-unrelated' issues, cynically called 'trade-related' issues, in trade treaties. These include intellectual property protection, domestic environmental issues, and labour standards, the last two often presented as if they were made for altruistic reasons aimed at benefiting foreign workers, even if they mask self-interest, and represent a new form of protectionism which raises the cost of production of foreign rivals by forcing on them the same standards as in the US (Bhagwati and Hudec, 1996; Krugman, 1997). Effectively, PTAs are now used by lobbies in the US and the EU to secure these agendas with weaker nations in particular because it would be more difficult to do so in the WTO (despite TRIPs precedent), as developing countries could better resist the pressure by the sheer force of their numbers.

In the end, an increased understanding of the magnitude of the cost of ROO in FTAs (and the cost of 'trade-unrelated' issues imposed on weaker countries through PTAs) is a necessary condition to inspire a stronger political leadership that will ensure that all countries come back to the WTO table and, through renewed MFN tariff liberalisation, progressively eliminate the perverse effects of preferential commerce, including its ROO gatekeepers, eventually neutralising the malign genie inside the bottle. This remains the best option available for weaker partners, including Mexico and Canada in North America.

APPENDIX: ROO LIBERALISATION – MODELLING AND CALIBRATION CHALLENGES

Assume a firm that belongs to an FTA which, without loss of generality, will be referred to as NAFTA. Suppose that the firm, when using an intermediary good X, might either purchase the intermediary good from NAFTA, X_{Nafta}, or from outside NAFTA, $X_{nonNafta}$, at existing prices P_{Nafta} and $P_{nonNafta}$. The firm has access to a constant return to scale technology to produce the composite intermediary X using X_{Nafta} and $X_{nonNafta}$, and one isoquant $\overline{X}$ is depicted by the curve in Figure A1.[25] Assume also that the firm must satisfy a ROO constraint that has to be met to obtain origin. From an analytical viewpoint the basic effect of a ROO is to raise the production costs of the good that meets the binding ROO (Francois, 2005; Krishna, 2005).

---

[25] A more formal presentation of the allocation between X_{Nafta} and $X_{nonNafta}$, where the firm must also choose between capital, labour and several composite intermediary inputs, is given in Georges (2008a).

FIGURE A1
Distortion Due to ROO

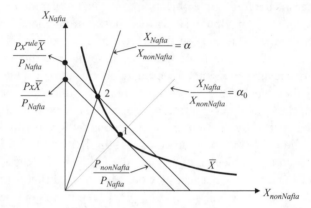

Suppose that at existing intermediary prices, an unconstrained firm chooses the input mix at the point labelled 1 using X_{Nafta} and $X_{nonNafta}$ so that their ratio equals α_0. The lowest cost to obtain $\overline{X}$ is given by the height of the isocost through point 1 and this cost expressed in terms of intermediary good originating from NAFTA is given by $Px\overline{X}/P_{Nafta}$, where Px is the minimum *unit* cost of the composite intermediary. A binding ROO would remove point 1 from the feasible set. If, for example, the ROO requires $X_{Nafta}/X_{nonNafta} \geq \alpha > \alpha_0$, then only points on or above the ray from the origin with slope α and on the isoquant would be feasible. In this case, costs are minimised by choosing the input mix given by point 2 and these costs, if the ROO are met, are given by the height of the isocost through point 2, $Px^{rule}\overline{X}/P_{Nafta}$, where Px^{rule} is the minimum unit cost of the composite intermediary given the binding ROO. Observe that a binding ROO acts like an implicit tax on the use of non-NAFTA intermediaries and an implicit subsidy on the use of NAFTA intermediaries. The implicit price distortion can be viewed graphically by comparing the slope of the isocost through point 1 with the slope of the price line (not drawn) tangent to the isoquant at point 2. More restrictive ROO would correspond to higher values for α, a steeper ray from the origin, and a higher minimum unit cost of production.

It is simple enough to realise that if a firm is strictly constrained by a ROO and is effectively at point 2 in Figure A1, then, removing the ROO would lead the firm to select the input combination given by point 1, increasing its purchase of non-NAFTA intermediary goods and decreasing the purchase of NAFTA intermediary goods, which would lower its total spending on intermediary goods. In effect, eliminating ROO implies eliminating the implicit tax on the use of non-NAFTA intermediaries and the implicit subsidy on the use of NAFTA intermediaries.

The simplicity of the argument is, however, deceptive, and Figure A2 illustrates this. Suppose for example that a dataset is available on the chosen intermediary

FIGURE A2
Calibration Issues

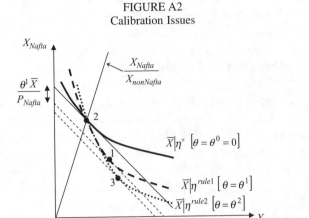

bundle at specific prices in a specific reference year and that this choice is given by point 2. (For the time being, ignore the isoquants drawn in Figure A2.) Point 2 is on a ray from the origin with slope $X_{Nafta}/X_{nonNafta}$. The ray's relative steepness reflects an observed *bias* for NAFTA versus non-NAFTA intermediary goods. However, we should not necessarily attribute this bias to a binding NAFTA ROO; that is, it is not because a firm utilises intensively NAFTA intermediary goods in its production process that this necessarily reflects a constrained behaviour due to a binding ROO. Alternatively, this means that if we compute the ratio: $X_{Nafta}/X_{nonNafta} = \alpha$ with X_{Nafta} and $X_{nonNafta}$ *observed* in the benchmark dataset, then α is simply the numerical value of this ratio and should not (necessarily) be taken as an institutional parameter reflecting *ex ante* ROO restrictiveness *per se*.

This naturally leads to the challenge of positioning the relevant isoquant in Figure A2, or, in other words, to calibrate the distribution parameters of the production function that links the composite intermediary good X to its input mix $(X_{Nafta}, X_{nonNafta})$ while assuming a cost-minimising behaviour of the firm that is *potentially* constrained by a ROO. For illustration, let us assume that such a technology is given by a constant elasticity of substitution (CES) function:

$$X = \left[\eta_{Nafta} \left(X_{Nafta} \right)^{\frac{\sigma-1}{\sigma}} + \eta_{nonNafta} \left(X_{nonNafta} \right)^{\frac{\sigma-1}{\sigma}} \right]^{\frac{\sigma}{\sigma-1}}, \qquad (A1)$$

where η_{Nafta} and $\eta_{nonNafta}$ are the distribution parameters and σ is the Armington elasticity of substitution between NAFTA and non-NAFTA intermediaries. The crucial assumption that must be made is whether the bias for NAFTA intermediary goods in Figure A2 is due, in part or entirely, to a binding ROO. For example, if ROO distortions that might have led the firm to select the combination given by point 2 are not introduced in the analysis (because, say, these rules are not the subject of the study), then the CGE modeller will calibrate the CES function by fixing η_{Nafta} and $\eta_{nonNafta}$ to $(\eta^{\circ}_{Nafta}, \eta^{\circ}_{nonNafta})$ in order to position the isoquant $\bar{X}|\eta^{\circ}$ at the tangency point with the isocost line at point 2.[26]

On the other hand, the modeller might assume that the observed bias at point 2 is due (in part or entirely) to a distorted behaviour of the firm facing a ROO such as $X_{Nafta}/X_{nonNafta} f \geq \alpha$ and which induced the firm to change the production process by substituting $X_{nonNafta}$ for X_{Nafta} in order to fulfil the ROO and benefit from the preferential NAFTA tariff when exporting the final good to its NAFTA partners. The calibration procedure must therefore be revised accordingly so that if point 2 observed in the data reflects an optimal behaviour under constraint of a distortionary ROO, then removing the distortion should induce some re-allocation out of X_{Nafta} and into $X_{nonNafta}$. Thus, the modeller must re-parameterise the CES function (1) by fixing the parameters $(\eta_{Nafta}, \eta_{nonNafta})$ to specific values $(\eta^{rule}_{Nafta}, \eta^{rule}_{nonNafta})$, therefore positioning the isoquant to, say: $\bar{X}|\eta^{rule1}$ or $\bar{X}|\eta^{rule2}$. These specific re-parameterisations suggest that, *ceteris paribus*, the removal of ROO would push the intermediary good bundle from point 2 to either point 1 or point 3.

Choosing between many different possible re-parameterisations is, therefore, a key challenge of this analysis. As Figure A2 illustrates, the indeterminacy between the two isoquants $(\bar{X}|\eta^{rule1}$ or $\bar{X}|\eta^{rule2})$ is the reason why a crucial additional assumption must be imposed in order to disentangle ROO distortions (that are only implicitly present in the dataset) versus any other factors that might have led the firm to choose point 2.

The proposed solution to the indeterminacy is as follows. As seen above, when ROO are distortionary there is an efficiency cost, which translates into an increase in the minimum unit cost of production in comparison to what it would be without the ROO. Therefore, we can argue that the ROO has increased the firm's minimum spending on intermediary goods by a pre-specified percentage $\theta \geq 0$, so that for example:

$$Px^{Rule}\bar{X} = Px(1+\theta)\bar{X},$$

or

$$Px^{Rule} = Px(1+\theta), \tag{A2}$$

where Px^{Rule} and Px, as defined before, are the unit costs of production of the composite intermediary good X, respectively with and without ROO, and where

---

[26] The calibration procedure consists of fitting the model to the database, which implies that the choice of the distribution parameters of the CES function in equation (A1) must be done so that if the modeller 'simulates' a parameterised model without shock, and assuming cost-minimising behaviour given a set of prices, then he/she will be able to replicate the observed dataset or benchmark (point 2).

$\theta \geq 0$ is the efficiency cost of the ROO. The parameter θ provides a measure of the distance between the two relevant isocost lines as shown in Figure A2. The assumption that $\theta = \theta^1 > 0$ corresponds to the parameterisation leading to the isoquant $\bar{X}|\eta^{rule1}$ so that removing ROO in the counterfactual pushes the firm from point 2 to point 1. If, on the other hand, the efficiency cost of ROO is assumed to be $\theta = \theta^2 > \theta^1$, then, the parameterised isoquant is $\bar{X}|\eta^{rule2}$ and removing ROO in the counterfactual pushes the firm (all else the same) from point 2 to point 3.

Finally, suppose that $\theta = \theta^0 = 0$ so that it is assumed that the initial introduction of ROO did not increase the costs of production, or, in other words, did not induce the firm to change its method of production (say, the ROO was not binding). Then, the high bias in favour of NAFTA intermediary goods as is observed at point 2 should not be attributed to ROO but to other (undetermined) factors. In this case, the calibration procedure would automatically set the shadow price of the ROO constraint equal to 0 and this would lead to a parameterised CES function given by $\bar{X}|\eta^\circ$ in Figure A2. Removing ROO in the counterfactual would therefore have no impact on the firm's choice between NAFTA and non-NAFTA intermediary goods and the firm would continue to optimally choose the allocation given by point 2.[27]

To implement the method described above we need information on the parameter θ – the efficiency cost of the ROO expressed as a percentage increase of the unit cost. This is an external parameter that must be estimated. Although there is very little information on the exact magnitude of this efficiency cost, the 'participation constraint' approach (Cadot et al., 2002; Anson et al., 2005) might be a good starting point. This literature closely links the cost of ROO with tariff preferences (i.e. the differences between MFN tariff and preferential (NAFTA) tariff). According to this approach, the terms of an FTA are set to leave partners close to or on their participation constraint (i.e. close to being indifferent between signing and not signing) so that there is a substitutability between tariff rates and ROO restrictiveness in terms of their impact on net revenues for exporters (larger net revenues due to deeper tariff preferences are just offset by the cost of more restrictive ROO). This approach leads to proxy the efficiency cost θ of the ROO with

---

[27] Recall that the bias given by α in Figure A2 represents *observed* data at the aggregate level. If we had used the alternative interpretation of an institutional parameter (say the cost of intermediates from outside the FTA must be less than or equal to x per cent of total cost), then the issue of whether the ROO is strictly binding or not would matter. Figure A1 shows a constrained firm which eventually chooses point 2, but we might also imagine an unconstrained firm with a technology such that its isoquant is tangent to the lowest isocost at the *left* of the α-ray. Detailed information on firms' use of NAFTA preferences would be necessary to disentangle the two types of firms in each sector and this would also require a modelling procedure that takes into account the heterogeneity of firms. Our approach, however, has the advantage of avoiding both the complication of whether ROO are strictly binding or not, and the problem of heterogeneous behaviour. A point such as point 2 in Figure A2 is *observable* for each sector, and we can assume that this is the choice of a 'representative' firm, which can be thought of as an 'average' of different types of firms with heterogeneous positions with respect to the sectoral ROO.

the tariff preference that can be obtained when exporting the final good to a NAFTA partner. This proxy is an upper bound to the cost of ROO, but the approach implies that it is not far off the true estimate because member countries are assumed to be 'close to', if not 'on', their participation constraint.[28]

As said previously, it is unlikely that ROO are the only factors explaining the high biases (the high values for α). Therefore, to re-emphasise, the key insight that is proposed is to consider that both the introduction of ROO and other (undetermined) factors have pushed the economy towards the high NAFTA-content that is observed in data. To disentangle ROO from other factors, it is assumed that ROO *per se* increased the unit cost of production in the order of magnitude $\theta (\geq 0)$ given by the appropriately weighted tariff preference as suggested above. With the information on parameter θ, the technological (distribution) parameters can be calibrated as discussed previously. For each sector of production, this method permits to compute the ROO's implicit tax for the use of non-FTA intermediaries and the implicit subsidy for the use of NAFTA-produced intermediary goods. From this, we can compute, for each sector, a distortionary factor given by the wedge formed by the (inverse of the) ratio of (1) the slope of the isocost tangent to the isoquant at a point such as 1 in Figures A1 or A2 and (2) the slope of the isocost tangent to the same isoquant at point 2 (not drawn). Distortionary factors have been computed in Georges (2008a), in a more general method that also includes the implicit subsidy for the use of domestic (NAFTA) labour and capital, using the GTAP5 database. These distortionary factors have been updated in Table A1 using the GTAP6 database and we can observe that they have generally decreased between 1997 and 2001, which illustrates a decrease in the implicit subsidies and taxes and thus a reduced *ex post* efficiency cost of NAFTA ROO. Note, as discussed in Section 2, that these distortionary factors should not be viewed as 'tariff equivalents' of NAFTA ROO.

Although estimating a sectoral θ to compute the efficiency cost of ROO is a key step to capture the effects of NAFTA's ROO, we need to go one step further to understand the general equilibrium impacts of removing these ROO. As seen above, a ROO acts as an implicit tax for the use of intermediary goods purchased outside NAFTA, an implicit subsidy to NAFTA firms for the use of intermediary goods purchased within NAFTA, and (in the generalised version proposed in Georges, 2008a) an implicit subsidy for the use of labour and capital. Given the

---

[28] θ is a percentage increase in the *average* (unit) cost of production (so that it applies to each unit produced), whereas tariff preference only applies to the production that is exported to NAFTA countries. Therefore, in order to use tariff preference as a proxy for the increase in unit cost of production, it must be weighted by the share of sectoral production that is exported to the NAFTA member (that provides the preference). If a firm sells its entire production domestically, then tariff preference *per se* has no value, so that the firm would not change its input mix and incur an increase in unit cost of production (weight = 0) in order to satisfy a ROO. The weight equals 1 in the other extreme scenario of a NAFTA firm that exports all its production to the two other NAFTA members.

TABLE A1
ROO Distortionary Factors

	Canada		Mexico	
	1997	2001	1997	2001
agri	1.39	1.24	1.52	1.37
reso	1.13	1.03	1.24	1.03
food	1.18	1.18	1.12	1.13
text	1.26	1.27	1.81	1.65
manu	1.23	1.19	1.19	1.13
tech	1.19	1.14	1.32	1.21
auto	1.18	1.16	1.23	1.19
serv	1.00	1.00	1.00	1.00

Source: Author's simulations.

interactions between agents and the likely repercussions on all markets in the domestic and foreign economies following the elimination of ROO, it appears to be essential to use a CGE model to gauge the impact of liberalising ROO.

REFERENCES

Anson, J., O. Cadot, A. Estevadeordal, J. de Melo, A. Suwa-Eisenmann and B. Tumurchudur (2005), 'Rules of Origin in North–South Preferential Trading Arrangements with an Application to NAFTA', *Review of International Economics*, **13**, 501–17.

Bhagwati, J. N. (1993), 'Regionalism and Multilateralism: An Overview', in J. de Melo and A. Panagariya (eds.), *New Dimensions in Regional Integration* (Cambridge: Cambridge University Press).

Bhagwati, J. N. (2008), *Termites in the Trading Systems – How Preferential Agreements Undermine Free Trade* (Oxford: Oxford University Press).

Bhagwati, J. N. and R. Hudec (eds.) (1996), *Fair Trade and Harmonization: Prerequisites for Free Trade?* (Cambridge, MA: MIT Press).

Brown, D., A. Deardorff and R. Stern (2001), 'Impact on NAFTA Members of Multilateral and Regional Trading Arrangements and Tariff Harmonization', in R. Harris (ed.), *North American Linkages: Opportunities and Challenges for Canada* (Calgary, AB: University of Calgary Press).

Cadot, O. and J. de Melo (2007), 'Why OECD Countries Should Reform Rules of Origin', *The World Bank Research Observer*, **23**, 77–105.

Cadot, O., J. de Melo, A. Estevadeordal, A. Suwa-Eisenmann and B. Tumurchudur (2002), 'Assessing the Effect of NAFTA's Rules of Origin', INRA Research Unit Working Paper No. 0306 (Laboratoire d'Économie Appliquée).

Cadot, O., A. Estevadeordal and A. Suwa-Eisenmann (2006a), 'Rules of Origin as Export Subsidies', in O. Cadot, A. Estevadeordal, A. Suwa-Eisenmann and T. Verdier (eds.), *The Origin of Goods: Rules of Origin in Regional Trade Agreements* (Oxford: Oxford University Press).

Cadot, O., A. Estevadeordal, A. Suwa-Eisenmann and T. Verdier (eds.) (2006b), *The Origin of Goods: Rules of Origin in Regional Trade Agreements* (Oxford: Oxford University Press).

Carrère, C. and J. de Melo (2004), 'Are Differential Rules of Origin Equally Costly? Estimates from NAFTA', CEPR Discussion Paper Series No. 4437 (London: CEPR).

Cornejo, R. and J. Harris (2007) 'Convergence in the Rules of Origin Spaghetti Bowl: A Methodological Proposal', INTAL-INT Working Paper No. 34 (Inter-American Development Bank).

Destler, I. M. (2006), 'Rules of Origin and US Trade Policy', in O. Cadot, A. Estevadeordal, A. Suwa-Eisenmann and T. Verdier (eds.), *The Origin of Goods: Rules of Origin in Regional Trade Agreements* (Oxford: Oxford University Press).

Dimaranan, B. V. and R. A. McDougall (eds.) (2002), *Global Trade, Assistance, and Production: The GTAP 5 Data Base*, Center for Global Trade Analysis (Purdue University, West Lafayette, Indiana).

Dimaranan, B. V. and R. A. McDougall (eds.) (2006), *Global Trade, Assistance, and Production: The GTAP 6 Data Base*, Center for Global Trade Analysis (Purdue University, West Lafayette, Indiana).

Estevadeordal, A. (2000), 'Negotiating Preferential Market Access – The Case of the North American Free Trade Agreement', *Journal of World Trade*, **34**, 141–66.

Estevadeordal, A. and K. Suominen (2006), 'Mapping and Measuring Rules of Origin Around the World', in O. Cadot, A. Estevadeordal, A. Suwa-Eisenmann and T. Verdier (eds.), *The Origin of Goods: Rules of Origin in Regional Trade Agreements* (Oxford: Oxford University Press).

Estevadeordal, A. and K. Suominen (2008), 'What are the Trade Effects of Rules of Origin?', in A. Estevadeordal and K. Suominen (eds.), *Gatekeepers of Global Commerce: Rules of Origin and International Economic Integration* (Washington, DC: Inter-American Development Bank).

Estevadeordal, A., J. Harris and K. Suominen (2008a), 'Multilateralizing Preferential Rules of Origin', in A. Estevadeordal and K. Suominen (eds.), *Gatekeepers of Global Commerce: Rules of Origin and International Economic Integration* (Washington, DC: Inter-American Development Bank).

Estevadeordal, A., J. E. López-Córdova and K. Suominen (2008b), 'How do Rules of Origin Affect Investment Flows? Some Hypotheses and the Case of Mexico', in A. Estevadeordal and K. Suominen (eds.), *Gatekeepers of Global Commerce: Rules of Origin and International Economic Integration* (Washington, DC: Inter-American Development Bank).

Falvey, R. and G. Reed (2002), 'Rules of Origin as Commercial Policy Instruments', *International Economic Review*, **43**, 393–407.

Francois, J. (2005), 'Preferential Trade Arrangements and the Pattern of Production and Trade When Inputs are Differentiated', Tinbergen Institute Discussion Paper No. 072/2.

Garay, L. J. and P. De Lombaerde (2004), 'Preferential Rules of Origin: Models and Levels of Rulemaking', Paper prepared for the Brussels UNU-CRIS/LSE Workshop on The Interaction between Levels of Rulemaking in International Trade and Investment.

Gasiorek, M., P. Augier and C. Lai-Tong (2007), 'Multilateralising Regionalism: Relaxing Rules of Origin or Can Those PECS be Flexed?', Paper presented at the Conference on Multilateralising Regionalism, 10–12 September, Geneva, Switzerland.

Georges, P. (2008a), 'Liberalizing NAFTA Rules of Origin: A Dynamic CGE Analysis', *Review of International Economics*, **16**, 672–86.

Georges, P. (2008b), 'Toward a North American Customs Union: Rules of Origin Liberalization Matters More than a Common External Tariff for Canada', *North American Journal of Economics and Finance*, **19**, 304–18.

Ghosh, M. and S. Rao (2005), 'A Canada–US Customs Union: Potential Economic Impacts in NAFTA Countries', *Journal of Policy Modeling*, **27**, 805–27.

Hirsch, M. (2002), 'International Trade Law, Political Economy and Rules of Origin: A Plea for a Reform of the WTO Regime on Rules of Origin', *Journal of World Trade*, **36**, 171–88.

Kemp, M. and H. Wan Jr. (1976), 'An Elementary Proposition Concerning the Formation of Customs Union', in M. Kemp (ed.), *Three Topics in the Theory of International Trade: Distribution, Welfare, and Uncertainty* (Amsterdam: North-Holland).

Krishna, K. (2005), 'Understanding Rules of Origin', NBER Working Paper No. 11150, Cambridge, MA: NBER.

Krishna, K. and A. Krueger (1995), 'Implementing Free Trade Areas: Rules of Origin and Hidden Protection', NBER Working Paper No. 4983, Cambridge, MA: NBER.

Krueger, A. (1993), 'Free Trade Agreements as Protectionist Devices: Rules of Origin', NBER Working Paper No. 4352, Cambridge, MA: NBER.

Krueger, A. (1995), 'Free Trade Agreements versus Customs Unions', NBER Working Paper No. 5084, Cambridge, MA: NBER.

Krugman, P. R. (1997), 'What Should Trade Negotiators Negotiate About?', *Journal of Economic Literature*, **35**, 113–20.

Kunimoto, R. and G. Sawchuk (2005), 'NAFTA Rules of Origin', Discussion Paper, Policy Research Initiative, Ottawa.

Meilke, K., J. Rude and S. Zahniser (2008), 'Is "NAFTA Plus" an Option in the North American Agrifood Sector?', *The World Economy*, **31**, 925–46.

Pastor, R. (2008), 'The Future of North America. Replacing a Bad Neighbour Policy', *Foreign Affairs*, **87**, 4, 84–98.

Pomfret, R. (2007), 'Is Regionalism an Increasing Feature of the World Economy?', *The World Economy*, **30**, 923–47.

Robson, W. (2007), 'Stuck on a Spoke: Proliferating Bilateral Trade Deals are a Dangerous Game for Canada', C. D. Howe Institute e-Brief.

Rodriguez, P. L. (2001), 'Rules of Origin with Multistage Production', *The World Economy*, **24**, 201–20.

World Bank (2005), *Global Economic Prospects – Trade, Regionalism, and Development* (Washington, DC: The World Bank).

Index

accreditation   29, 30, 37, 41
   see also EA; EAL; TURKAK
ACP (African, Caribbean and Pacific) countries
   86, 89–90
   compensation for preference erosion   165
   see also EPA
Africa   195, 204
   see also Egypt; Ethiopia; Ghana; Kenya;
   Morocco; South Africa; Sub-Saharan
   Africa
Agenda 2000   151
agricultural products   47, 86, 88, 137, 231
   price increase on   139
   processed   2, 13, 14, 19, 20
   tariffs on   12, 16, 19, 78, 134, 156, 159,
   232
   see also AMA
Aid for Trade package   165, 174
Albania   19, 240
AMA (agricultural market access)   155, 156,
   172, 173
AMS (Aggregate Measurement of Support)
   132–44
Andean Community   256
   see also Bolivia; Colombia; Ecuador; Peru;
   Venezuela
Anderson, J. E.   101, 105, 106, 107
Ankara Agreement Additional Protocol (1970)
   2
anti-dumping measures   19, 27, 95, 110, 231,
   232

AoA (UR Agreement on Agriculture)   132,
   136, 140, 143, 144
Argentina   151, 257
Arnold, J. M.   195
ASEAN (Association of Southeast Asian
   Nations)   252
   trade with China   59, 69, 70
   see also CAFTA
Australia   54, 67, 70, 147, 149, 151
Austria   254
Aw, B. Y.   194–5

backbone services   4, 92–3
Bagwell, K.   152, 177, 202, 250, 251
Baier, S. L.   97, 98
Baldwin, R. E.   31, 112, 148, 177, 191, 204,
   205
Baltic Republics   204
Bandyopadhyay, U.   54
Bangladesh   152, 162, 164–5, 167, 172–3
bargaining process   148, 149, 160–9, 173
barriers to trade   88, 151, 190
   bilateral   206
   bloc-lateral   206
   effects on TFP   191
   high in agriculture   285
   iceberg cost type   101
   MFN   250
   policy-induced   107
   protectionism and   200–1
   see also NTBs; tariff barriers; TBTs

The World Economy: Global Trade Policy 2010, First Edition. Edited by David Greenaway.
© 2011 Blackwell Publishing Ltd. Published 2011 by Blackwell Publishing Ltd.